drawnandquarterly.com

ISBN 978-1-77046-407-0 | First edition: September 2020 | Printed in Turkey | 10 9 8 7 6 5 4 3 2 1

Cataloguing data available from Library and Archives Canada

Published in the USA by Drawn & Quarterly, a client publisher of Farrar, Straus and Giroux | Published in
Canada by Drawn & Quarterly, a client publisher of Raincoast Books | Published in the United Kingdom by
Drawn & Quarterly, a client publisher of Publishers Group UK

The CONTRADICTIONS

SOPHIE YANOW

DRAWN & QUARTERLY

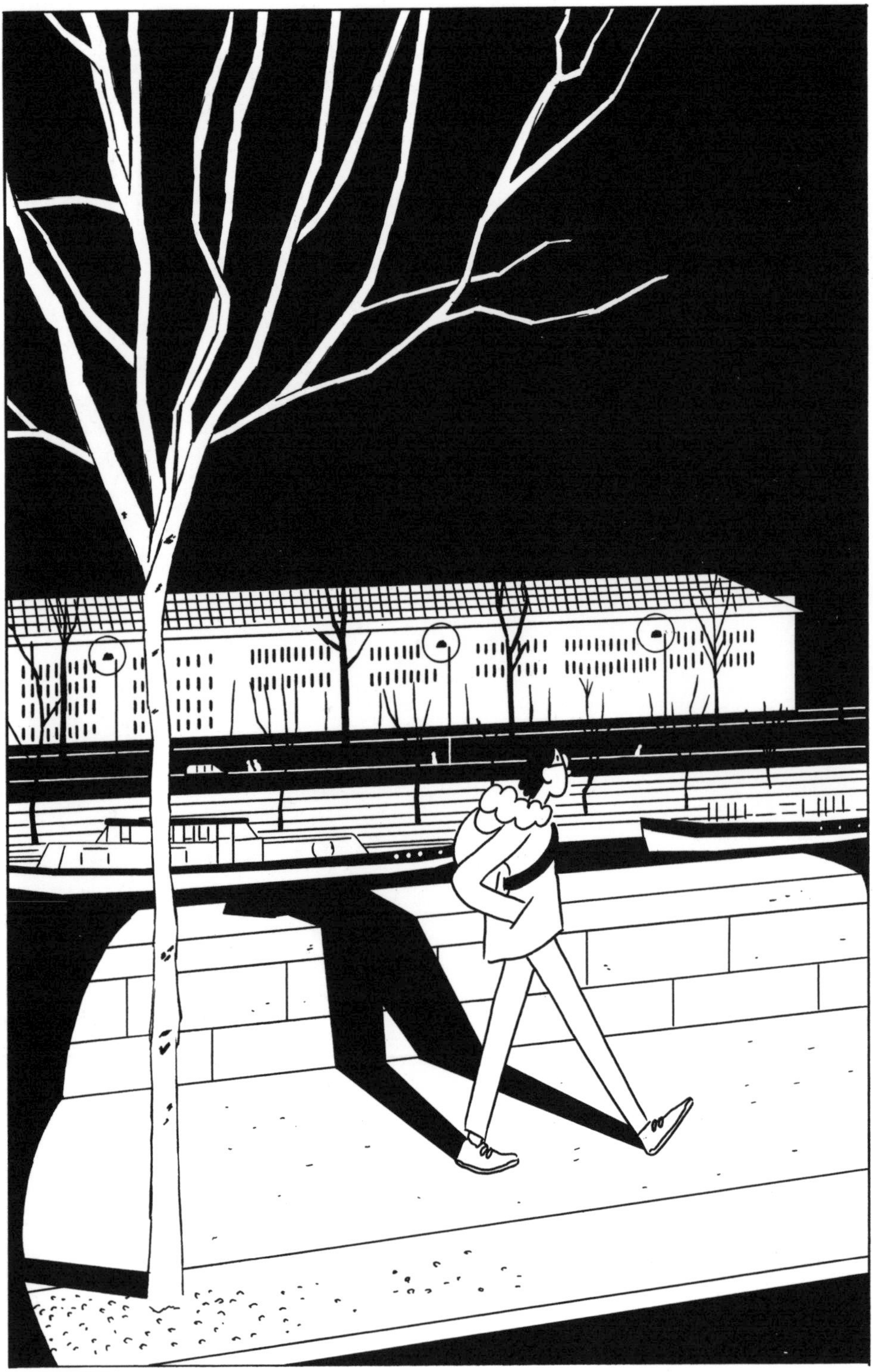

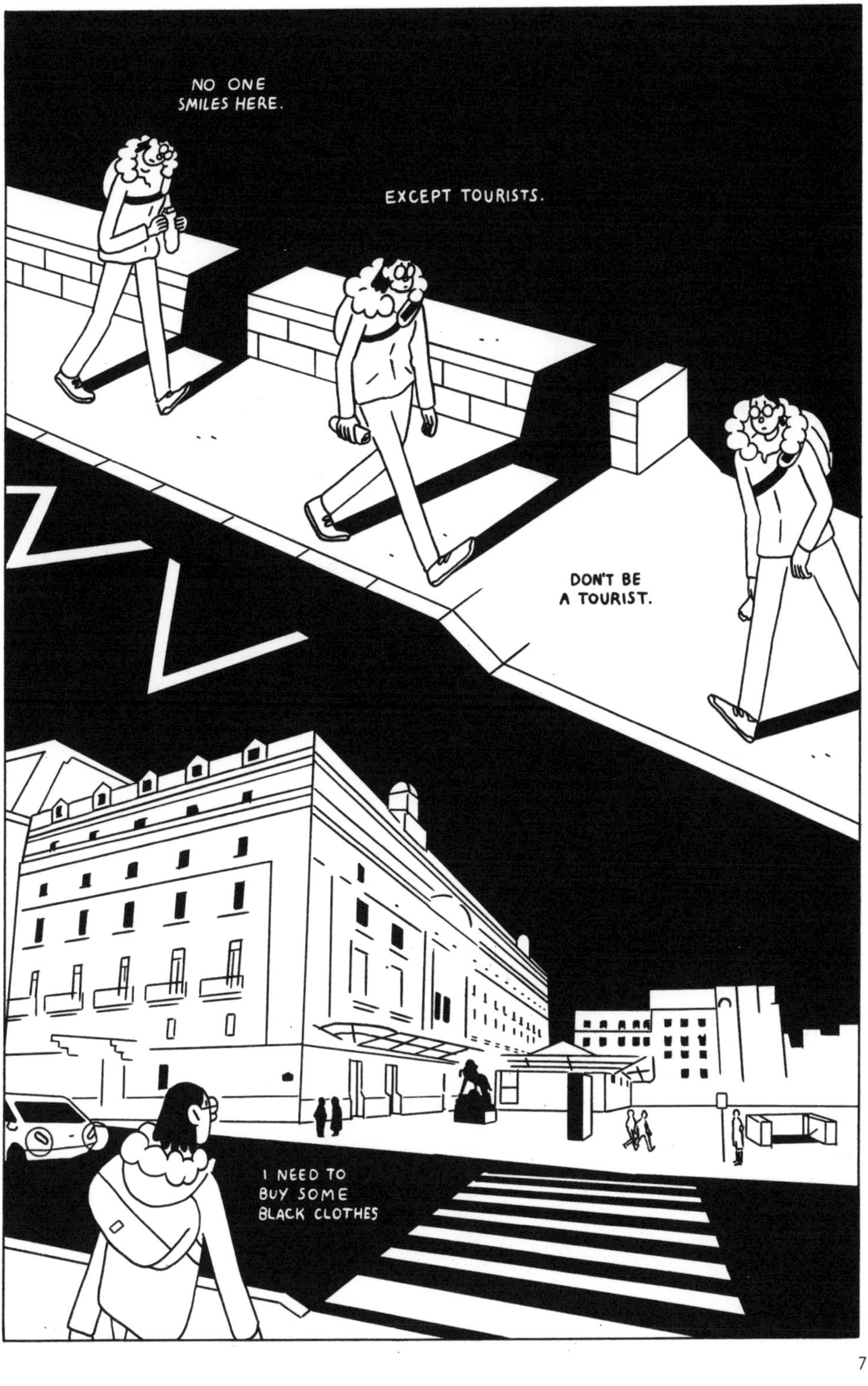
NO ONE
SMILES HERE.
EXCEPT TOURISTS.
DON'T BE
A TOURIST.
I NEED TO
BUY SOME
BLACK CLOTHES

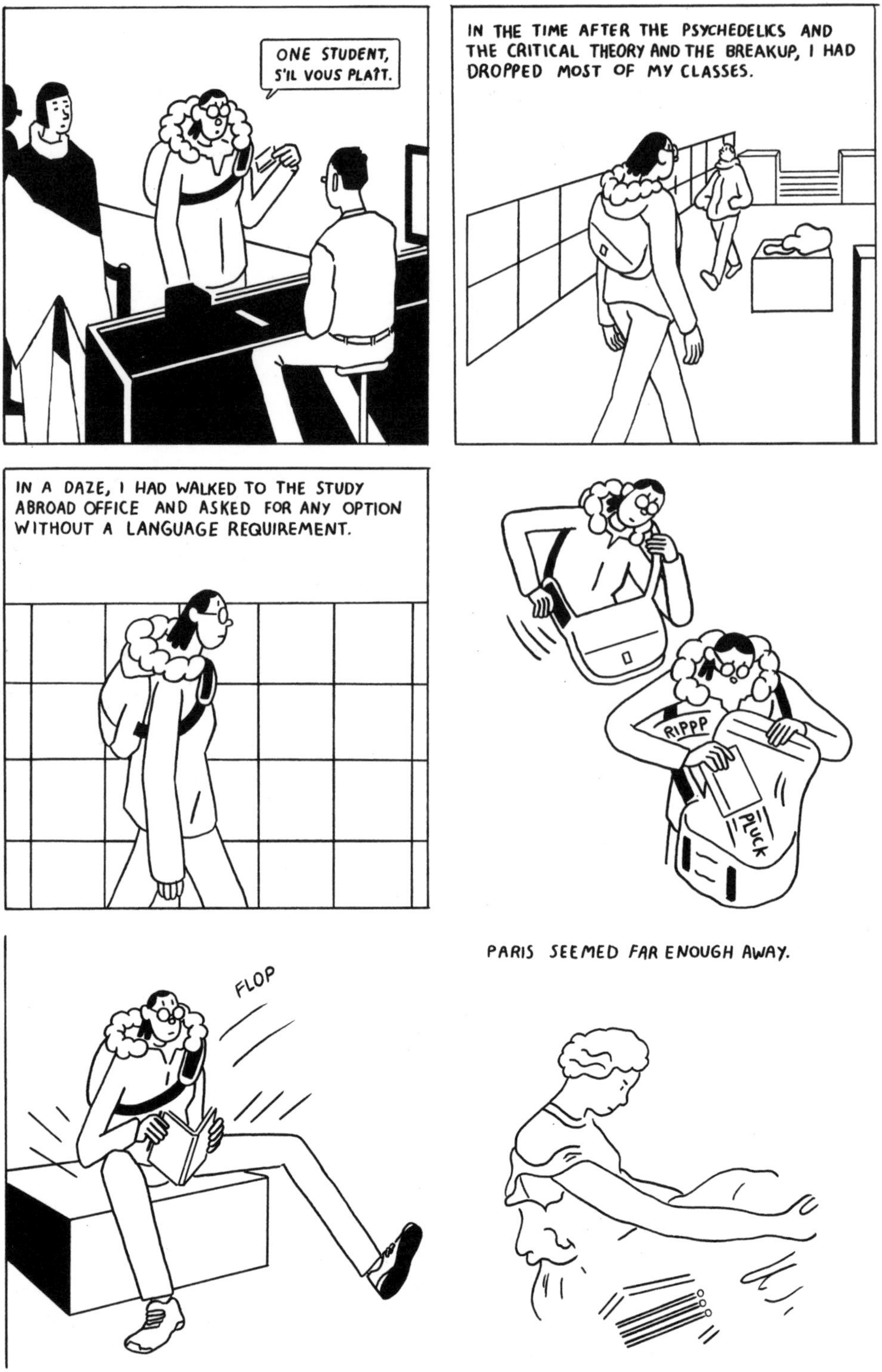
ONE STUDENT, S'IL VOUS PLAÎT.
IN THE TIME AFTER THE PSYCHEDELICS AND THE CRITICAL THEORY AND THE BREAKUP, I HAD DROPPED MOST OF MY CLASSES.
IN A DAZE, I HAD WALKED TO THE STUDY ABROAD OFFICE AND ASKED FOR ANY OPTION WITHOUT A LANGUAGE REQUIREMENT.
RIPPP
PLUCK
FLOP
PARIS SEEMED FAR ENOUGH AWAY.

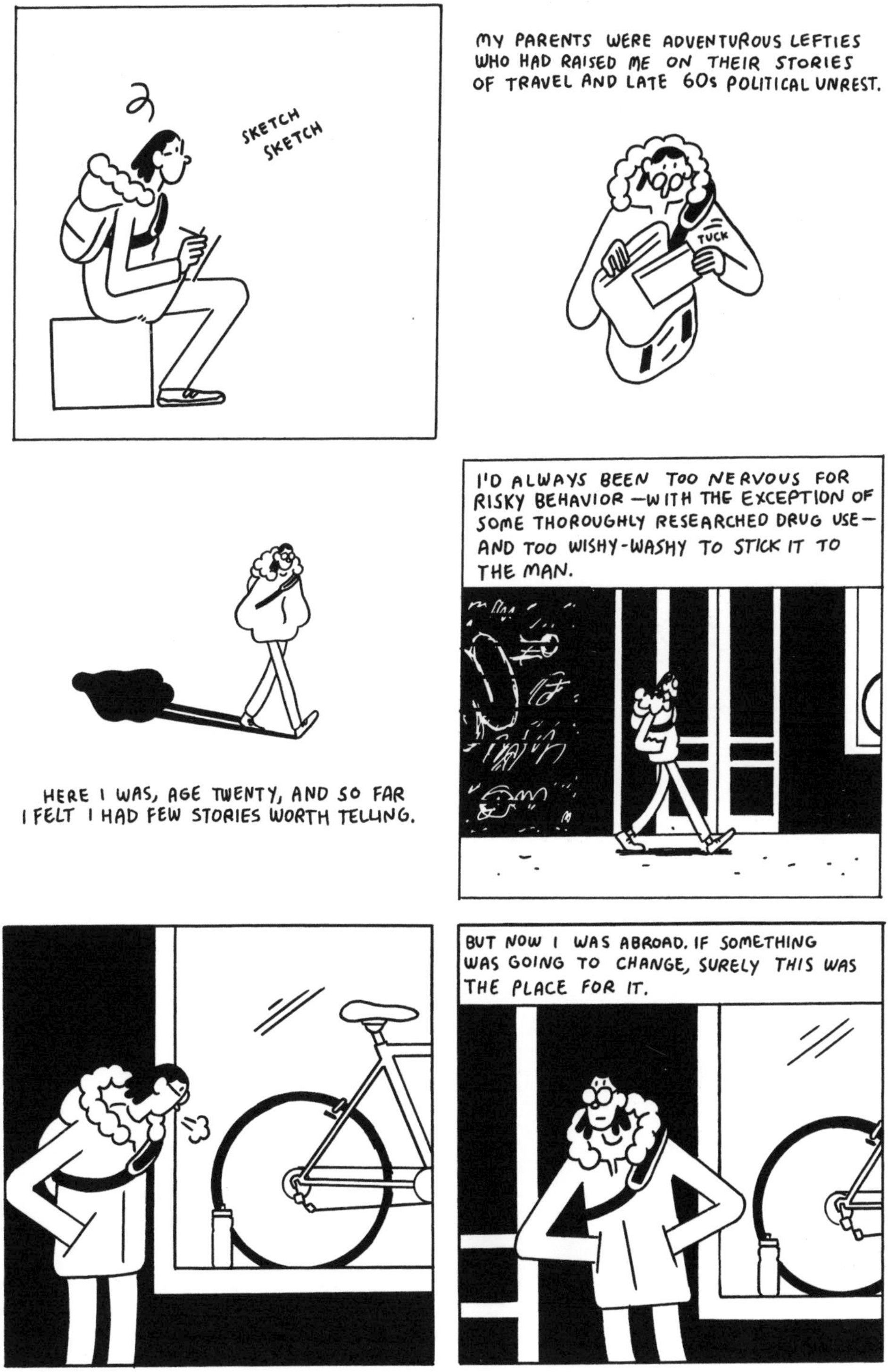
SKETCH
SKETCH
MY PARENTS WERE ADVENTUROUS LEFTIES WHO HAD RAISED ME ON THEIR STORIES OF TRAVEL AND LATE 60s POLITICAL UNREST.
TUCK
HERE I WAS, AGE TWENTY, AND SO FAR I FELT I HAD FEW STORIES WORTH TELLING.
I'D ALWAYS BEEN TOO NERVOUS FOR RISKY BEHAVIOR—WITH THE EXCEPTION OF SOME THOROUGHLY RESEARCHED DRUG USE—AND TOO WISHY-WASHY TO STICK IT TO THE MAN.
BUT NOW I WAS ABROAD. IF SOMETHING WAS GOING TO CHANGE, SURELY THIS WAS THE PLACE FOR IT.

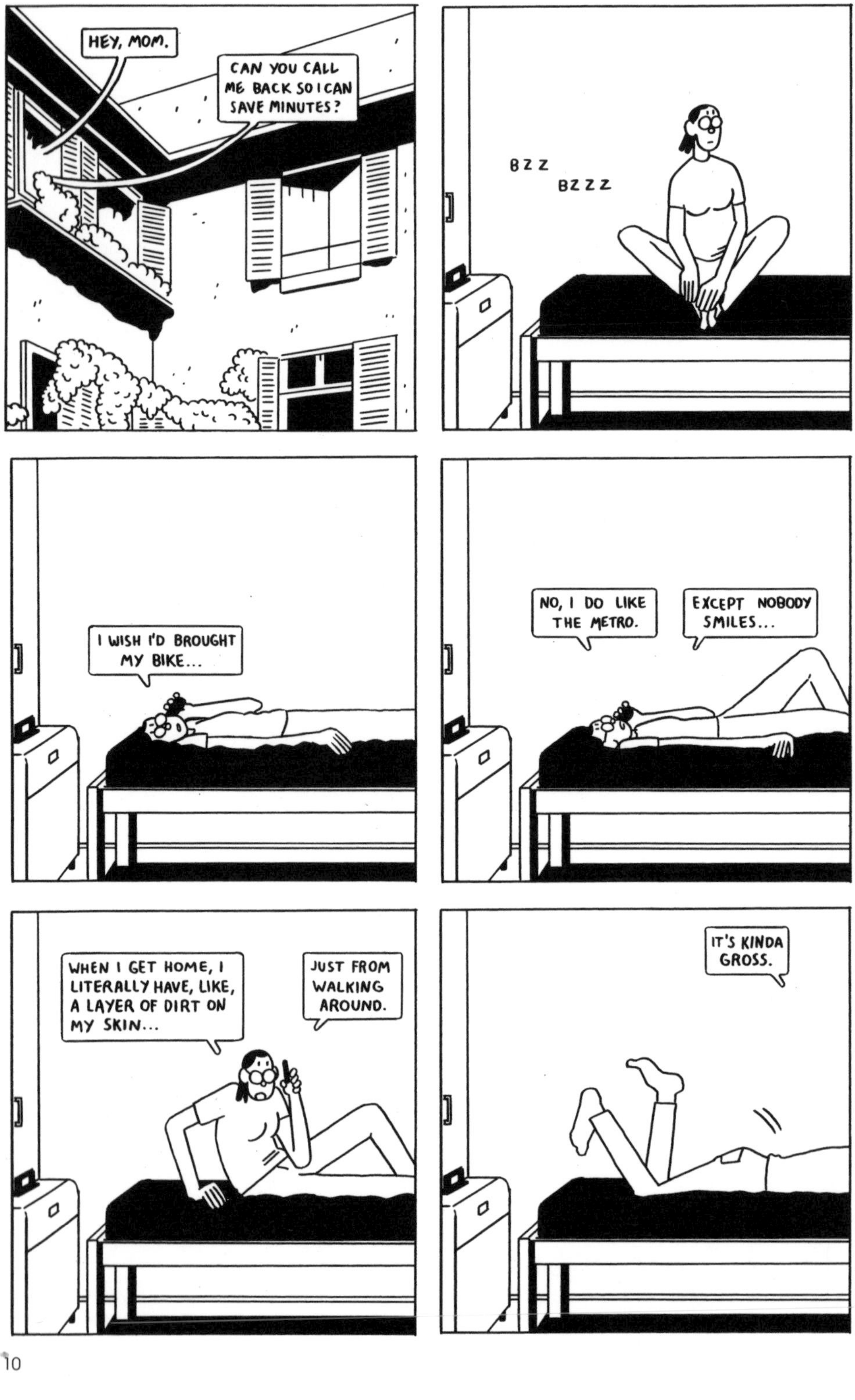
HEY, MOM.
CAN YOU CALL ME BACK SO I CAN SAVE MINUTES?
BZZ
BZZZ
I WISH I'D BROUGHT MY BIKE...
NO, I DO LIKE THE METRO.
EXCEPT NOBODY SMILES...
WHEN I GET HOME, I LITERALLY HAVE, LIKE, A LAYER OF DIRT ON MY SKIN...
JUST FROM WALKING AROUND.
IT'S KINDA GROSS.

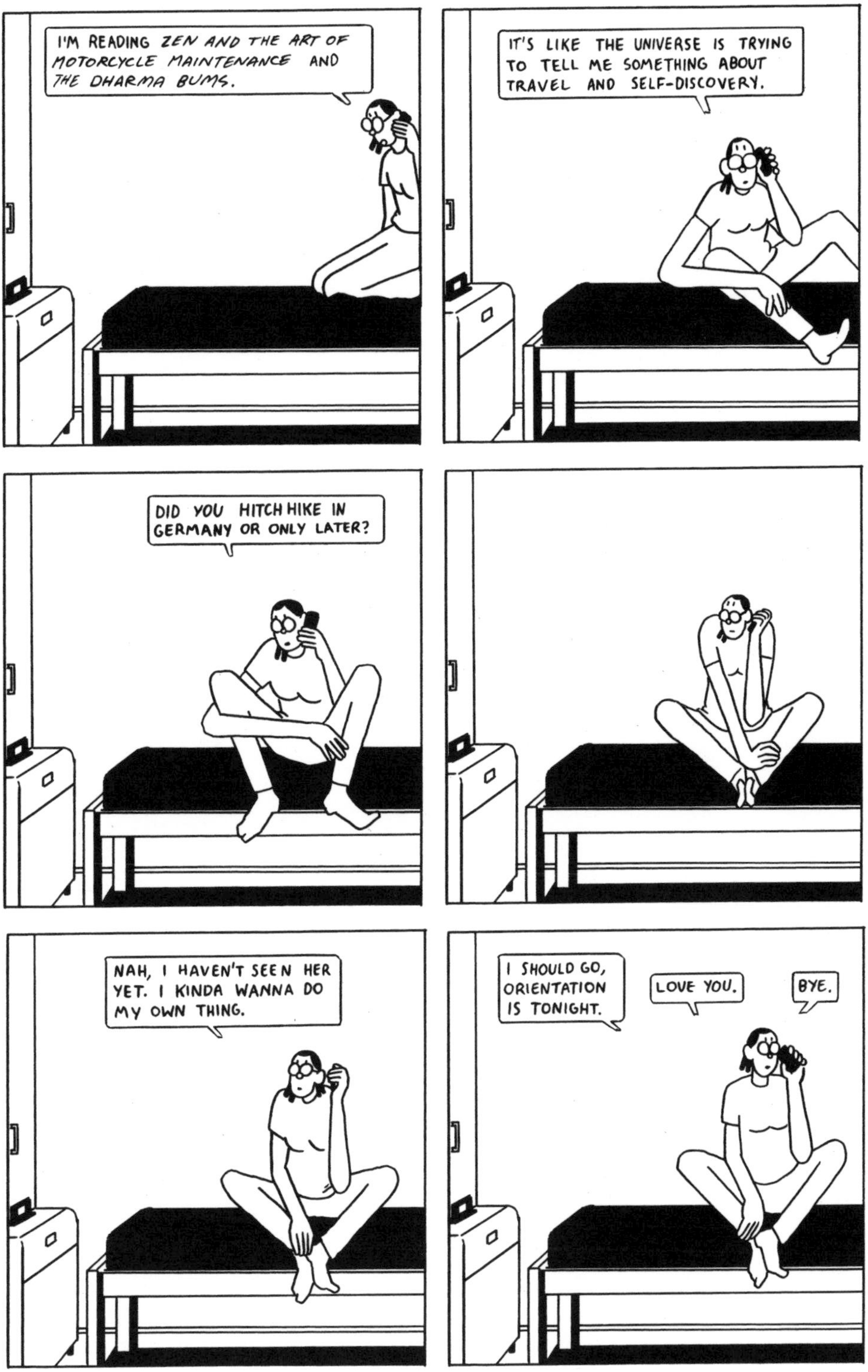

I'M READING *ZEN AND THE ART OF MOTORCYCLE MAINTENANCE* AND *THE DHARMA BUMS*.
IT'S LIKE THE UNIVERSE IS TRYING TO TELL ME SOMETHING ABOUT TRAVEL AND SELF-DISCOVERY.
DID YOU HITCHHIKE IN GERMANY OR ONLY LATER?
NAH, I HAVEN'T SEEN HER YET. I KINDA WANNA DO MY OWN THING.
I SHOULD GO, ORIENTATION IS TONIGHT.
LOVE YOU.
BYE.

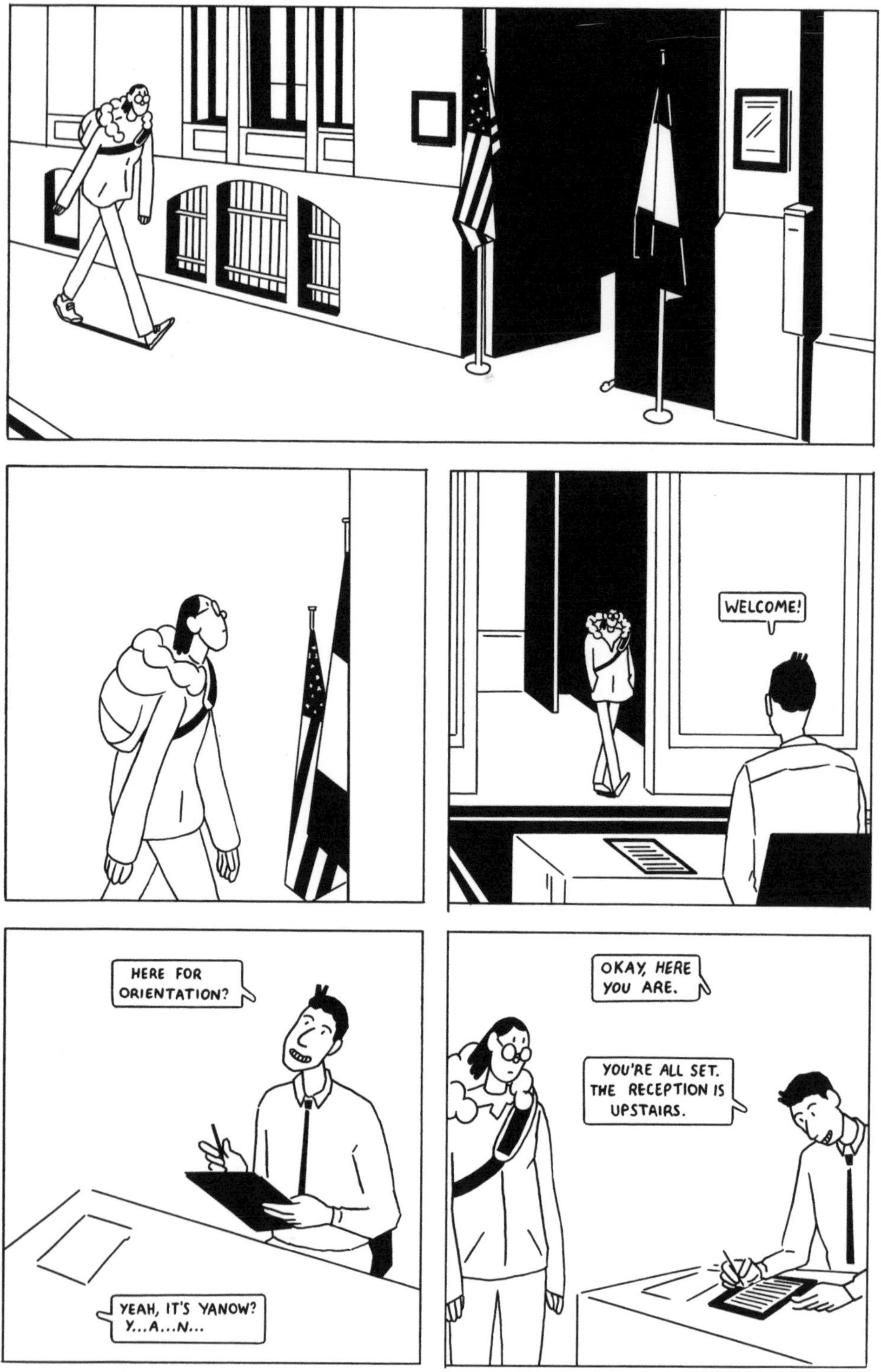
WELCOME!
HERE FOR ORIENTATION?
YEAH, IT'S YANOW? Y...A...N...
OKAY, HERE YOU ARE.
YOU'RE ALL SET. THE RECEPTION IS UPSTAIRS.

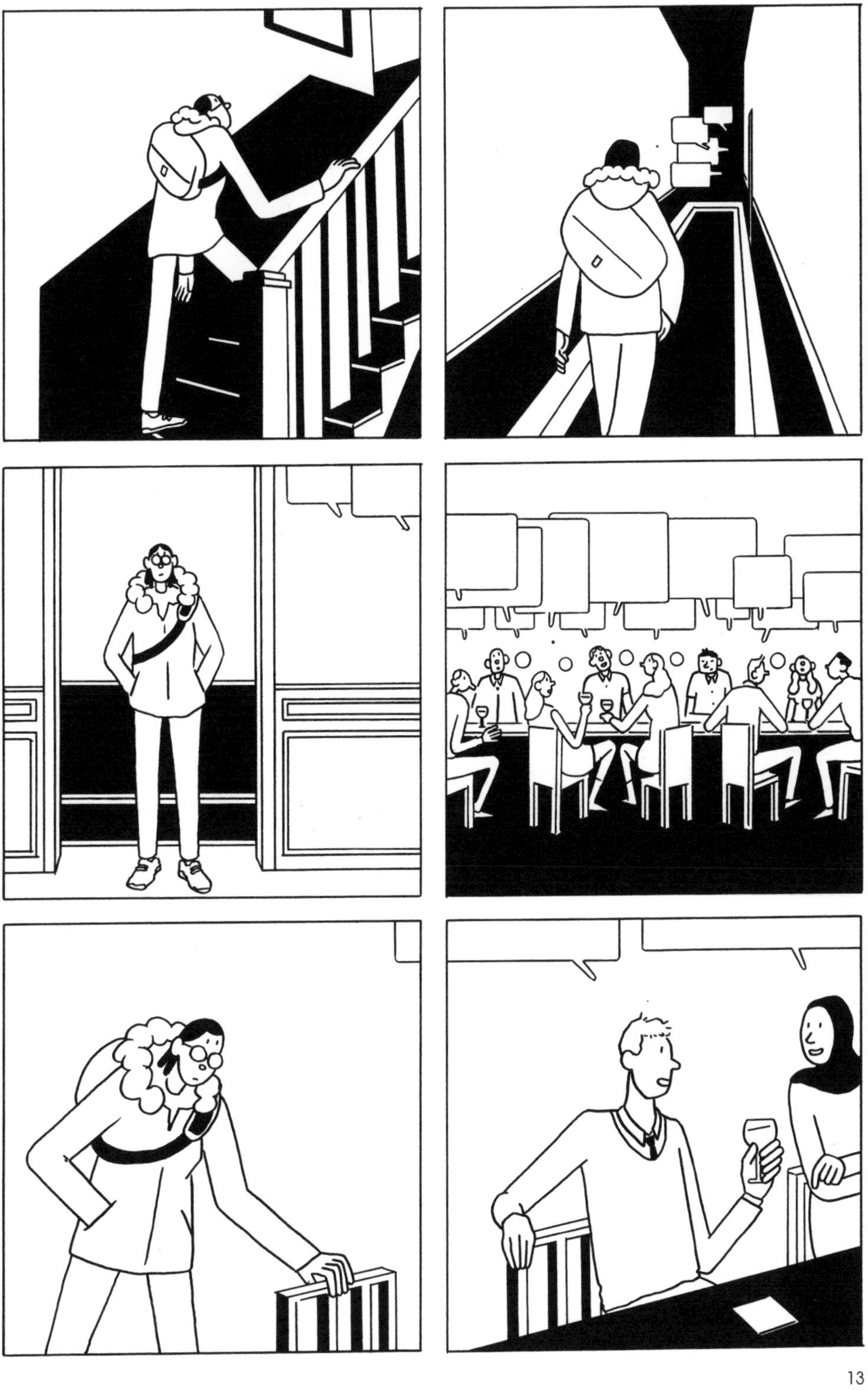

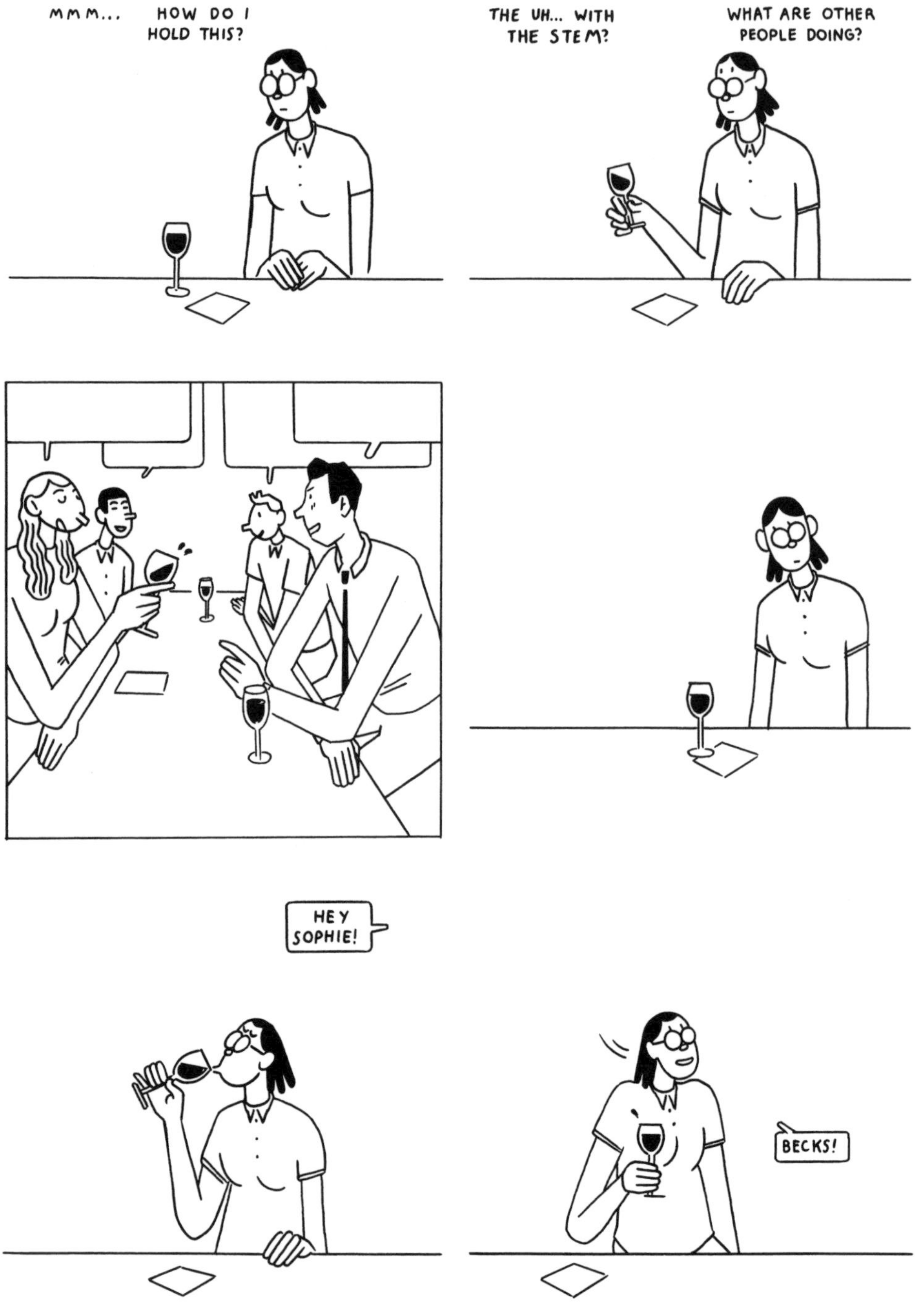
MMM...
HOW DO I HOLD THIS?
THE UH... WITH THE STEM?
WHAT ARE OTHER PEOPLE DOING?
HEY SOPHIE!
BECKS!

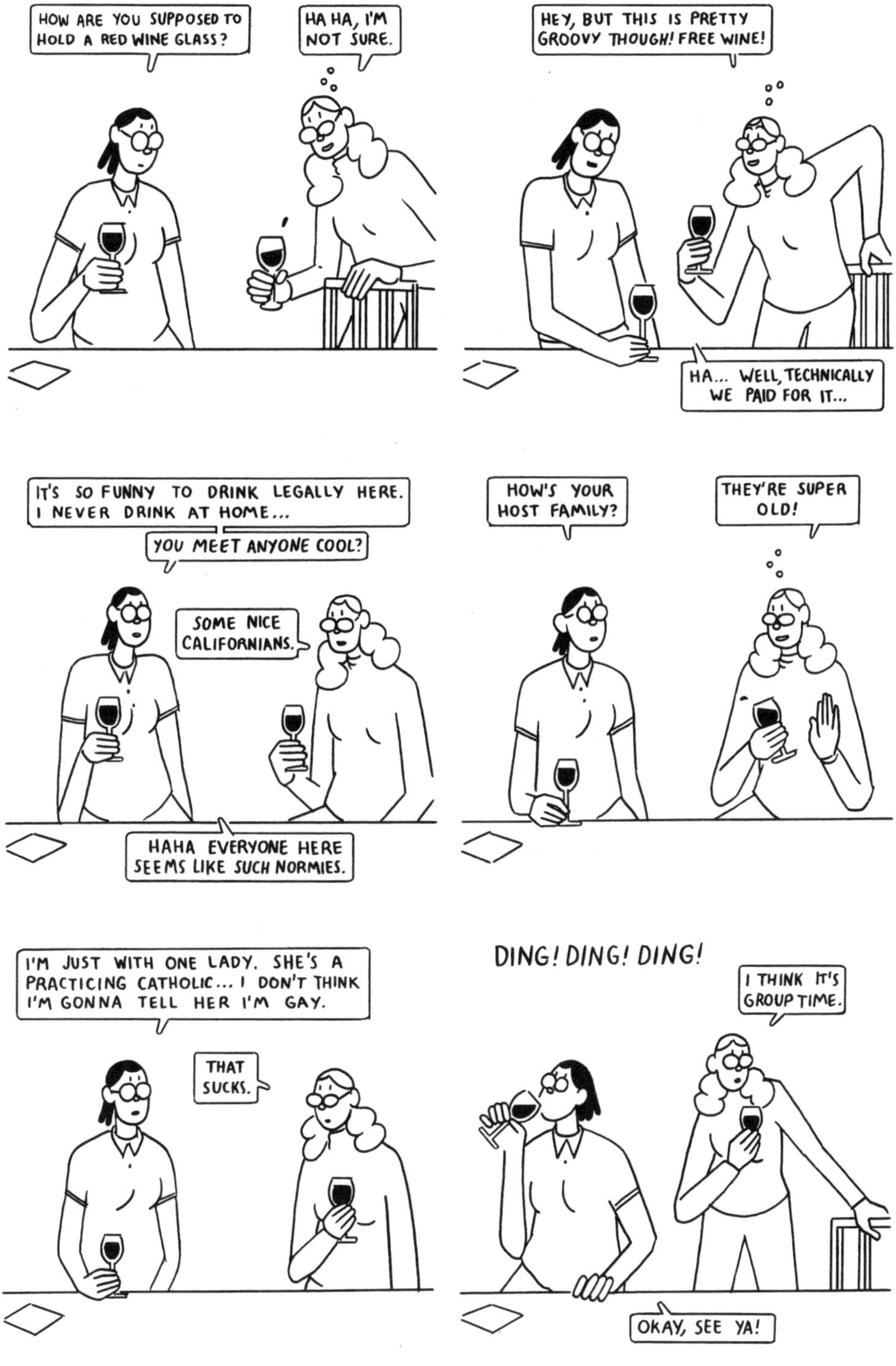
HOW ARE YOU SUPPOSED TO HOLD A RED WINE GLASS?
HA HA, I'M NOT SURE.
HEY, BUT THIS IS PRETTY GROOVY THOUGH! FREE WINE!
HA... WELL, TECHNICALLY WE PAID FOR IT...
IT'S SO FUNNY TO DRINK LEGALLY HERE. I NEVER DRINK AT HOME...
YOU MEET ANYONE COOL?
SOME NICE CALIFORNIANS.
HAHA EVERYONE HERE SEEMS LIKE SUCH NORMIES.
HOW'S YOUR HOST FAMILY?
THEY'RE SUPER OLD!
I'M JUST WITH ONE LADY. SHE'S A PRACTICING CATHOLIC... I DON'T THINK I'M GONNA TELL HER I'M GAY.
THAT SUCKS.
DING! DING! DING!
I THINK IT'S GROUP TIME.
OKAY, SEE YA!

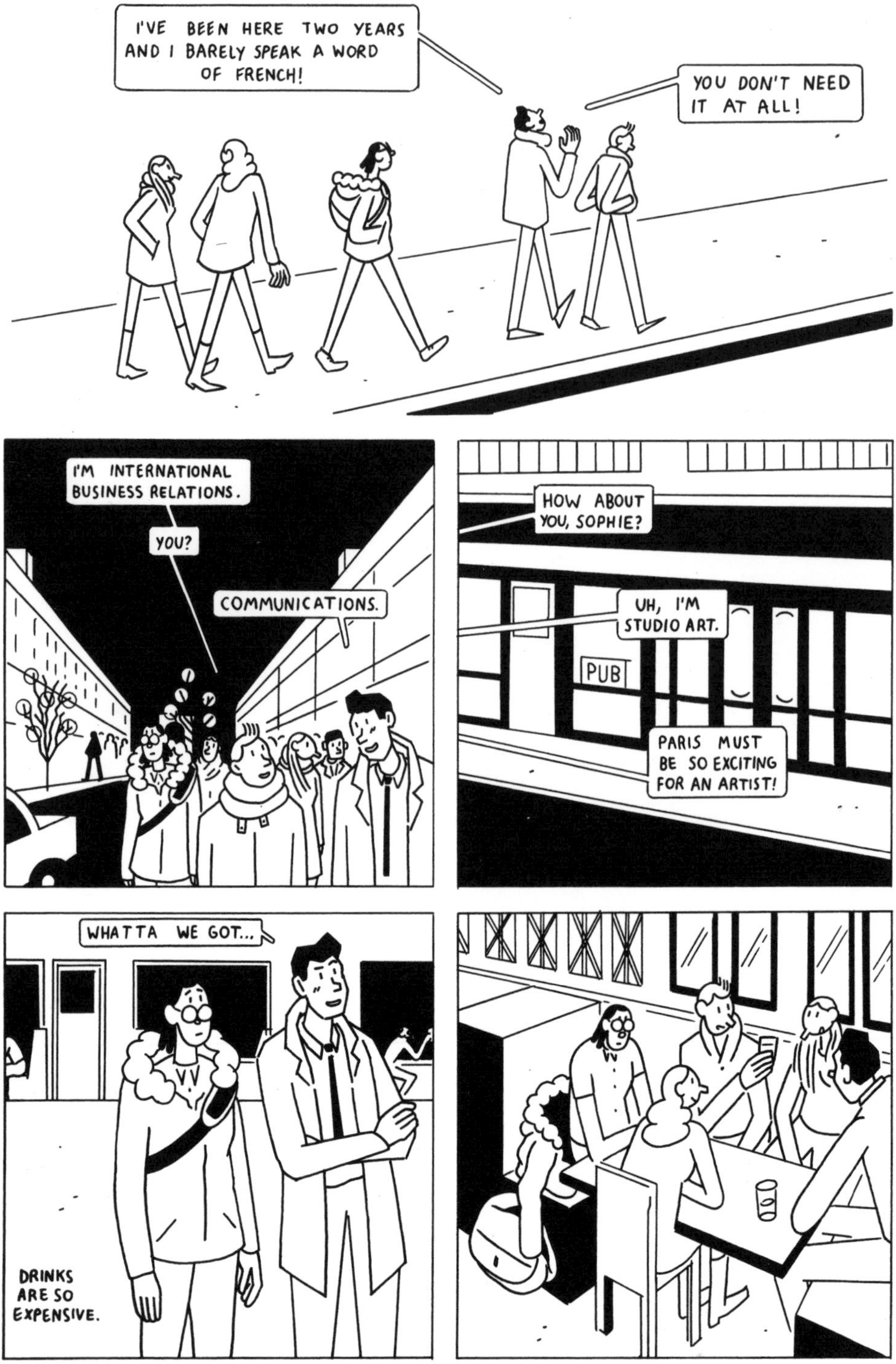
I'VE BEEN HERE TWO YEARS AND I BARELY SPEAK A WORD OF FRENCH!
YOU DON'T NEED IT AT ALL!
I'M INTERNATIONAL BUSINESS RELATIONS.
YOU?
COMMUNICATIONS.
HOW ABOUT YOU, SOPHIE?
UH, I'M STUDIO ART.
PUB
PARIS MUST BE SO EXCITING FOR AN ARTIST!
WHATTA WE GOT...
DRINKS ARE SO EXPENSIVE.

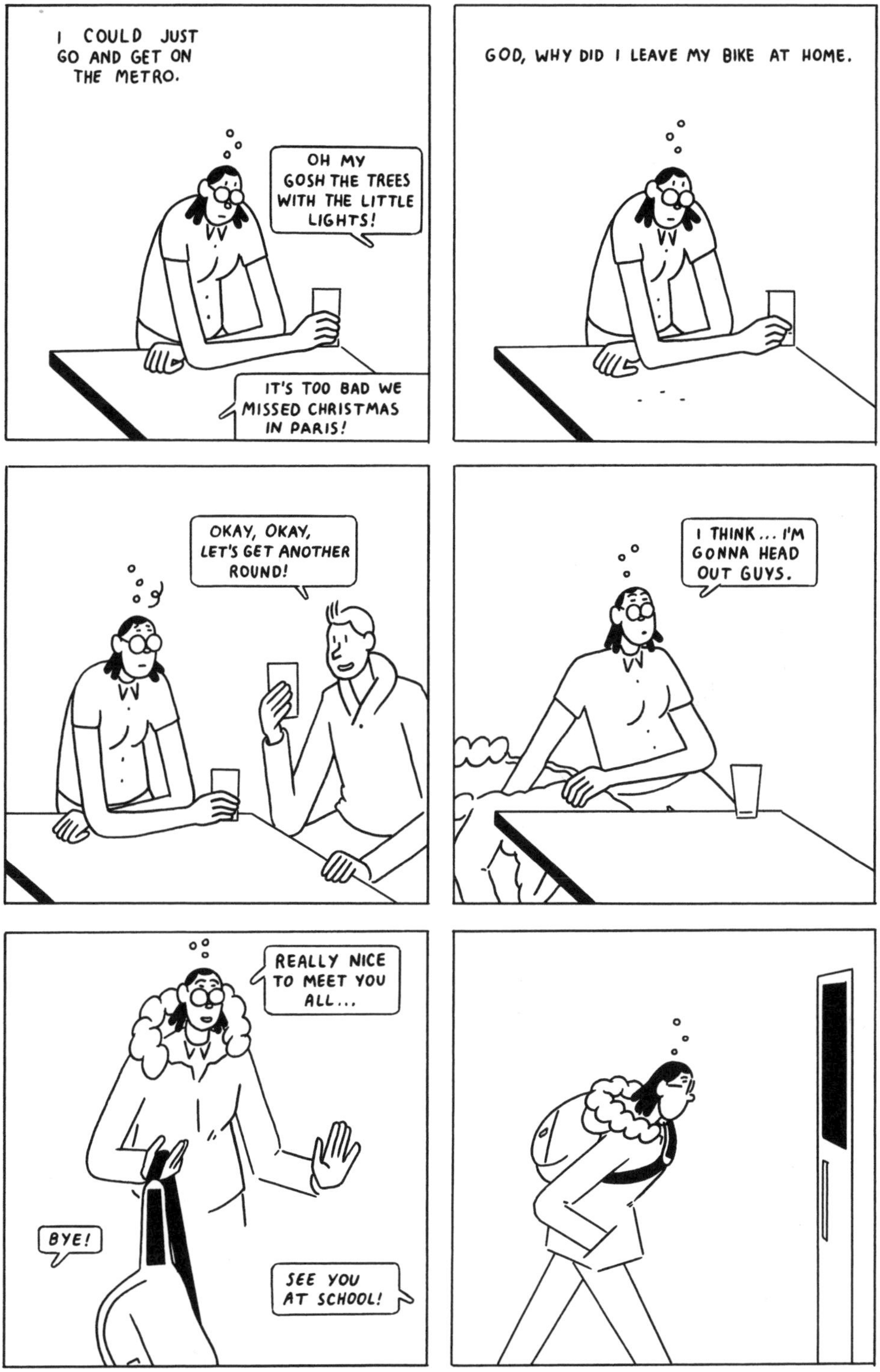
I COULD JUST GO AND GET ON THE METRO.
OH MY GOSH THE TREES WITH THE LITTLE LIGHTS!
IT'S TOO BAD WE MISSED CHRISTMAS IN PARIS!
GOD, WHY DID I LEAVE MY BIKE AT HOME.
OKAY, OKAY, LET'S GET ANOTHER ROUND!
I THINK... I'M GONNA HEAD OUT GUYS.
REALLY NICE TO MEET YOU ALL...
BYE!
SEE YOU AT SCHOOL!

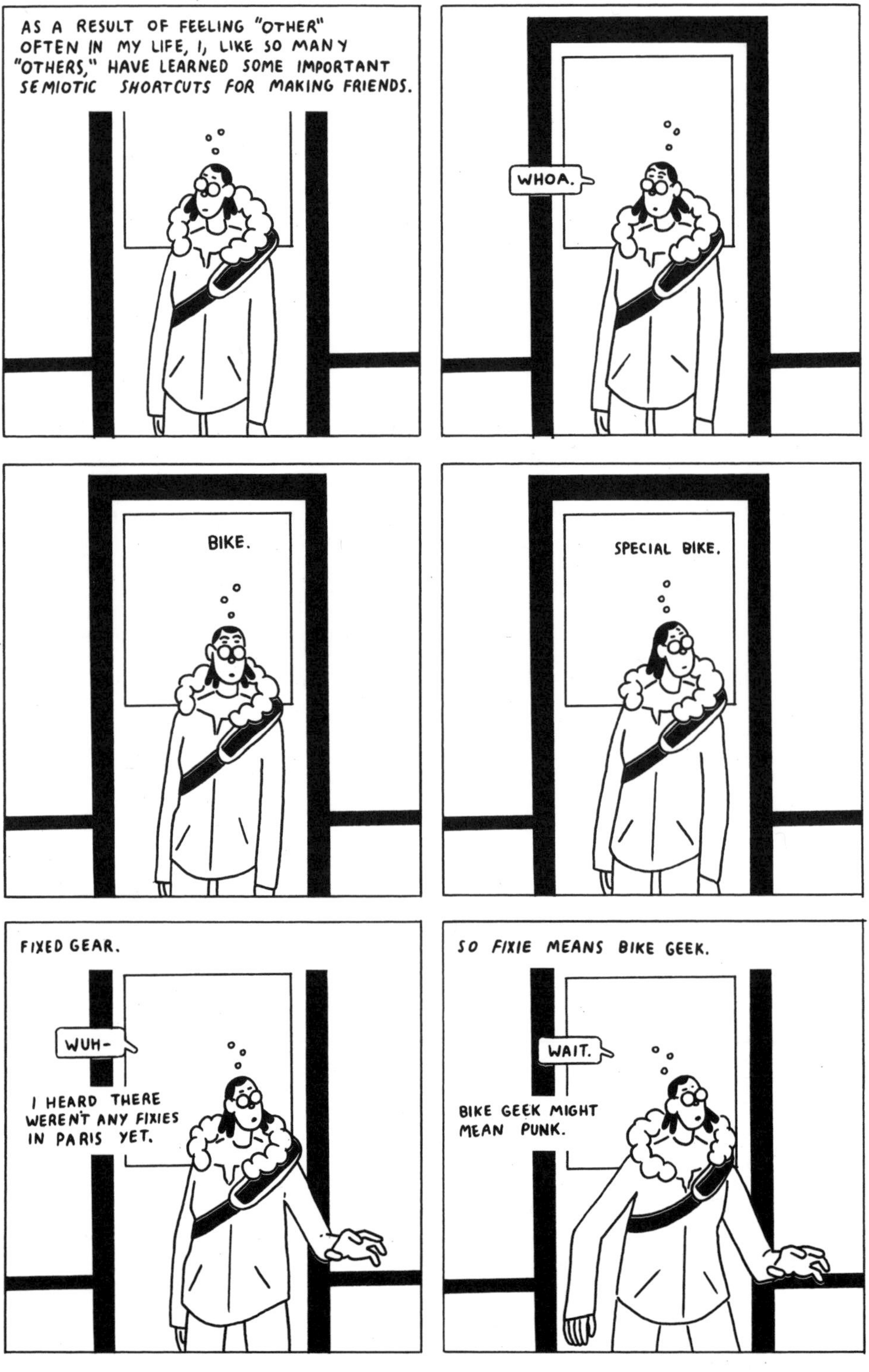
AS A RESULT OF FEELING "OTHER" OFTEN IN MY LIFE, I, LIKE SO MANY "OTHERS," HAVE LEARNED SOME IMPORTANT SEMIOTIC SHORTCUTS FOR MAKING FRIENDS.
WHOA.
BIKE.
SPECIAL BIKE.
FIXED GEAR.
WUH-
I HEARD THERE WEREN'T ANY FIXIES IN PARIS YET.
SO FIXIE MEANS BIKE GEEK.
WAIT.
BIKE GEEK MIGHT MEAN PUNK.

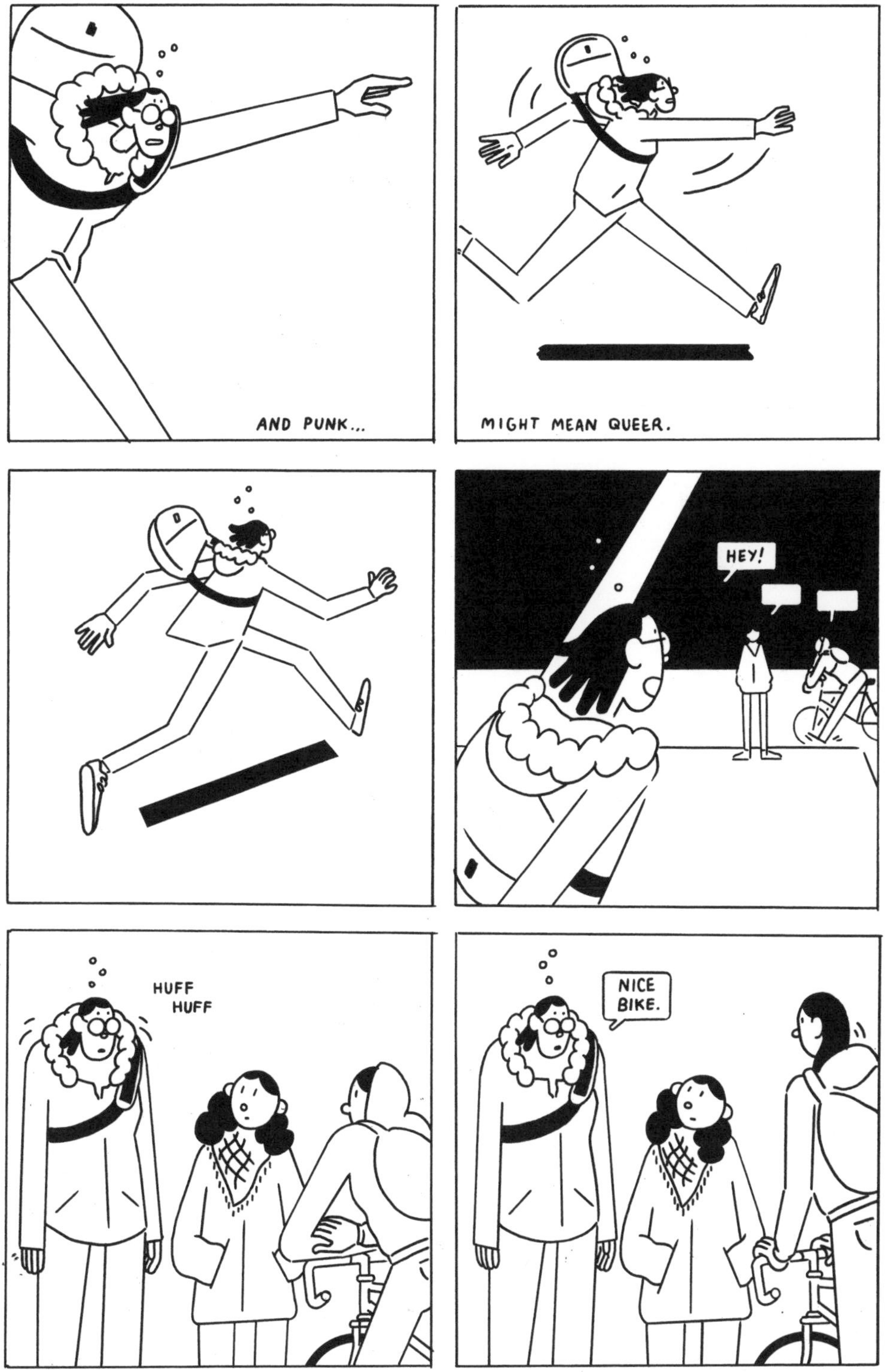
AND PUNK...
MIGHT MEAN QUEER.
HEY!
HUFF
HUFF
NICE
BIKE.

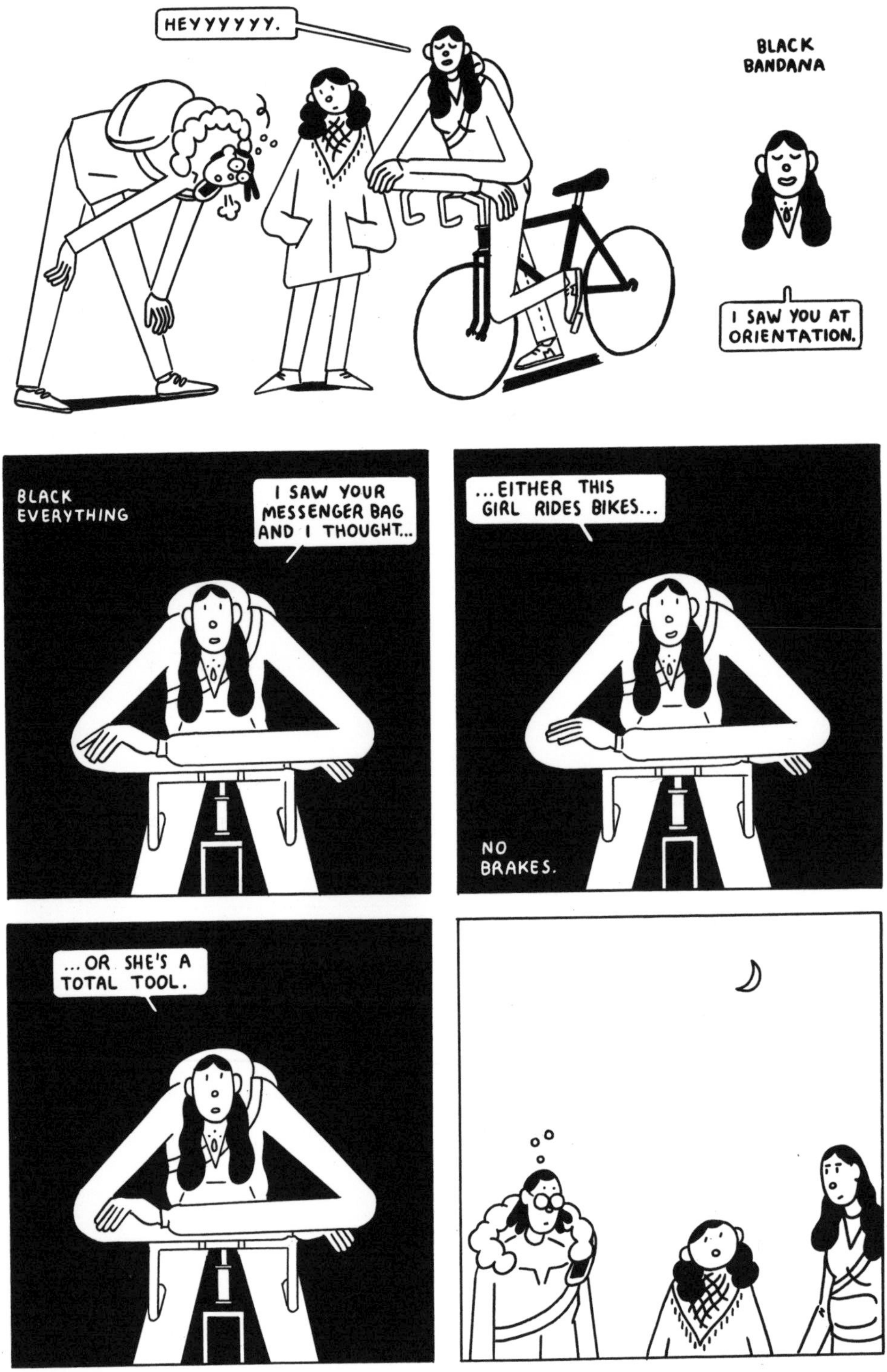
HEYYYYYY.
BLACK BANDANA
I SAW YOU AT ORIENTATION.
BLACK EVERYTHING
I SAW YOUR MESSENGER BAG AND I THOUGHT...
...EITHER THIS GIRL RIDES BIKES...
NO BRAKES.
...OR SHE'S A TOTAL TOOL.

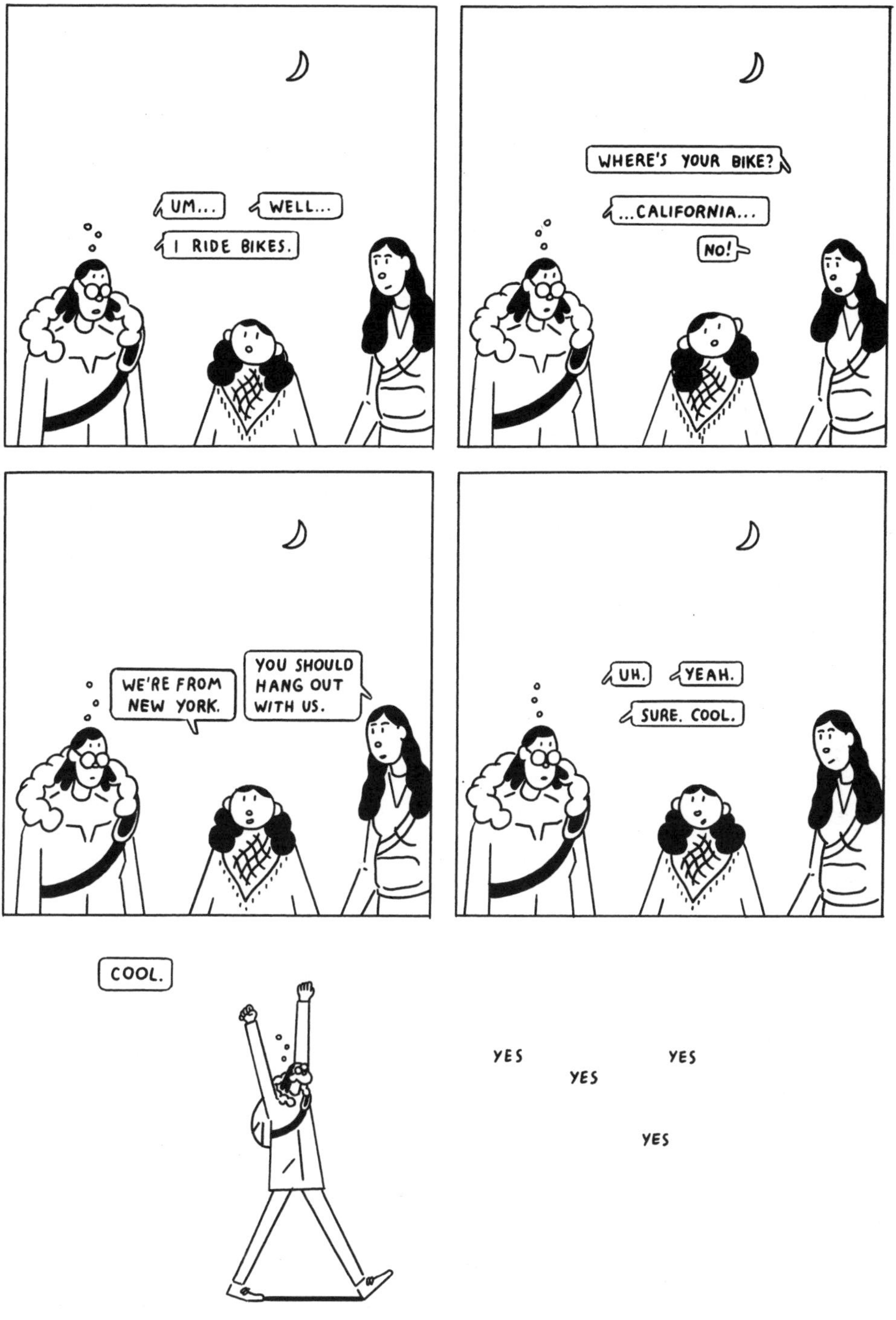

UM...
WELL...
I RIDE BIKES.
WHERE'S YOUR BIKE?
...CALIFORNIA...
NO!
WE'RE FROM NEW YORK.
YOU SHOULD HANG OUT WITH US.
UH.
YEAH.
SURE. COOL.
COOL.
YES
YES
YES
YES

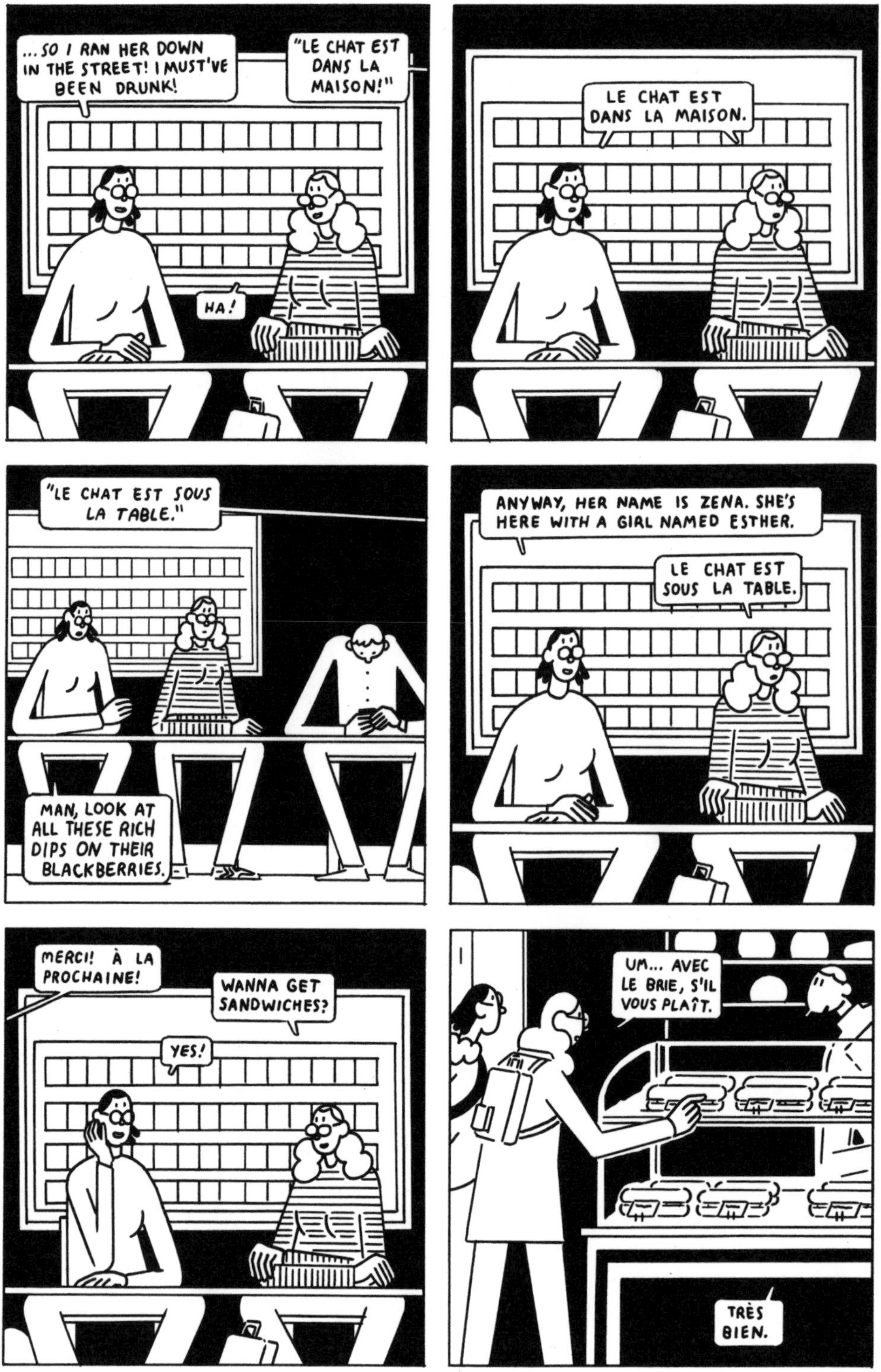
...SO I RAN HER DOWN IN THE STREET! I MUST'VE BEEN DRUNK!
"LE CHAT EST DANS LA MAISON!"
HA!
LE CHAT EST DANS LA MAISON.
"LE CHAT EST SOUS LA TABLE."
MAN, LOOK AT ALL THESE RICH DIPS ON THEIR BLACKBERRIES.
ANYWAY, HER NAME IS ZENA. SHE'S HERE WITH A GIRL NAMED ESTHER.
LE CHAT EST SOUS LA TABLE.
MERCI! À LA PROCHAINE!
WANNA GET SANDWICHES?
YES!
UM... AVEC LE BRIE, S'IL VOUS PLAÎT.
TRÈS BIEN.

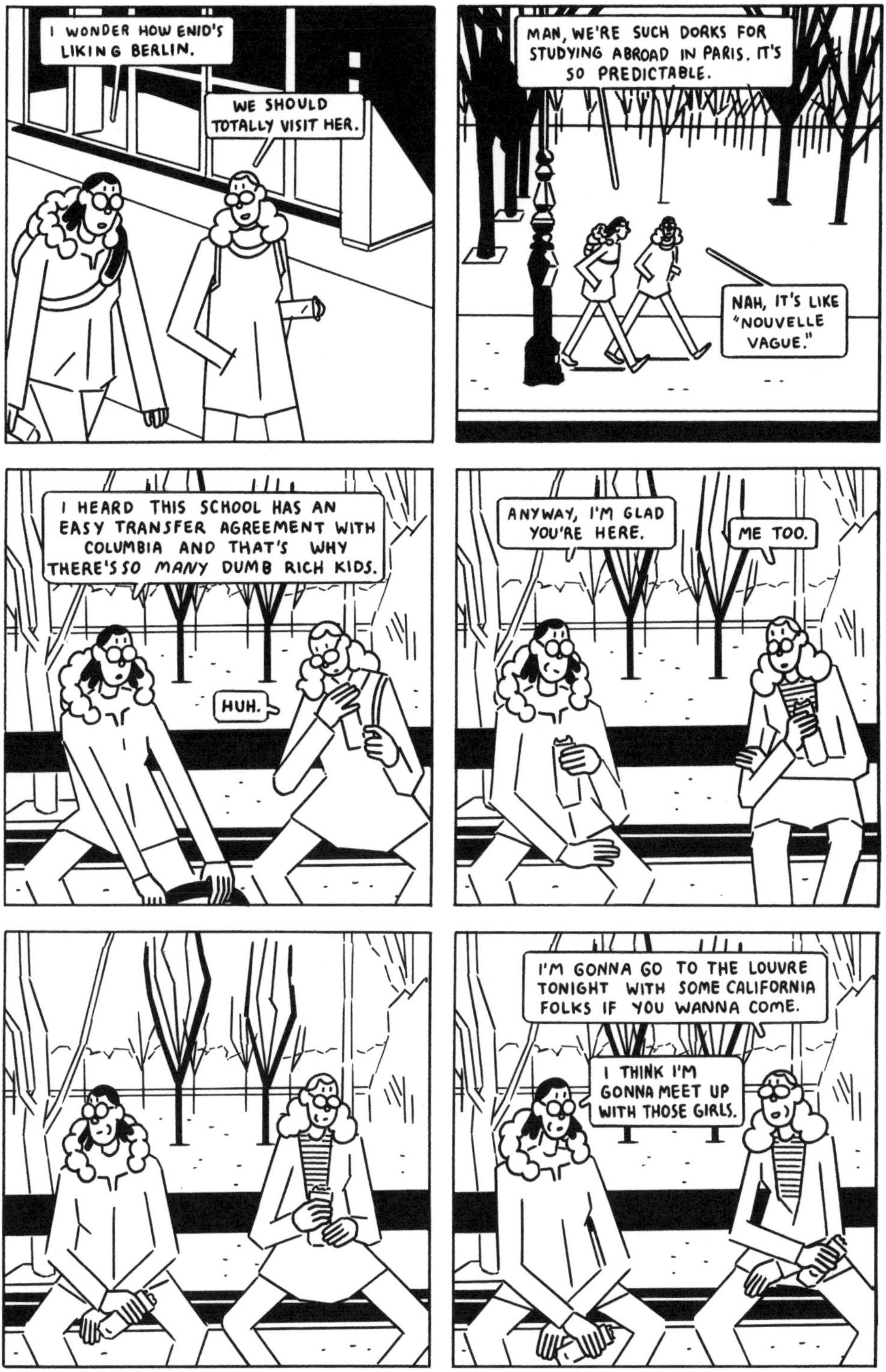
I WONDER HOW ENID'S LIKING BERLIN.
WE SHOULD TOTALLY VISIT HER.
MAN, WE'RE SUCH DORKS FOR STUDYING ABROAD IN PARIS. IT'S SO PREDICTABLE.
NAH, IT'S LIKE "NOUVELLE VAGUE."
I HEARD THIS SCHOOL HAS AN EASY TRANSFER AGREEMENT WITH COLUMBIA AND THAT'S WHY THERE'S SO MANY DUMB RICH KIDS.
HUH.
ANYWAY, I'M GLAD YOU'RE HERE.
ME TOO.
I'M GONNA GO TO THE LOUVRE TONIGHT WITH SOME CALIFORNIA FOLKS IF YOU WANNA COME.
I THINK I'M GONNA MEET UP WITH THOSE GIRLS.

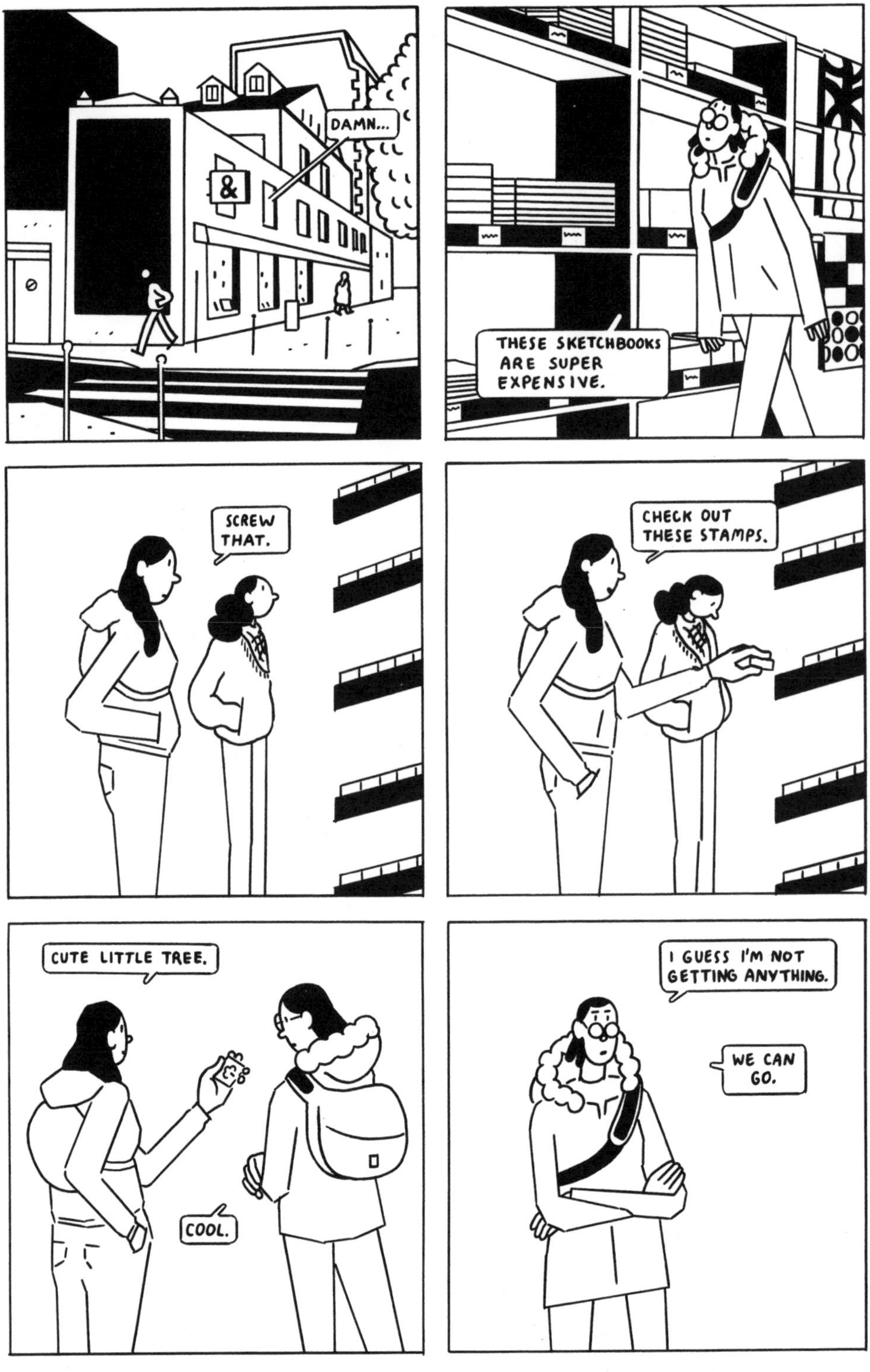
DAMN...
THESE SKETCHBOOKS ARE SUPER EXPENSIVE.
SCREW THAT.
CHECK OUT THESE STAMPS.
CUTE LITTLE TREE.
COOL.
I GUESS I'M NOT GETTING ANYTHING.
WE CAN GO.

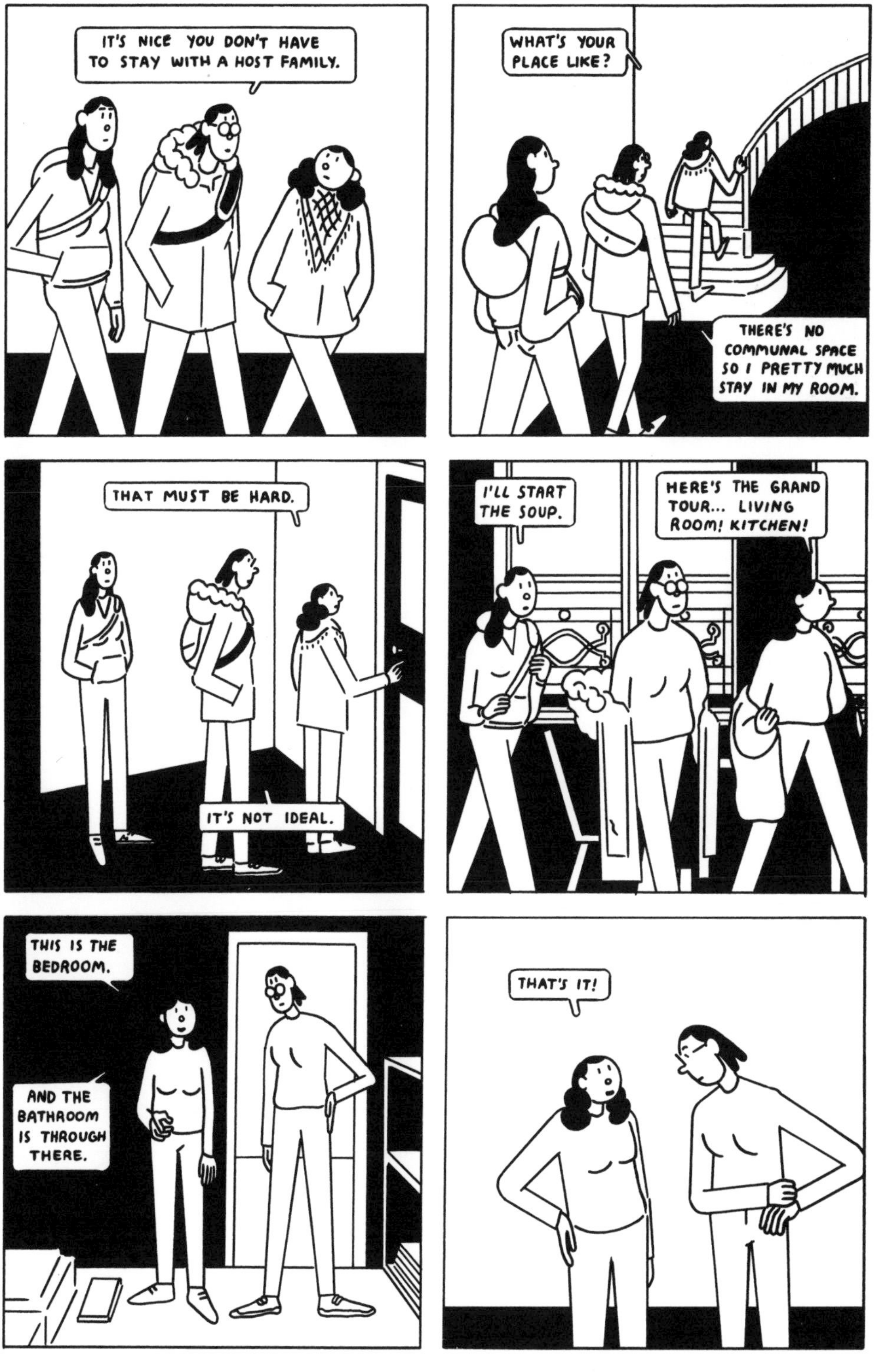
IT'S NICE YOU DON'T HAVE TO STAY WITH A HOST FAMILY.
WHAT'S YOUR PLACE LIKE?
THERE'S NO COMMUNAL SPACE SO I PRETTY MUCH STAY IN MY ROOM.
THAT MUST BE HARD.
IT'S NOT IDEAL.
I'LL START THE SOUP.
HERE'S THE GRAND TOUR... LIVING ROOM! KITCHEN!
THIS IS THE BEDROOM.
AND THE BATHROOM IS THROUGH THERE.
THAT'S IT!

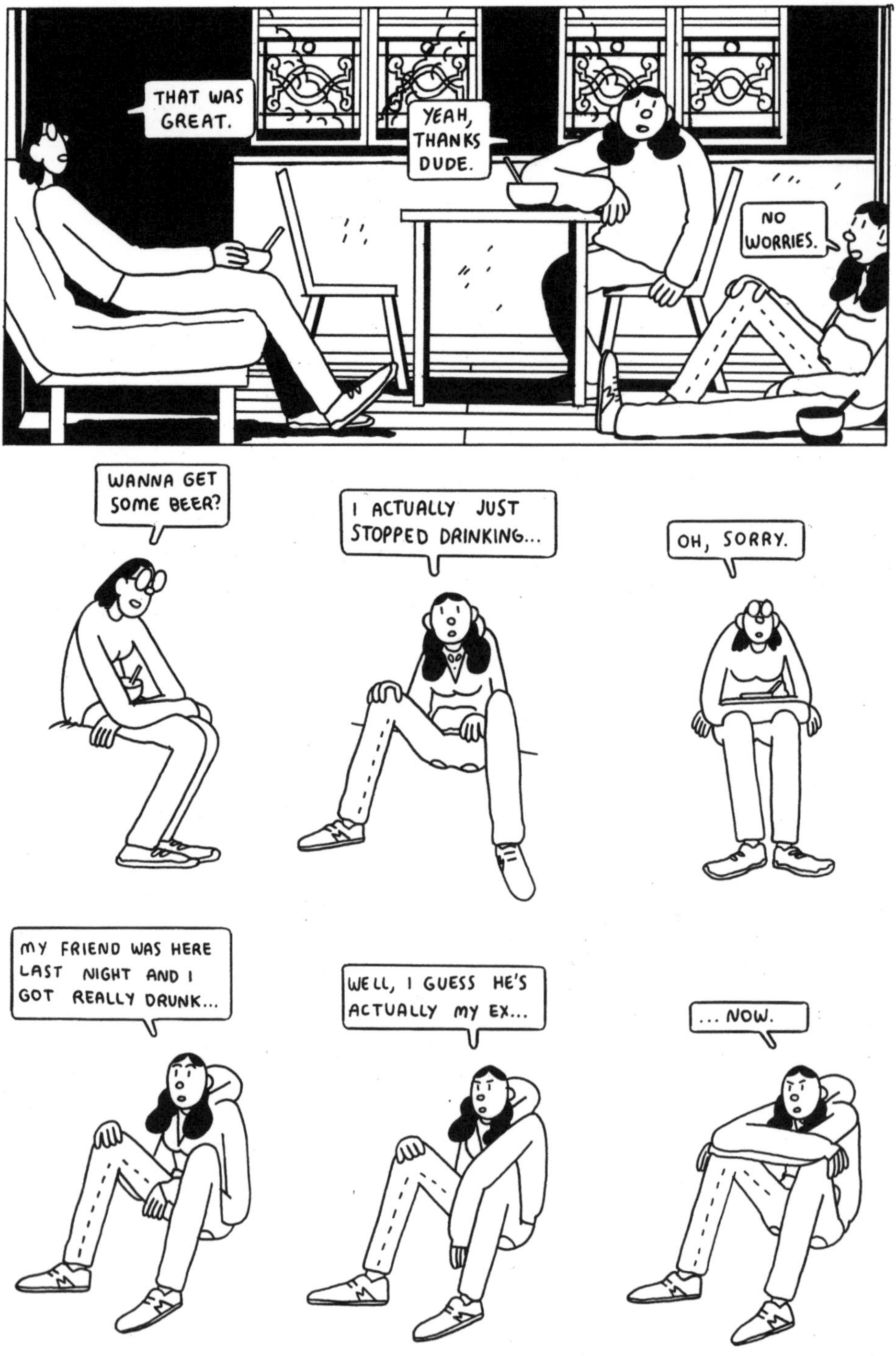
THAT WAS GREAT.
YEAH, THANKS DUDE.
NO WORRIES.
WANNA GET SOME BEER?
I ACTUALLY JUST STOPPED DRINKING...
OH, SORRY.
MY FRIEND WAS HERE LAST NIGHT AND I GOT REALLY DRUNK...
WELL, I GUESS HE'S ACTUALLY MY EX...
... NOW.

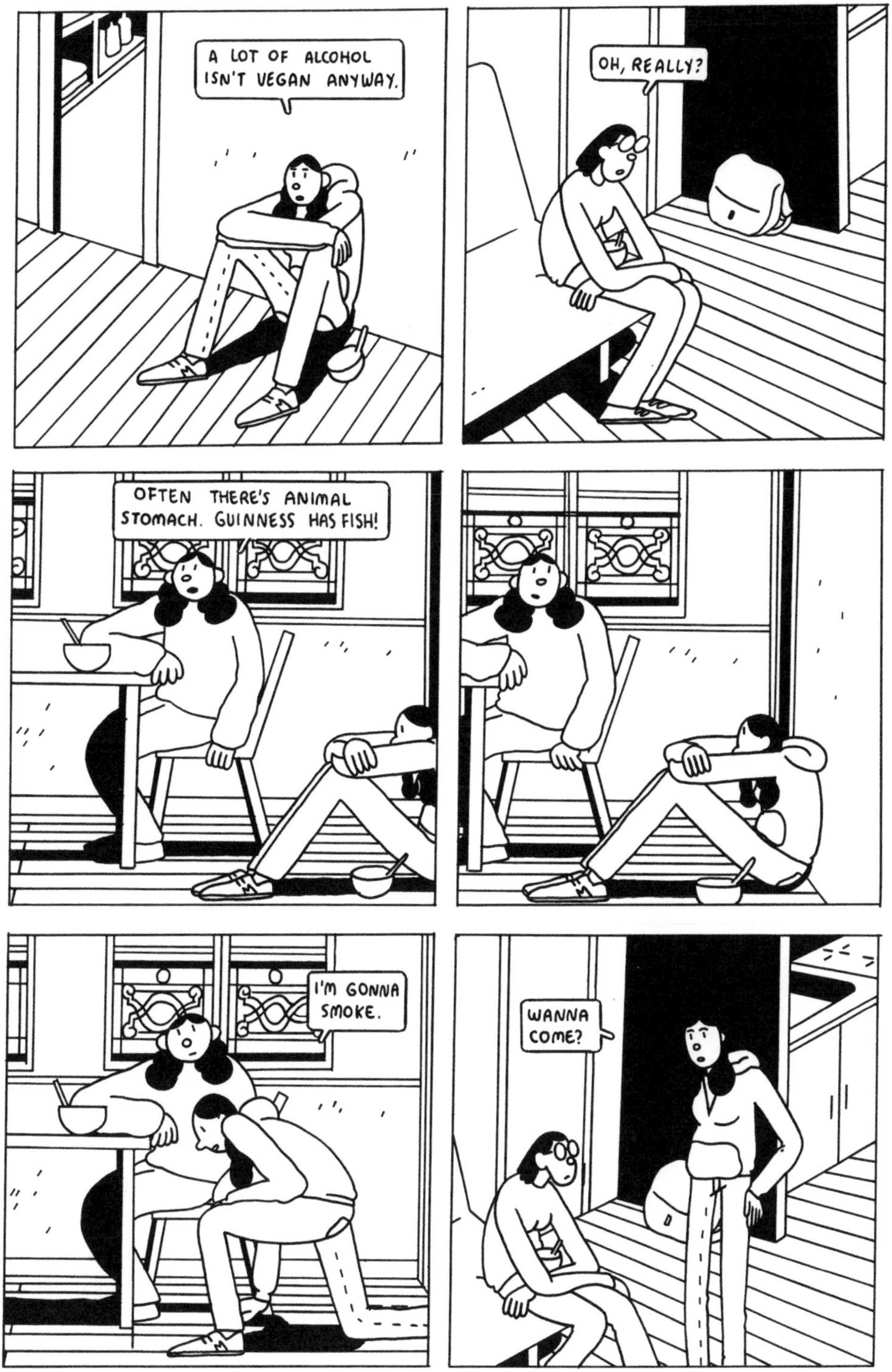
A LOT OF ALCOHOL ISN'T VEGAN ANYWAY.
OH, REALLY?
OFTEN THERE'S ANIMAL STOMACH. GUINNESS HAS FISH!
I'M GONNA SMOKE.
WANNA COME?

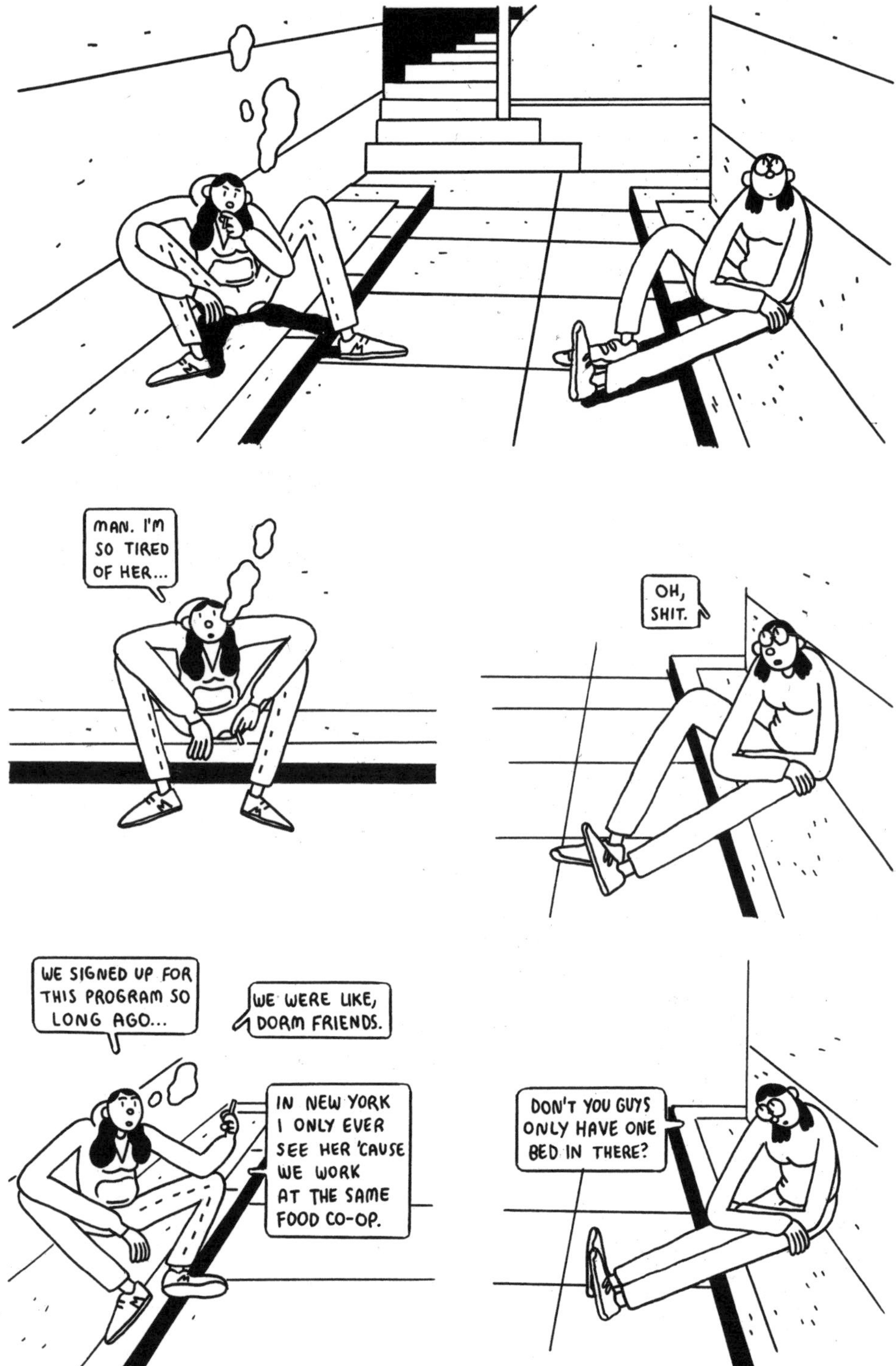
MAN. I'M SO TIRED OF HER...
OH, SHIT.
WE SIGNED UP FOR THIS PROGRAM SO LONG AGO...
WE WERE LIKE, DORM FRIENDS.
IN NEW YORK I ONLY EVER SEE HER 'CAUSE WE WORK AT THE SAME FOOD CO-OP.
DON'T YOU GUYS ONLY HAVE ONE BED IN THERE?

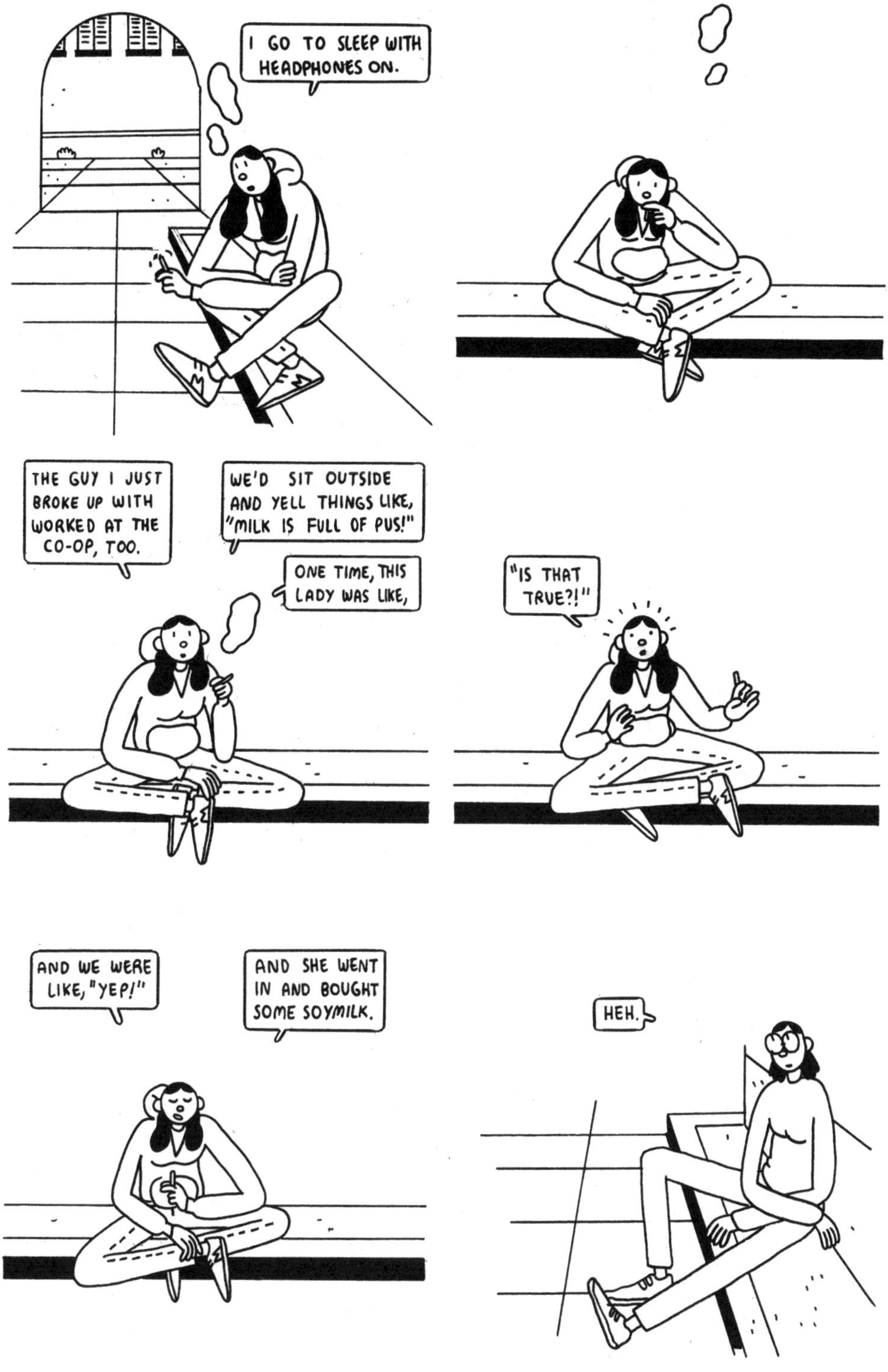
I GO TO SLEEP WITH HEADPHONES ON.
THE GUY I JUST BROKE UP WITH WORKED AT THE CO-OP, TOO.
WE'D SIT OUTSIDE AND YELL THINGS LIKE, "MILK IS FULL OF PUS!"
ONE TIME, THIS LADY WAS LIKE,
"IS THAT TRUE?!"
AND WE WERE LIKE, "YEP!"
AND SHE WENT IN AND BOUGHT SOME SOYMILK.
HEH.

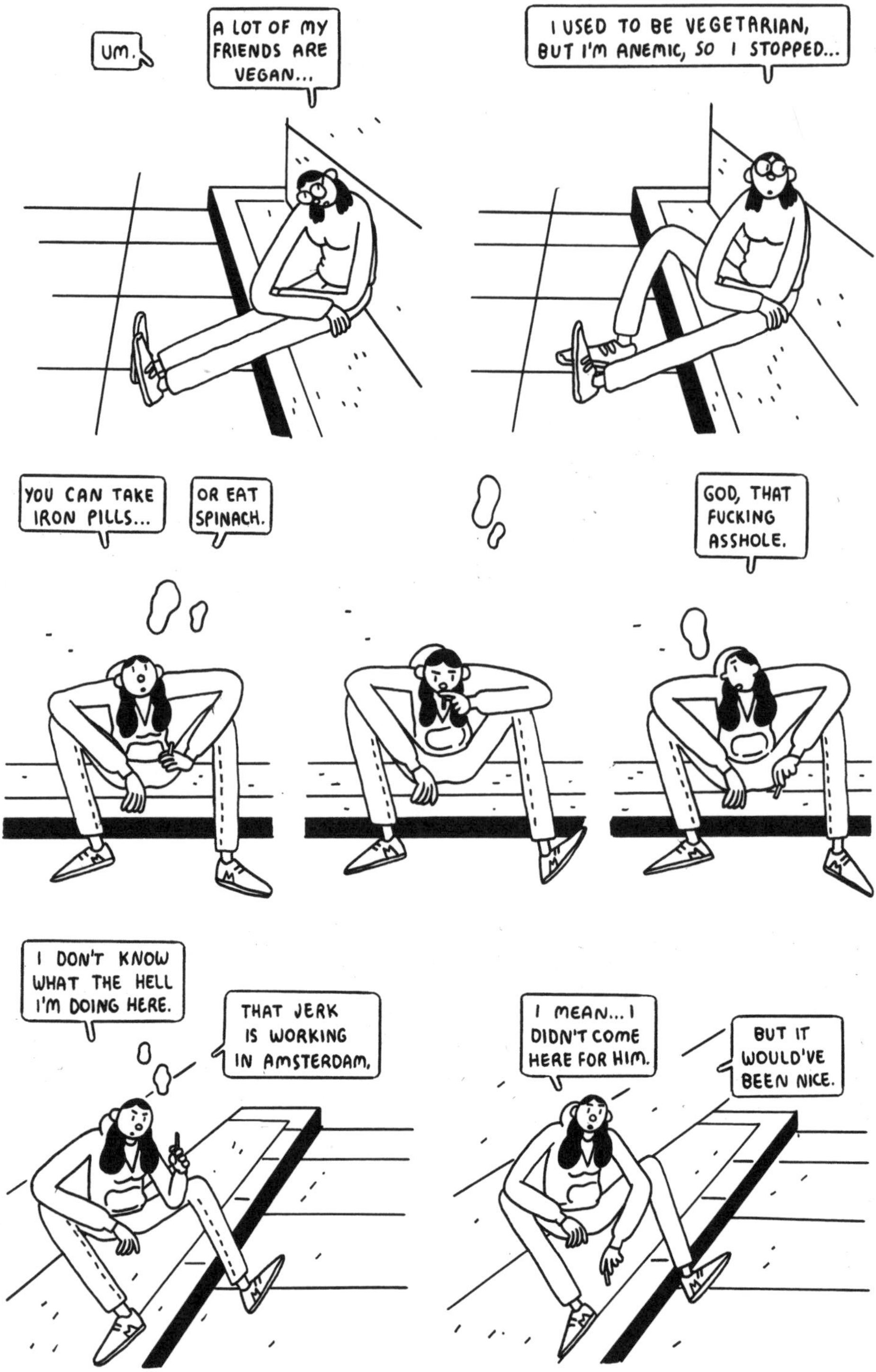
UM.
A LOT OF MY FRIENDS ARE VEGAN...
I USED TO BE VEGETARIAN, BUT I'M ANEMIC, SO I STOPPED...
YOU CAN TAKE IRON PILLS...
OR EAT SPINACH.
GOD, THAT FUCKING ASSHOLE.
I DON'T KNOW WHAT THE HELL I'M DOING HERE.
THAT JERK IS WORKING IN AMSTERDAM.
I MEAN... I DIDN'T COME HERE FOR HIM.
BUT IT WOULD'VE BEEN NICE.

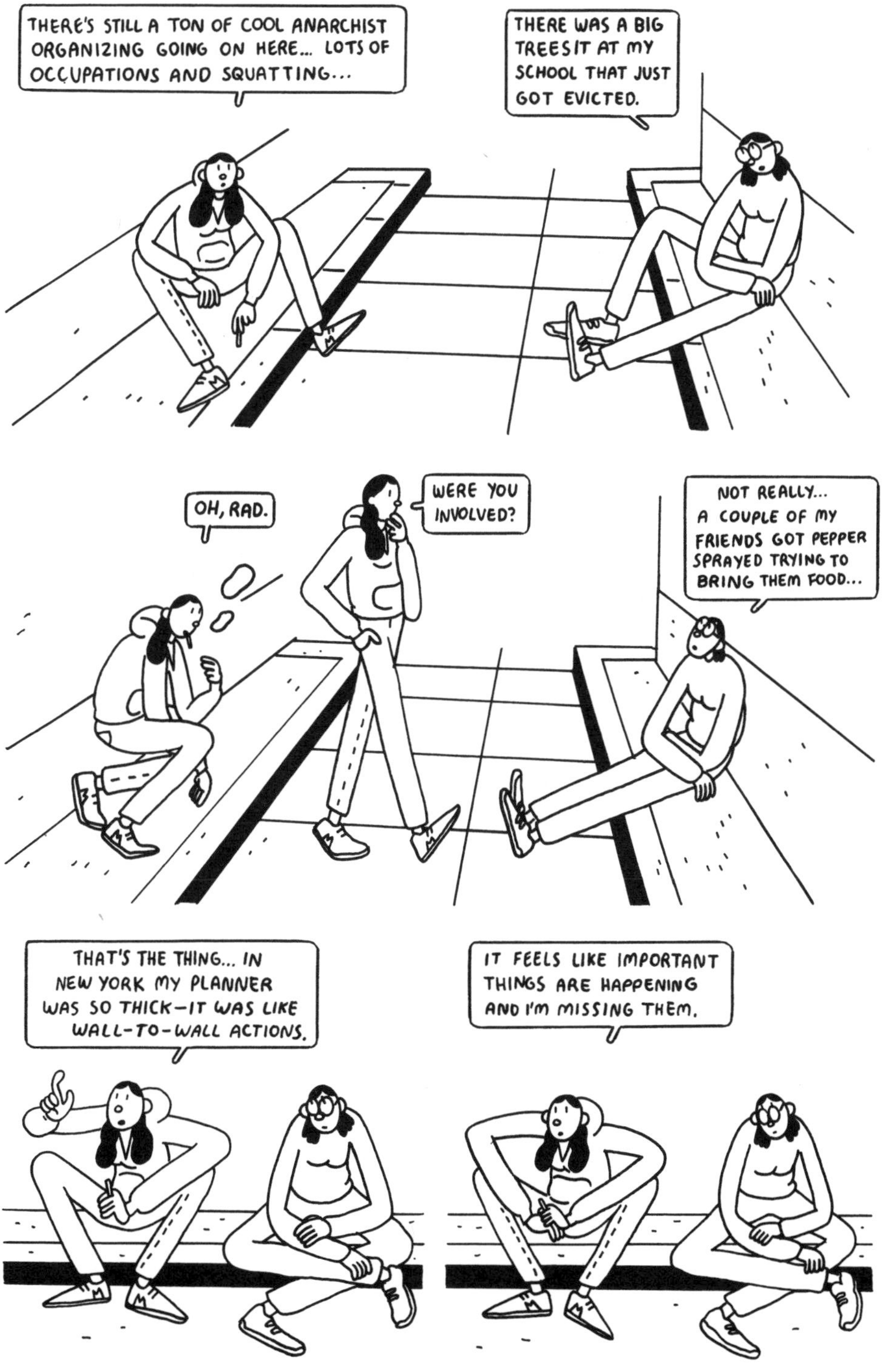
THERE'S STILL A TON OF COOL ANARCHIST ORGANIZING GOING ON HERE... LOTS OF OCCUPATIONS AND SQUATTING...
THERE WAS A BIG TREESIT AT MY SCHOOL THAT JUST GOT EVICTED.
OH, RAD.
WERE YOU INVOLVED?
NOT REALLY... A COUPLE OF MY FRIENDS GOT PEPPER SPRAYED TRYING TO BRING THEM FOOD...
THAT'S THE THING... IN NEW YORK MY PLANNER WAS SO THICK—IT WAS LIKE WALL-TO-WALL ACTIONS.
IT FEELS LIKE IMPORTANT THINGS ARE HAPPENING AND I'M MISSING THEM.

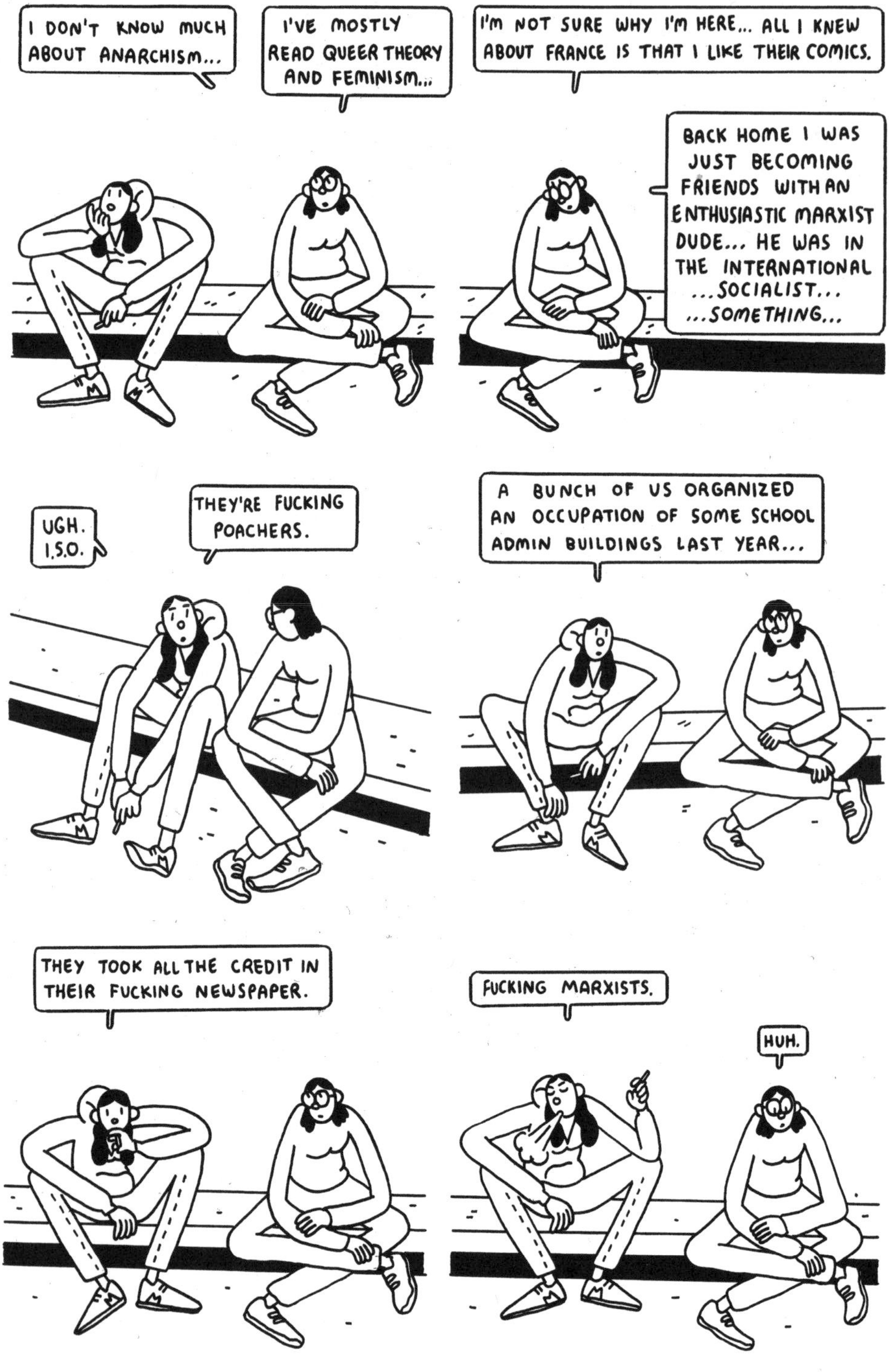

I DON'T KNOW MUCH ABOUT ANARCHISM...
I'VE MOSTLY READ QUEER THEORY AND FEMINISM...
I'M NOT SURE WHY I'M HERE... ALL I KNEW ABOUT FRANCE IS THAT I LIKE THEIR COMICS.
BACK HOME I WAS JUST BECOMING FRIENDS WITH AN ENTHUSIASTIC MARXIST DUDE... HE WAS IN THE INTERNATIONAL ...SOCIALIST... ...SOMETHING...
UGH. I.S.O.
THEY'RE FUCKING POACHERS.
A BUNCH OF US ORGANIZED AN OCCUPATION OF SOME SCHOOL ADMIN BUILDINGS LAST YEAR...
THEY TOOK ALL THE CREDIT IN THEIR FUCKING NEWSPAPER.
FUCKING MARXISTS.
HUH.

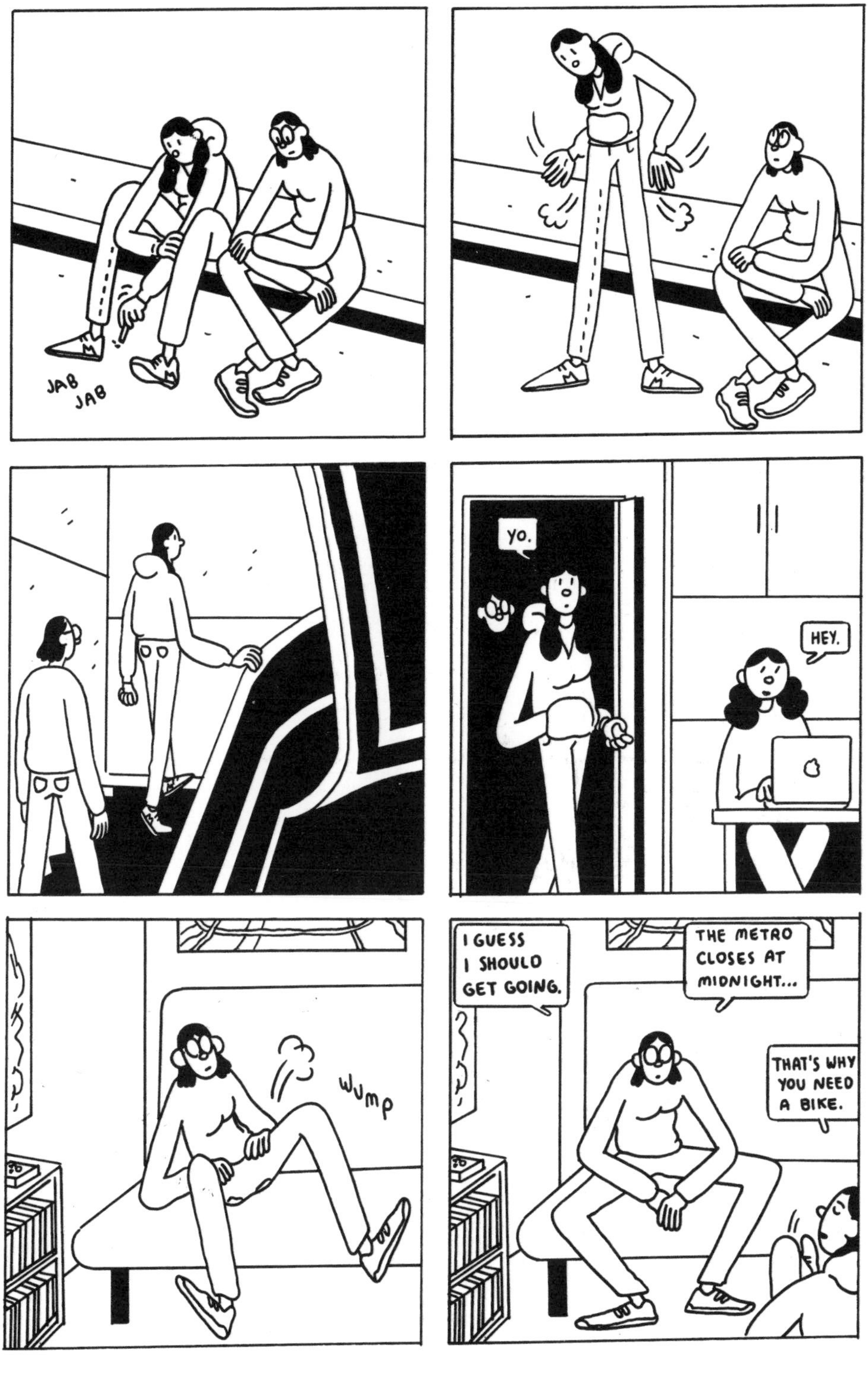
JAB
JAB
YO.
HEY.
WUMP
I GUESS I SHOULD GET GOING.
THE METRO CLOSES AT MIDNIGHT...
THAT'S WHY YOU NEED A BIKE.

I DO NEED A BIKE...
I'M GONNA GO TO THE FLEA MARKET IN THE SUBURBS SOON. THEY HAVE USED BIKES.
OH, COOL.
IS THIS THAT STAMP FROM THE STORE?
YEP.
COOL.

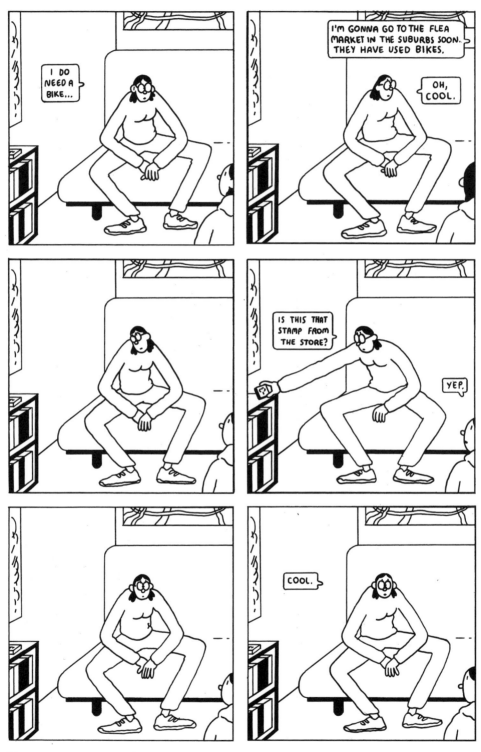

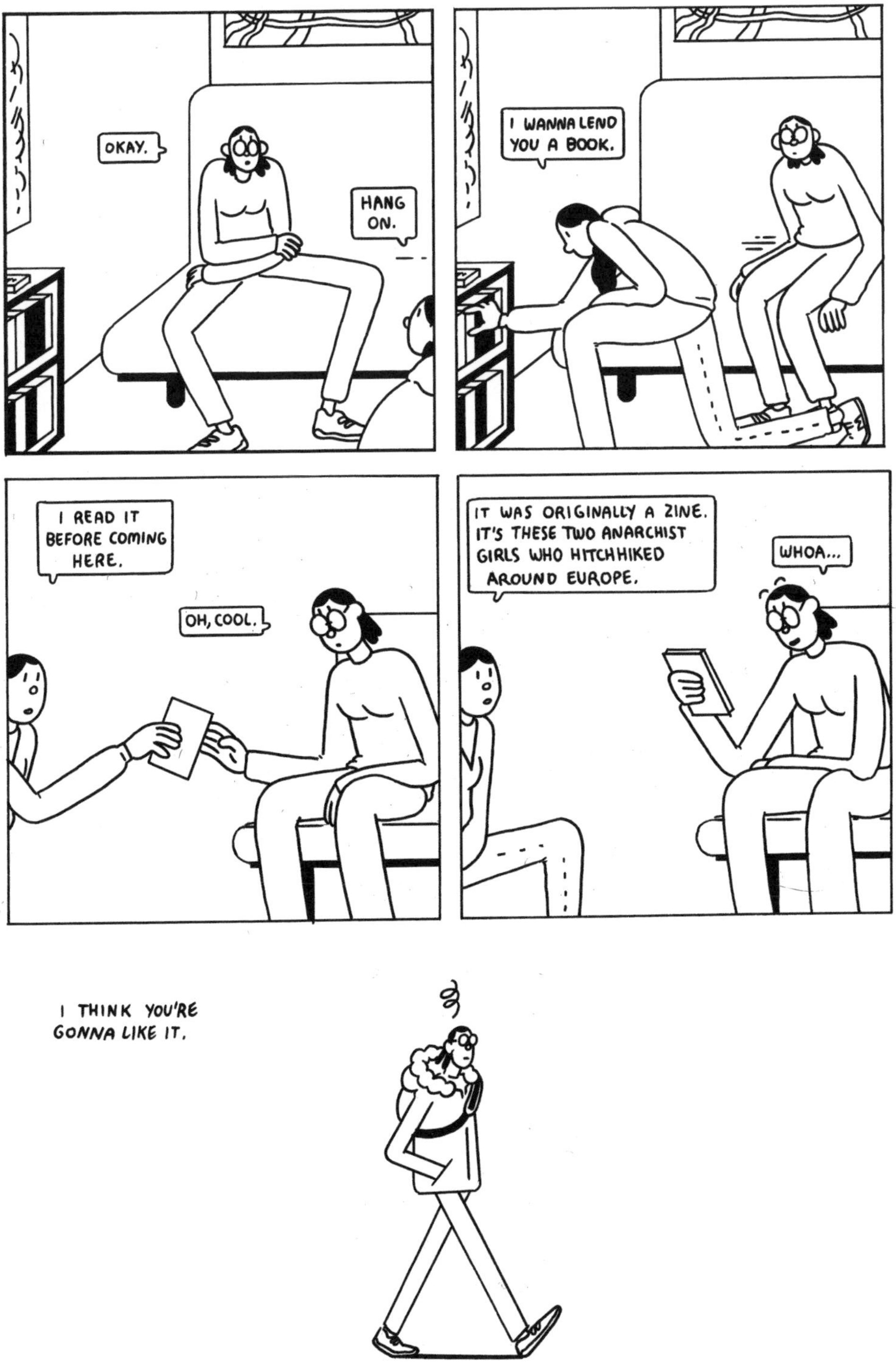
OKAY.
HANG ON.
I WANNA LEND YOU A BOOK.
I READ IT BEFORE COMING HERE.
OH, COOL.
IT WAS ORIGINALLY A ZINE. IT'S THESE TWO ANARCHIST GIRLS WHO HITCHHIKED AROUND EUROPE.
WHOA...
I THINK YOU'RE GONNA LIKE IT.

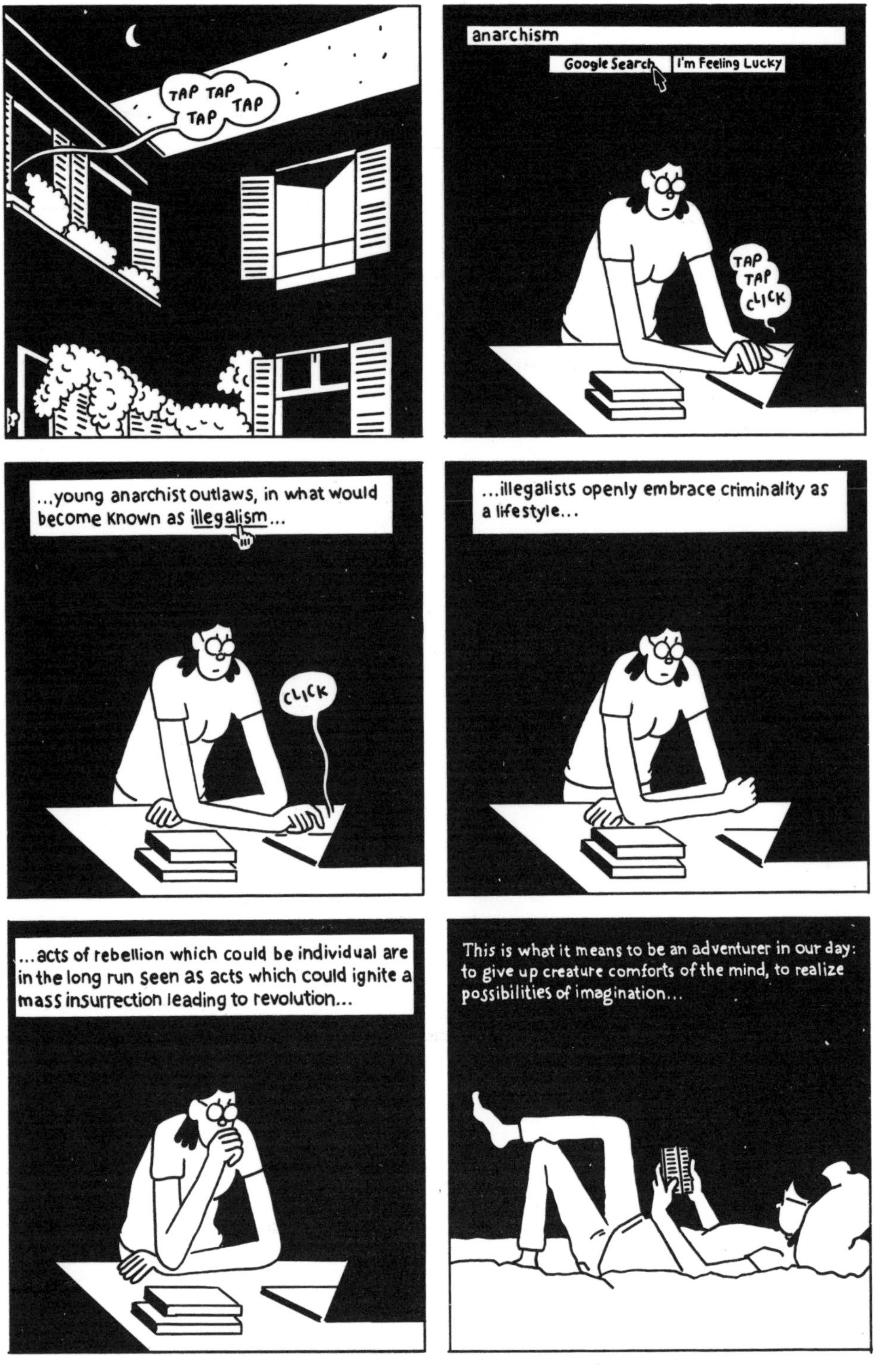
TAP TAP TAP TAP
anarchism
Google Search
I'm Feeling Lucky
TAP TAP CLICK
...young anarchist outlaws, in what would become known as illegalism...
CLICK
...illegalists openly embrace criminality as a lifestyle...
...acts of rebellion which could be individual are in the long run seen as acts which could ignite a mass insurrection leading to revolution...
This is what it means to be an adventurer in our day: to give up creature comforts of the mind, to realize possibilities of imagination...

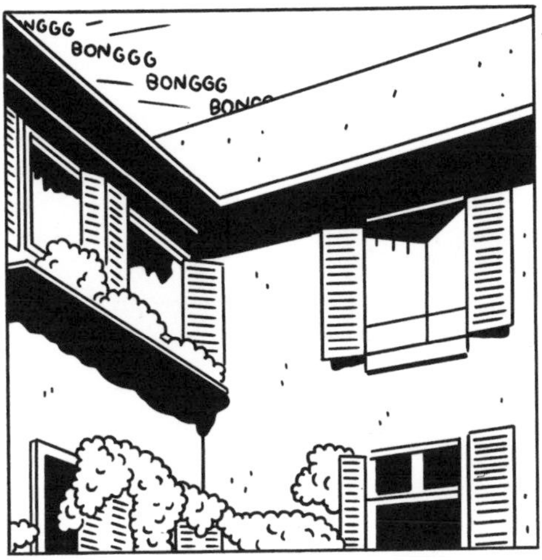
NGGG
BONGGG
BONGGG

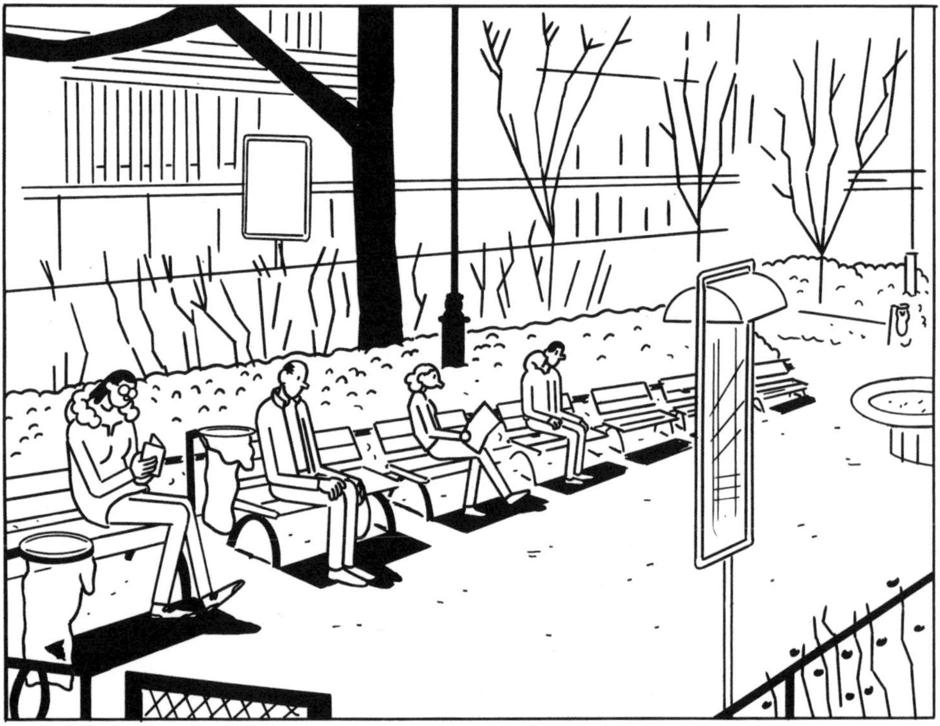

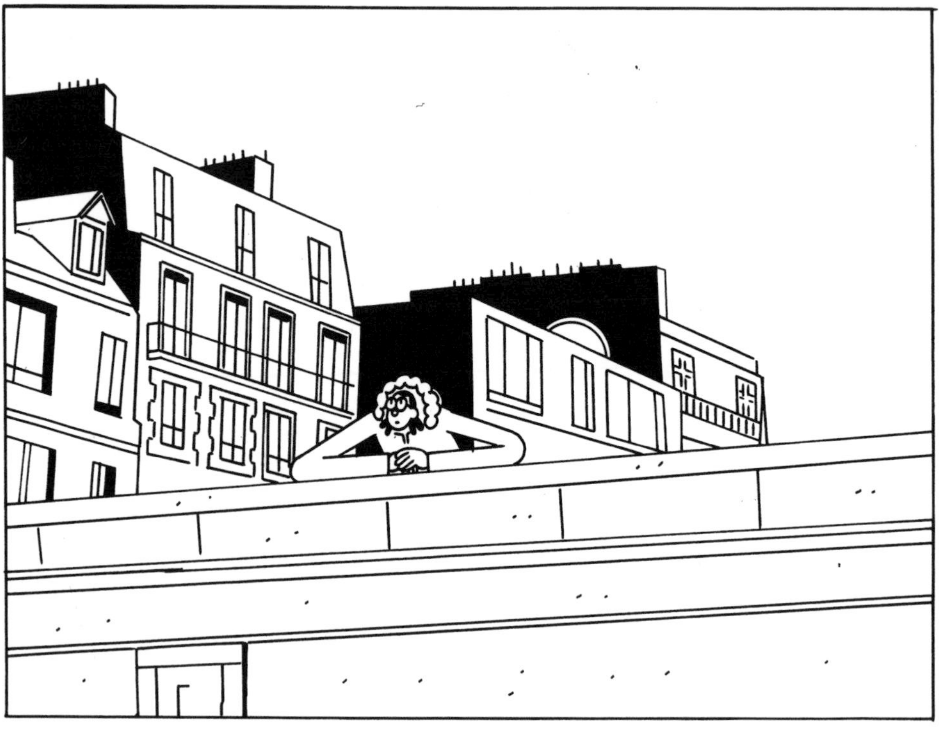

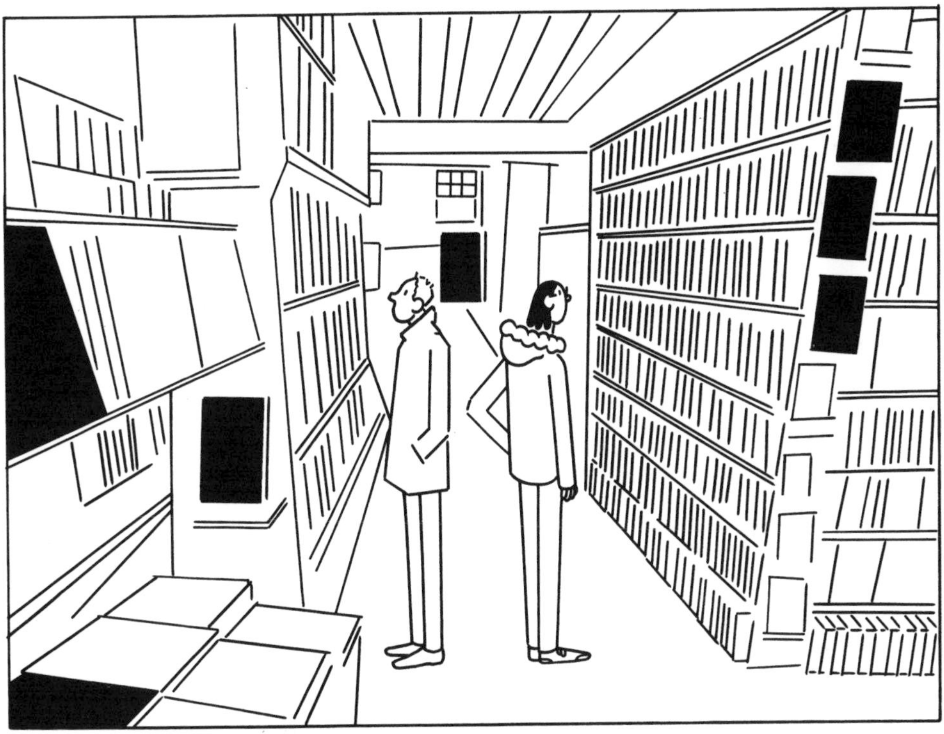

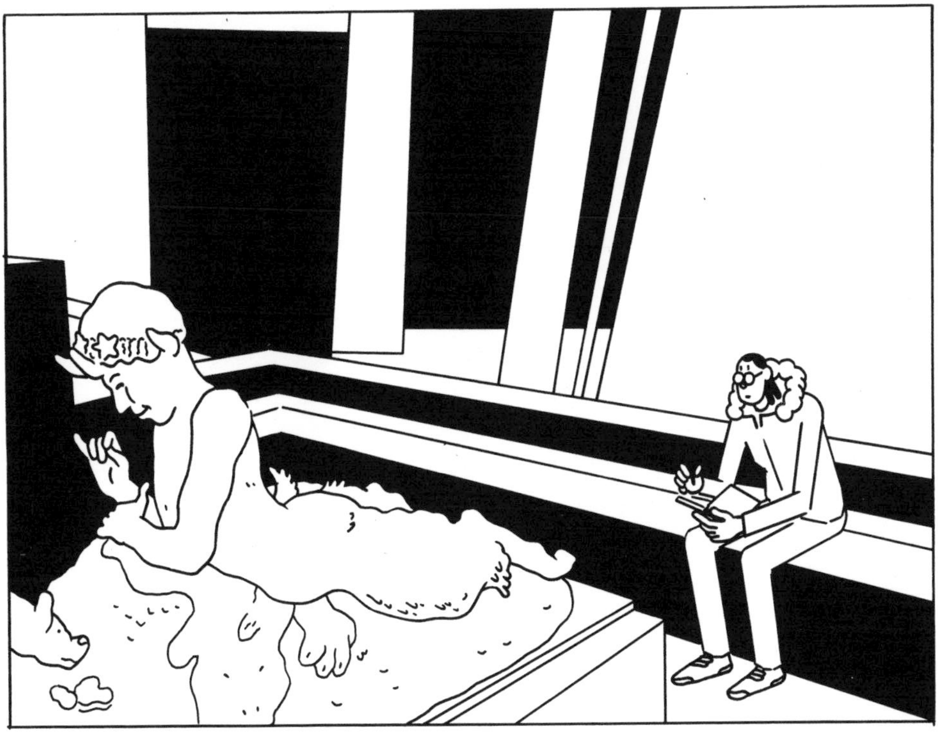

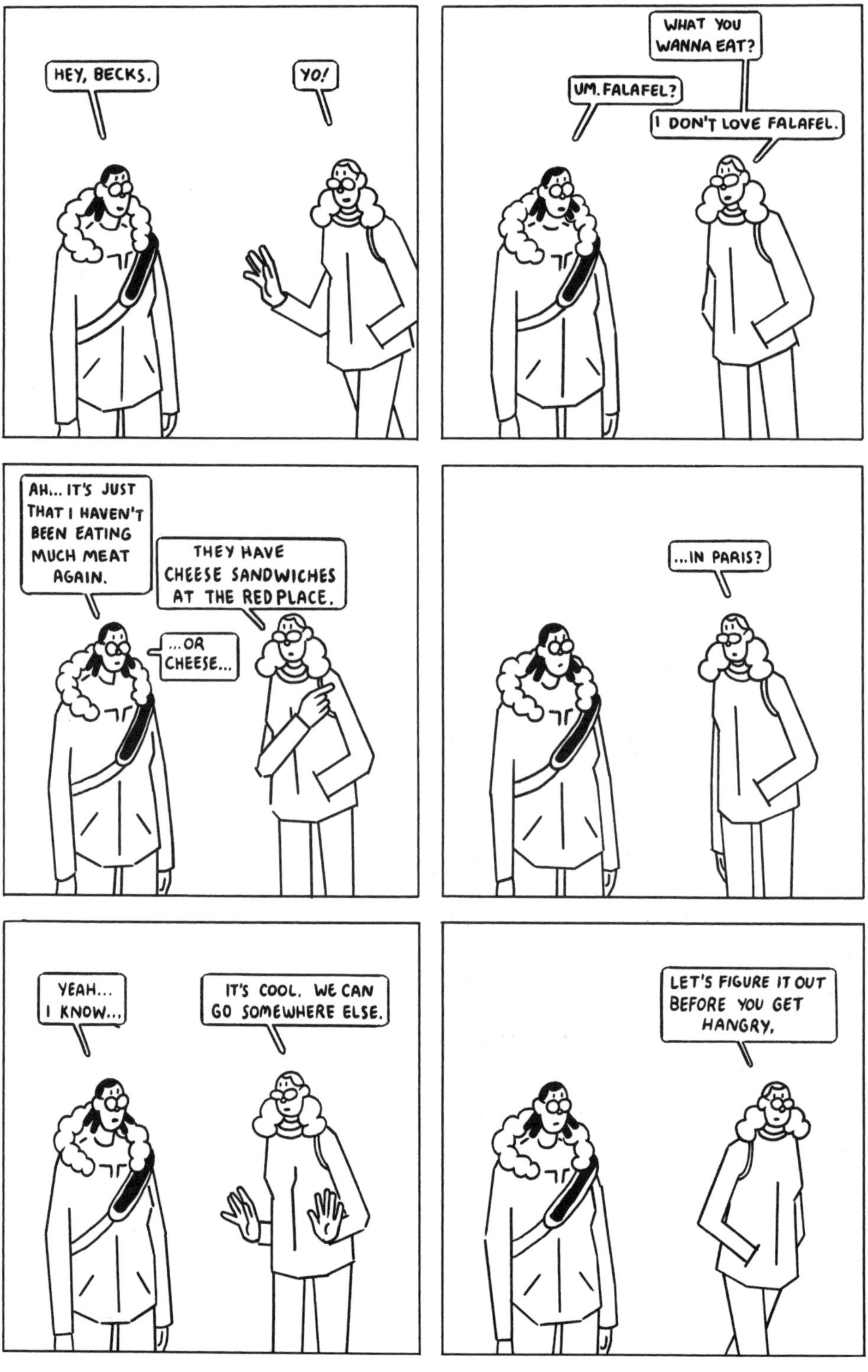
HEY, BECKS.
YO!
WHAT YOU WANNA EAT?
UM. FALAFEL?
I DON'T LOVE FALAFEL.
AH... IT'S JUST THAT I HAVEN'T BEEN EATING MUCH MEAT AGAIN.
THEY HAVE CHEESE SANDWICHES AT THE RED PLACE.
...OR CHEESE...
...IN PARIS?
YEAH... I KNOW...
IT'S COOL. WE CAN GO SOMEWHERE ELSE.
LET'S FIGURE IT OUT BEFORE YOU GET HANGRY.

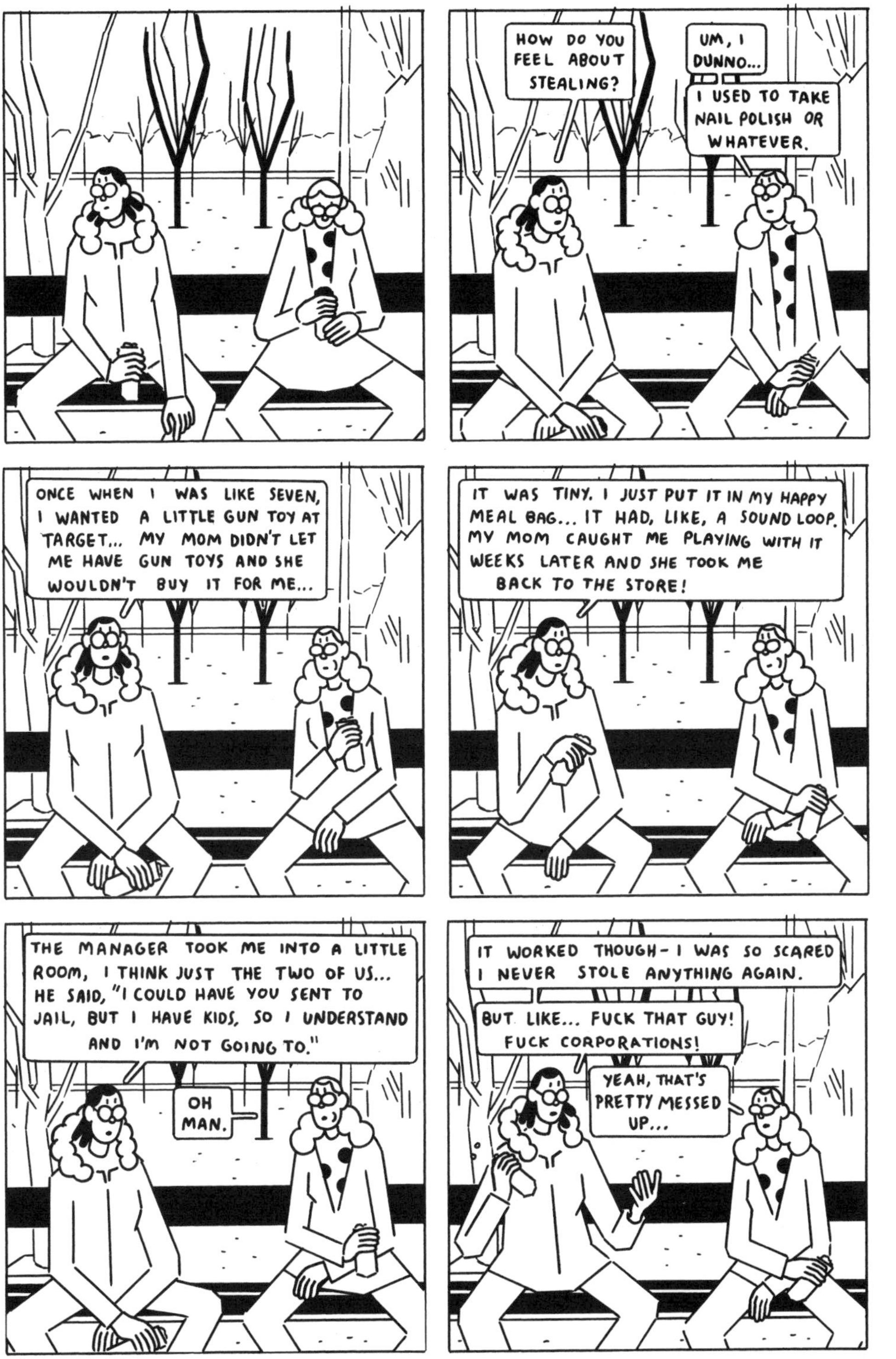
HOW DO YOU FEEL ABOUT STEALING?
UM, I DUNNO...
I USED TO TAKE NAIL POLISH OR WHATEVER.
ONCE WHEN I WAS LIKE SEVEN, I WANTED A LITTLE GUN TOY AT TARGET... MY MOM DIDN'T LET ME HAVE GUN TOYS AND SHE WOULDN'T BUY IT FOR ME...
IT WAS TINY. I JUST PUT IT IN MY HAPPY MEAL BAG... IT HAD, LIKE, A SOUND LOOP. MY MOM CAUGHT ME PLAYING WITH IT WEEKS LATER AND SHE TOOK ME BACK TO THE STORE!
THE MANAGER TOOK ME INTO A LITTLE ROOM, I THINK JUST THE TWO OF US... HE SAID, "I COULD HAVE YOU SENT TO JAIL, BUT I HAVE KIDS, SO I UNDERSTAND AND I'M NOT GOING TO."
OH MAN.
IT WORKED THOUGH- I WAS SO SCARED I NEVER STOLE ANYTHING AGAIN.
BUT LIKE... FUCK THAT GUY! FUCK CORPORATIONS!
YEAH, THAT'S PRETTY MESSED UP...

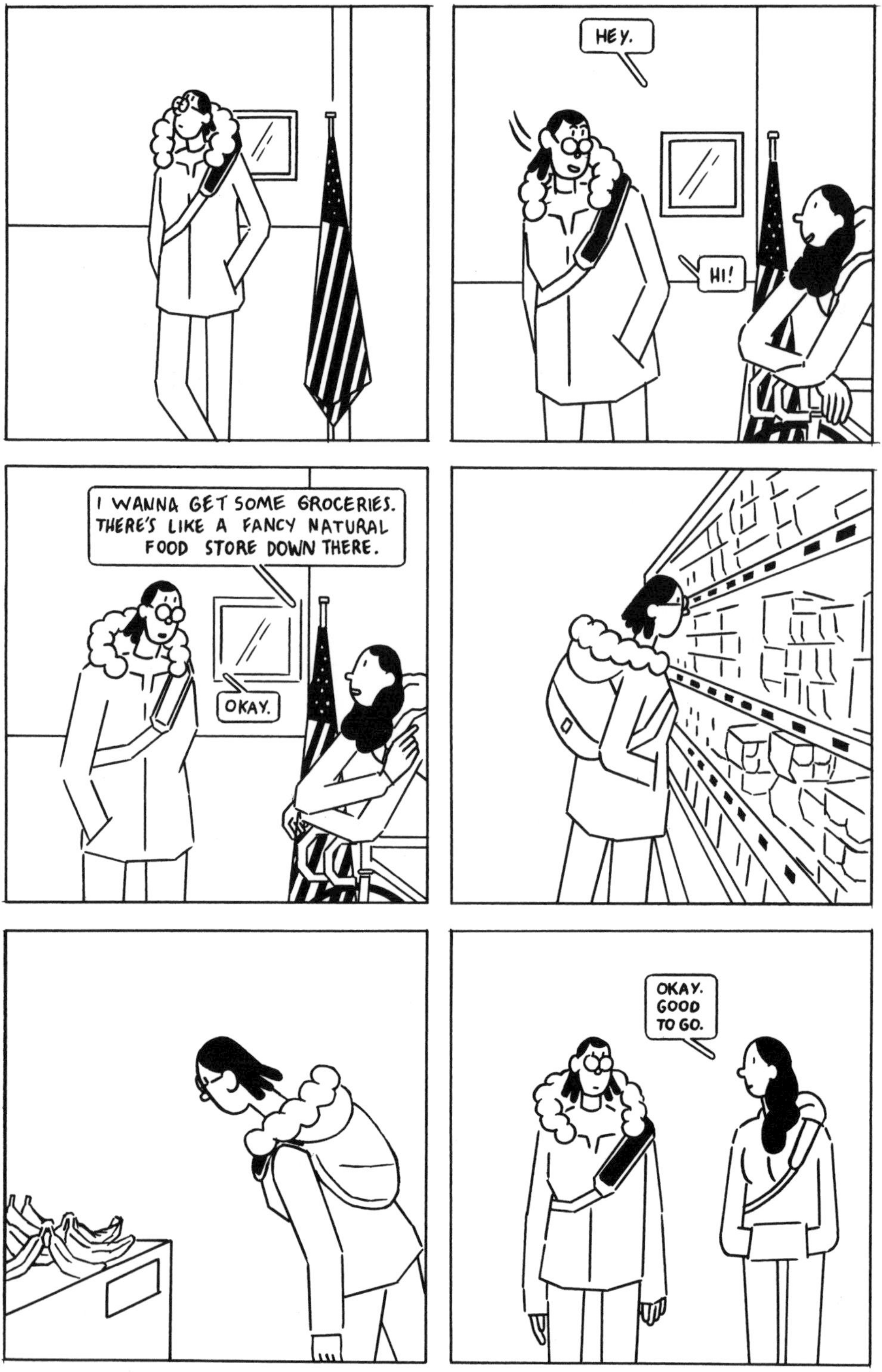
HEY.
HI!
I WANNA GET SOME GROCERIES. THERE'S LIKE A FANCY NATURAL FOOD STORE DOWN THERE.
OKAY.
OKAY. GOOD TO GO.

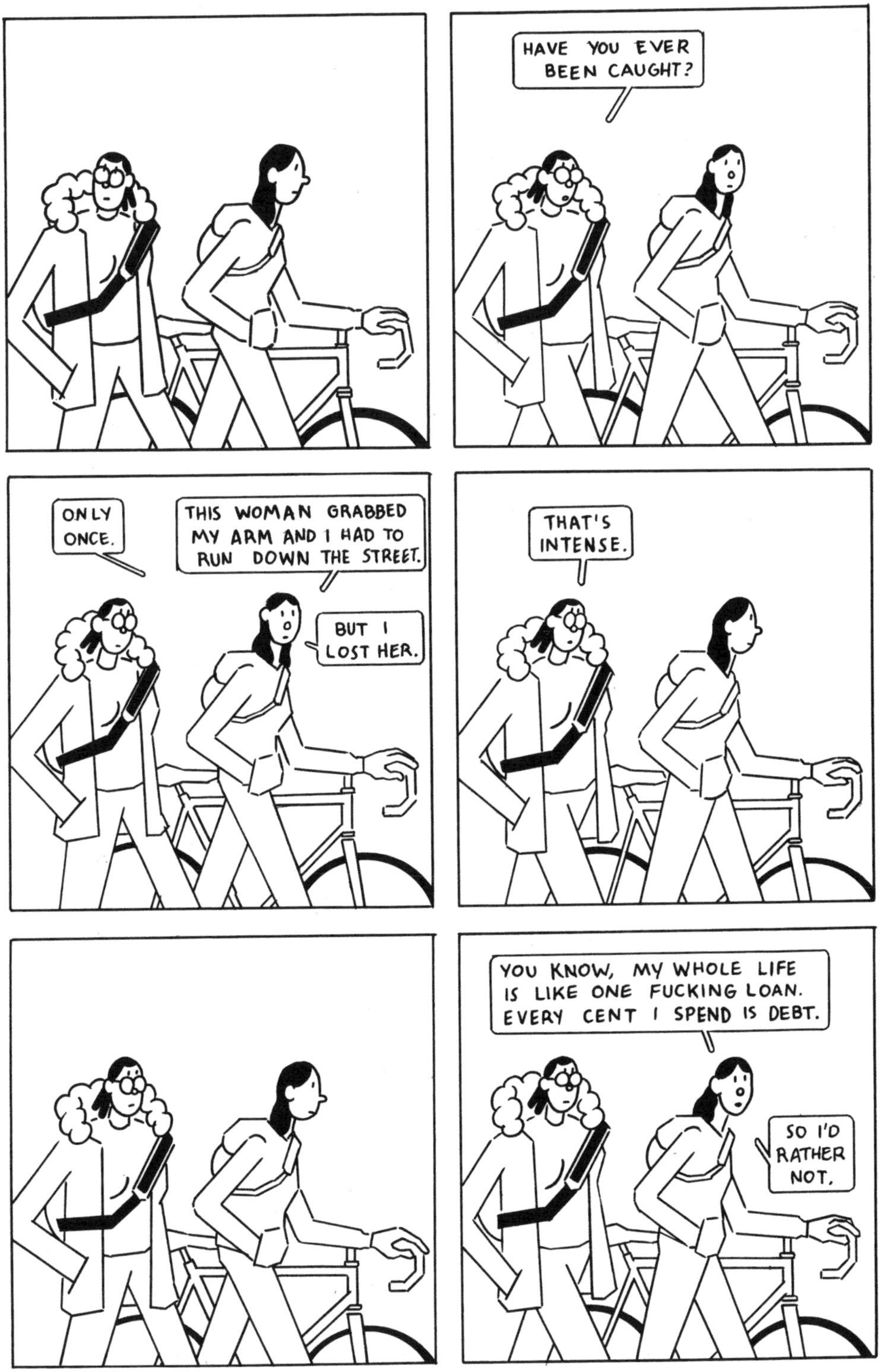
HAVE YOU EVER BEEN CAUGHT?
ONLY ONCE.
THIS WOMAN GRABBED MY ARM AND I HAD TO RUN DOWN THE STREET.
BUT I LOST HER.
THAT'S INTENSE.
YOU KNOW, MY WHOLE LIFE IS LIKE ONE FUCKING LOAN. EVERY CENT I SPEND IS DEBT.
SO I'D RATHER NOT.

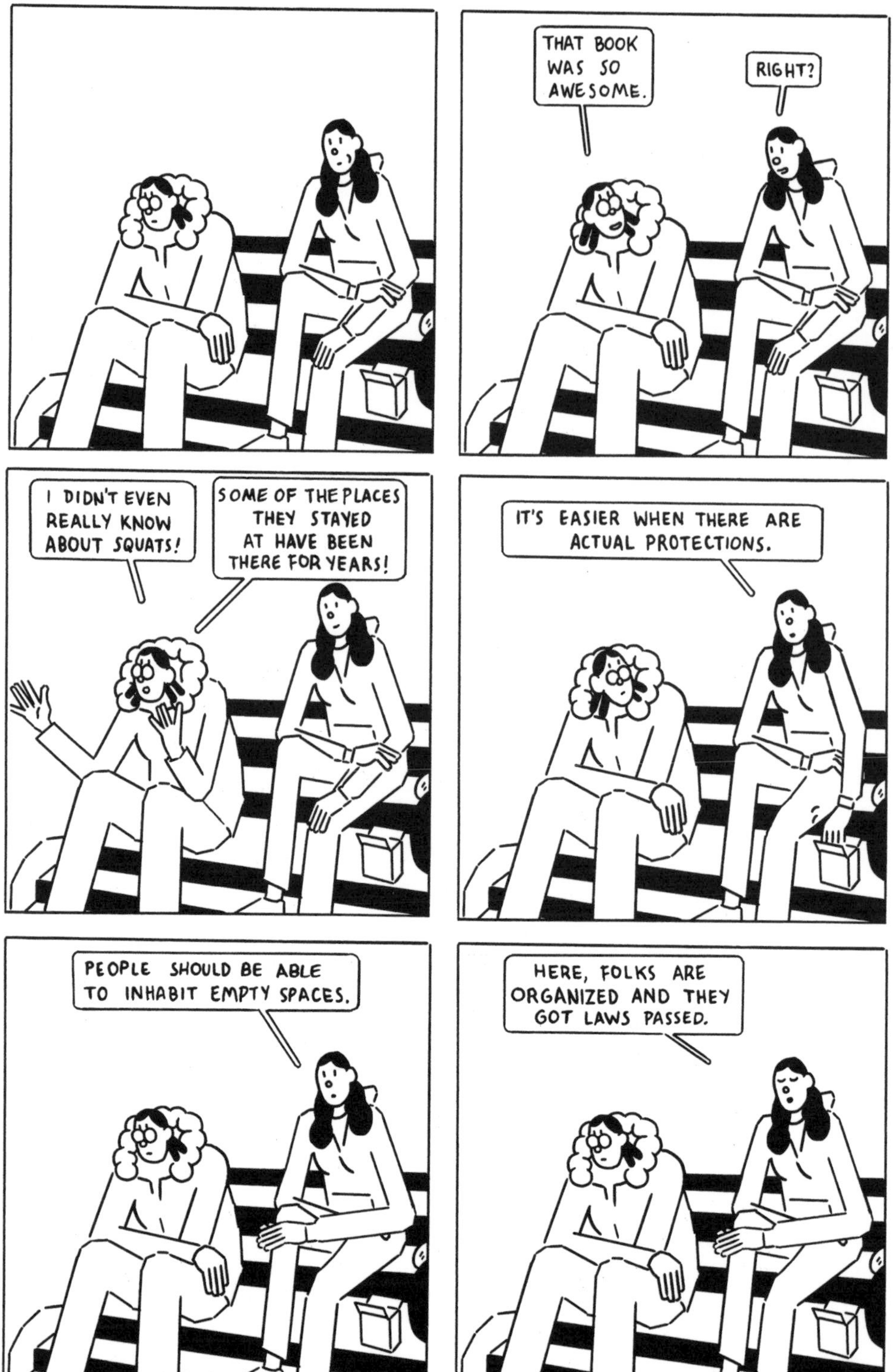
THAT BOOK WAS SO AWESOME.
RIGHT?
I DIDN'T EVEN REALLY KNOW ABOUT SQUATS!
SOME OF THE PLACES THEY STAYED AT HAVE BEEN THERE FOR YEARS!
IT'S EASIER WHEN THERE ARE ACTUAL PROTECTIONS.
PEOPLE SHOULD BE ABLE TO INHABIT EMPTY SPACES.
HERE, FOLKS ARE ORGANIZED AND THEY GOT LAWS PASSED.

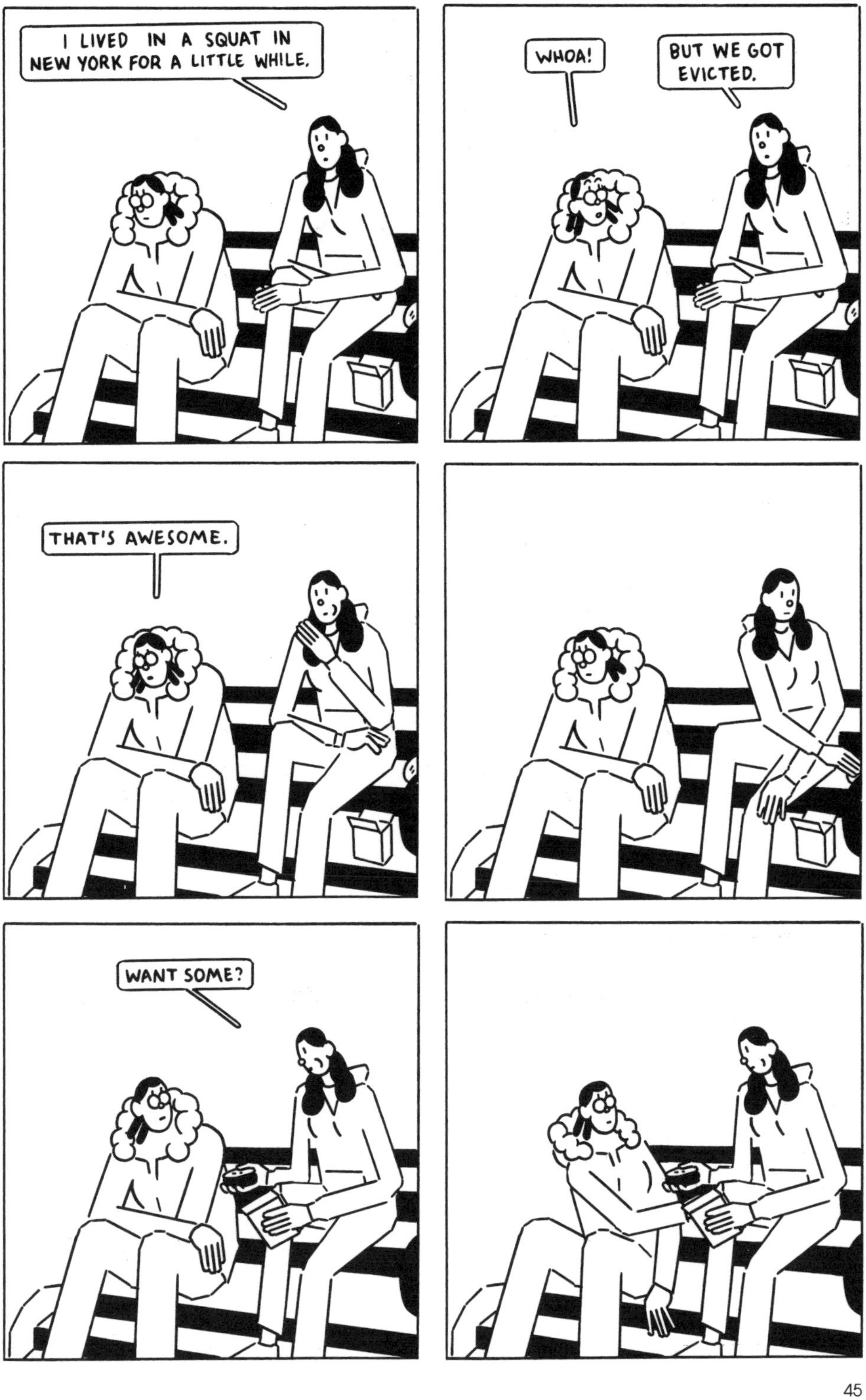
I LIVED IN A SQUAT IN NEW YORK FOR A LITTLE WHILE.
WHOA!
BUT WE GOT EVICTED.
THAT'S AWESOME.
WANT SOME?

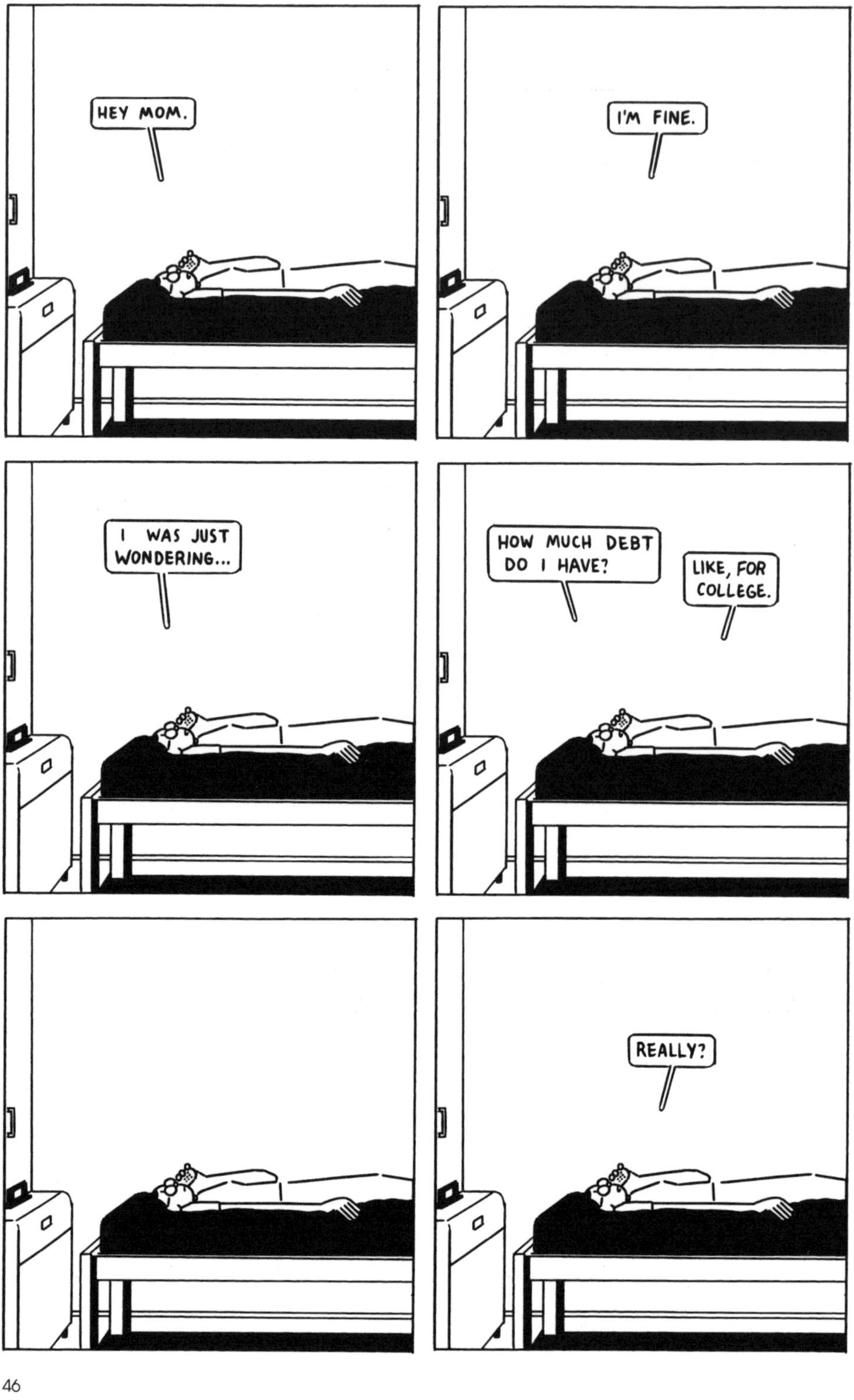
HEY MOM.
I'M FINE.
I WAS JUST WONDERING...
HOW MUCH DEBT DO I HAVE?
LIKE, FOR COLLEGE.
REALLY?

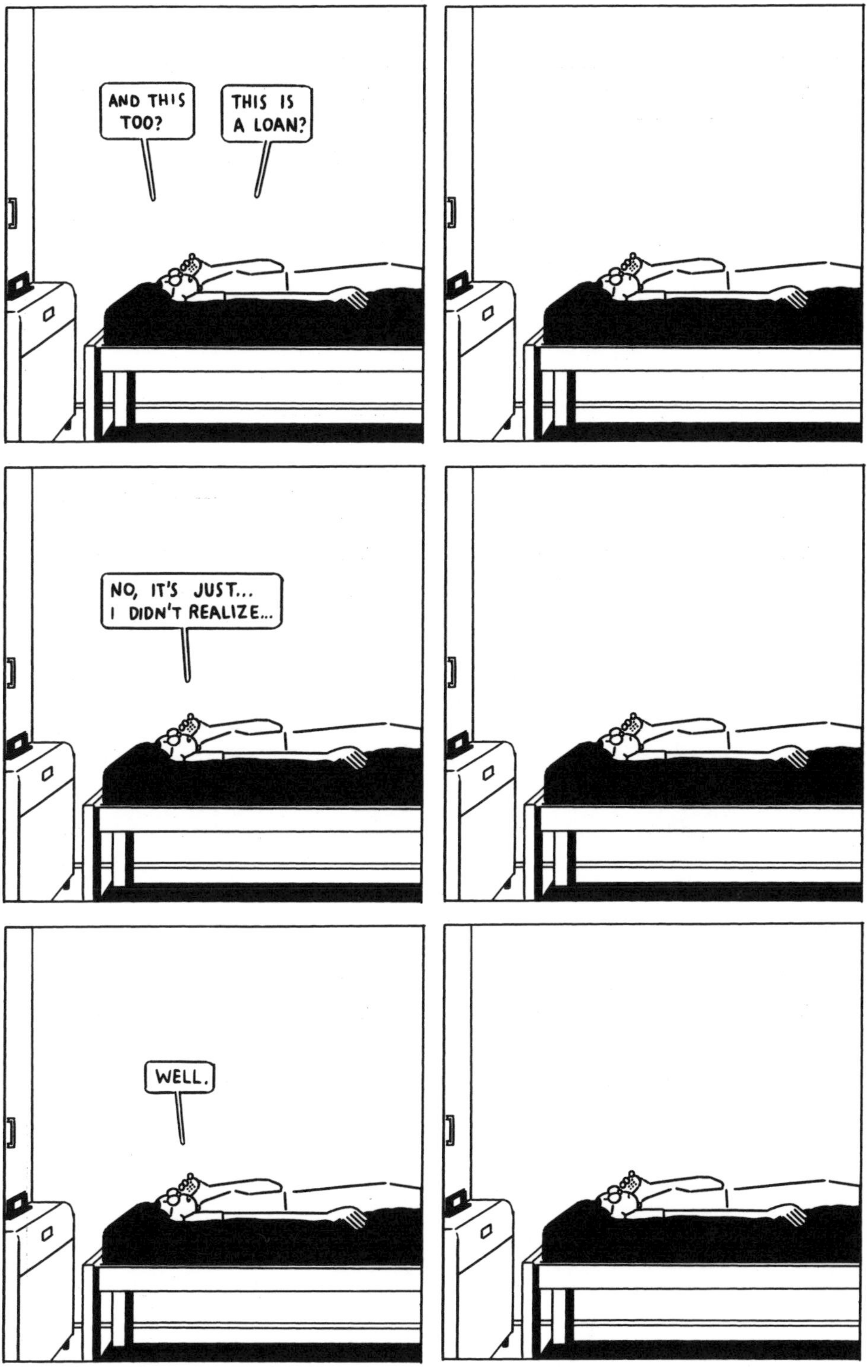
AND THIS TOO?
THIS IS A LOAN?
NO, IT'S JUST... I DIDN'T REALIZE...
WELL.

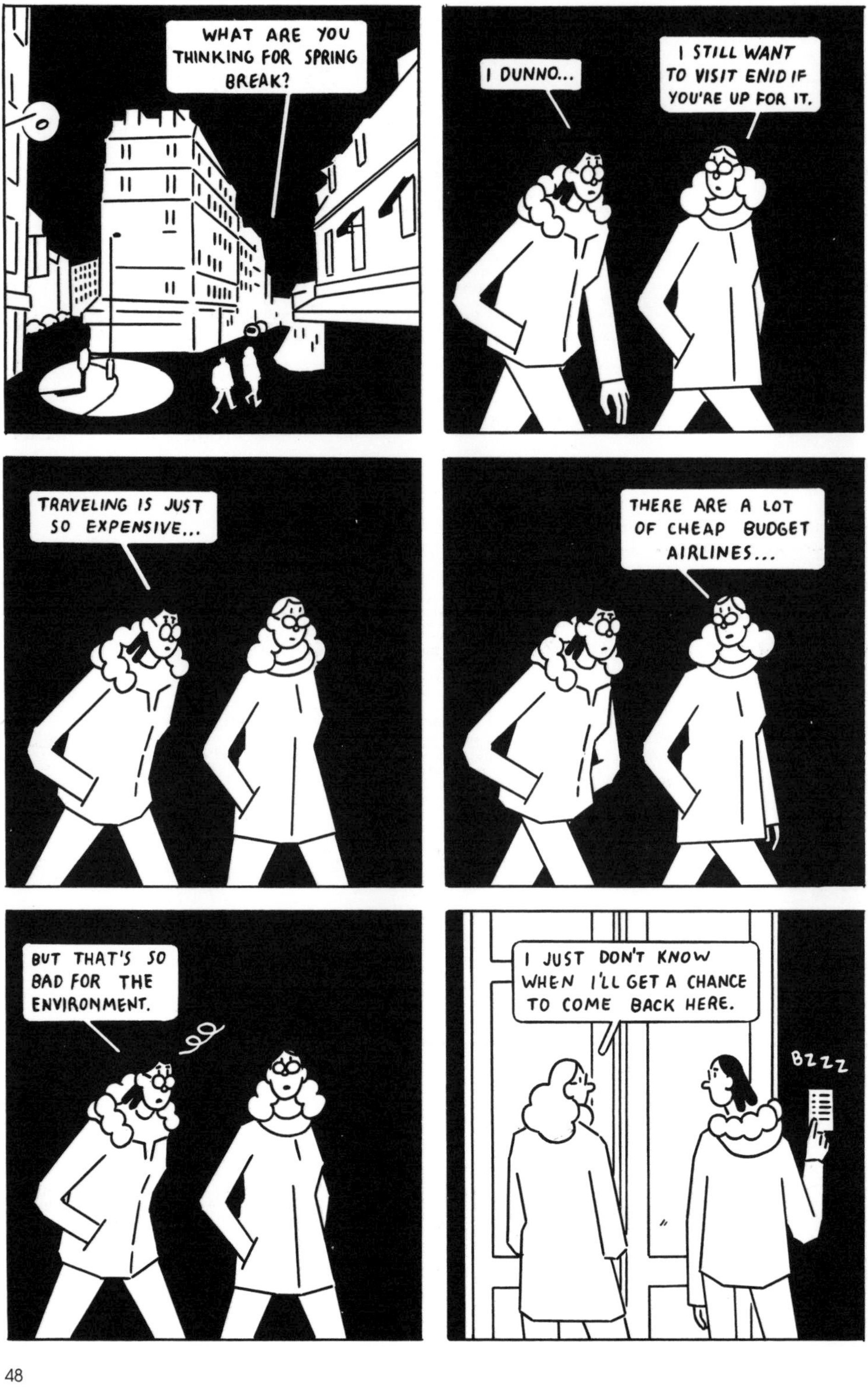
WHAT ARE YOU THINKING FOR SPRING BREAK?
I DUNNO...
I STILL WANT TO VISIT ENID IF YOU'RE UP FOR IT.
TRAVELING IS JUST SO EXPENSIVE...
THERE ARE A LOT OF CHEAP BUDGET AIRLINES...
BUT THAT'S SO BAD FOR THE ENVIRONMENT.
I JUST DON'T KNOW WHEN I'LL GET A CHANCE TO COME BACK HERE.
BZZZ

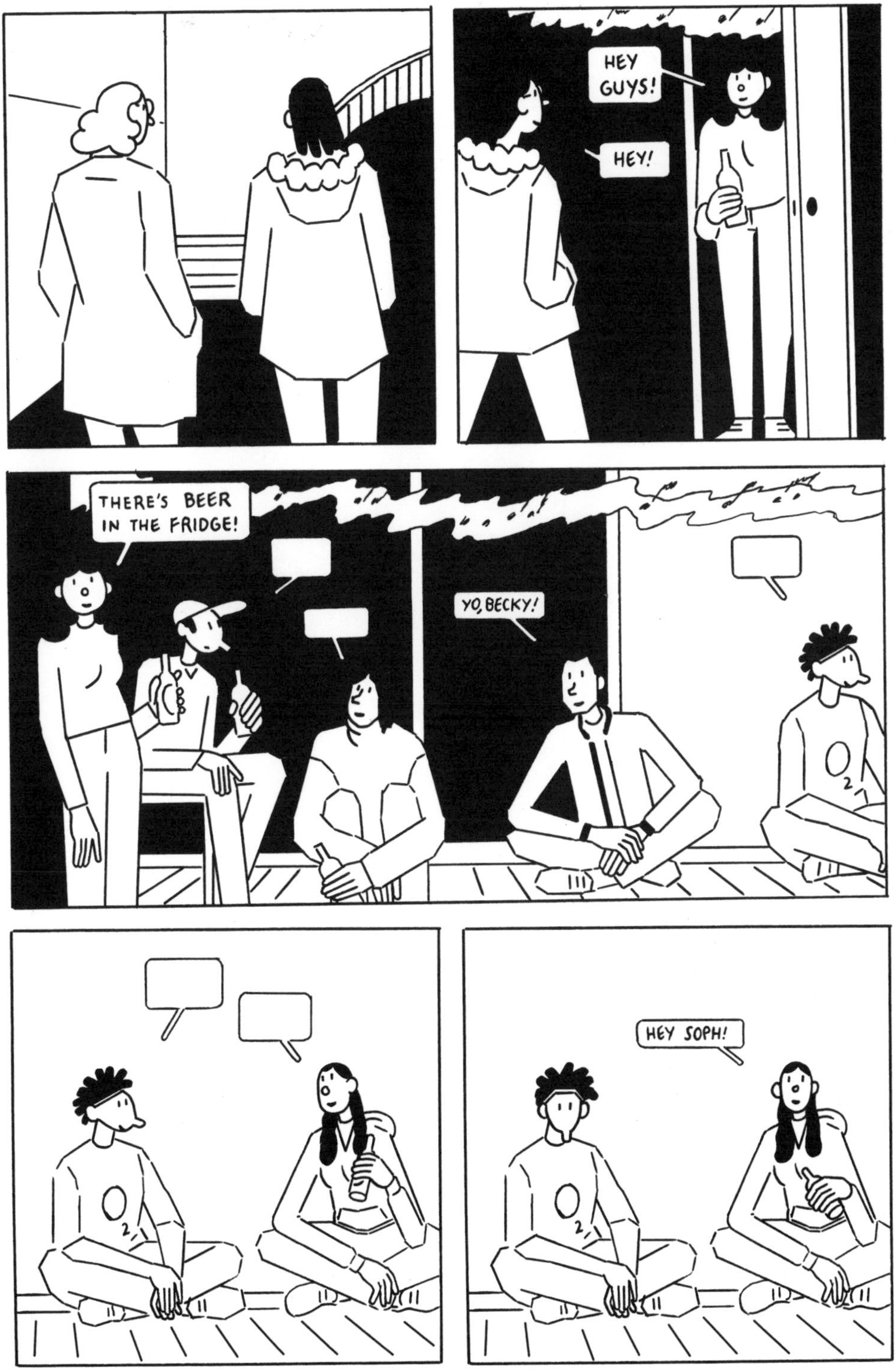
HEY GUYS!
HEY!
THERE'S BEER IN THE FRIDGE!
YO, BECKY!
HEY SOPH!

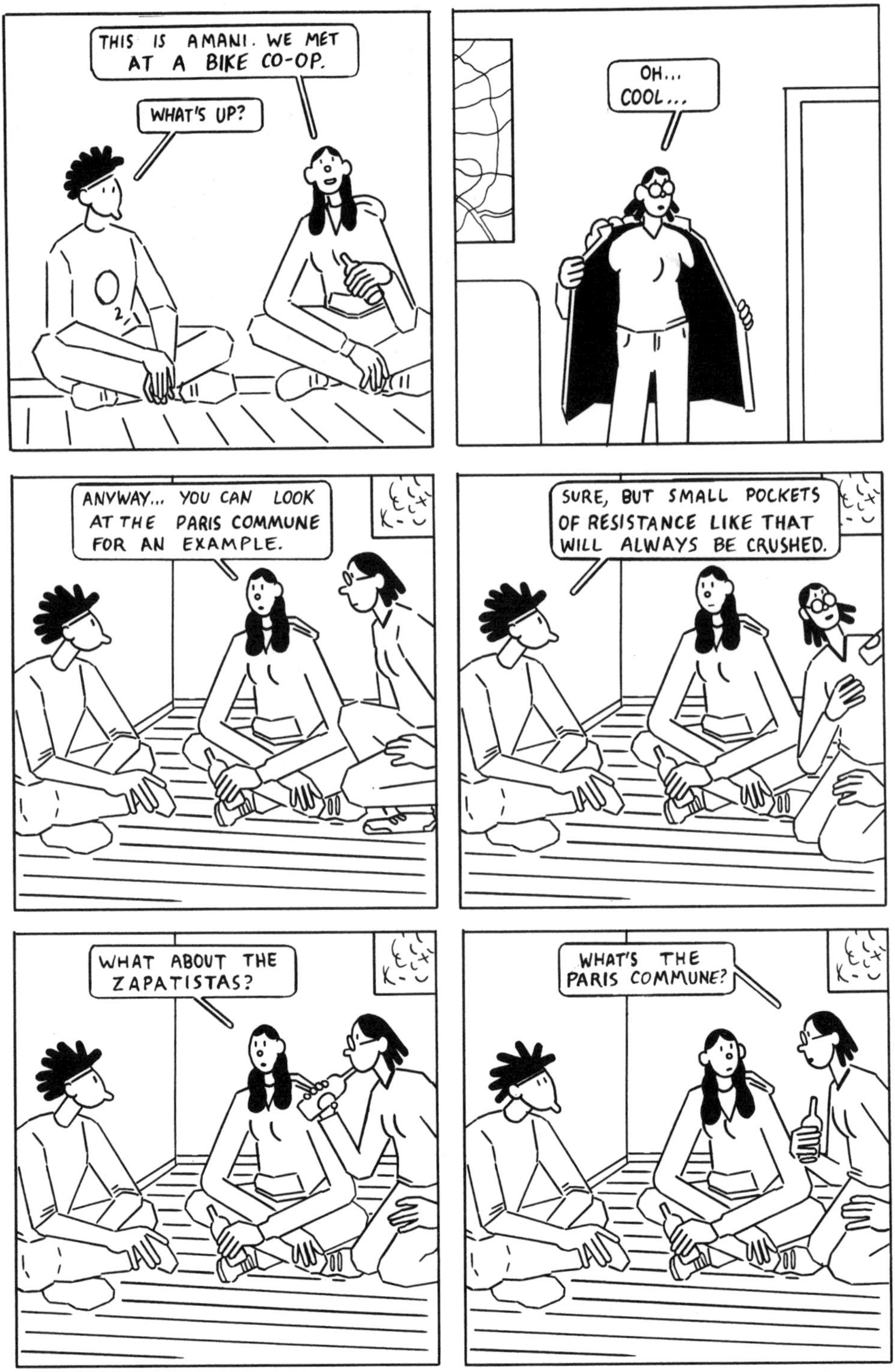
THIS IS AMANI. WE MET AT A BIKE CO-OP.
WHAT'S UP?
OH... COOL...
ANYWAY... YOU CAN LOOK AT THE PARIS COMMUNE FOR AN EXAMPLE.
SURE, BUT SMALL POCKETS OF RESISTANCE LIKE THAT WILL ALWAYS BE CRUSHED.
WHAT ABOUT THE ZAPATISTAS?
WHAT'S THE PARIS COMMUNE?

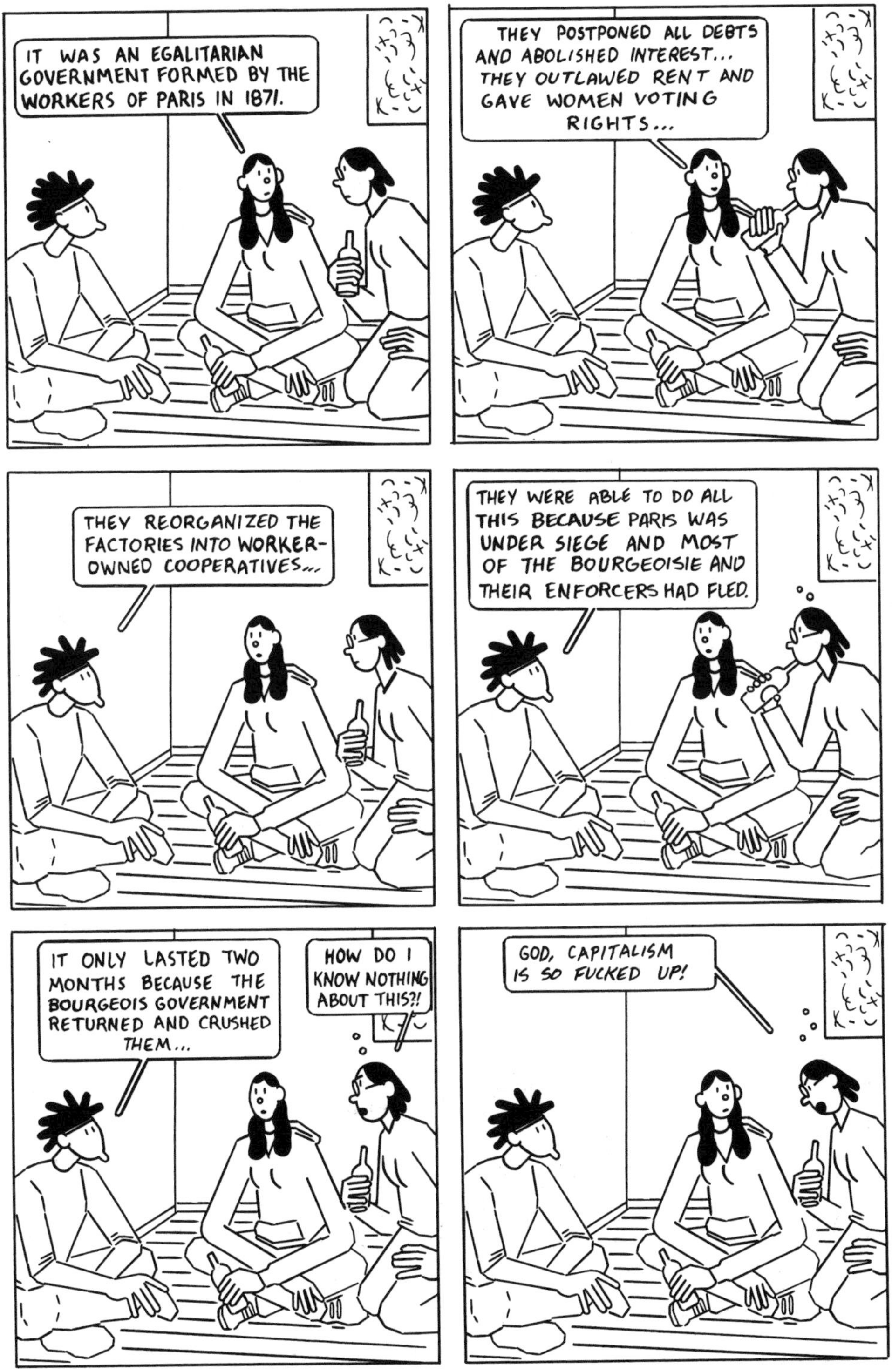
IT WAS AN EGALITARIAN GOVERNMENT FORMED BY THE WORKERS OF PARIS IN 1871.
THEY POSTPONED ALL DEBTS AND ABOLISHED INTEREST... THEY OUTLAWED RENT AND GAVE WOMEN VOTING RIGHTS...
THEY REORGANIZED THE FACTORIES INTO WORKER-OWNED COOPERATIVES...
THEY WERE ABLE TO DO ALL THIS BECAUSE PARIS WAS UNDER SIEGE AND MOST OF THE BOURGEOISIE AND THEIR ENFORCERS HAD FLED.
IT ONLY LASTED TWO MONTHS BECAUSE THE BOURGEOIS GOVERNMENT RETURNED AND CRUSHED THEM...
HOW DO I KNOW NOTHING ABOUT THIS?!
GOD, CAPITALISM IS SO FUCKED UP!

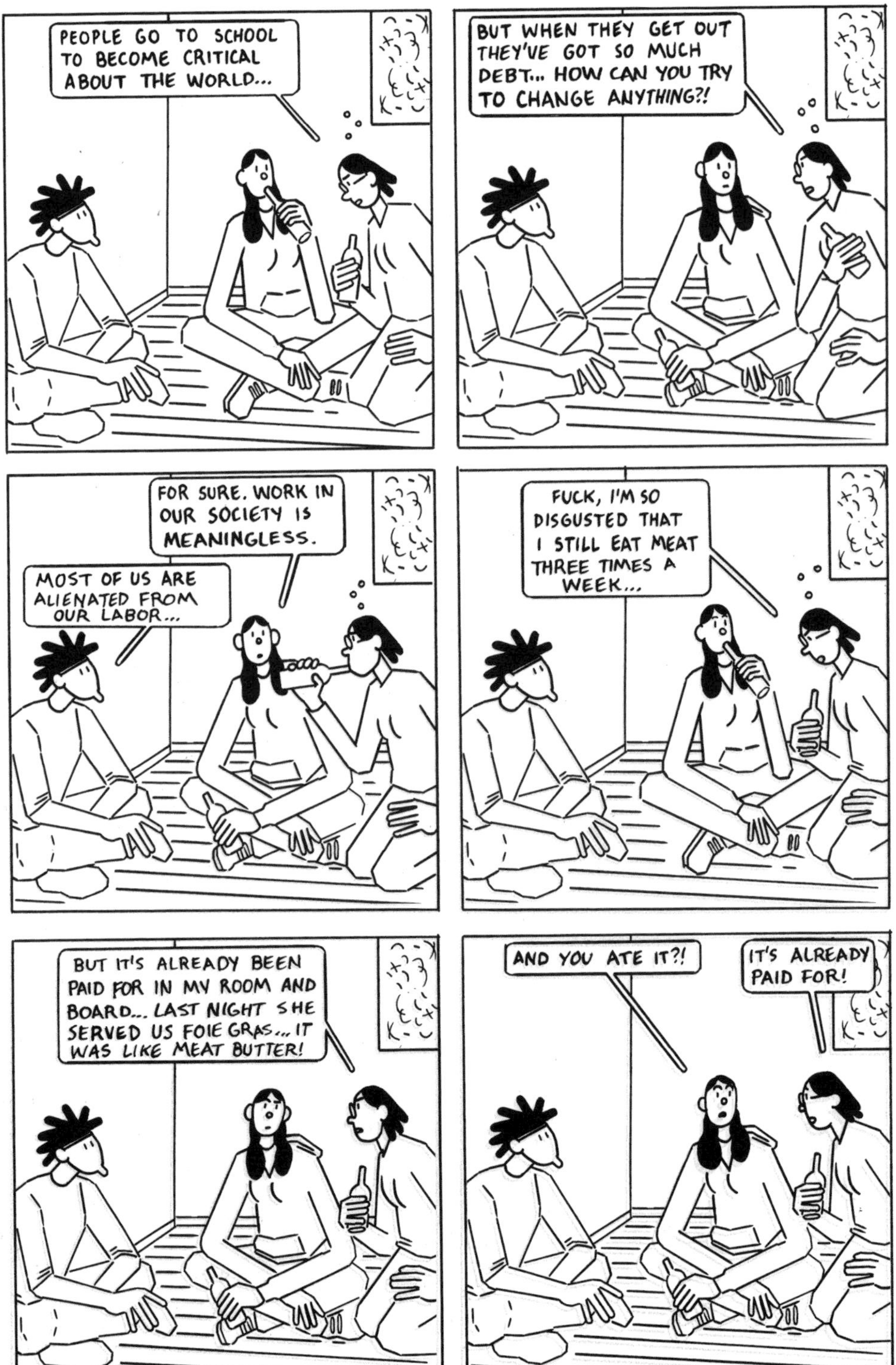
PEOPLE GO TO SCHOOL TO BECOME CRITICAL ABOUT THE WORLD...
BUT WHEN THEY GET OUT THEY'VE GOT SO MUCH DEBT... HOW CAN YOU TRY TO CHANGE ANYTHING?!
MOST OF US ARE ALIENATED FROM OUR LABOR...
FOR SURE. WORK IN OUR SOCIETY IS MEANINGLESS.
FUCK, I'M SO DISGUSTED THAT I STILL EAT MEAT THREE TIMES A WEEK...
BUT IT'S ALREADY BEEN PAID FOR IN MY ROOM AND BOARD... LAST NIGHT SHE SERVED US FOIE GRAS... IT WAS LIKE MEAT BUTTER!
AND YOU ATE IT?!
IT'S ALREADY PAID FOR!

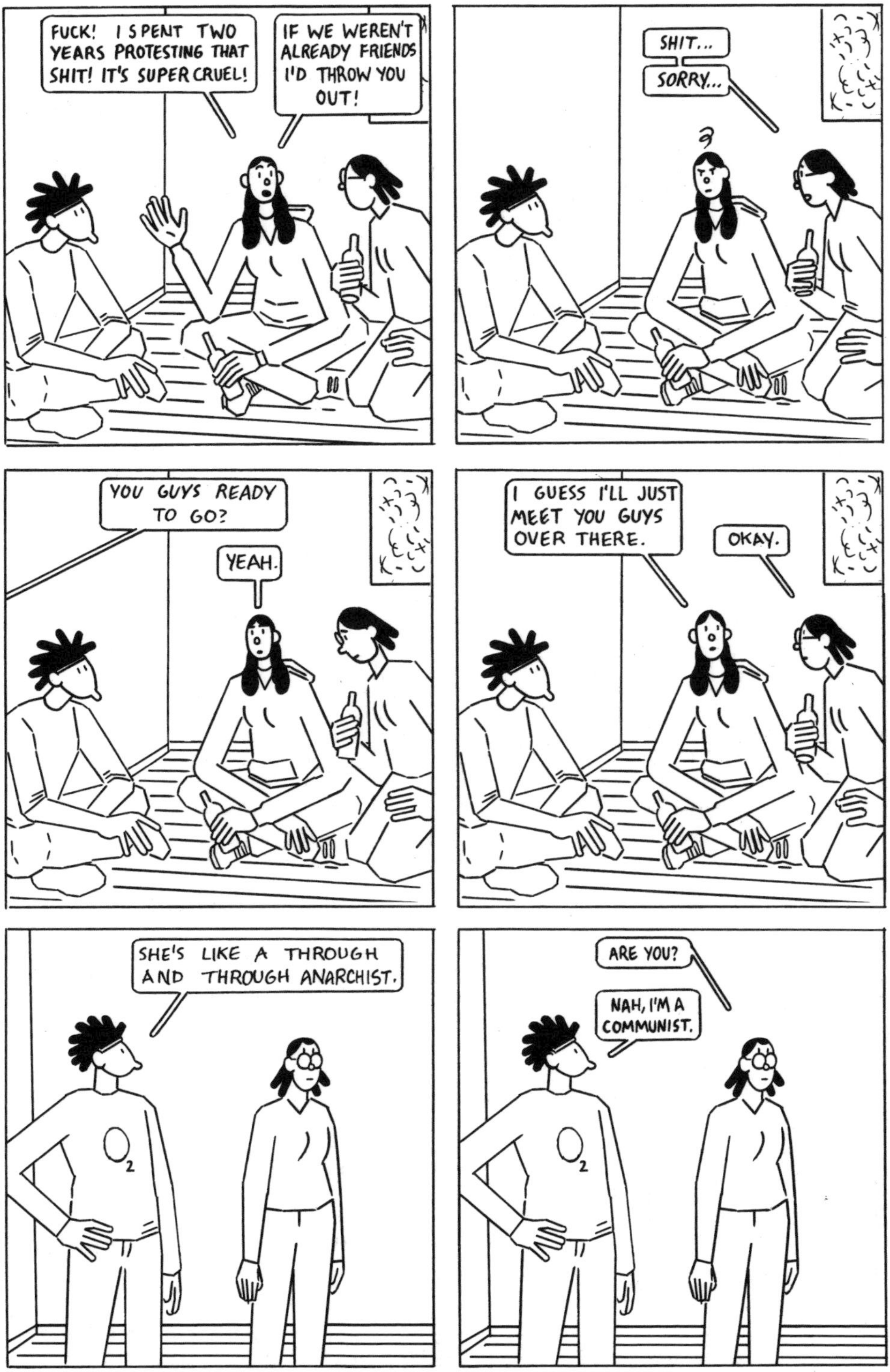
FUCK! I SPENT TWO YEARS PROTESTING THAT SHIT! IT'S SUPER CRUEL!
IF WE WEREN'T ALREADY FRIENDS I'D THROW YOU OUT!
SHIT...
SORRY...
YOU GUYS READY TO GO?
YEAH.
I GUESS I'LL JUST MEET YOU GUYS OVER THERE.
OKAY.
SHE'S LIKE A THROUGH AND THROUGH ANARCHIST.
O_2
ARE YOU?
NAH, I'M A COMMUNIST.
O_2

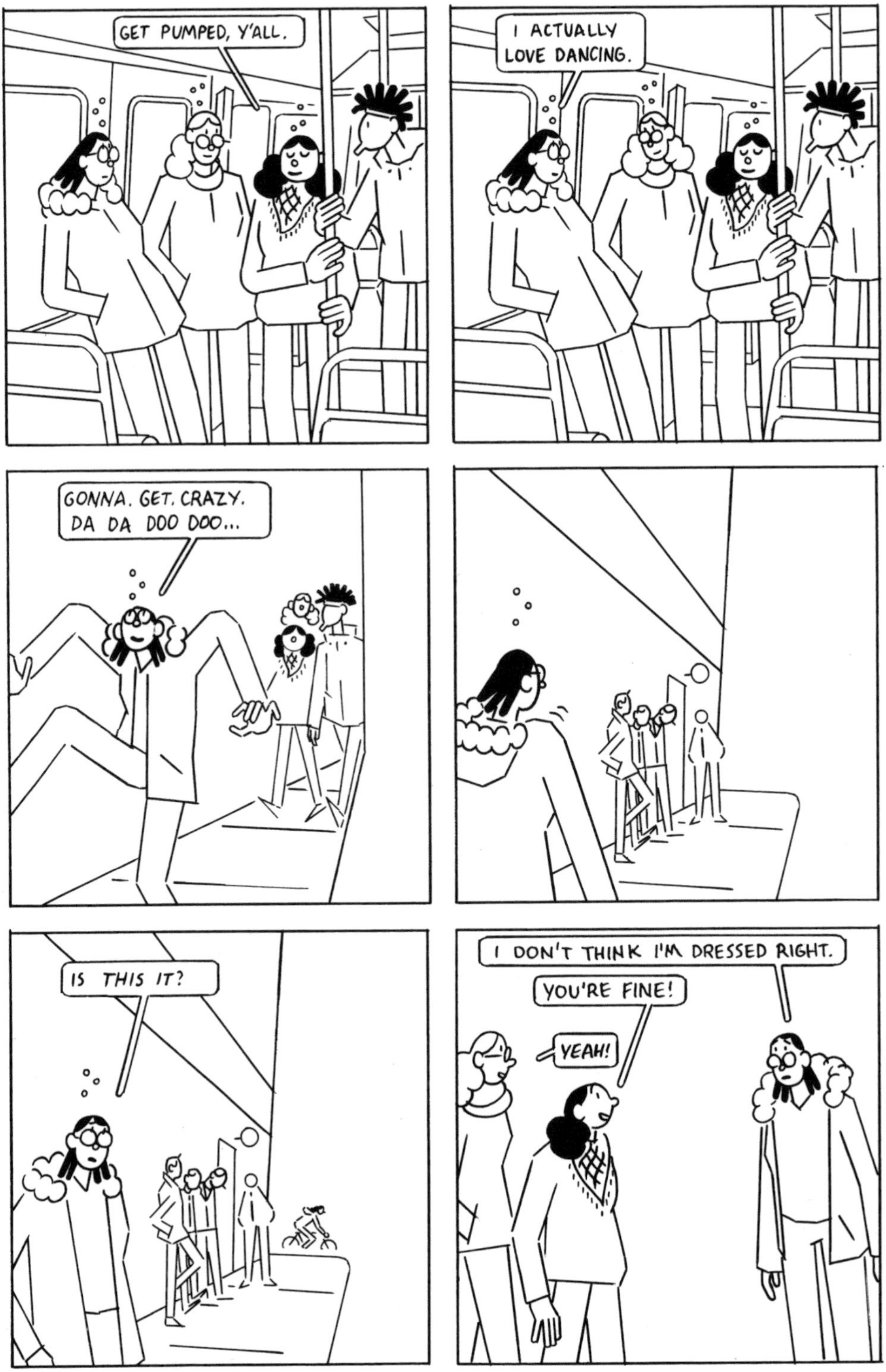
GET PUMPED, Y'ALL.
I ACTUALLY LOVE DANCING.
GONNA. GET. CRAZY. DA DA DOO DOO...
IS THIS IT?
I DON'T THINK I'M DRESSED RIGHT.
YOU'RE FINE!
YEAH!

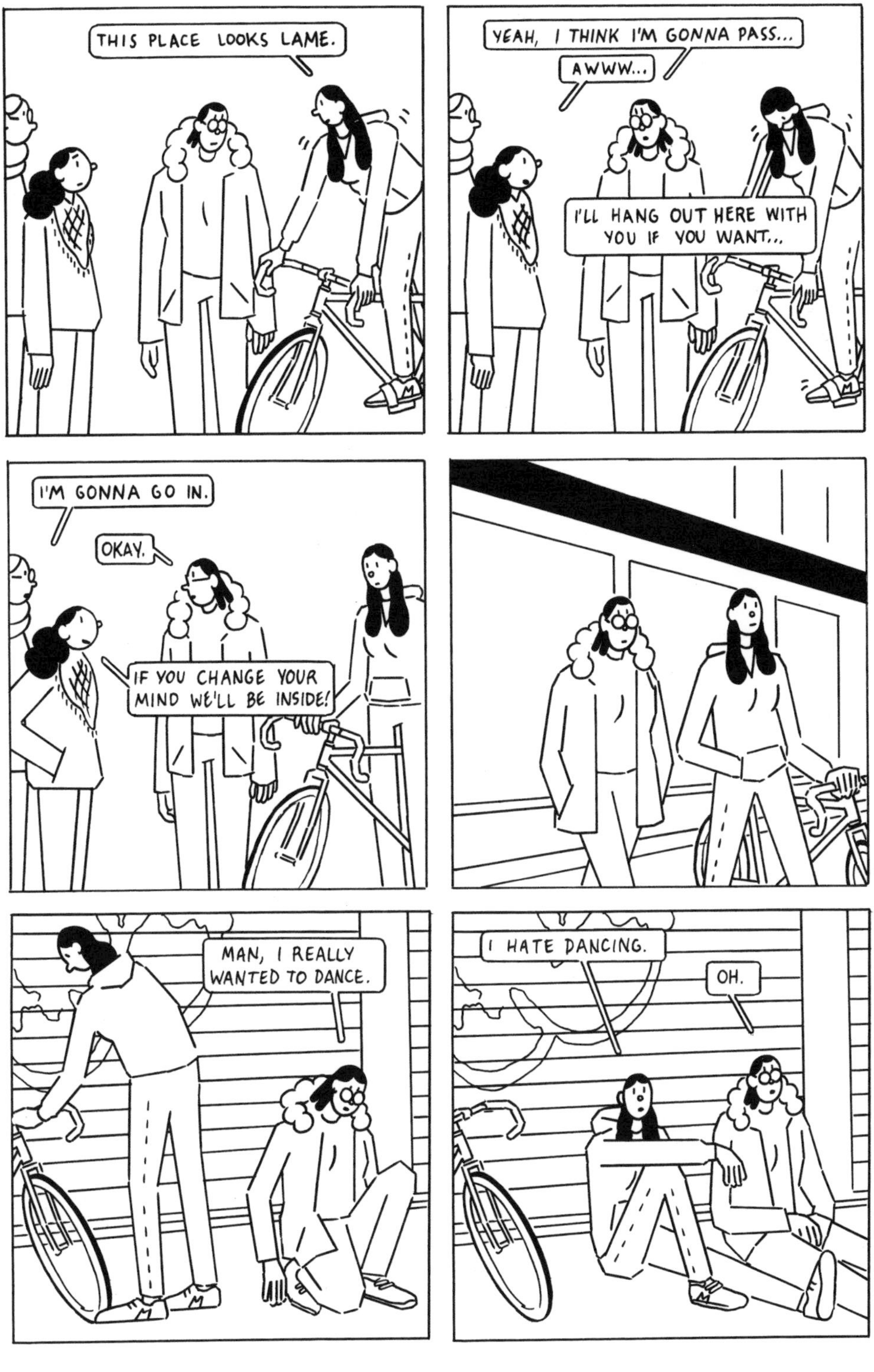
THIS PLACE LOOKS LAME.
YEAH, I THINK I'M GONNA PASS...
AWWW...
I'LL HANG OUT HERE WITH YOU IF YOU WANT...
I'M GONNA GO IN.
OKAY.
IF YOU CHANGE YOUR MIND WE'LL BE INSIDE!
MAN, I REALLY WANTED TO DANCE.
I HATE DANCING.
OH.

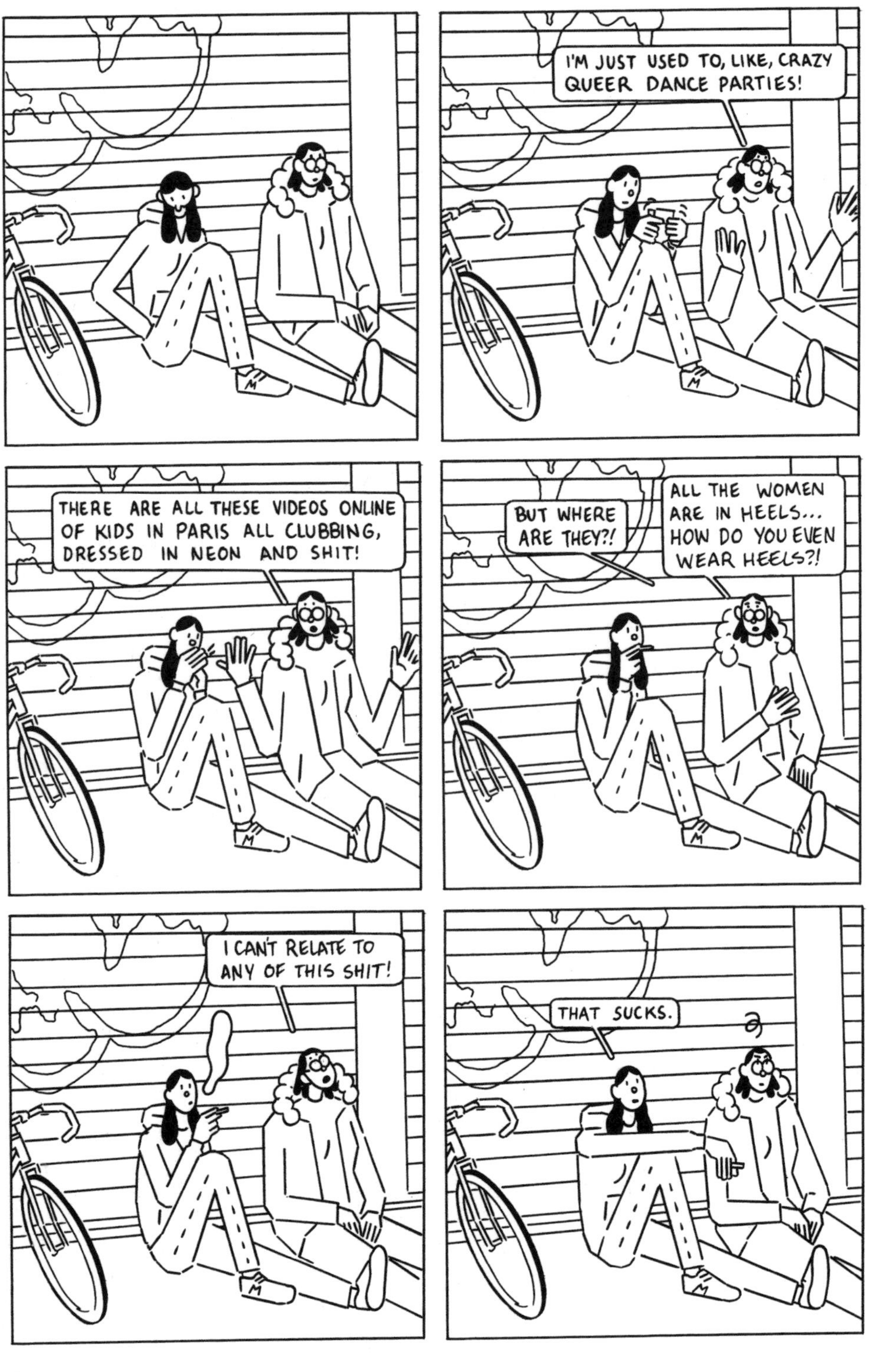
I'M JUST USED TO, LIKE, CRAZY QUEER DANCE PARTIES!
THERE ARE ALL THESE VIDEOS ONLINE OF KIDS IN PARIS ALL CLUBBING, DRESSED IN NEON AND SHIT!
BUT WHERE ARE THEY?!
ALL THE WOMEN ARE IN HEELS... HOW DO YOU EVEN WEAR HEELS?!
I CAN'T RELATE TO ANY OF THIS SHIT!
THAT SUCKS.

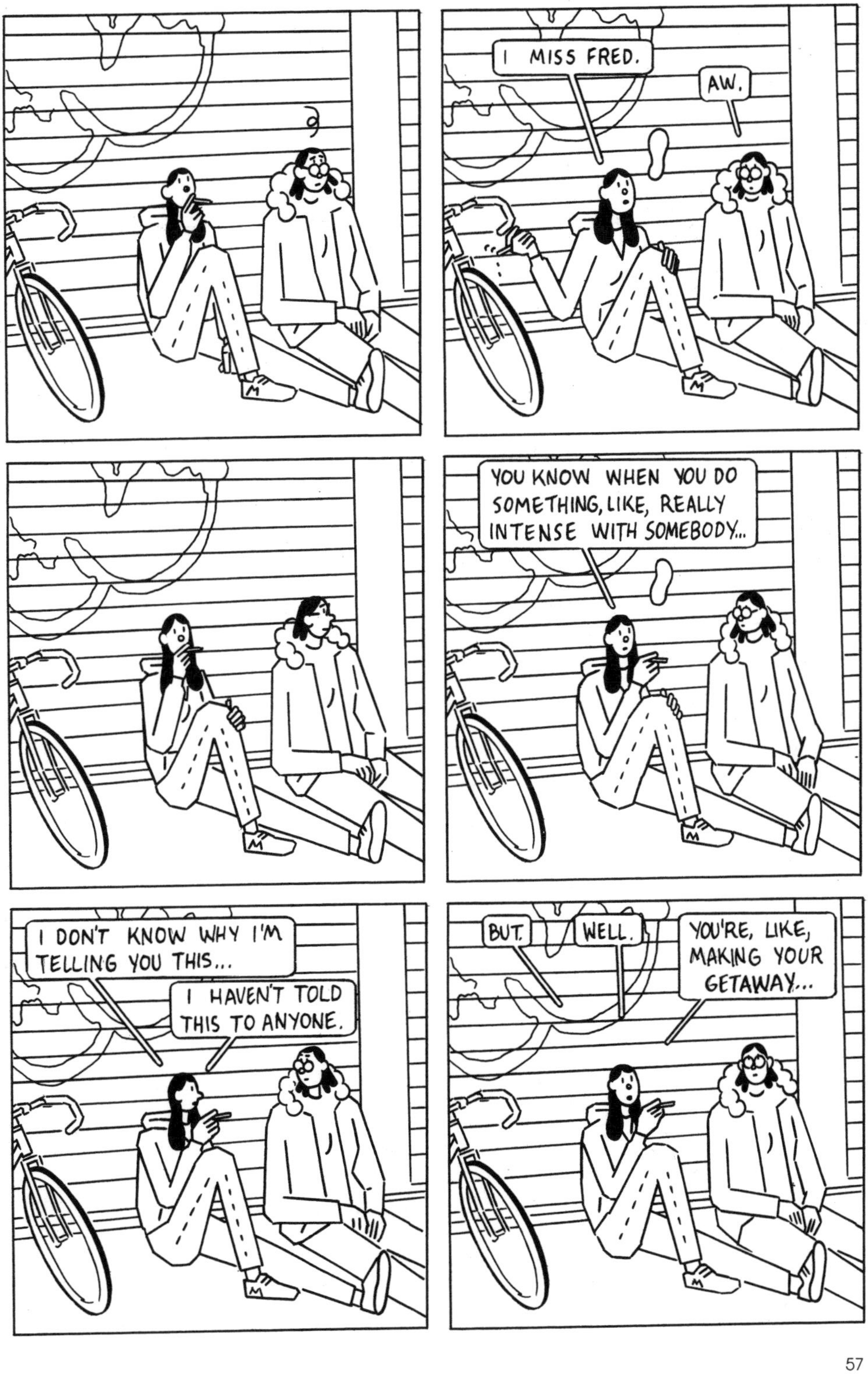
I MISS FRED.
AW.
YOU KNOW WHEN YOU DO SOMETHING, LIKE, REALLY INTENSE WITH SOMEBODY...
I DON'T KNOW WHY I'M TELLING YOU THIS...
I HAVEN'T TOLD THIS TO ANYONE.
BUT.
WELL.
YOU'RE, LIKE, MAKING YOUR GETAWAY...

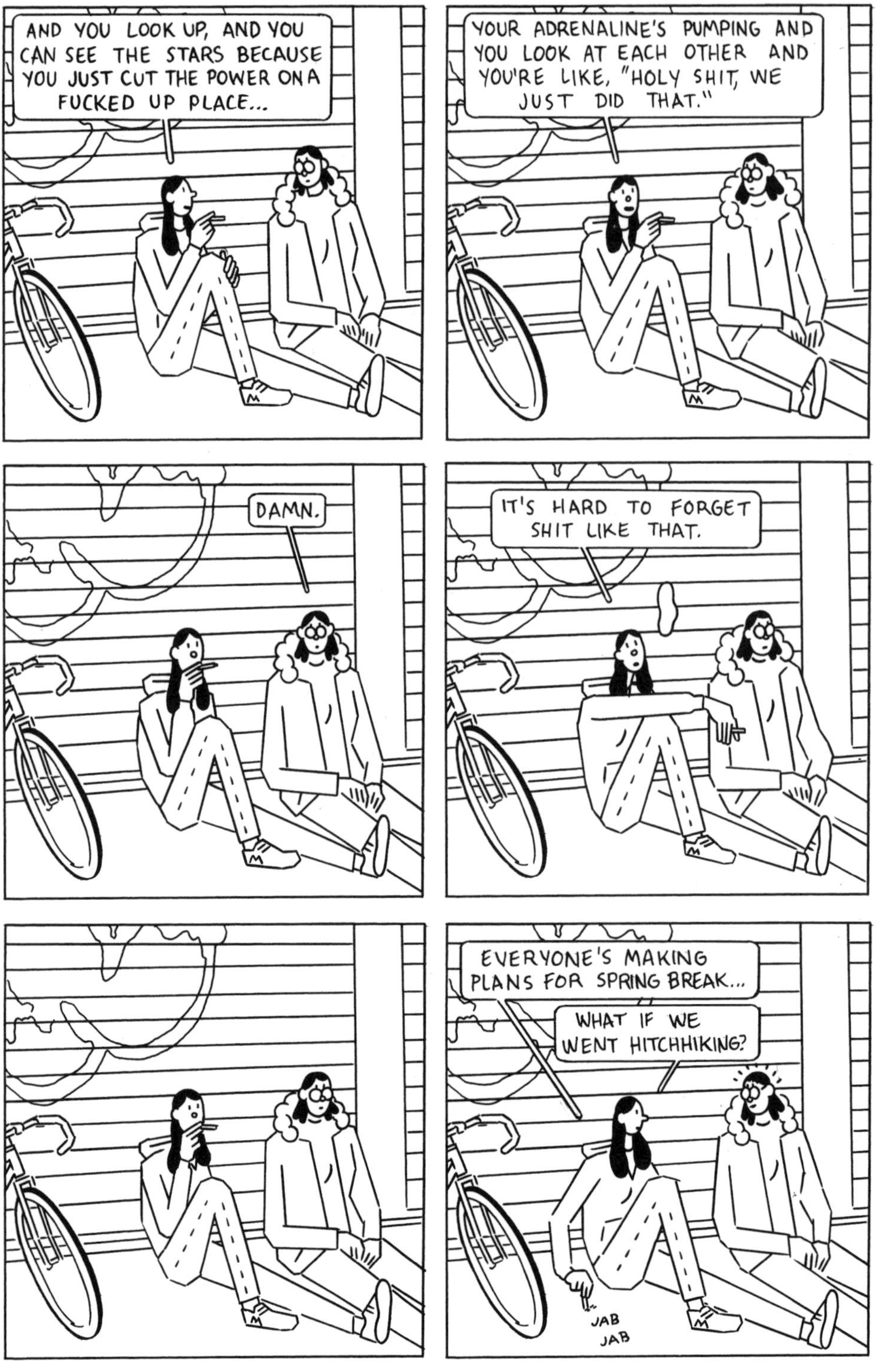

AND YOU LOOK UP, AND YOU CAN SEE THE STARS BECAUSE YOU JUST CUT THE POWER ON A FUCKED UP PLACE...
YOUR ADRENALINE'S PUMPING AND YOU LOOK AT EACH OTHER AND YOU'RE LIKE, "HOLY SHIT, WE JUST DID THAT."
DAMN.
IT'S HARD TO FORGET SHIT LIKE THAT.
EVERYONE'S MAKING PLANS FOR SPRING BREAK...
WHAT IF WE WENT HITCHHIKING?
JAB
JAB

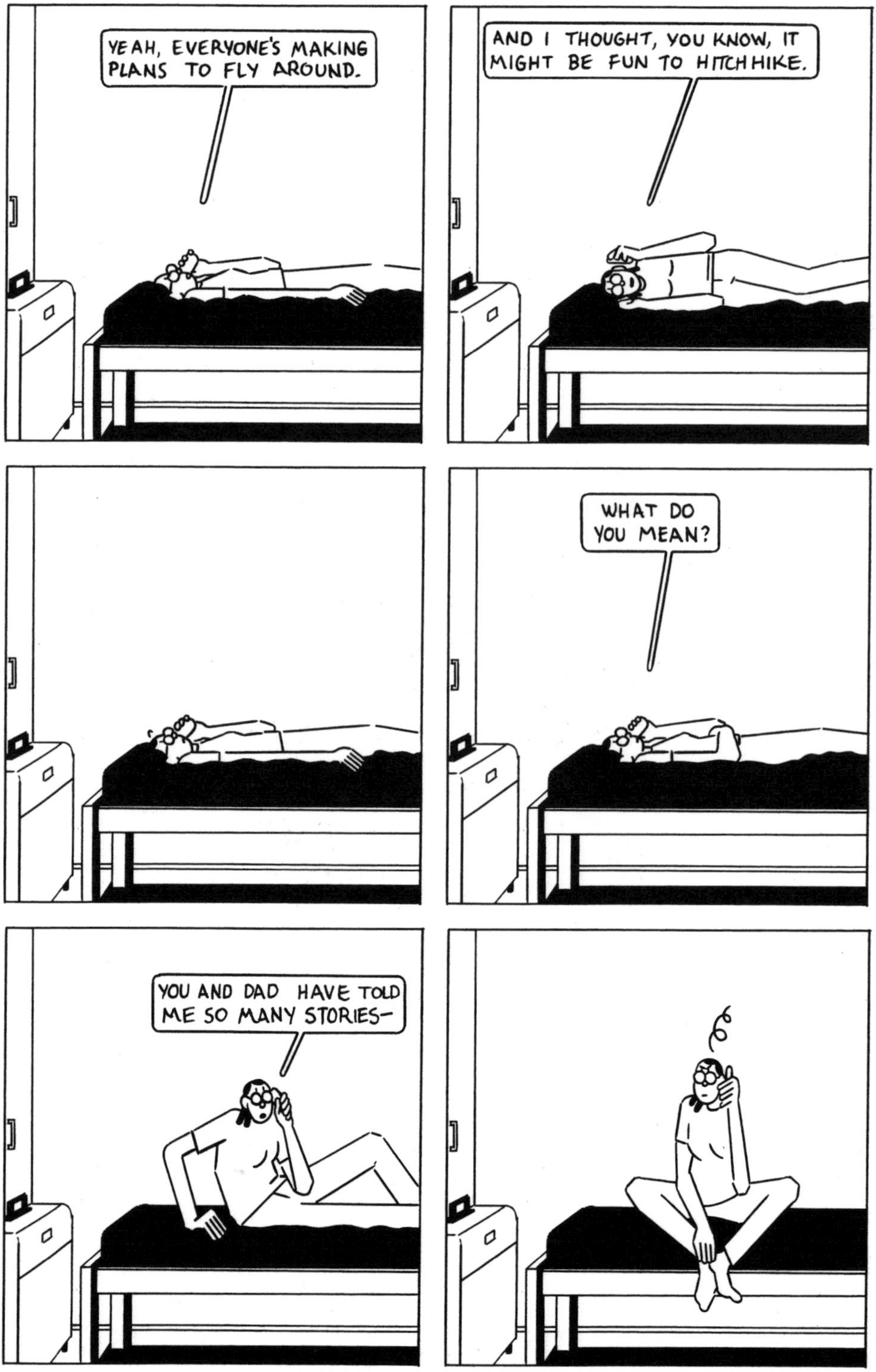
YEAH, EVERYONE'S MAKING PLANS TO FLY AROUND.
AND I THOUGHT, YOU KNOW, IT MIGHT BE FUN TO HITCHHIKE.
WHAT DO YOU MEAN?
YOU AND DAD HAVE TOLD ME SO MANY STORIES—

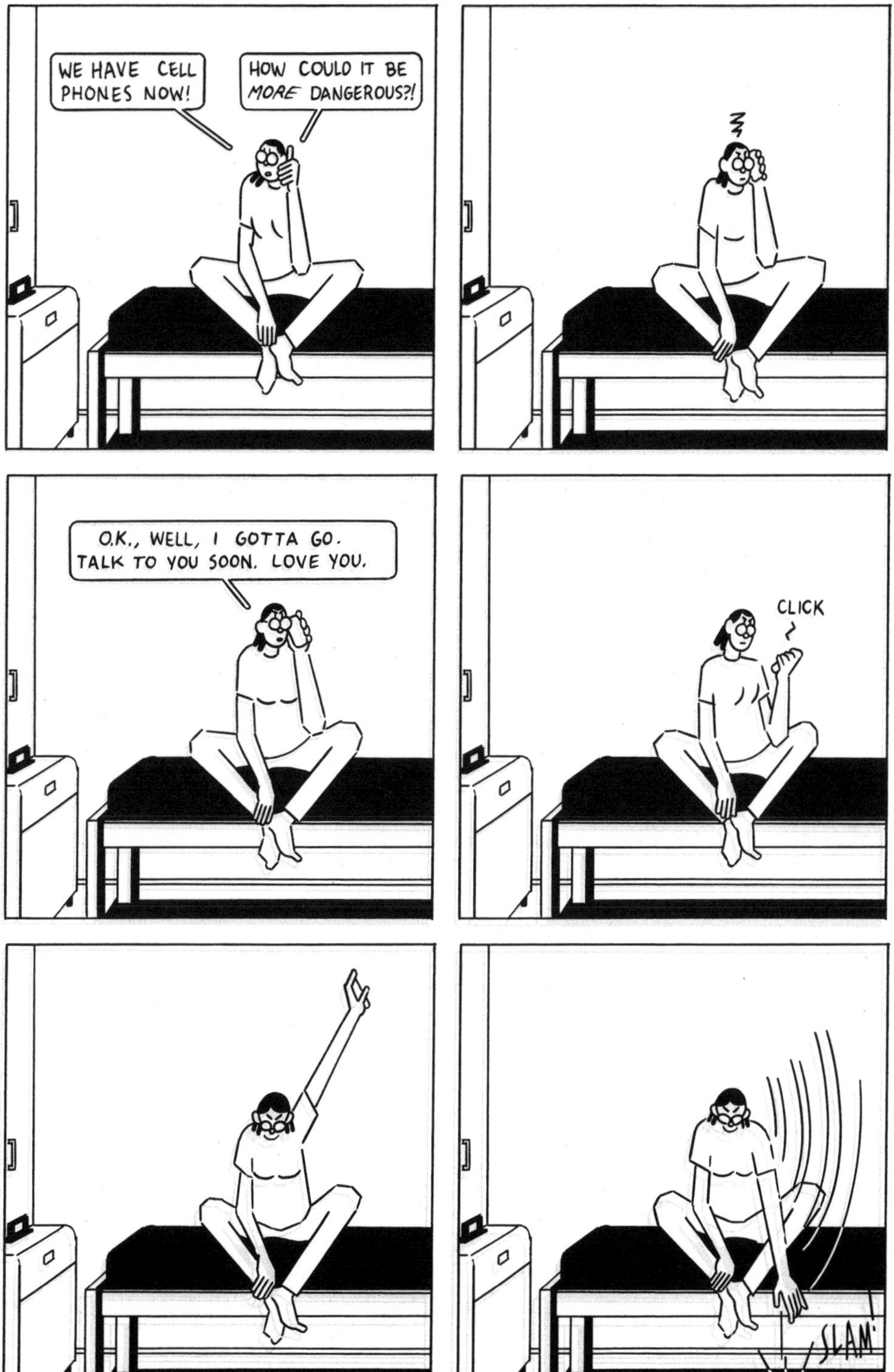
WE HAVE CELL PHONES NOW!
HOW COULD IT BE MORE DANGEROUS?!
O.K., WELL, I GOTTA GO. TALK TO YOU SOON. LOVE YOU.
CLICK
SLAM!

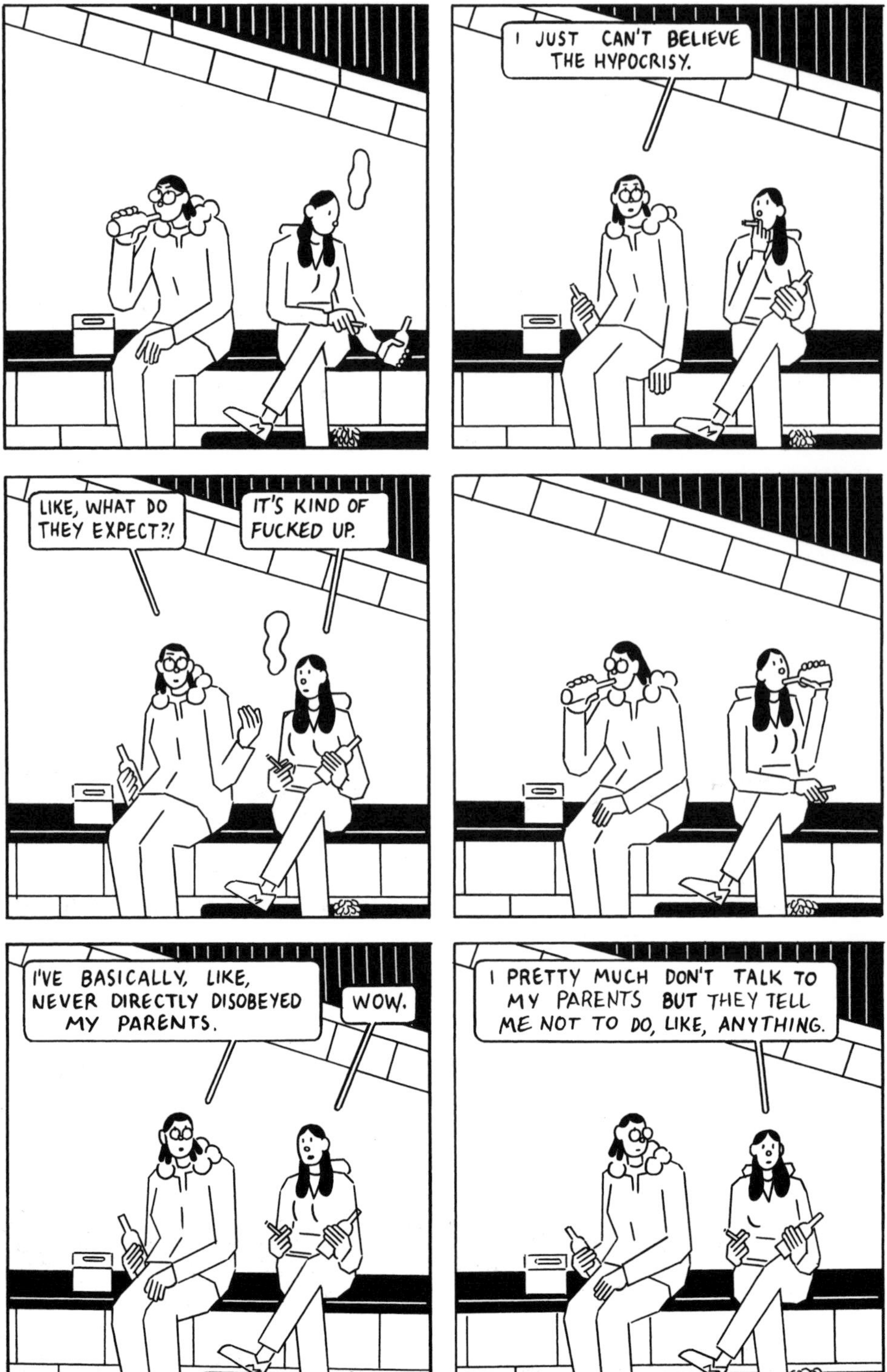
I JUST CAN'T BELIEVE THE HYPOCRISY.
LIKE, WHAT DO THEY EXPECT?!
IT'S KIND OF FUCKED UP.
I'VE BASICALLY, LIKE, NEVER DIRECTLY DISOBEYED MY PARENTS.
WOW.
I PRETTY MUCH DON'T TALK TO MY PARENTS BUT THEY TELL ME NOT TO DO, LIKE, ANYTHING.

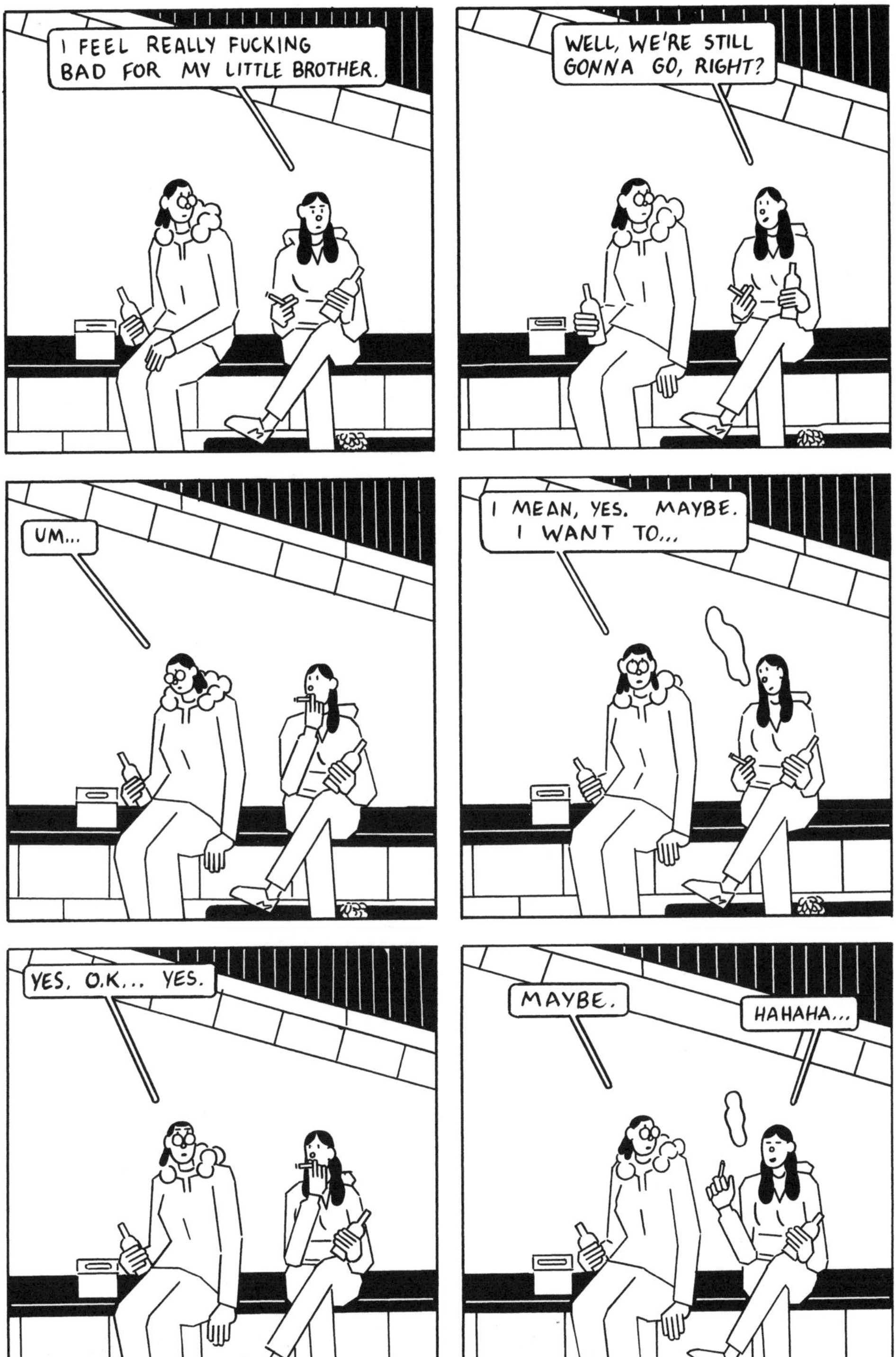
I FEEL REALLY FUCKING BAD FOR MY LITTLE BROTHER.
WELL, WE'RE STILL GONNA GO, RIGHT?
UM...
I MEAN, YES. MAYBE. I WANT TO...
YES. O.K... YES.
MAYBE.
HAHAHA...

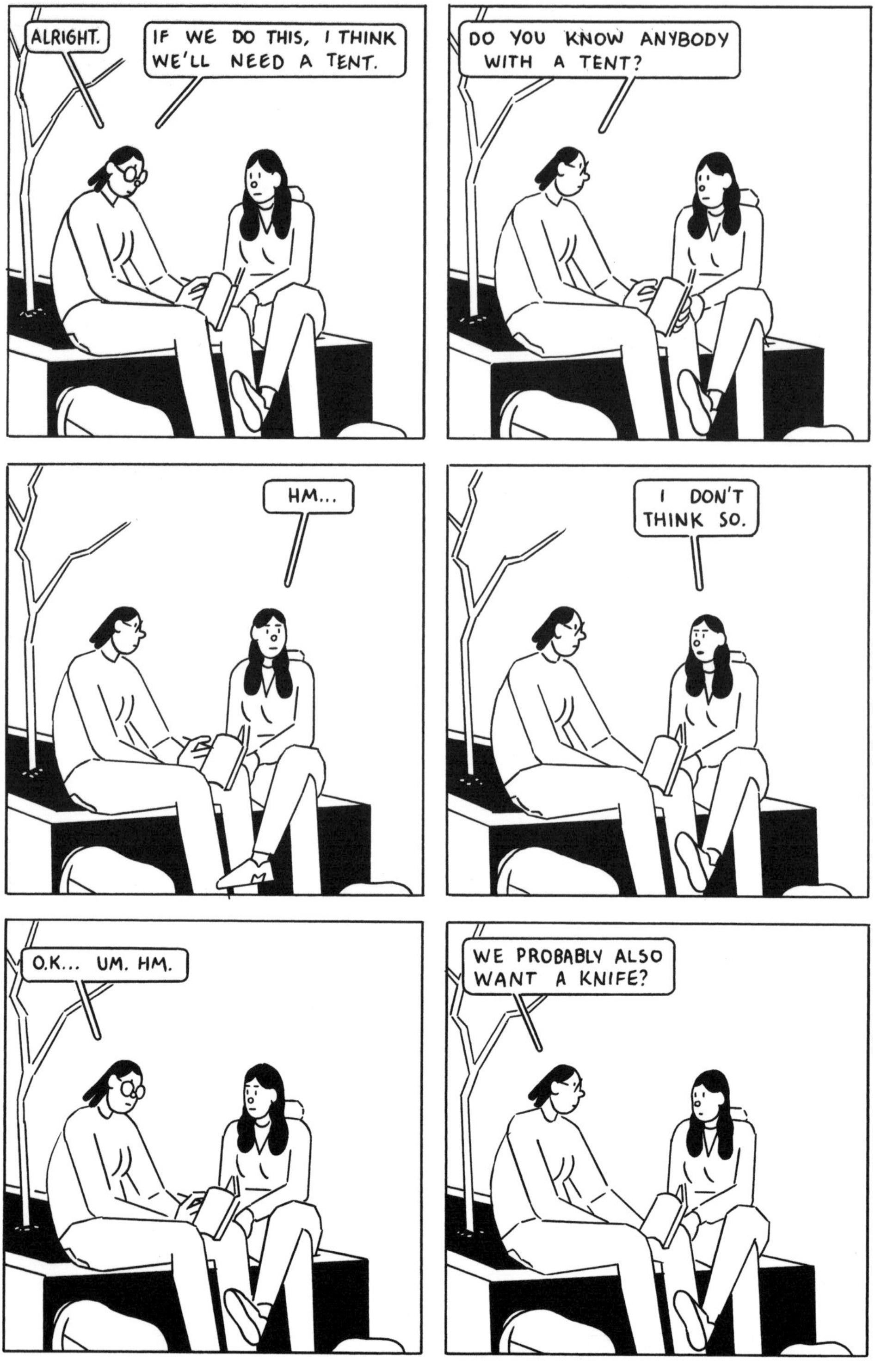
ALRIGHT.
IF WE DO THIS, I THINK WE'LL NEED A TENT.
DO YOU KNOW ANYBODY WITH A TENT?
HM...
I DON'T THINK SO.
O.K... UM. HM.
WE PROBABLY ALSO WANT A KNIFE?

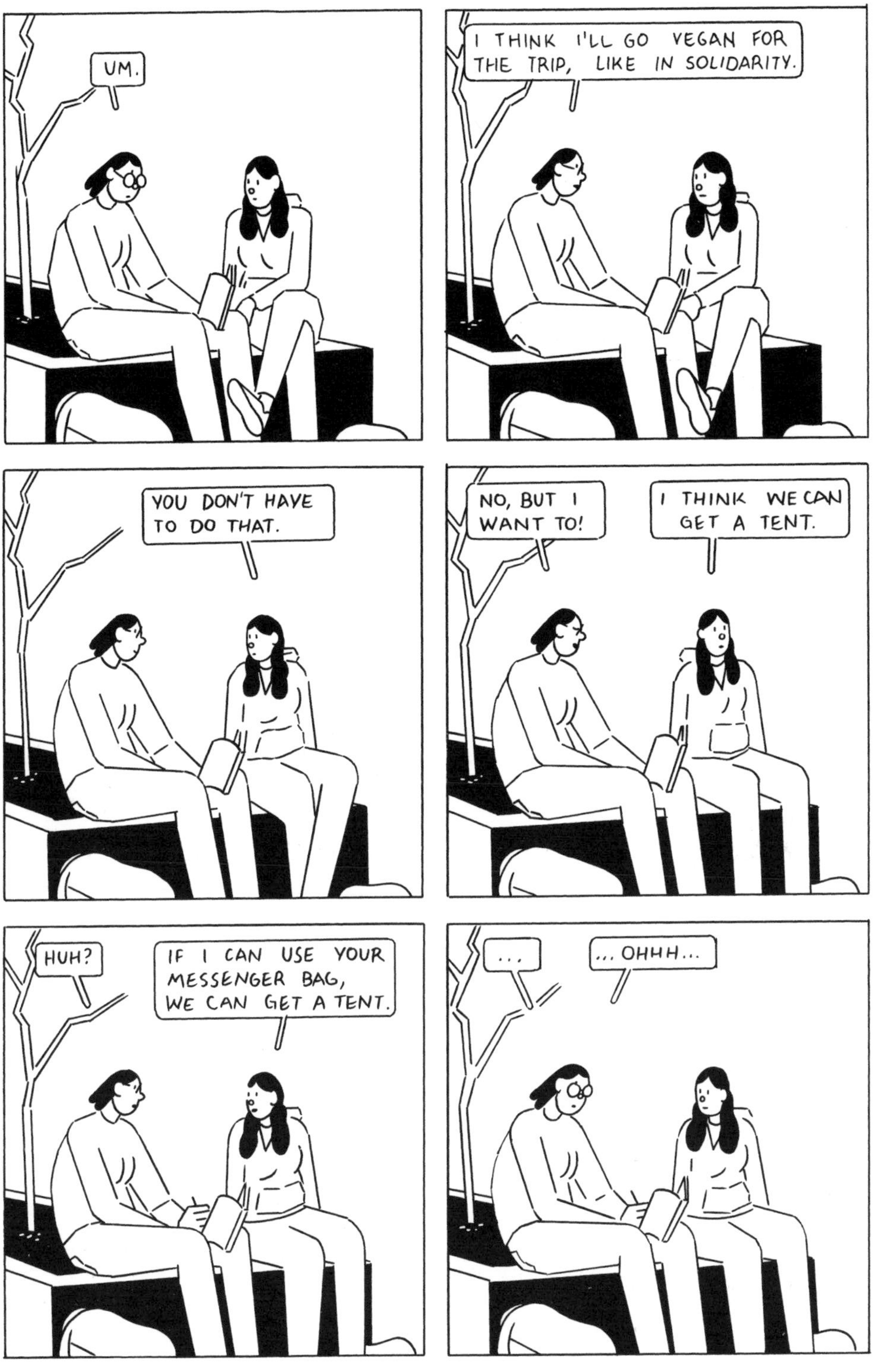
UM.
I THINK I'LL GO VEGAN FOR THE TRIP, LIKE IN SOLIDARITY.
YOU DON'T HAVE TO DO THAT.
NO, BUT I WANT TO!
I THINK WE CAN GET A TENT.
HUH?
IF I CAN USE YOUR MESSENGER BAG, WE CAN GET A TENT.
...
...OHHH...

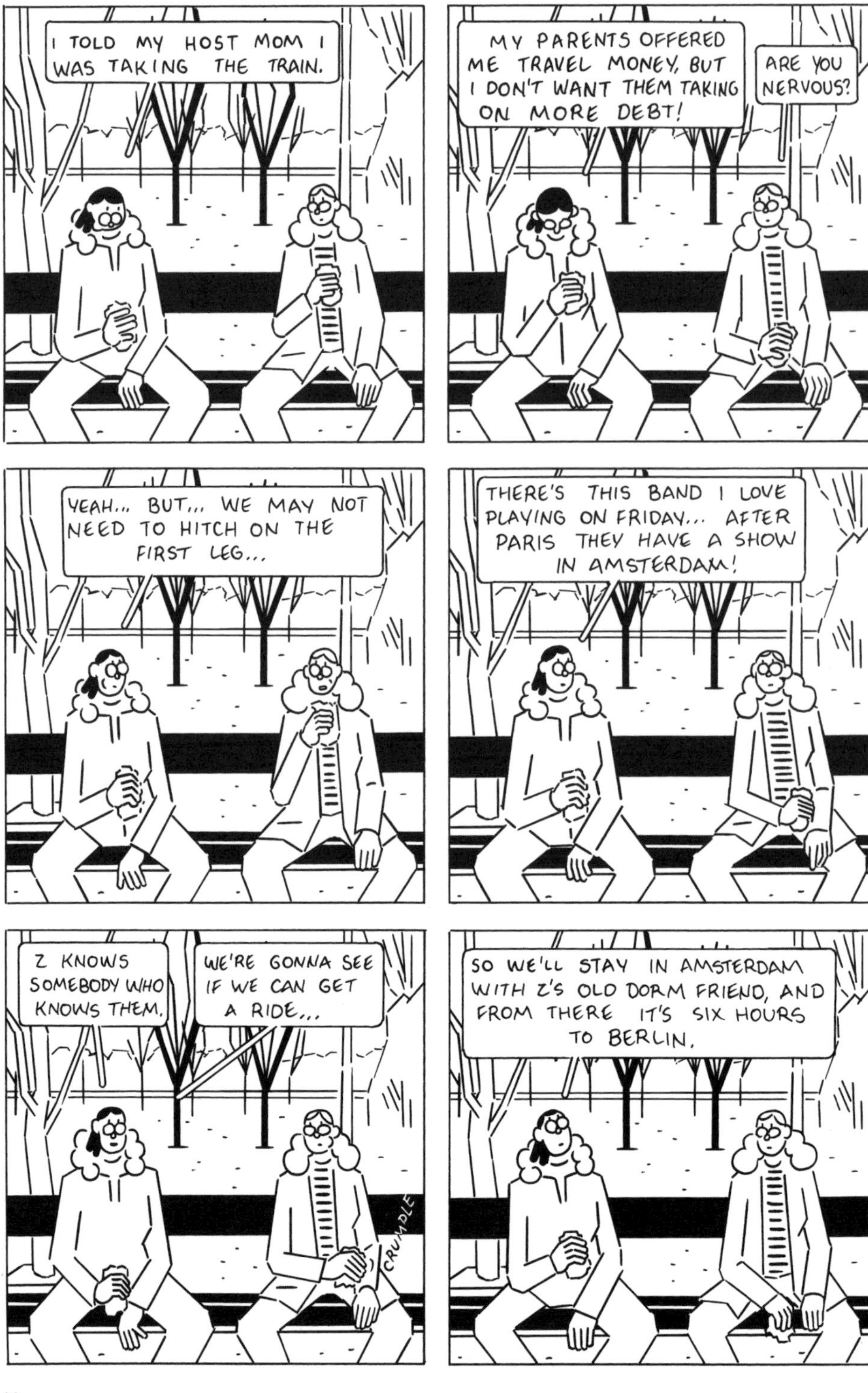
I TOLD MY HOST MOM I WAS TAKING THE TRAIN.
MY PARENTS OFFERED ME TRAVEL MONEY, BUT I DON'T WANT THEM TAKING ON MORE DEBT!
ARE YOU NERVOUS?
YEAH... BUT... WE MAY NOT NEED TO HITCH ON THE FIRST LEG...
THERE'S THIS BAND I LOVE PLAYING ON FRIDAY... AFTER PARIS THEY HAVE A SHOW IN AMSTERDAM!
Z KNOWS SOMEBODY WHO KNOWS THEM.
WE'RE GONNA SEE IF WE CAN GET A RIDE...
CRUMBLE
SO WE'LL STAY IN AMSTERDAM WITH Z'S OLD DORM FRIEND, AND FROM THERE IT'S SIX HOURS TO BERLIN.

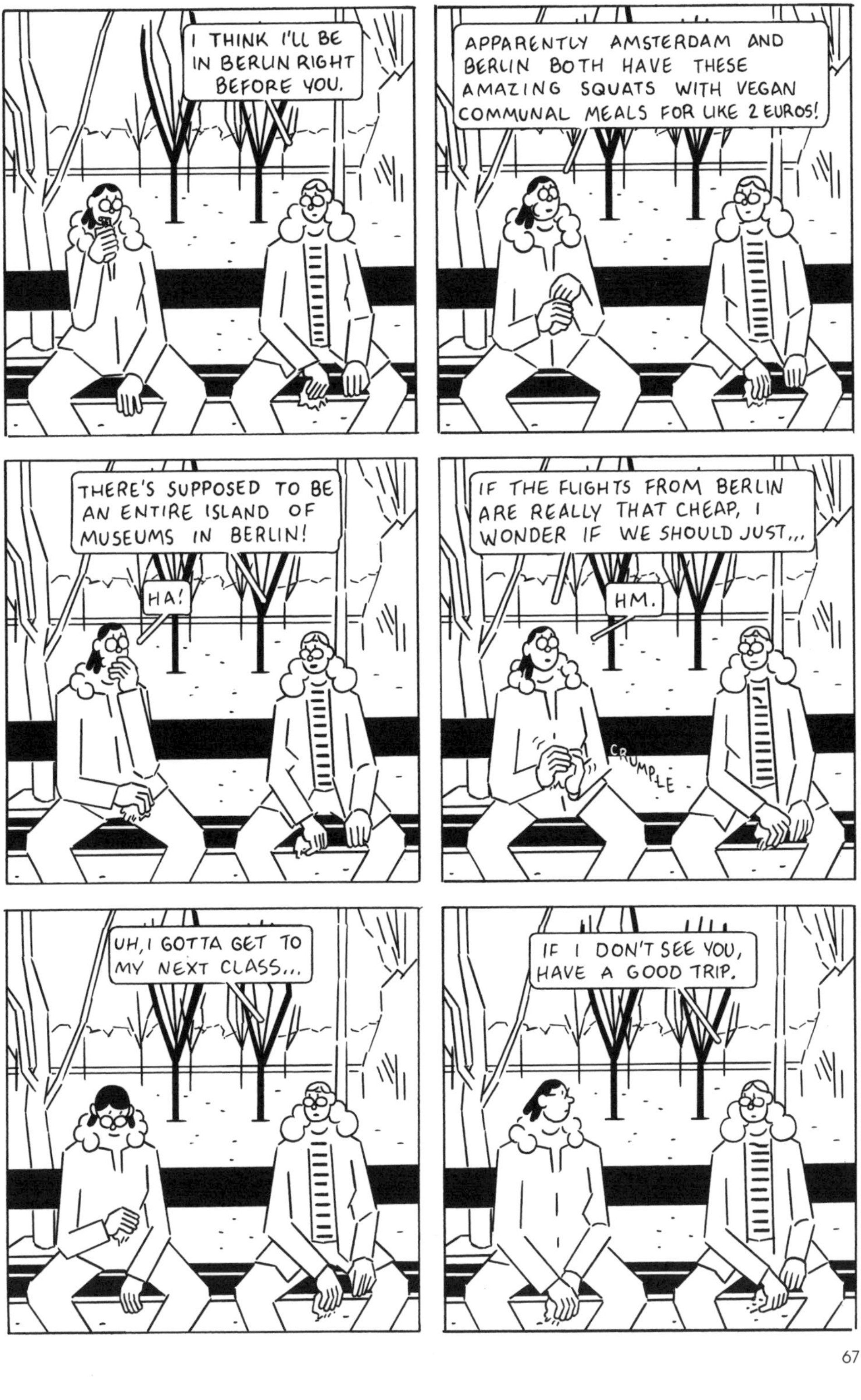
I THINK I'LL BE IN BERLIN RIGHT BEFORE YOU.
APPARENTLY AMSTERDAM AND BERLIN BOTH HAVE THESE AMAZING SQUATS WITH VEGAN COMMUNAL MEALS FOR LIKE 2 EUROS!
THERE'S SUPPOSED TO BE AN ENTIRE ISLAND OF MUSEUMS IN BERLIN!
HA!
IF THE FLIGHTS FROM BERLIN ARE REALLY THAT CHEAP, I WONDER IF WE SHOULD JUST...
HM.
CRUMPLE
UH, I GOTTA GET TO MY NEXT CLASS...
IF I DON'T SEE YOU, HAVE A GOOD TRIP.

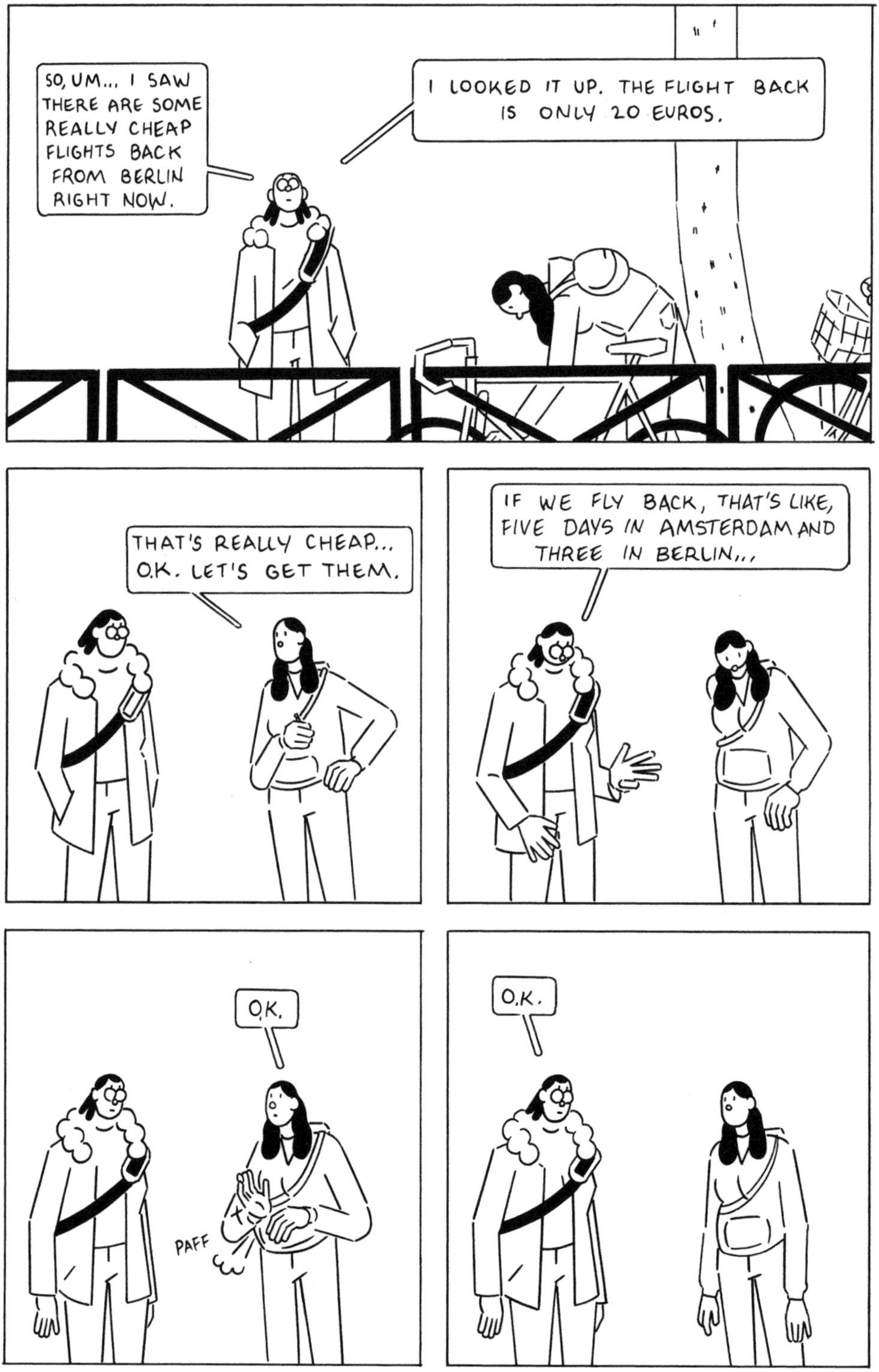
SO, UM... I SAW THERE ARE SOME REALLY CHEAP FLIGHTS BACK FROM BERLIN RIGHT NOW.
I LOOKED IT UP. THE FLIGHT BACK IS ONLY 20 EUROS.
THAT'S REALLY CHEAP... O.K. LET'S GET THEM.
IF WE FLY BACK, THAT'S LIKE, FIVE DAYS IN AMSTERDAM AND THREE IN BERLIN...
O.K.
PAFF
O.K.

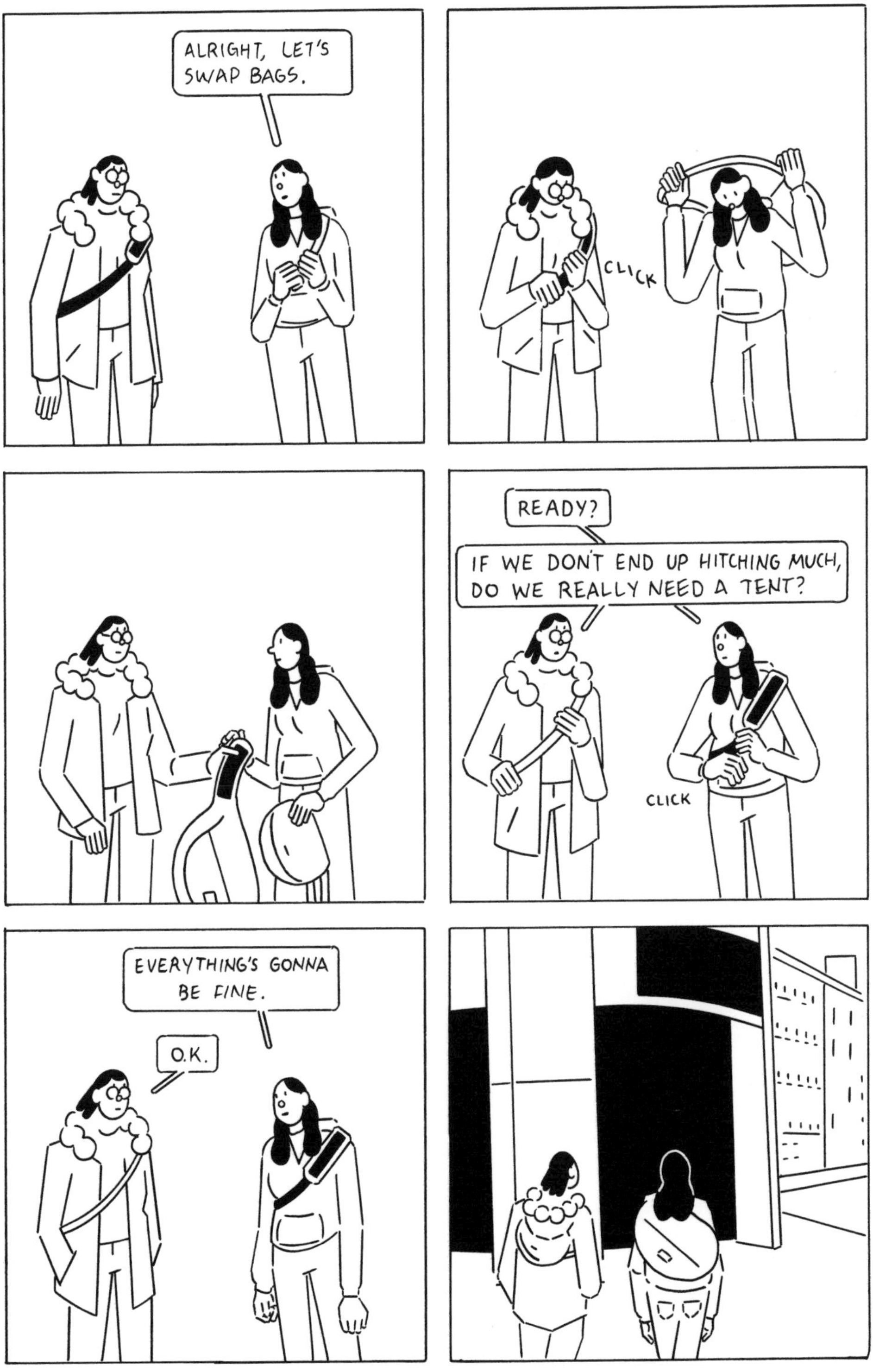
ALRIGHT, LET'S SWAP BAGS.
CLICK
READY?
IF WE DON'T END UP HITCHING MUCH, DO WE REALLY NEED A TENT?
CLICK
EVERYTHING'S GONNA BE FINE.
O.K.

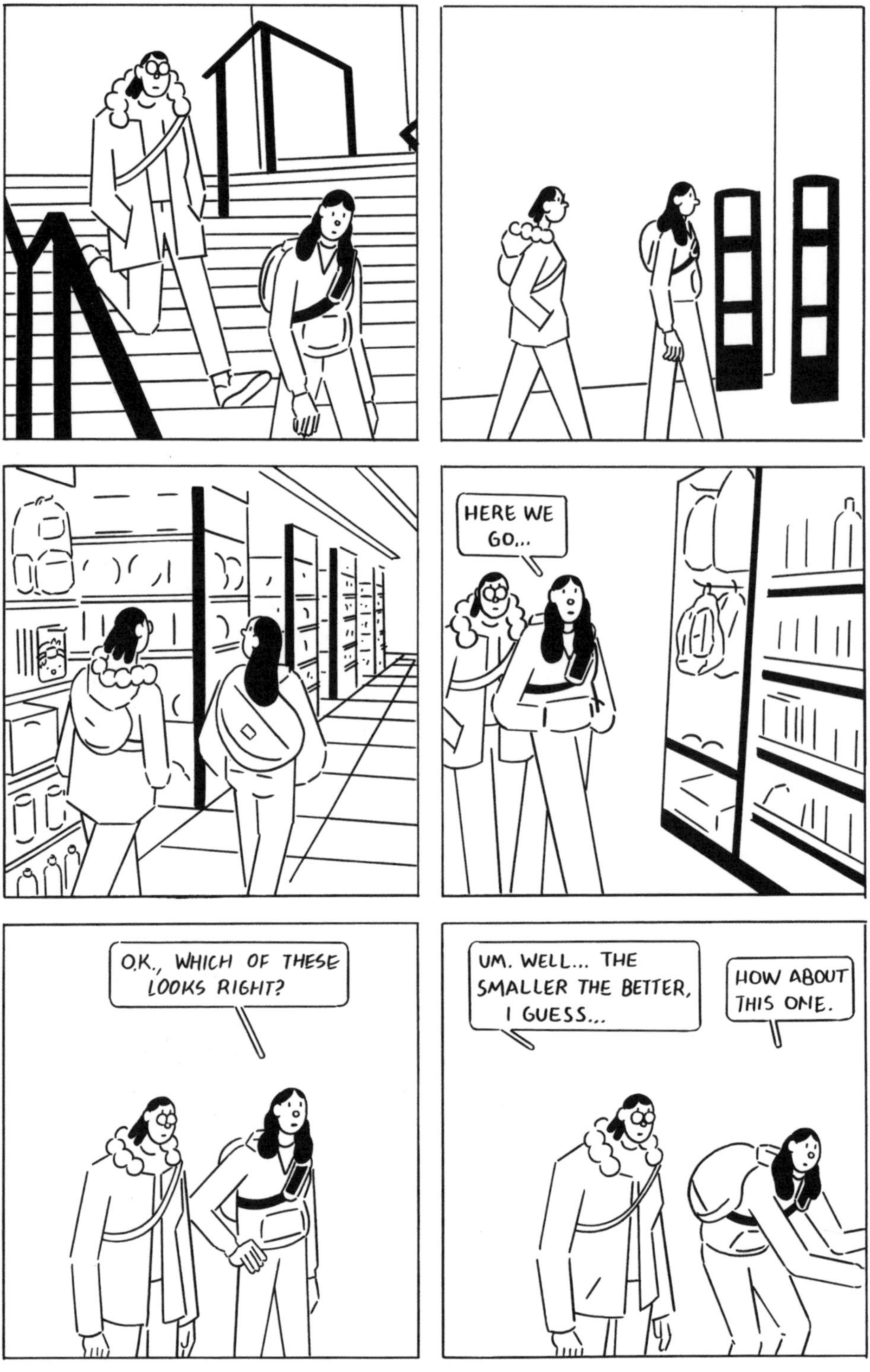
HERE WE GO...
O.K., WHICH OF THESE LOOKS RIGHT?
UM. WELL... THE SMALLER THE BETTER, I GUESS...
HOW ABOUT THIS ONE.

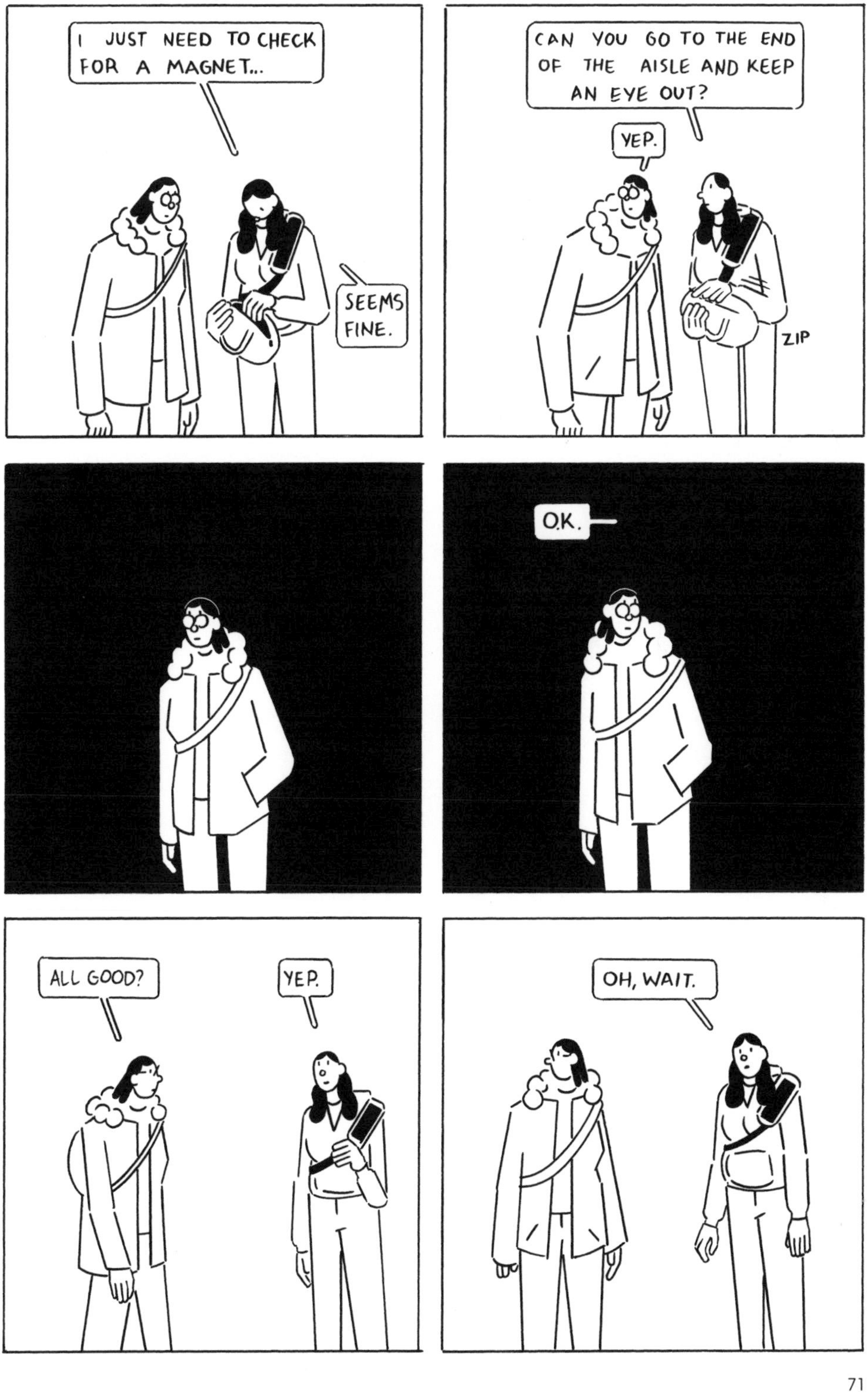
I JUST NEED TO CHECK FOR A MAGNET...
SEEMS FINE.
CAN YOU GO TO THE END OF THE AISLE AND KEEP AN EYE OUT?
YEP.
ZIP
O.K.
ALL GOOD?
YEP.
OH, WAIT.

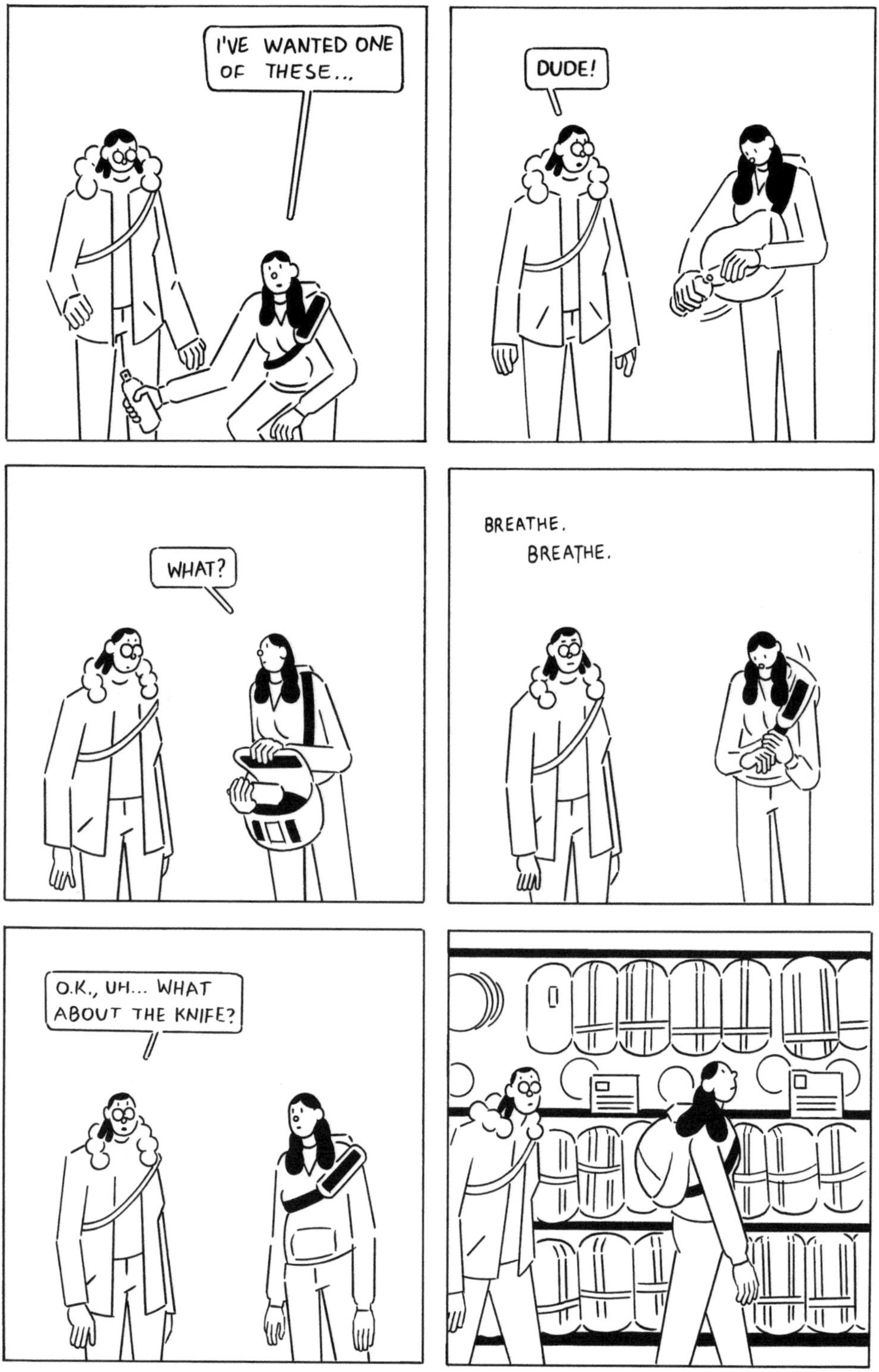
I'VE WANTED ONE OF THESE...
DUDE!
WHAT?
BREATHE.
BREATHE.
O.K., UH... WHAT ABOUT THE KNIFE?

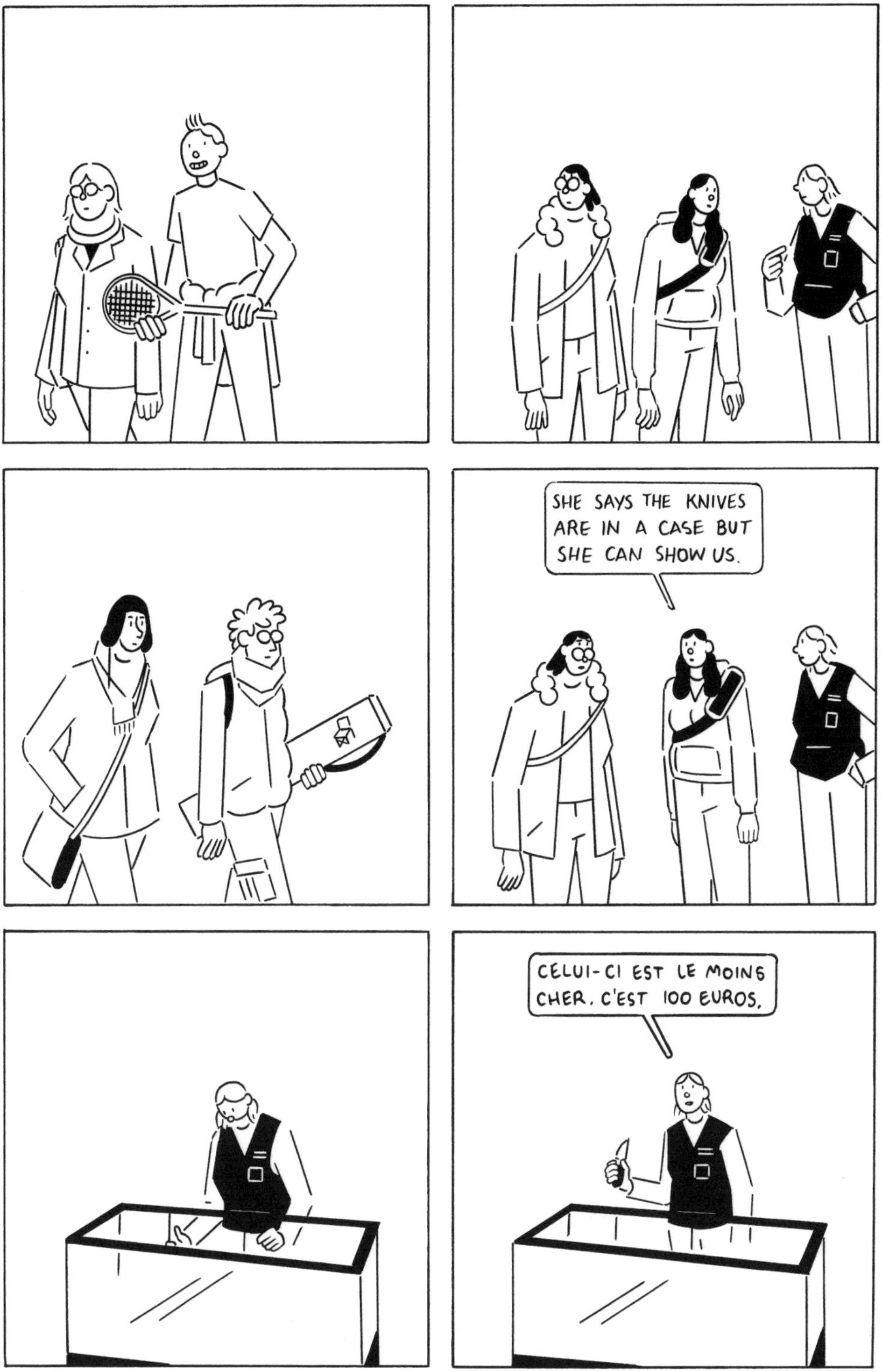
SHE SAYS THE KNIVES ARE IN A CASE BUT SHE CAN SHOW US.
CELUI-CI EST LE MOINS CHER. C'EST 100 EUROS.

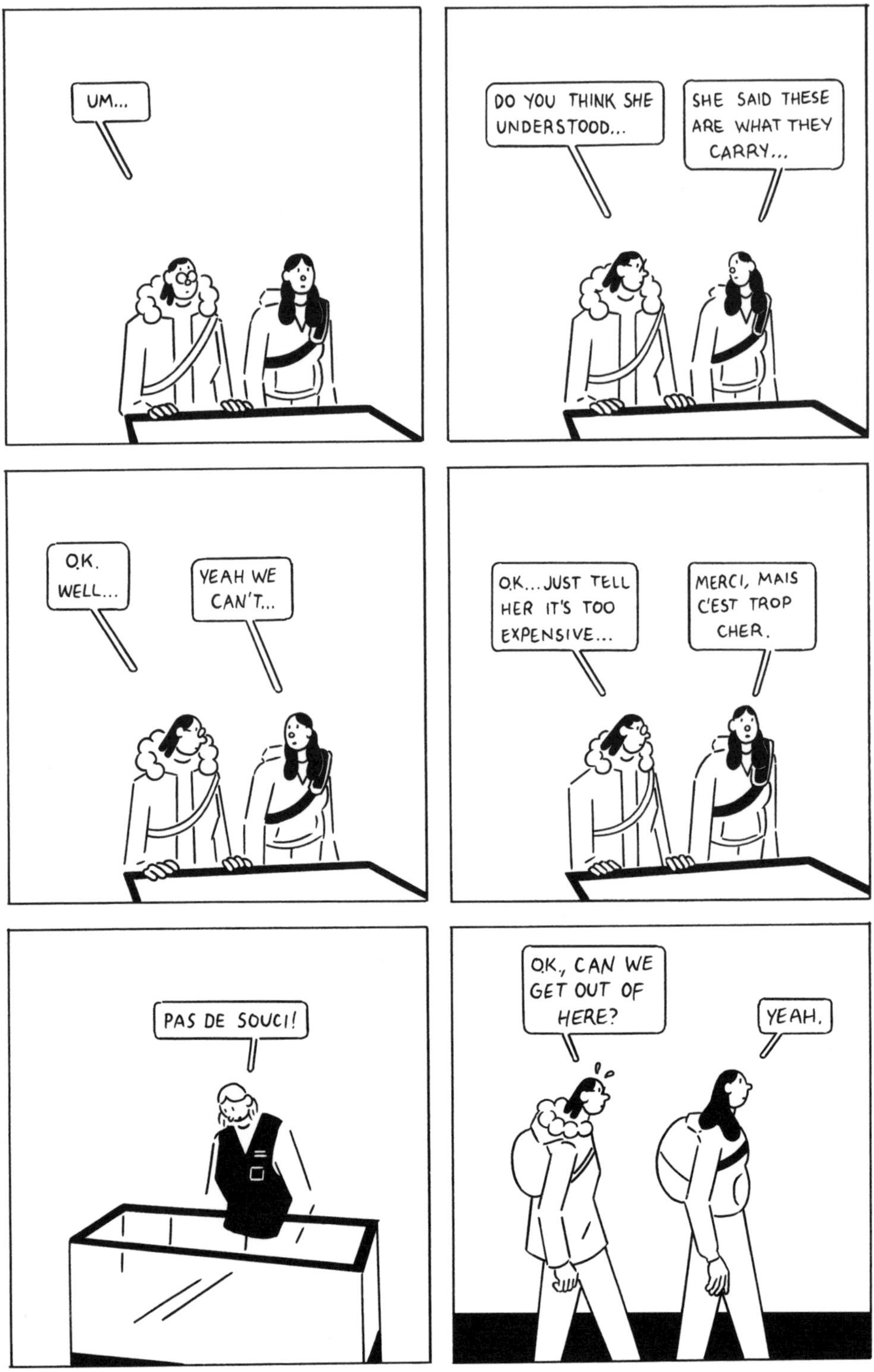
UM...
DO YOU THINK SHE UNDERSTOOD...
SHE SAID THESE ARE WHAT THEY CARRY...
O.K. WELL...
YEAH WE CAN'T...
O.K... JUST TELL HER IT'S TOO EXPENSIVE...
MERCI, MAIS C'EST TROP CHER.
PAS DE SOUCI!
O.K., CAN WE GET OUT OF HERE?
YEAH.

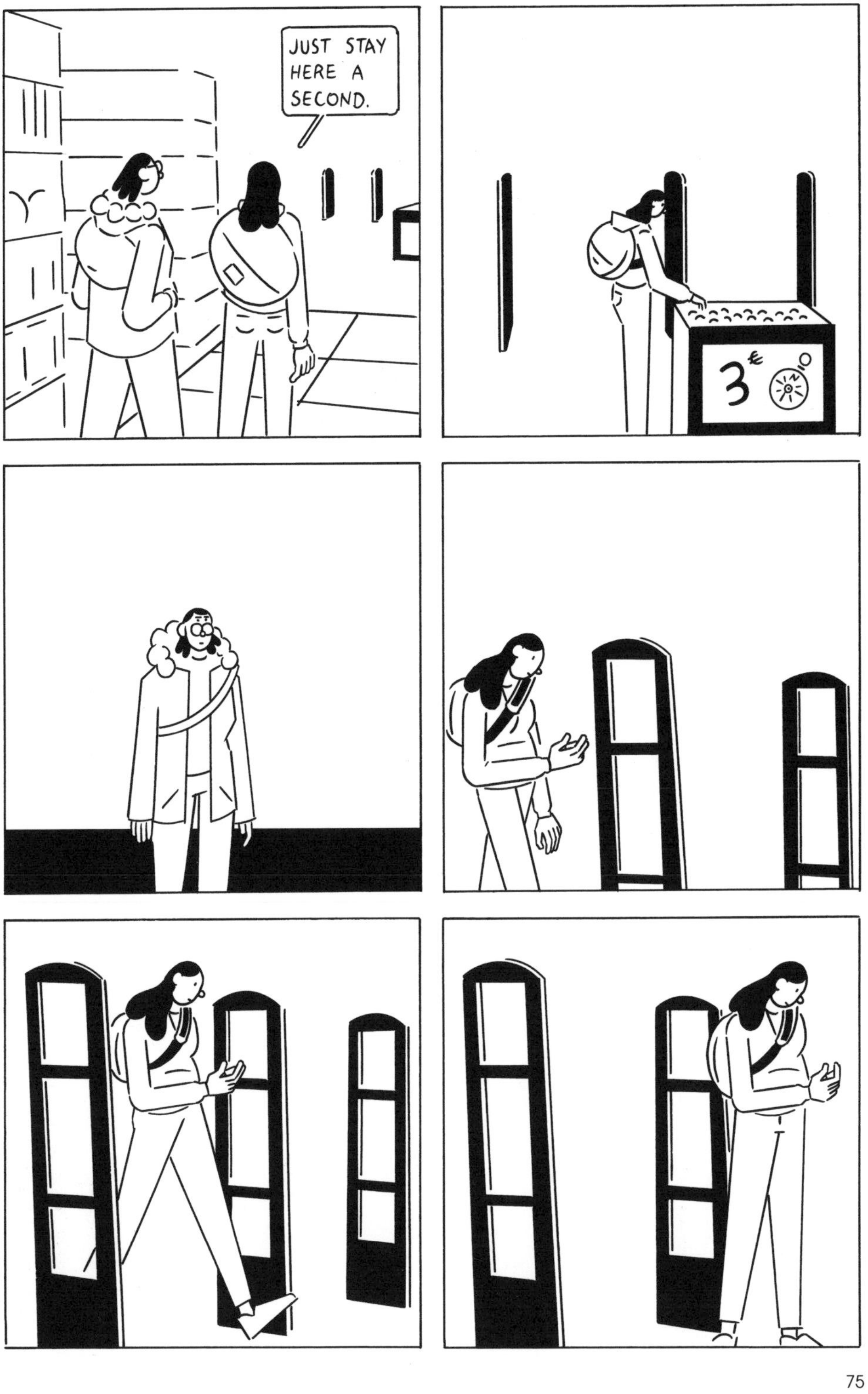
JUST STAY HERE A SECOND.
3€

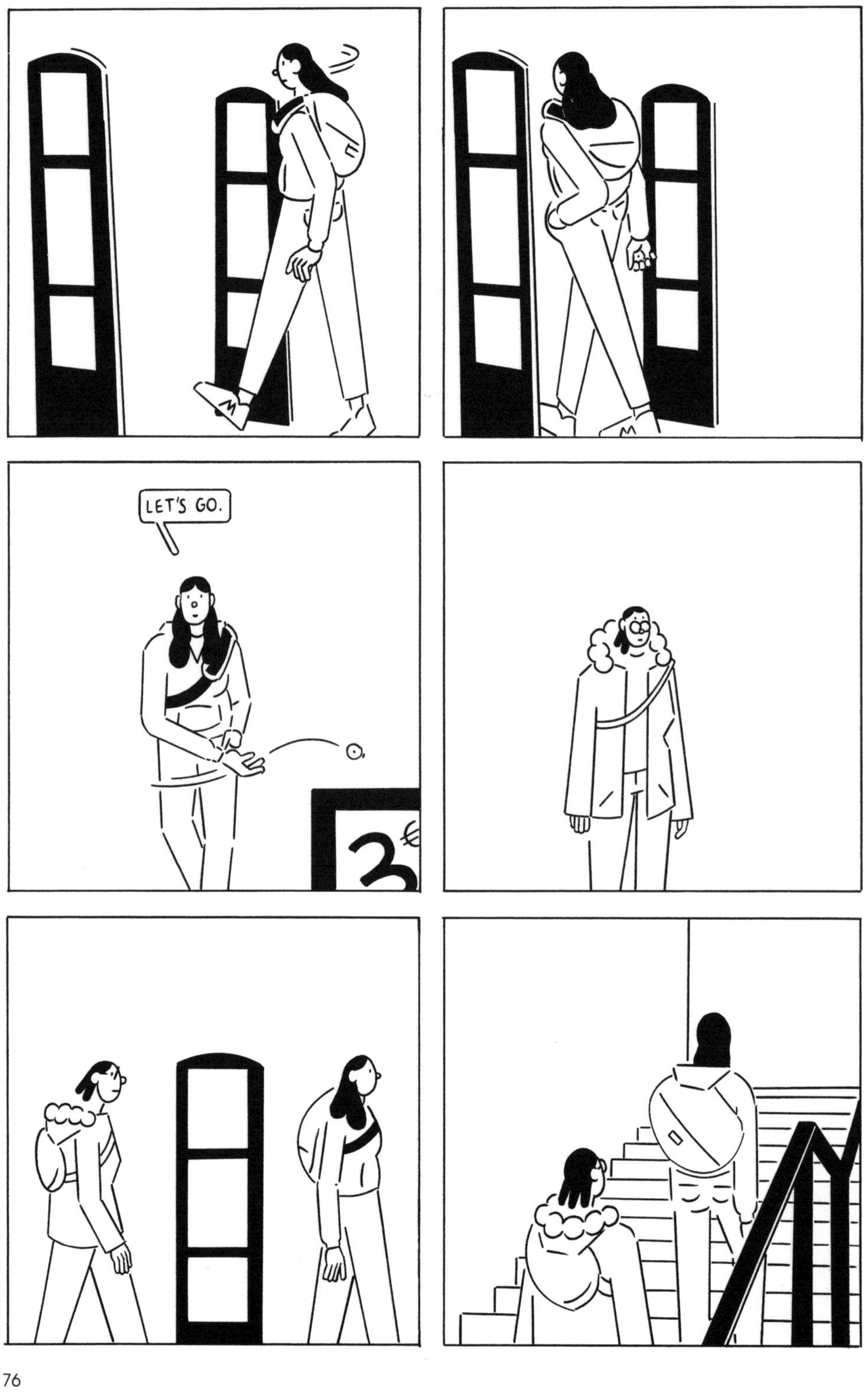
LET'S GO.
3€

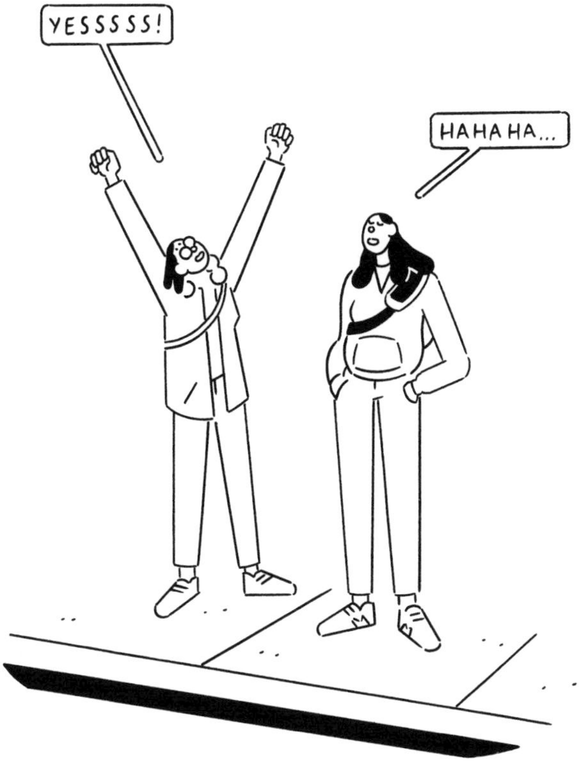
YESSSSSS!
HAHAHA...

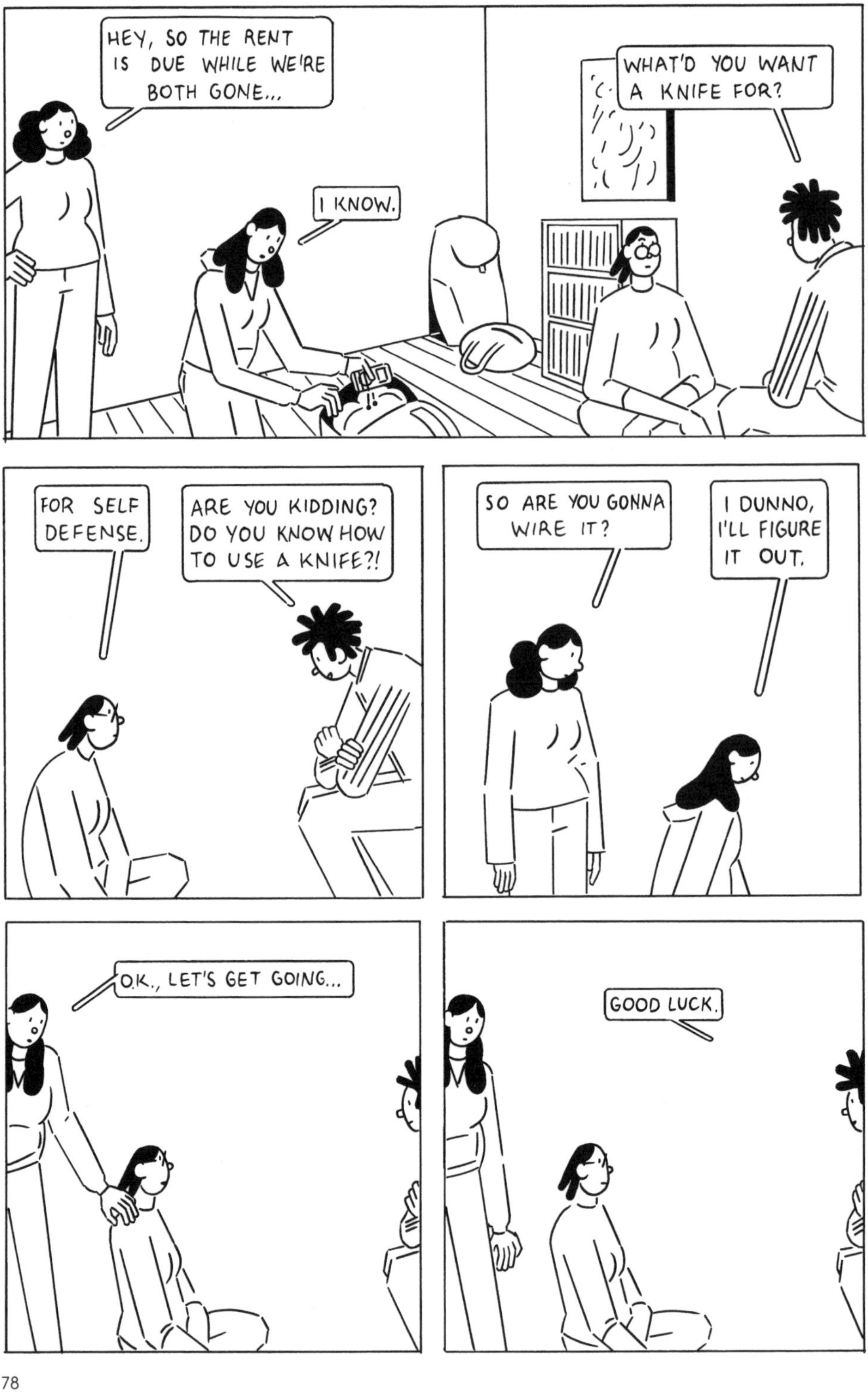
HEY, SO THE RENT IS DUE WHILE WE'RE BOTH GONE...
I KNOW.
WHAT'D YOU WANT A KNIFE FOR?
FOR SELF DEFENSE.
ARE YOU KIDDING? DO YOU KNOW HOW TO USE A KNIFE?!
SO ARE YOU GONNA WIRE IT?
I DUNNO, I'LL FIGURE IT OUT.
O.K., LET'S GET GOING...
GOOD LUCK.

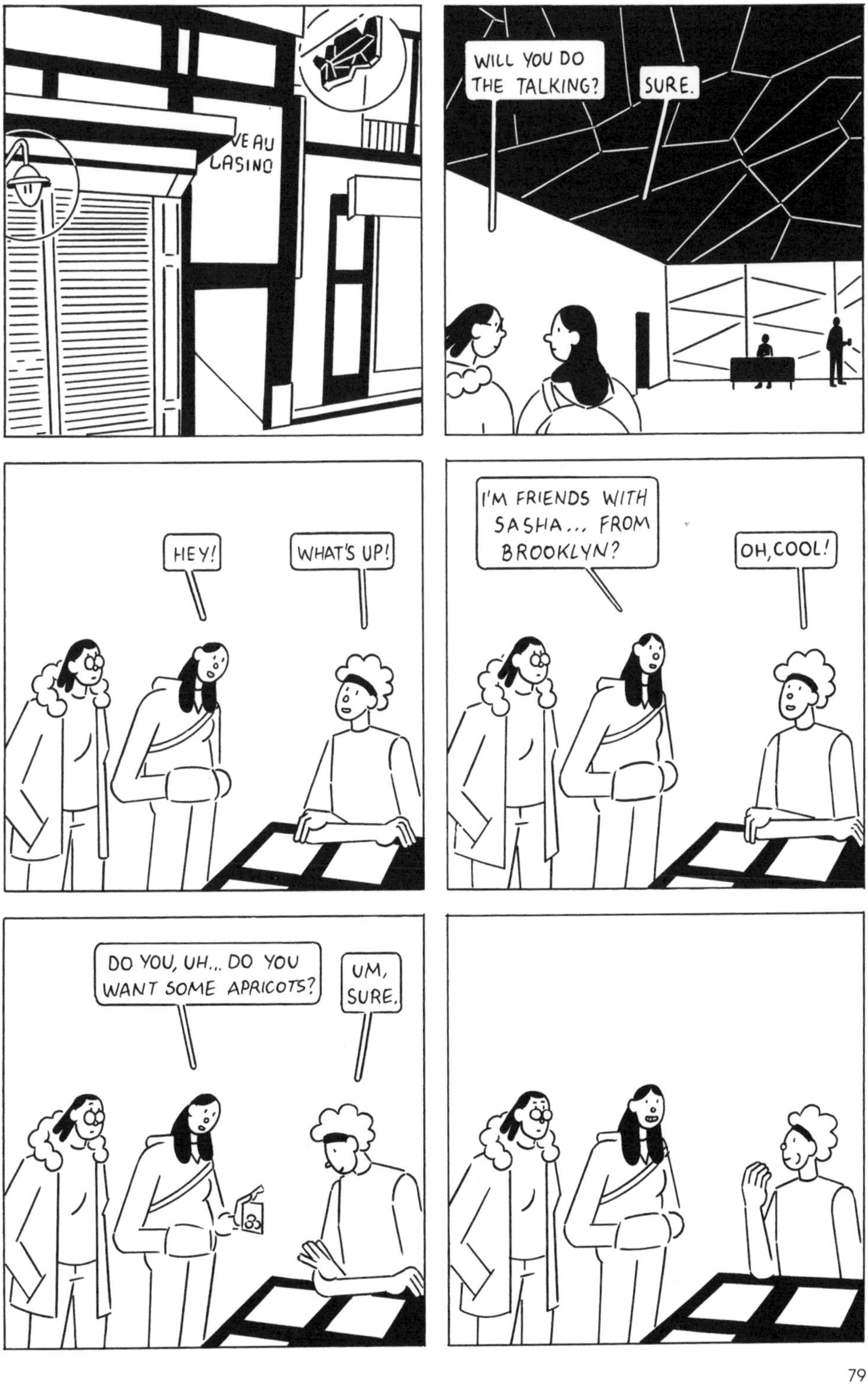
VEAU
LASINO
WILL YOU DO THE TALKING?
SURE.
HEY!
WHAT'S UP!
I'M FRIENDS WITH SASHA... FROM BROOKLYN?
OH, COOL!
DO YOU, UH... DO YOU WANT SOME APRICOTS?
UM, SURE.

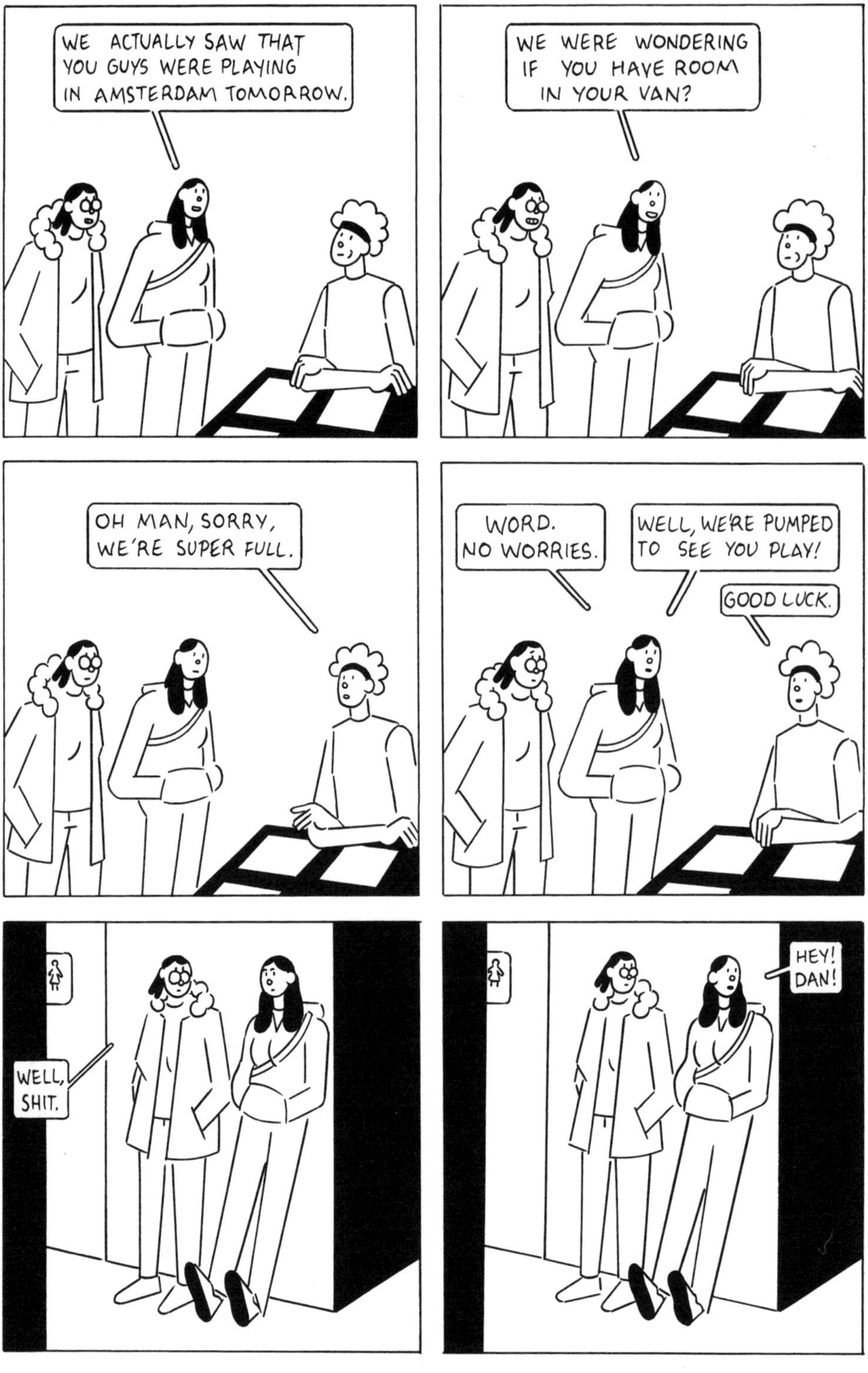
WE ACTUALLY SAW THAT YOU GUYS WERE PLAYING IN AMSTERDAM TOMORROW.
WE WERE WONDERING IF YOU HAVE ROOM IN YOUR VAN?
OH MAN, SORRY, WE'RE SUPER FULL.
WORD. NO WORRIES.
WELL, WE'RE PUMPED TO SEE YOU PLAY!
GOOD LUCK.
WELL, SHIT.
HEY! DAN!

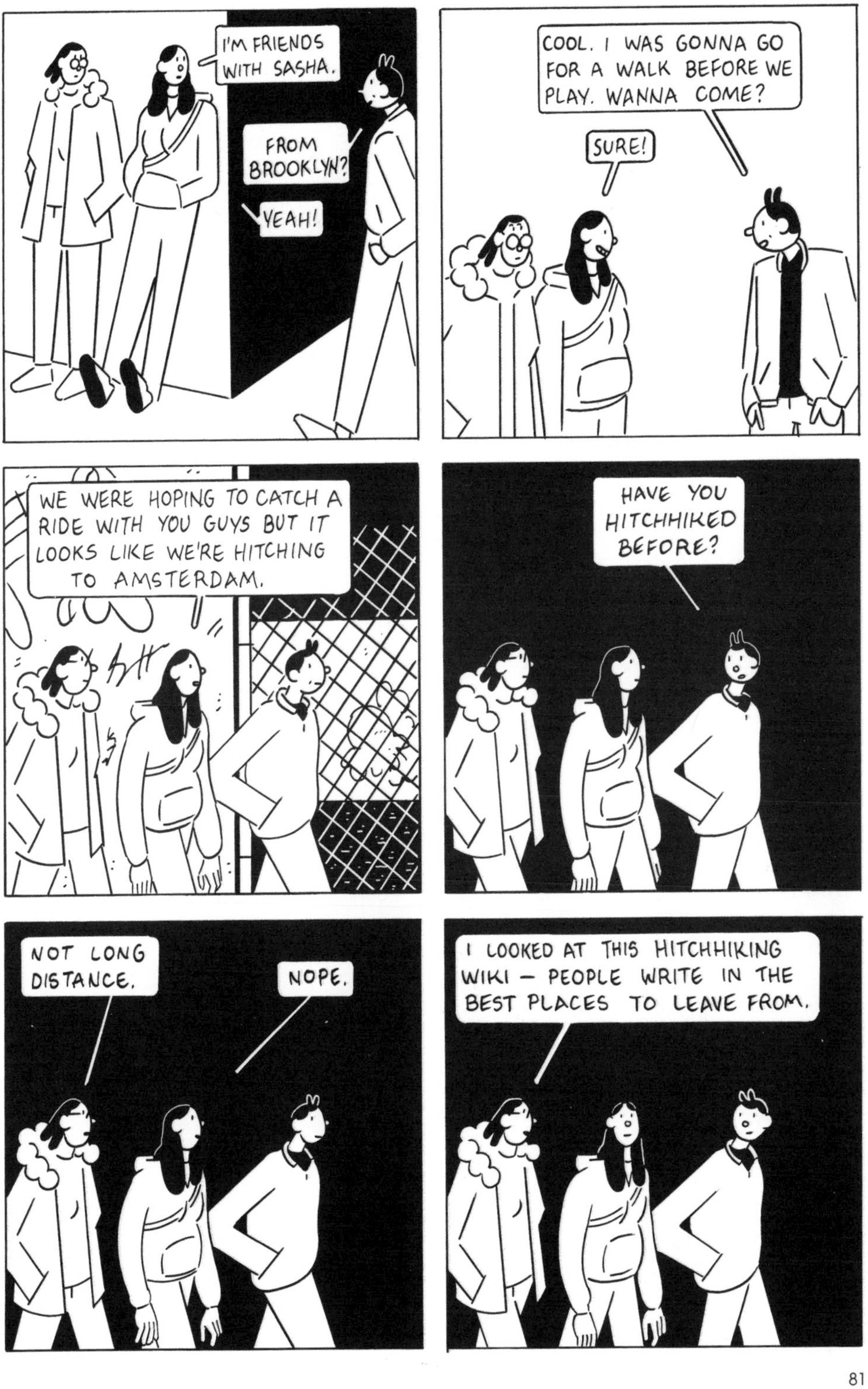
I'M FRIENDS WITH SASHA.
FROM BROOKLYN?
YEAH!
COOL. I WAS GONNA GO FOR A WALK BEFORE WE PLAY. WANNA COME?
SURE!
WE WERE HOPING TO CATCH A RIDE WITH YOU GUYS BUT IT LOOKS LIKE WE'RE HITCHING TO AMSTERDAM.
HAVE YOU HITCHHIKED BEFORE?
NOT LONG DISTANCE.
NOPE.
I LOOKED AT THIS HITCHHIKING WIKI — PEOPLE WRITE IN THE BEST PLACES TO LEAVE FROM.

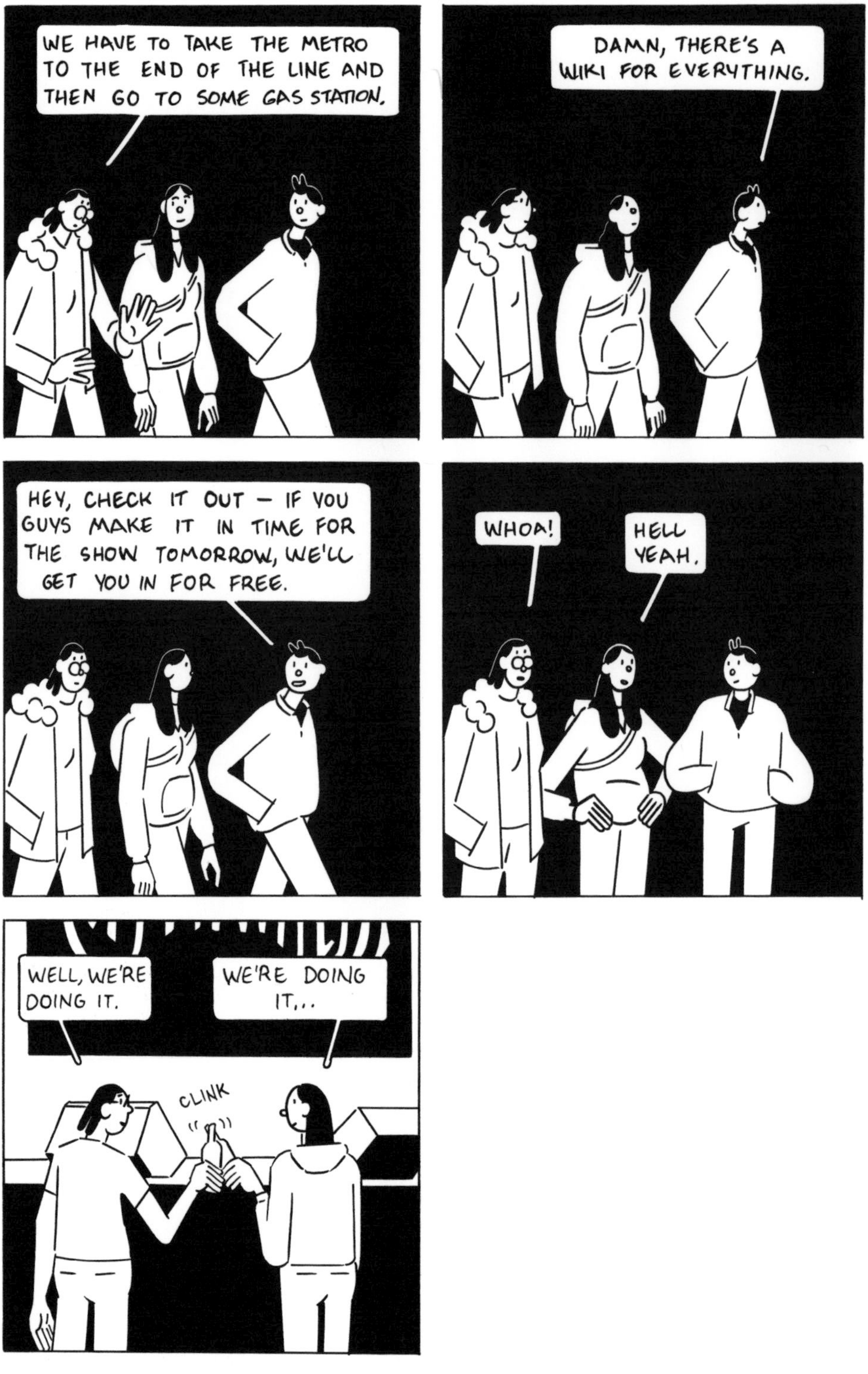
WE HAVE TO TAKE THE METRO TO THE END OF THE LINE AND THEN GO TO SOME GAS STATION.
DAMN, THERE'S A WIKI FOR EVERYTHING.
HEY, CHECK IT OUT – IF YOU GUYS MAKE IT IN TIME FOR THE SHOW TOMORROW, WE'LL GET YOU IN FOR FREE.
WHOA!
HELL YEAH.
WELL, WE'RE DOING IT.
WE'RE DOING IT...
CLINK

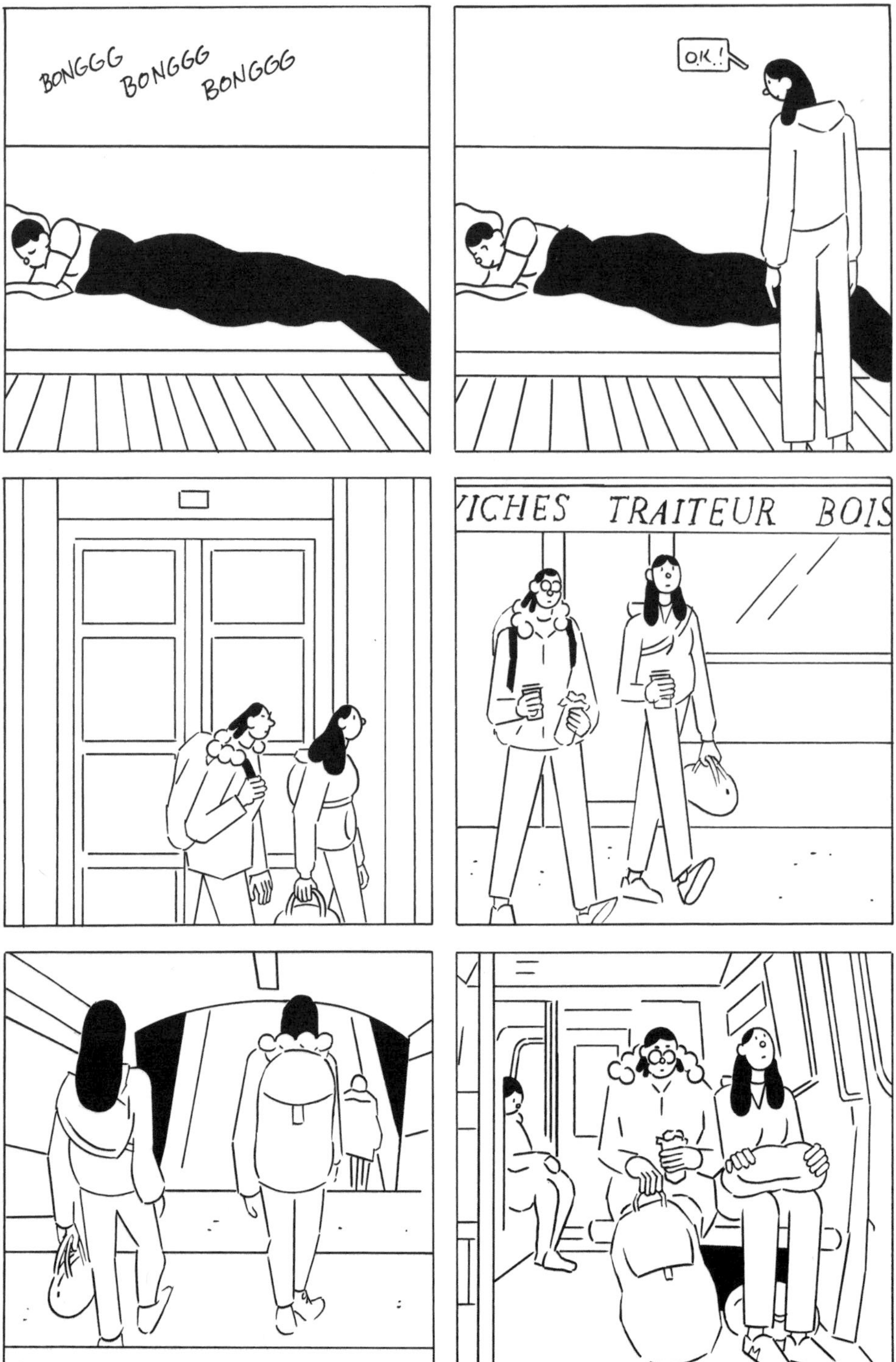
BONGGG
BONGGG
BONGGG
OK!
VICHES TRAITEUR BOIS

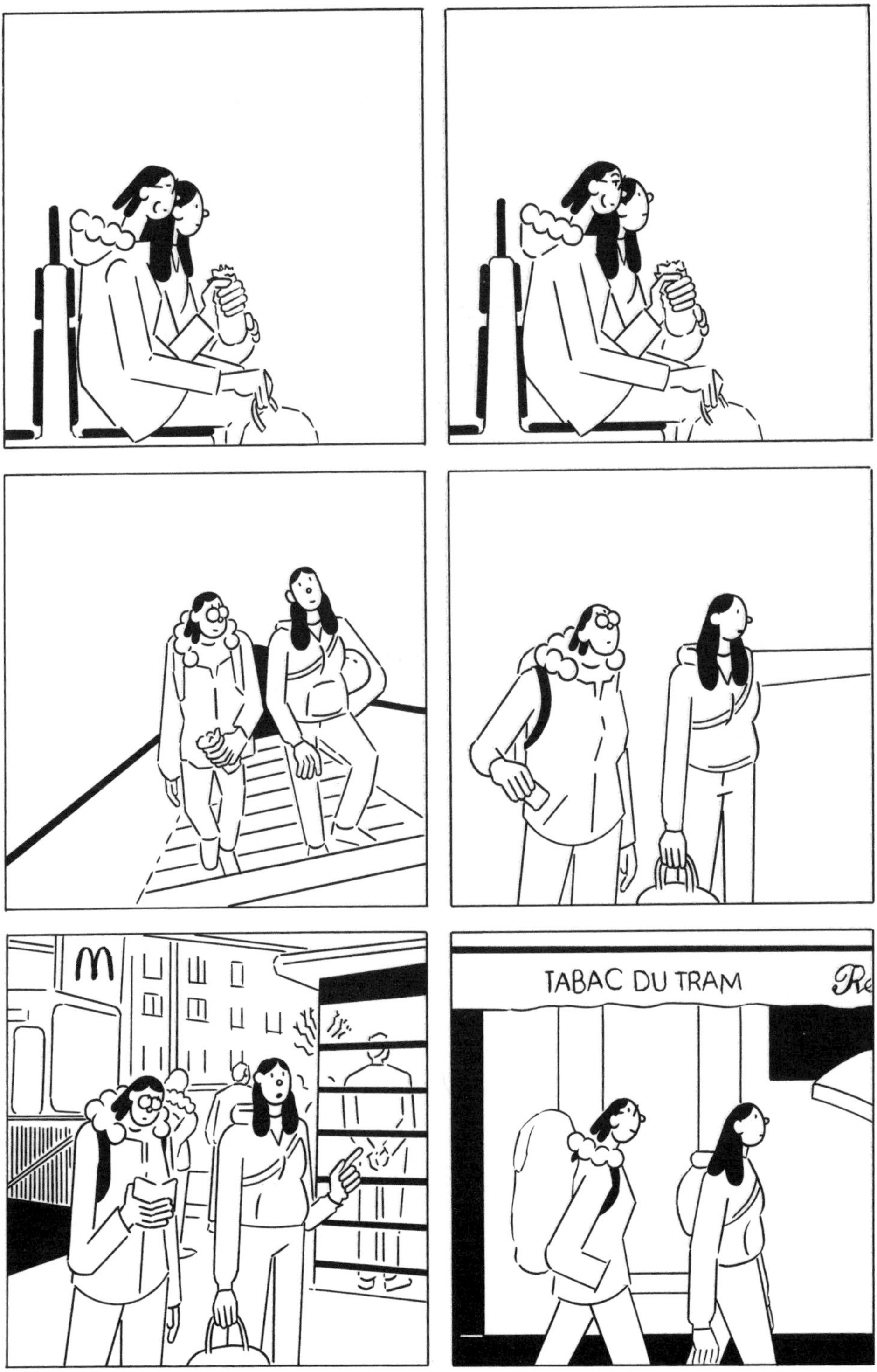
TABAC DU TRAM

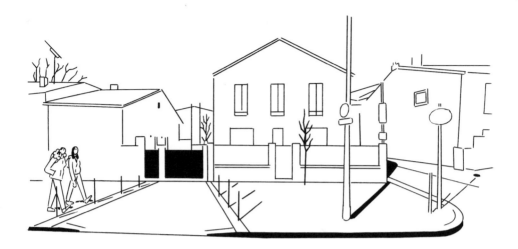

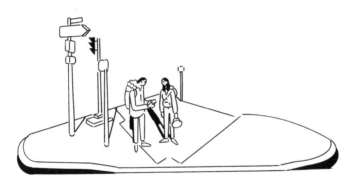

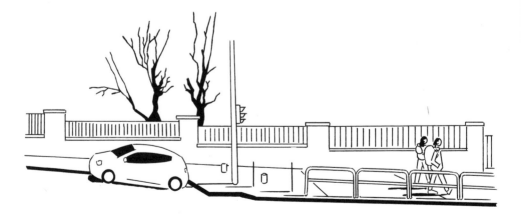

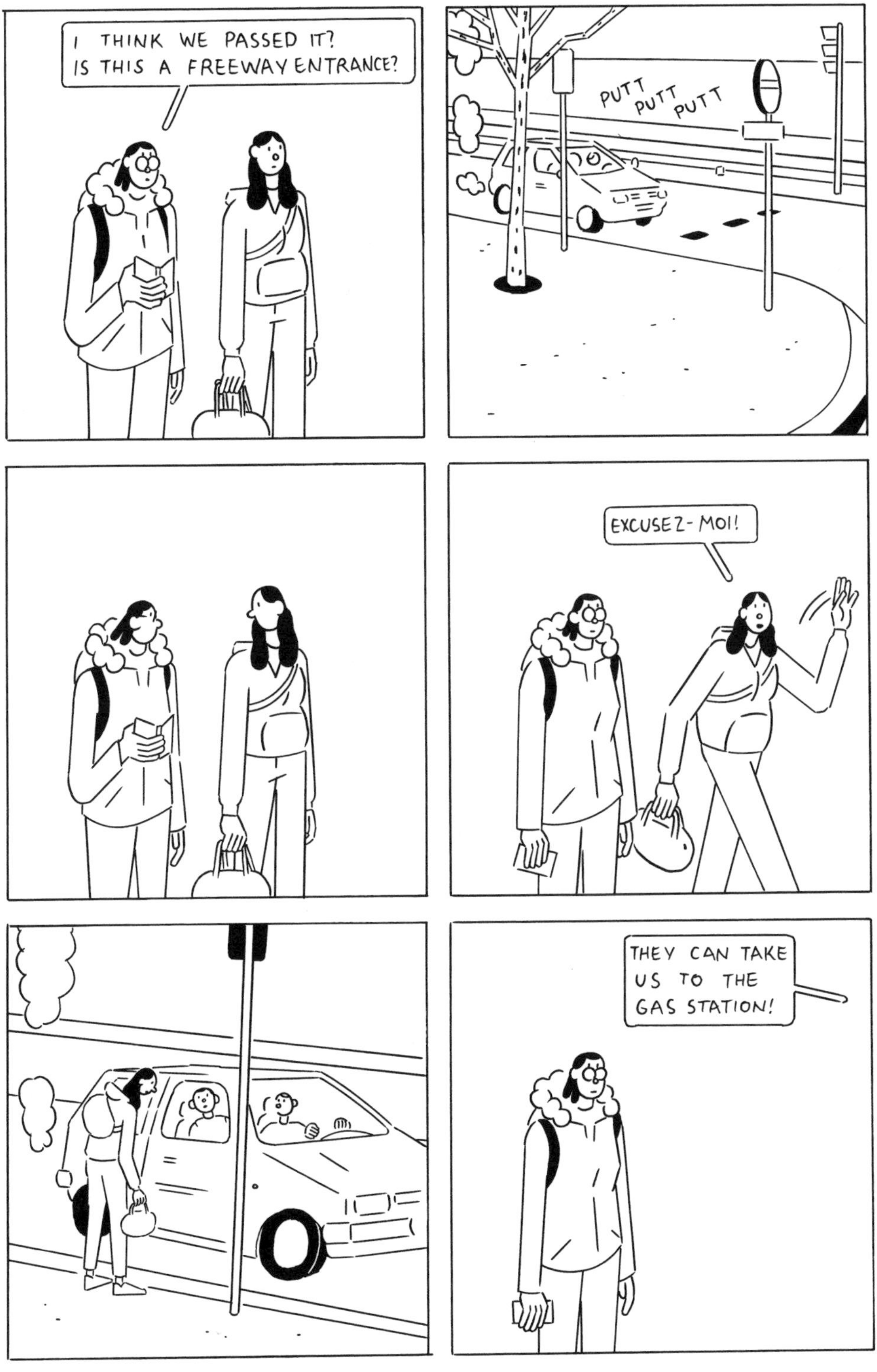
I THINK WE PASSED IT?
IS THIS A FREEWAY ENTRANCE?
PUTT PUTT PUTT
EXCUSEZ-MOI!
THEY CAN TAKE US TO THE GAS STATION!

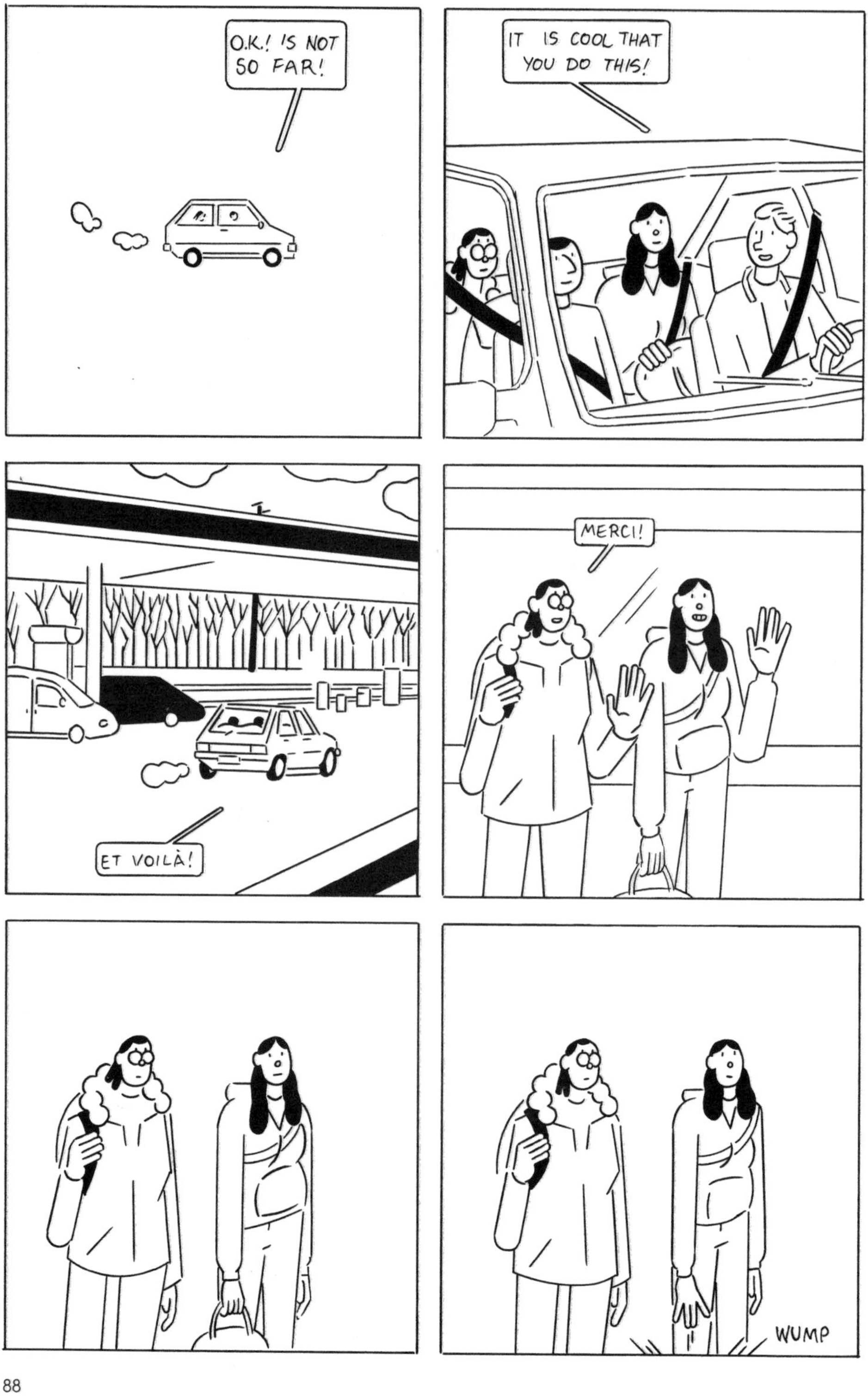
O.K.! IS NOT SO FAR!
IT IS COOL THAT YOU DO THIS!
ET VOILÀ!
MERCI!
WUMP

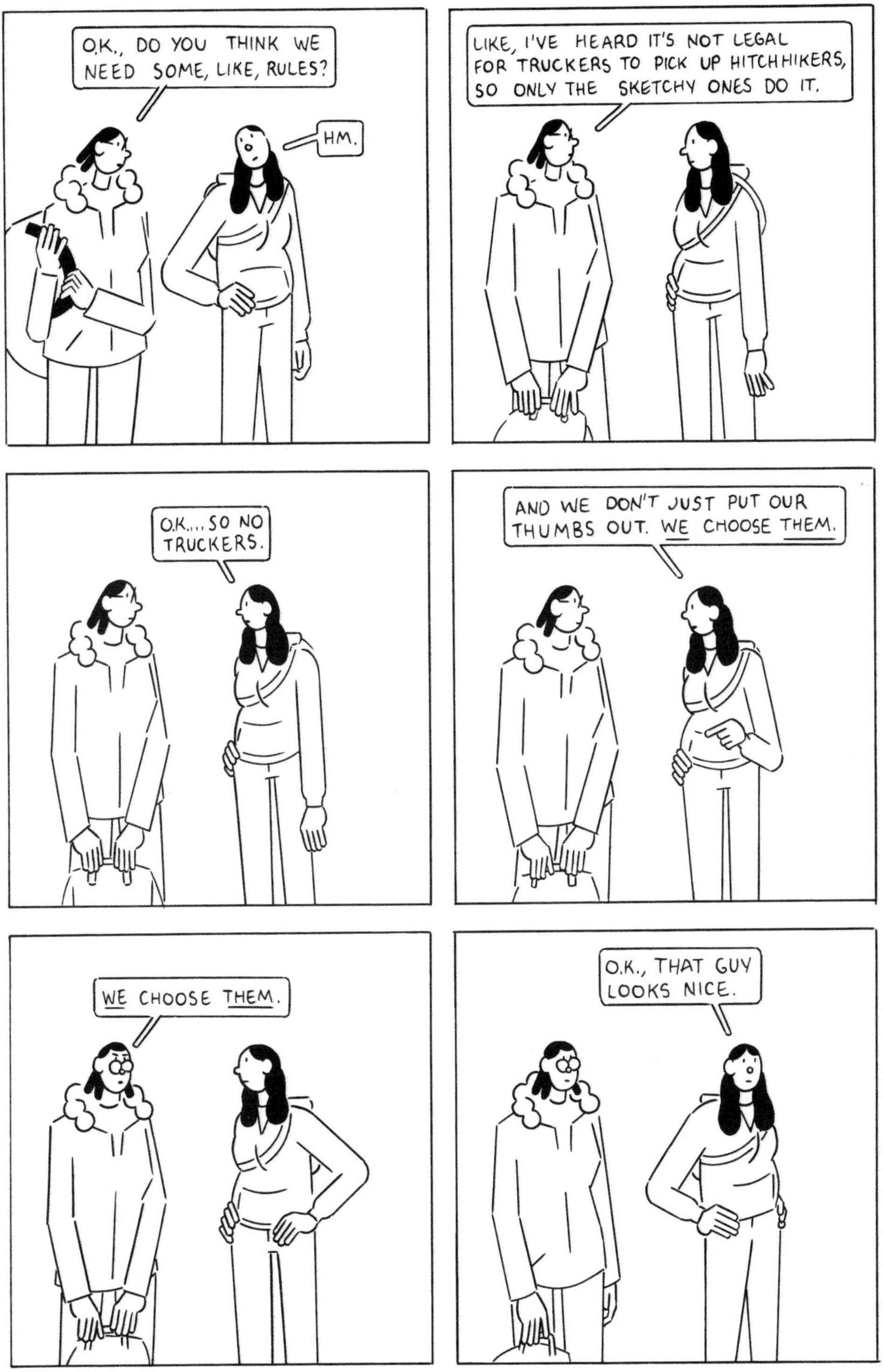
O.K., DO YOU THINK WE NEED SOME, LIKE, RULES?
HM.
LIKE, I'VE HEARD IT'S NOT LEGAL FOR TRUCKERS TO PICK UP HITCHHIKERS, SO ONLY THE SKETCHY ONES DO IT.
O.K.... SO NO TRUCKERS.
AND WE DON'T JUST PUT OUR THUMBS OUT. WE CHOOSE THEM.
WE CHOOSE THEM.
O.K., THAT GUY LOOKS NICE.

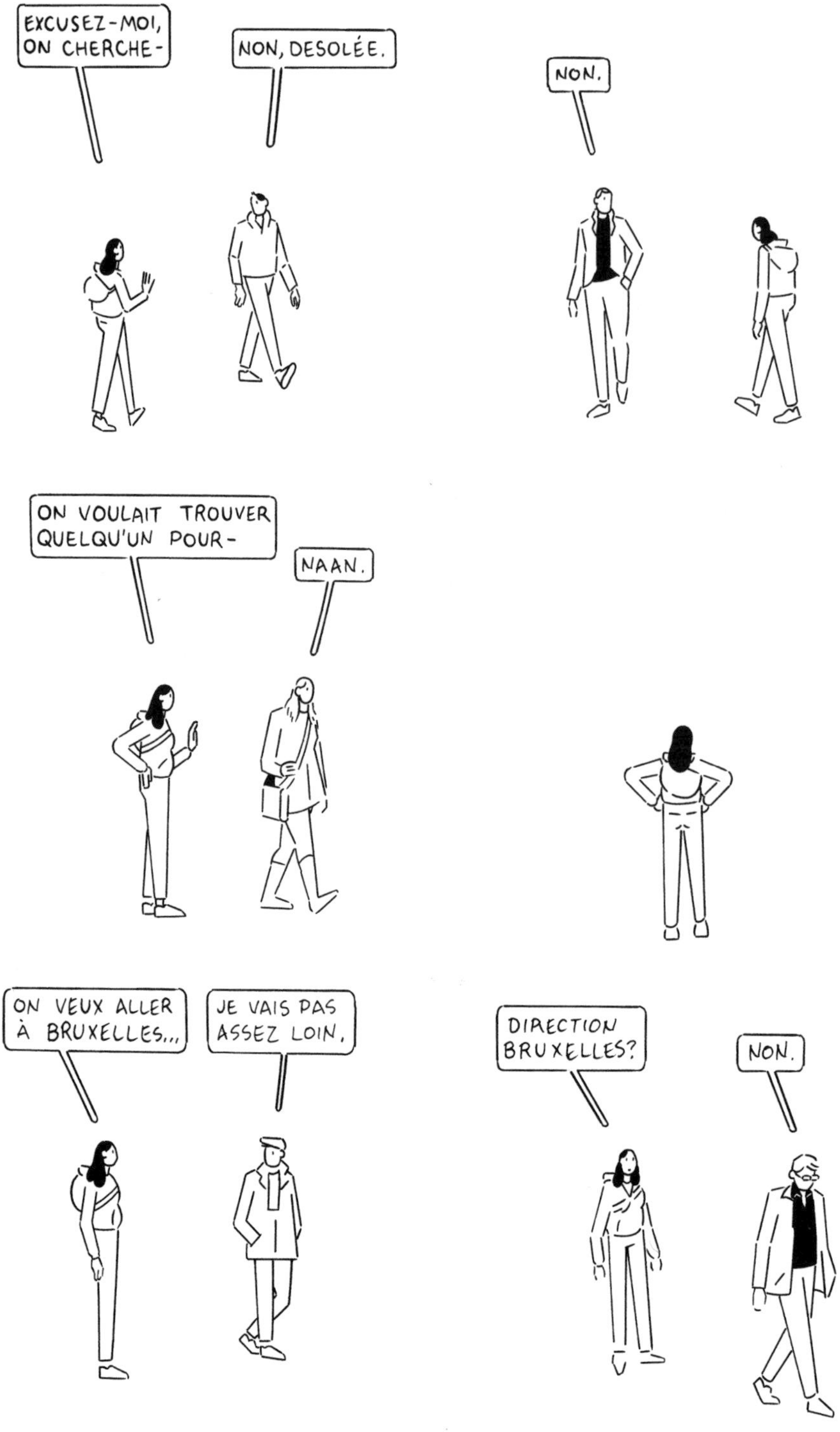
EXCUSEZ-MOI, ON CHERCHE-
NON, DESOLÉE.
NON.
ON VOULAIT TROUVER QUELQU'UN POUR-
NAAN.
ON VEUX ALLER À BRUXELLES...
JE VAIS PAS ASSEZ LOIN.
DIRECTION BRUXELLES?
NON.

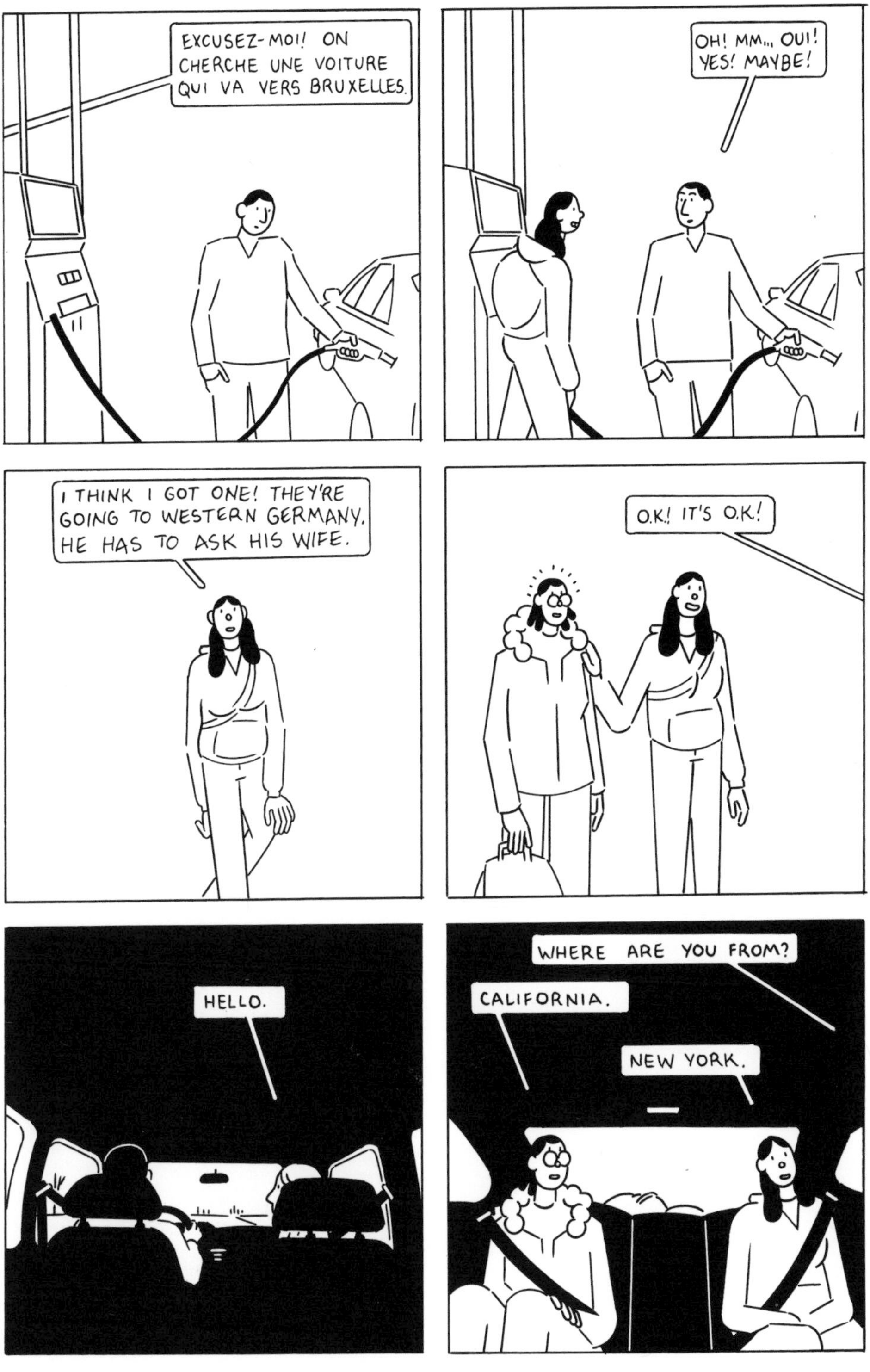
EXCUSEZ-MOI! ON CHERCHE UNE VOITURE QUI VA VERS BRUXELLES.
OH! MM... OUI! YES! MAYBE!
I THINK I GOT ONE! THEY'RE GOING TO WESTERN GERMANY. HE HAS TO ASK HIS WIFE.
O.K.! IT'S O.K.!
HELLO.
WHERE ARE YOU FROM?
CALIFORNIA.
NEW YORK.

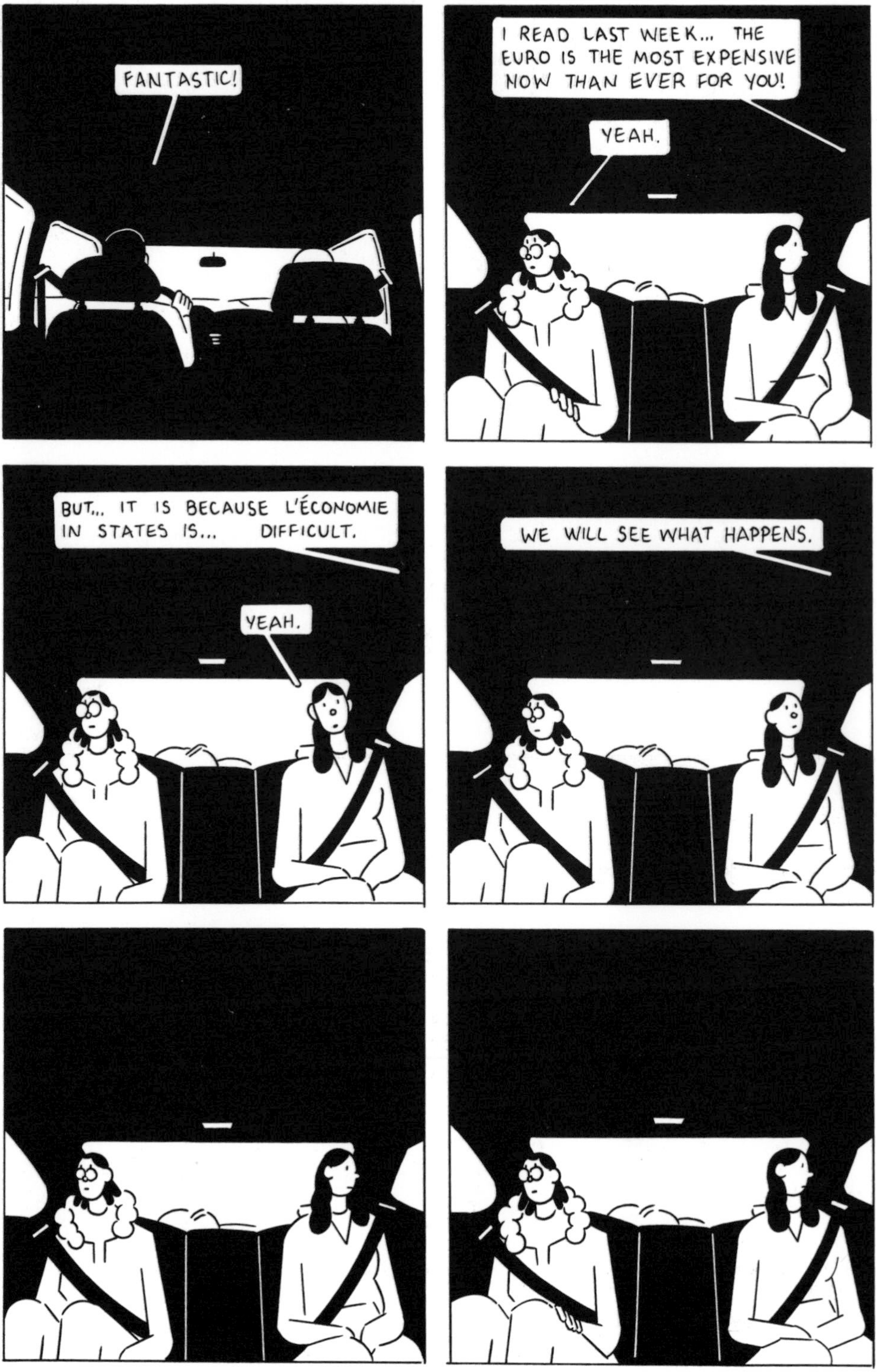
FANTASTIC!
I READ LAST WEEK... THE EURO IS THE MOST EXPENSIVE NOW THAN EVER FOR YOU!
YEAH.
BUT... IT IS BECAUSE L'ÉCONOMIE IN STATES IS... DIFFICULT.
YEAH.
WE WILL SEE WHAT HAPPENS.

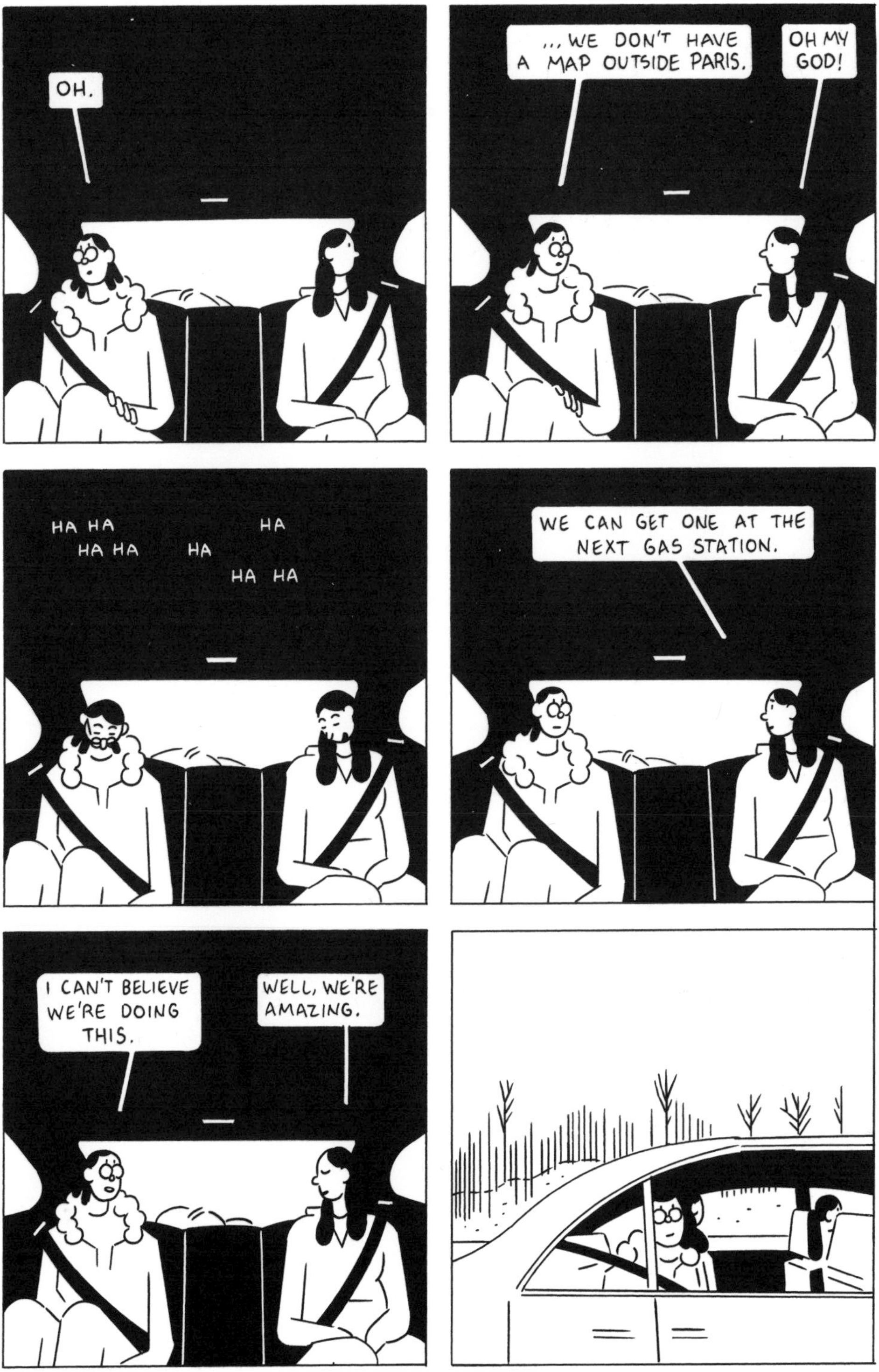
OH.
..., WE DON'T HAVE A MAP OUTSIDE PARIS.
OH MY GOD!
HA HA HA HA HA HA HA HA
WE CAN GET ONE AT THE NEXT GAS STATION.
I CAN'T BELIEVE WE'RE DOING THIS.
WELL, WE'RE AMAZING.

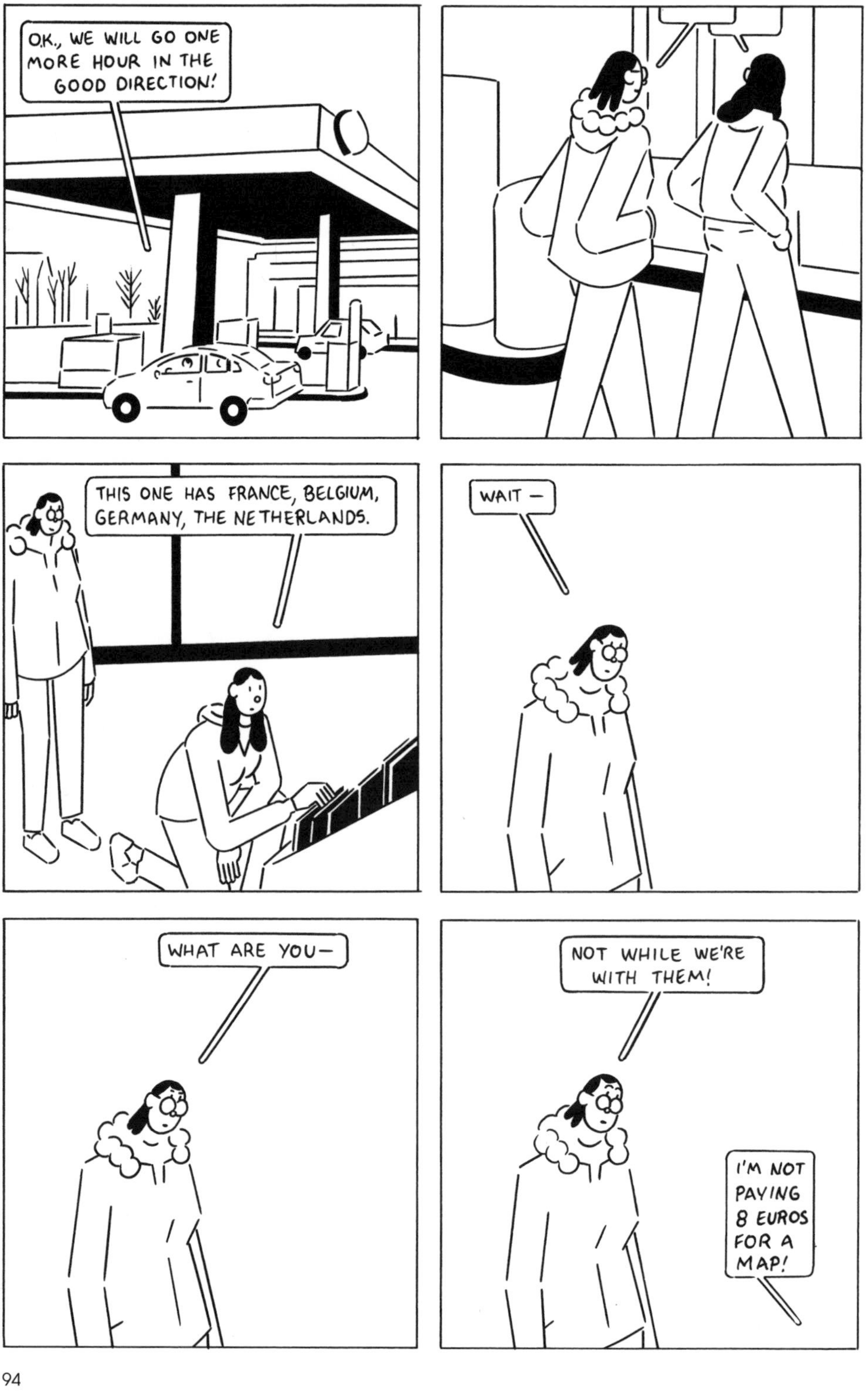
O.K., WE WILL GO ONE MORE HOUR IN THE GOOD DIRECTION!
THIS ONE HAS FRANCE, BELGIUM, GERMANY, THE NETHERLANDS.
WAIT —
WHAT ARE YOU—
NOT WHILE WE'RE WITH THEM!
I'M NOT PAYING 8 EUROS FOR A MAP!

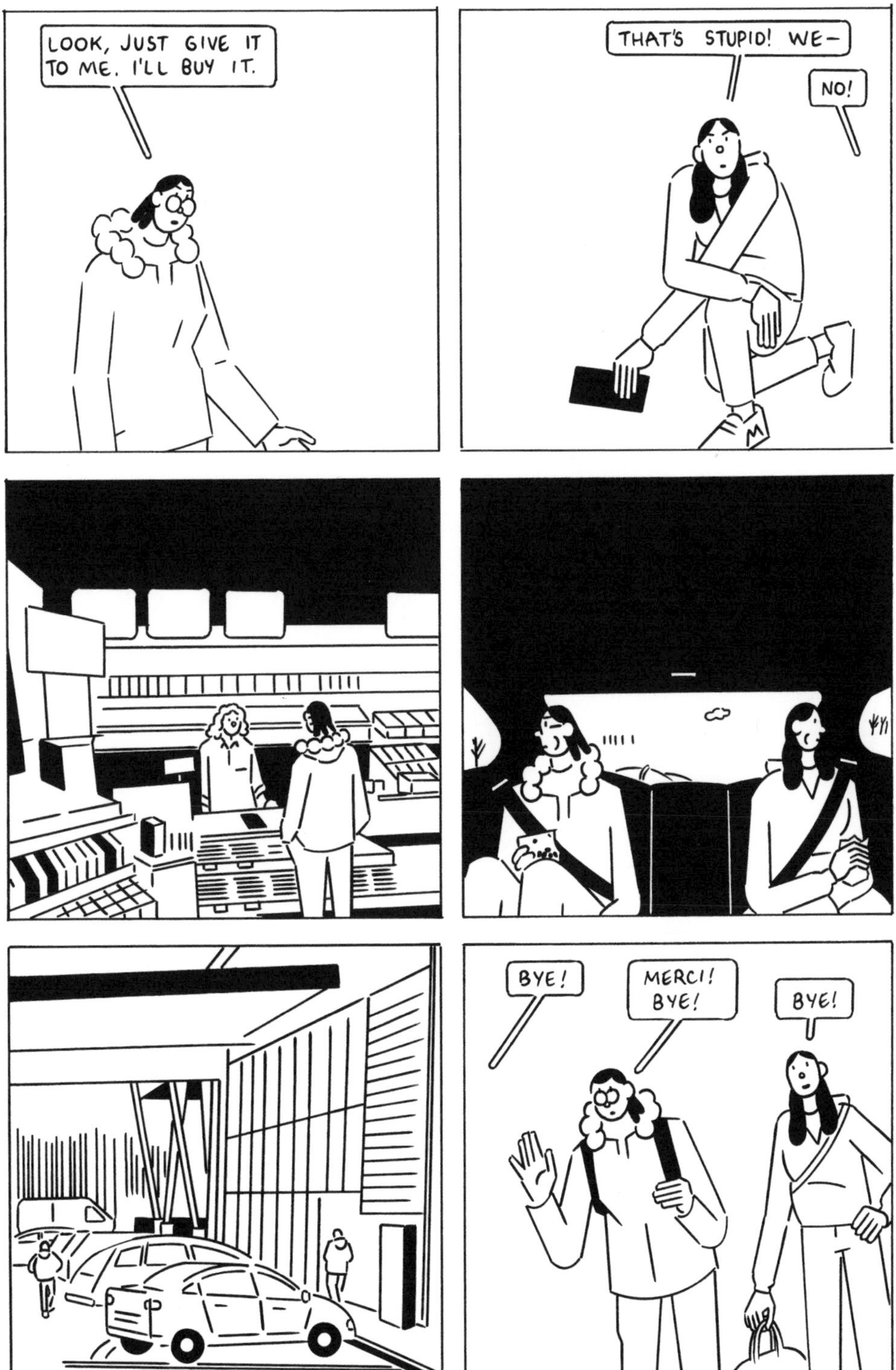
LOOK, JUST GIVE IT TO ME. I'LL BUY IT.
THAT'S STUPID! WE—
NO!
BYE!
MERCI! BYE!
BYE!

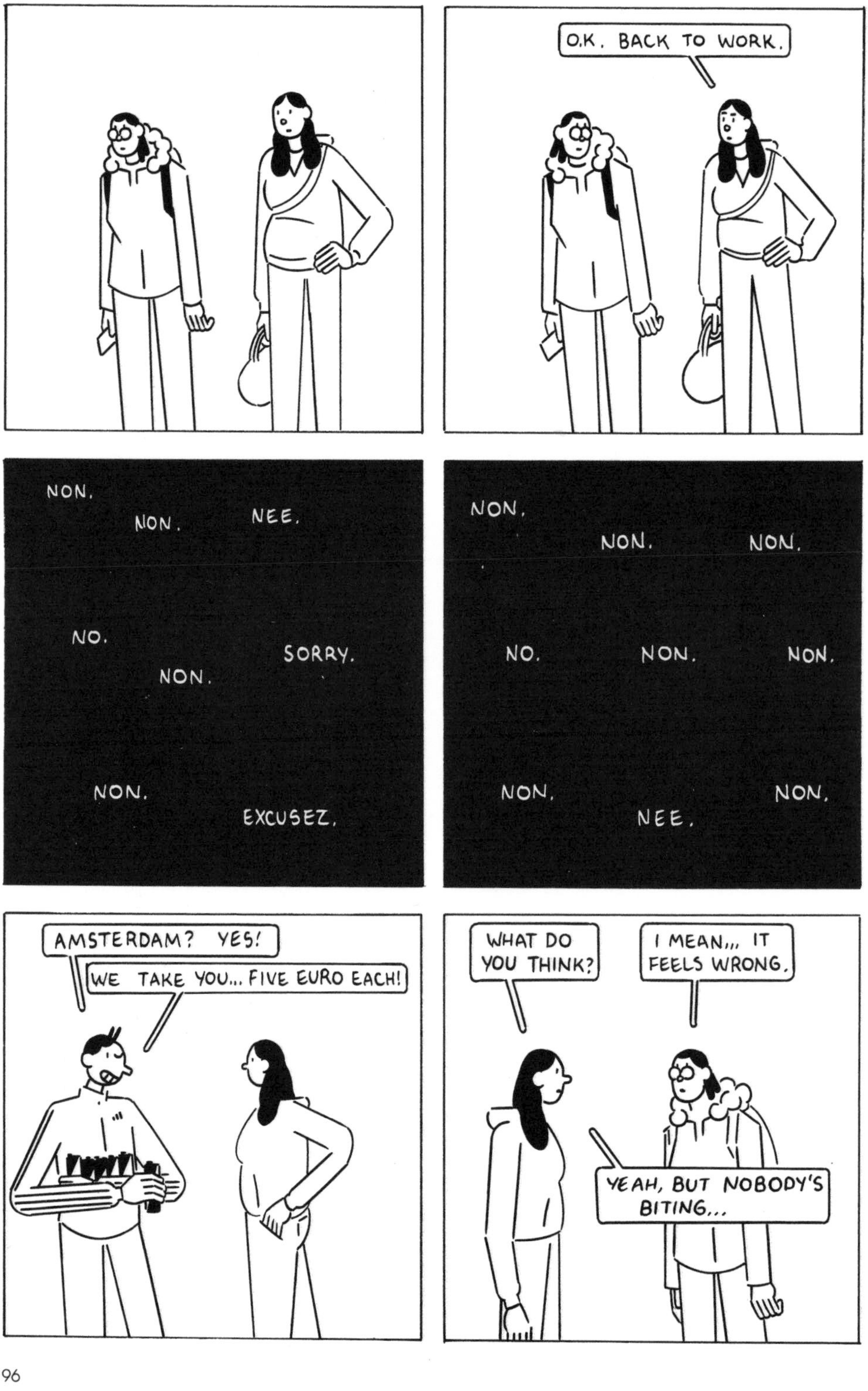
O.K. BACK TO WORK.
NON.
NON.
NEE.
NO.
NON.
SORRY.
NON.
EXCUSEZ.
NON.
NON.
NON.
NO.
NON.
NON.
NON.
NEE.
NON.
AMSTERDAM? YES!
WE TAKE YOU... FIVE EURO EACH!
WHAT DO YOU THINK?
I MEAN,,, IT FEELS WRONG.
YEAH, BUT NOBODY'S BITING...

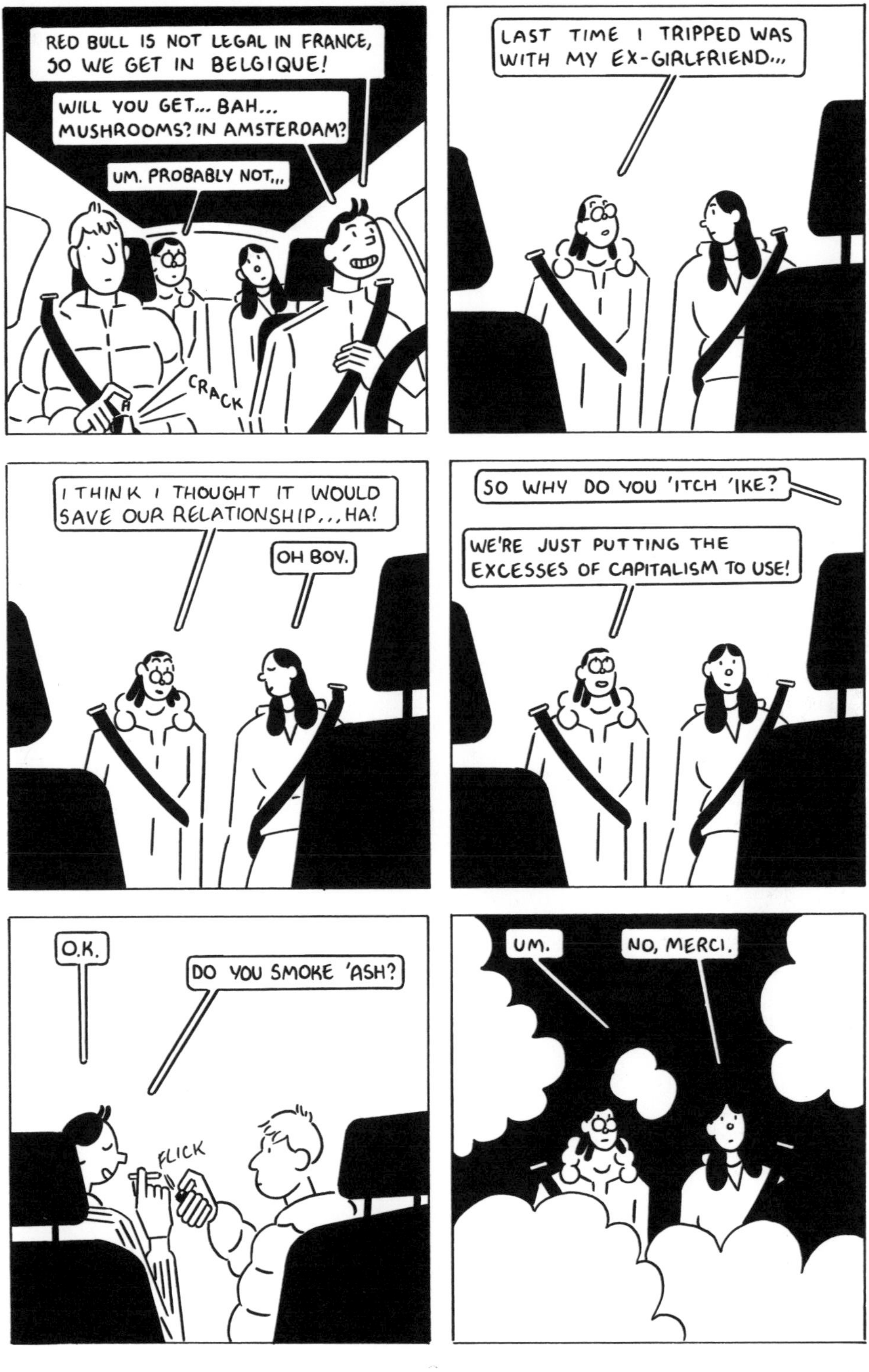
RED BULL IS NOT LEGAL IN FRANCE, SO WE GET IN BELGIQUE!
WILL YOU GET... BAH... MUSHROOMS? IN AMSTERDAM?
UM. PROBABLY NOT...
CRACK
LAST TIME I TRIPPED WAS WITH MY EX-GIRLFRIEND...
I THINK I THOUGHT IT WOULD SAVE OUR RELATIONSHIP... HA!
OH BOY.
SO WHY DO YOU 'ITCH 'IKE?
WE'RE JUST PUTTING THE EXCESSES OF CAPITALISM TO USE!
O.K.
DO YOU SMOKE 'ASH?
FLICK
UM.
NO, MERCI.

97

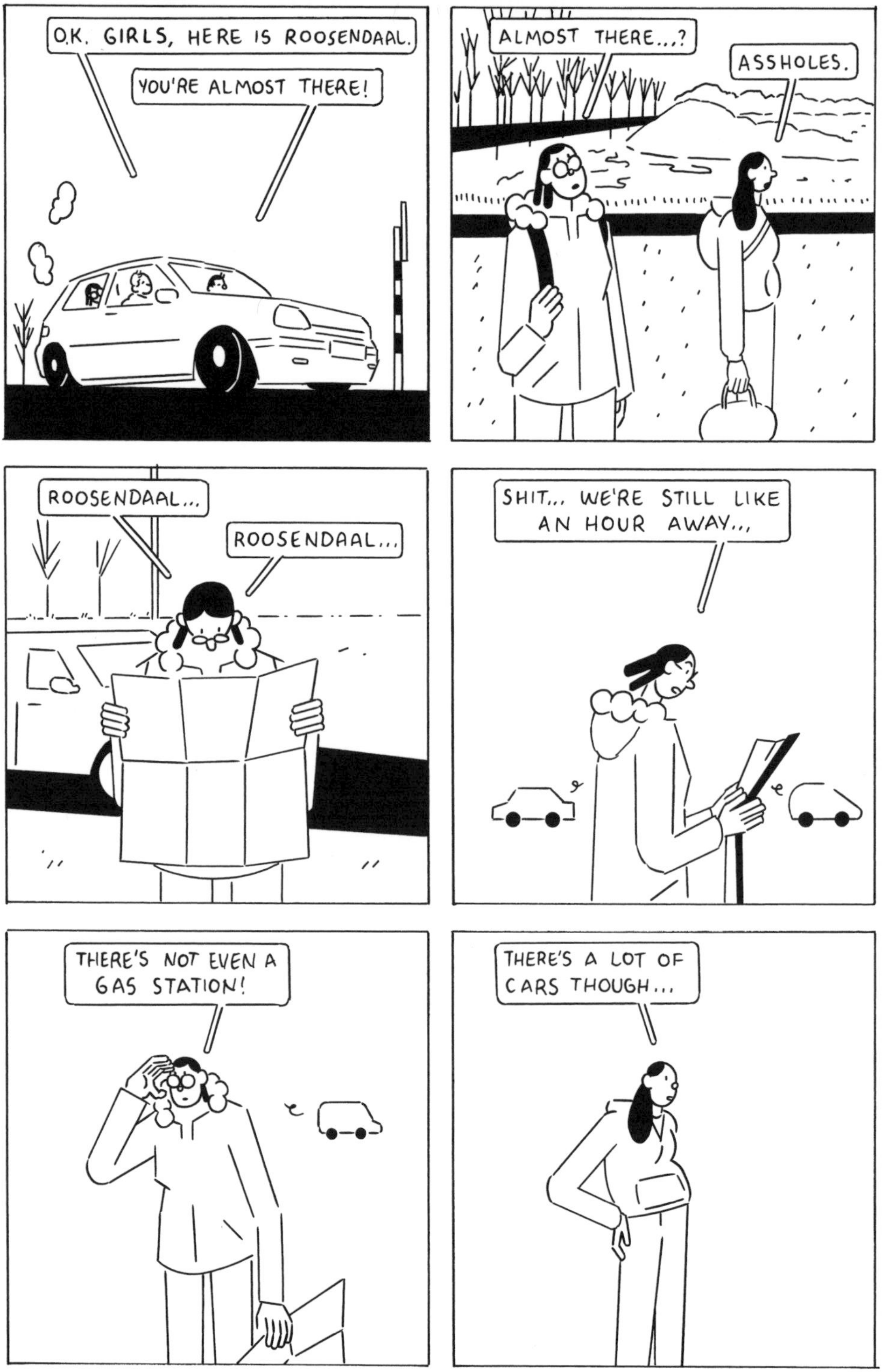
O.K. GIRLS, HERE IS ROOSENDAAL.
YOU'RE ALMOST THERE!
ALMOST THERE...?
ASSHOLES.
ROOSENDAAL...
ROOSENDAAL...
SHIT... WE'RE STILL LIKE AN HOUR AWAY...
THERE'S NOT EVEN A GAS STATION!
THERE'S A LOT OF CARS THOUGH...

98

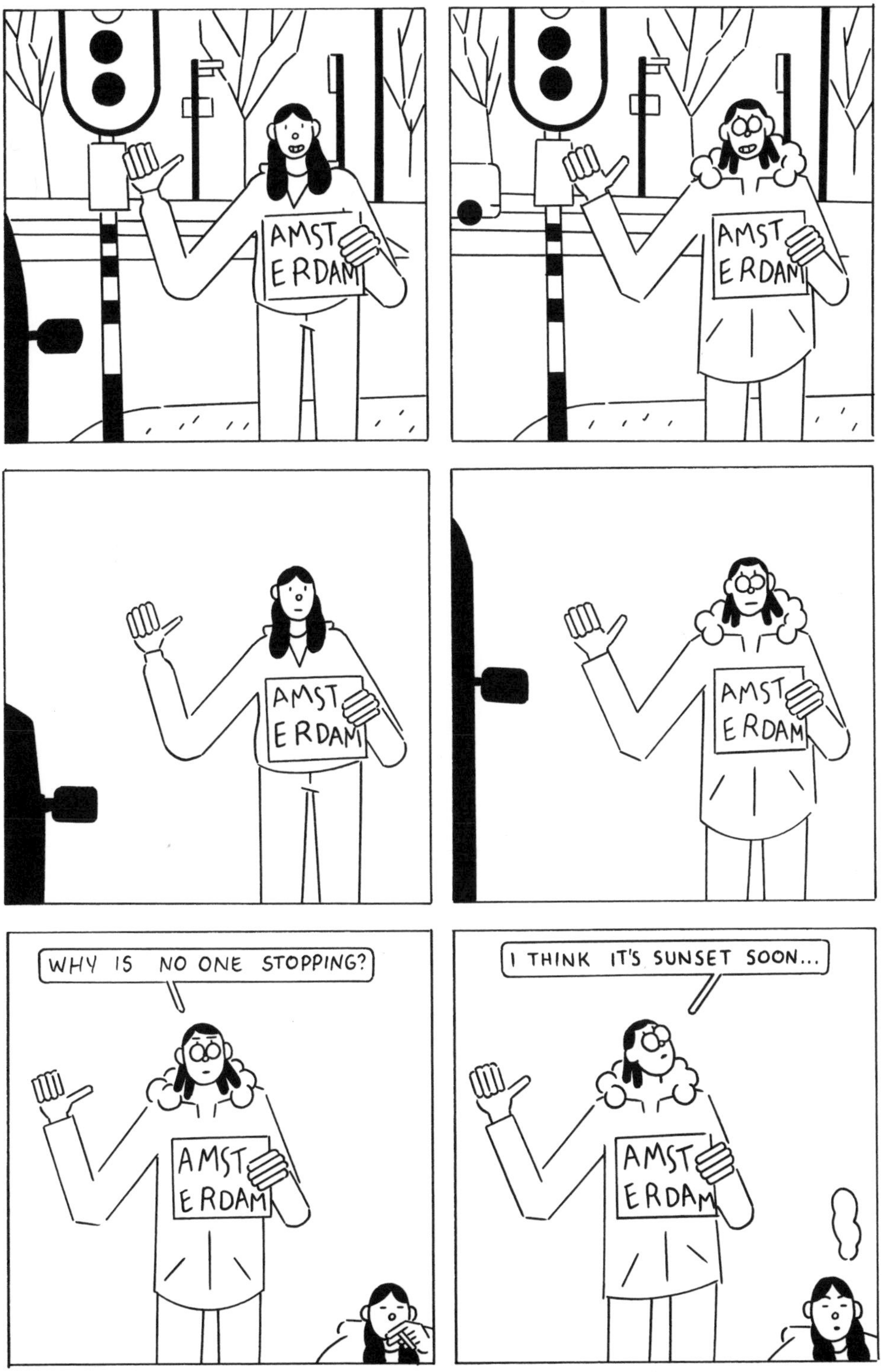
AMST ERDAM
AMST ERDAM
AMST ERDAM
AMST ERDAM
WHY IS NO ONE STOPPING?
AMST ERDAM
I THINK IT'S SUNSET SOON...
AMST ERDAM

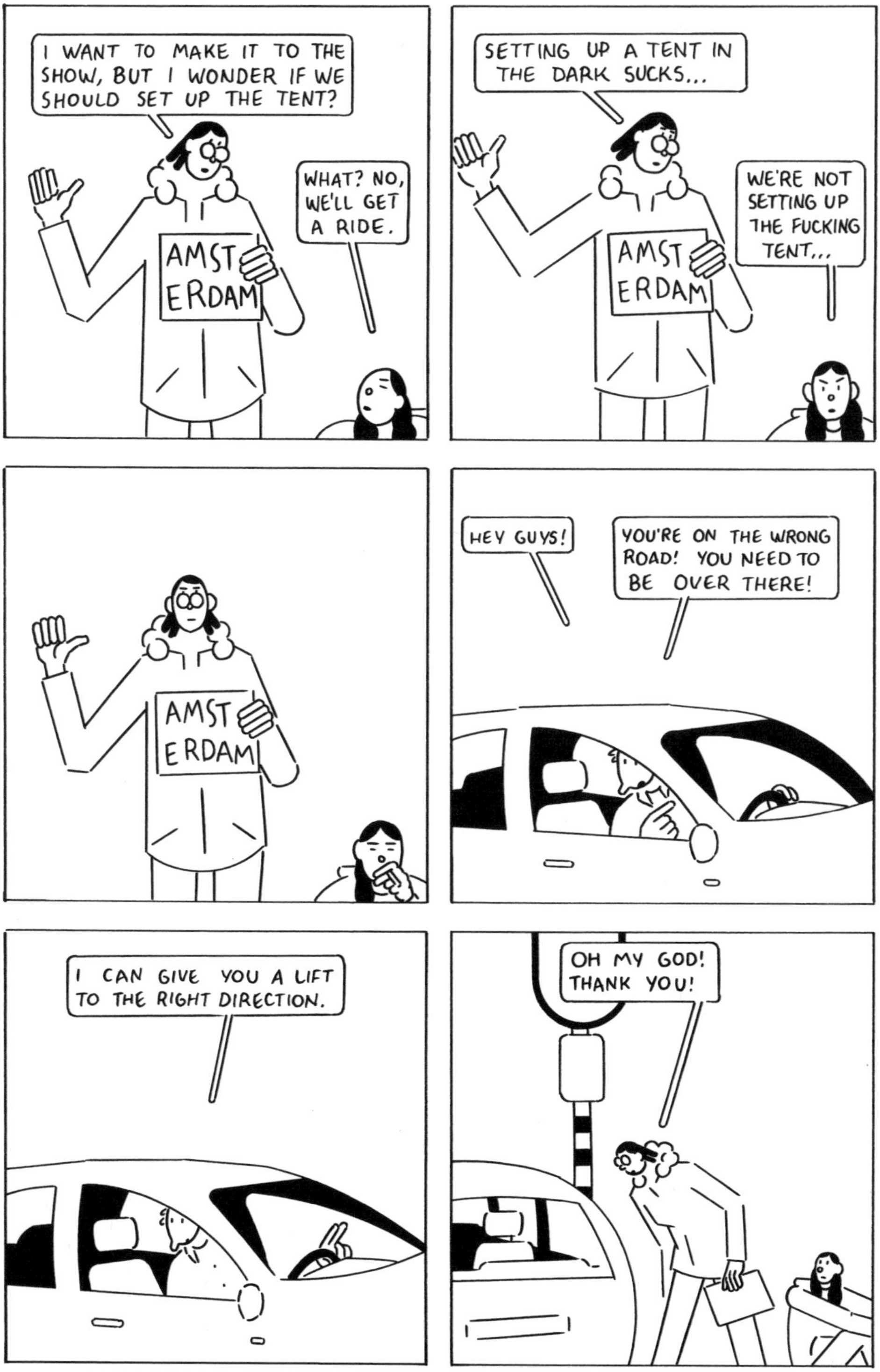
I WANT TO MAKE IT TO THE SHOW, BUT I WONDER IF WE SHOULD SET UP THE TENT?
WHAT? NO, WE'LL GET A RIDE.
AMST ERDAM
SETTING UP A TENT IN THE DARK SUCKS...
WE'RE NOT SETTING UP THE FUCKING TENT...
AMST ERDAM
AMST ERDAM
HEY GUYS!
YOU'RE ON THE WRONG ROAD! YOU NEED TO BE OVER THERE!
I CAN GIVE YOU A LIFT TO THE RIGHT DIRECTION.
OH MY GOD! THANK YOU!

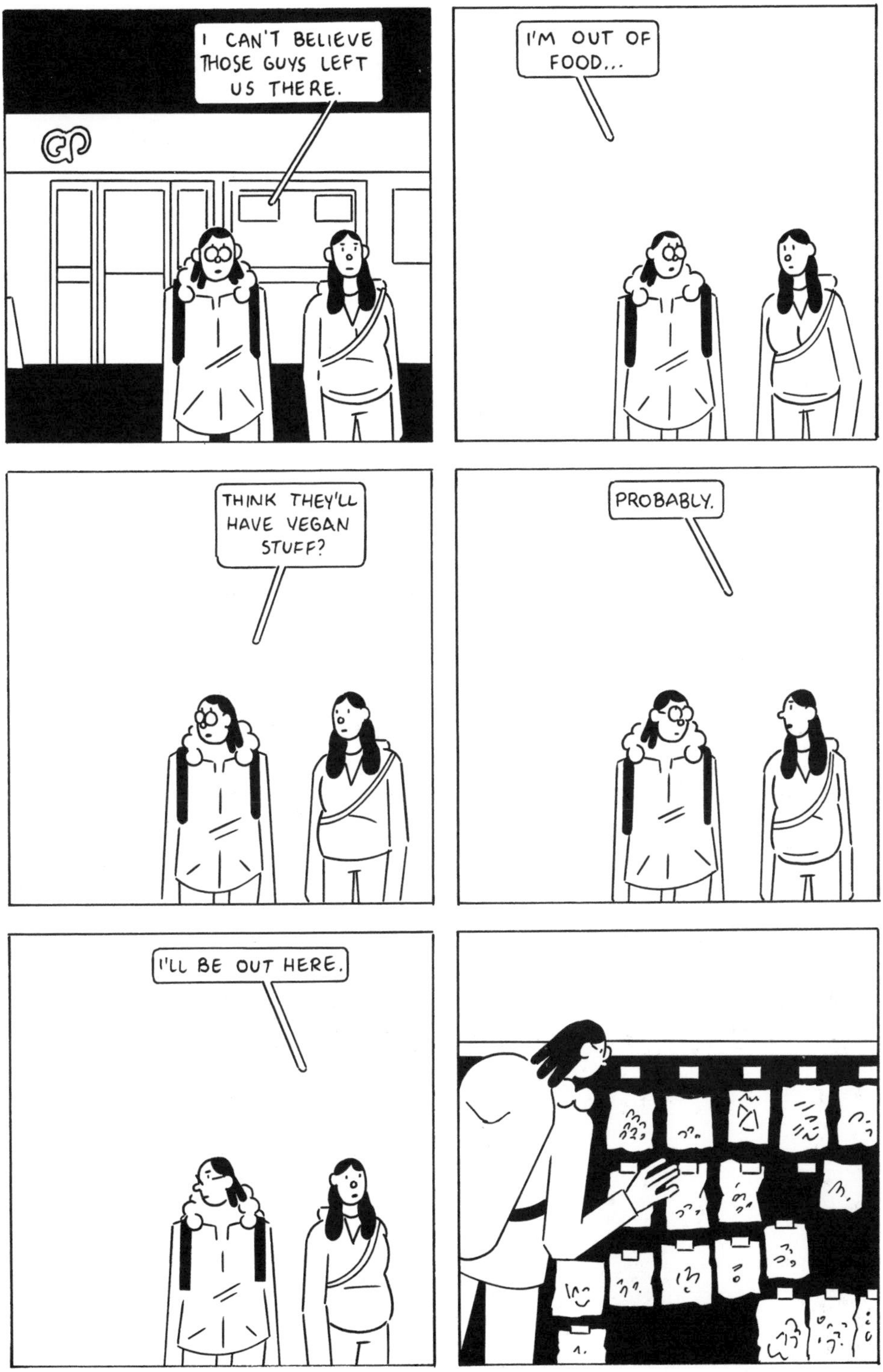
I CAN'T BELIEVE THOSE GUYS LEFT US THERE.
I'M OUT OF FOOD...
THINK THEY'LL HAVE VEGAN STUFF?
PROBABLY.
I'LL BE OUT HERE.

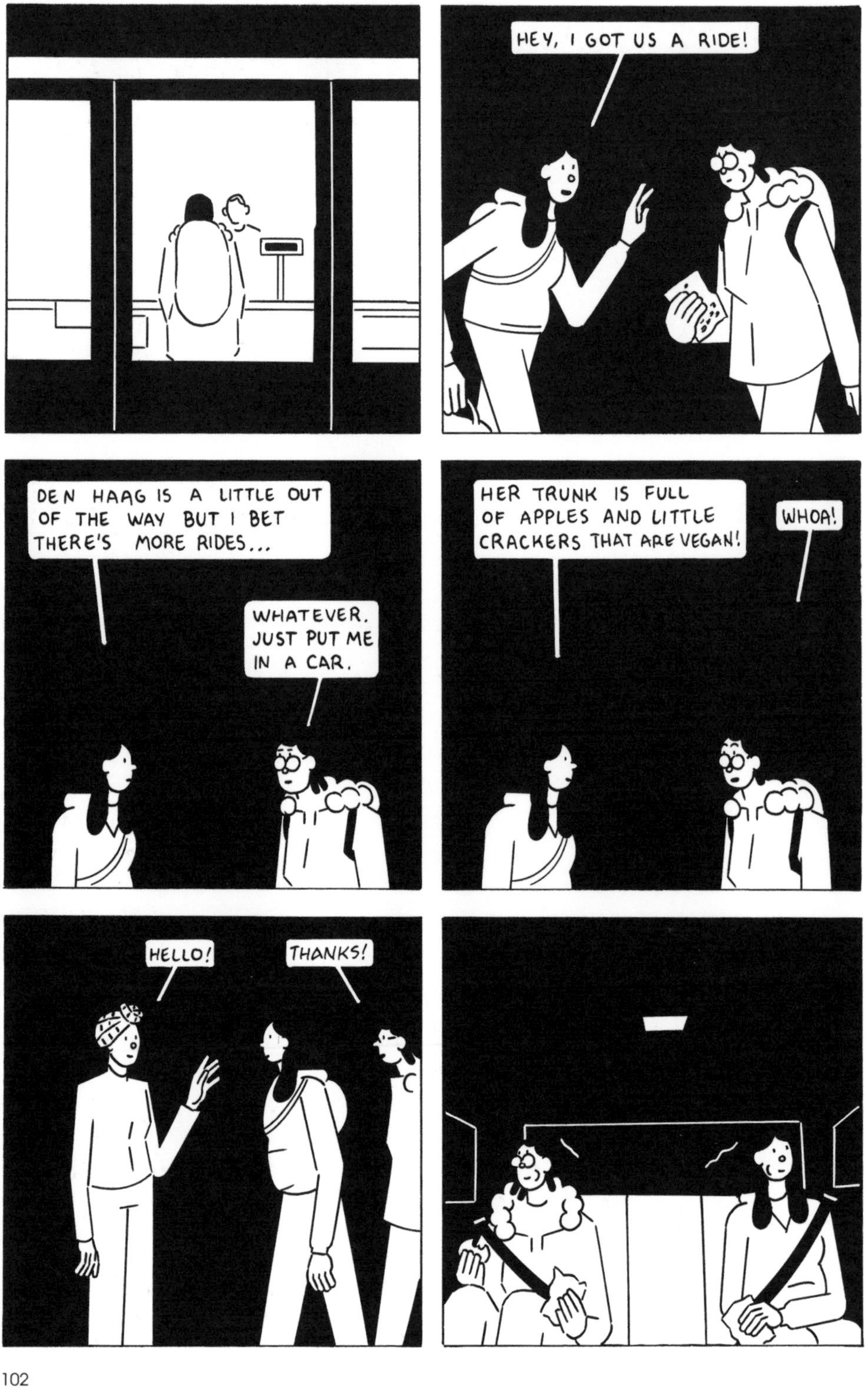
HEY, I GOT US A RIDE!
DEN HAAG IS A LITTLE OUT OF THE WAY BUT I BET THERE'S MORE RIDES...
WHATEVER. JUST PUT ME IN A CAR.
HER TRUNK IS FULL OF APPLES AND LITTLE CRACKERS THAT ARE VEGAN!
WHOA!
HELLO!
THANKS!

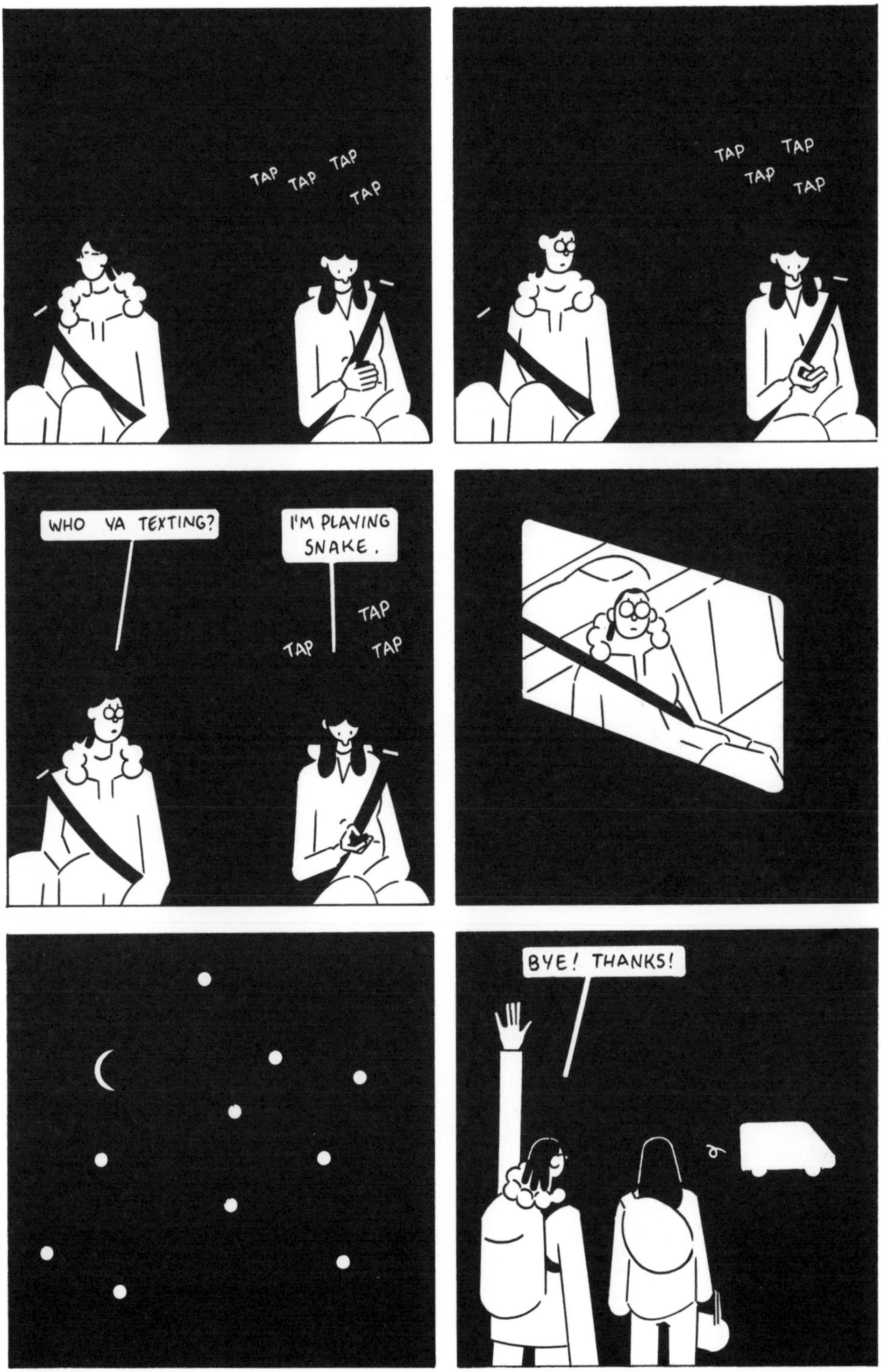
TAP TAP TAP
TAP
TAP TAP
TAP TAP
WHO YA TEXTING?
I'M PLAYING SNAKE.
TAP TAP TAP
BYE! THANKS!

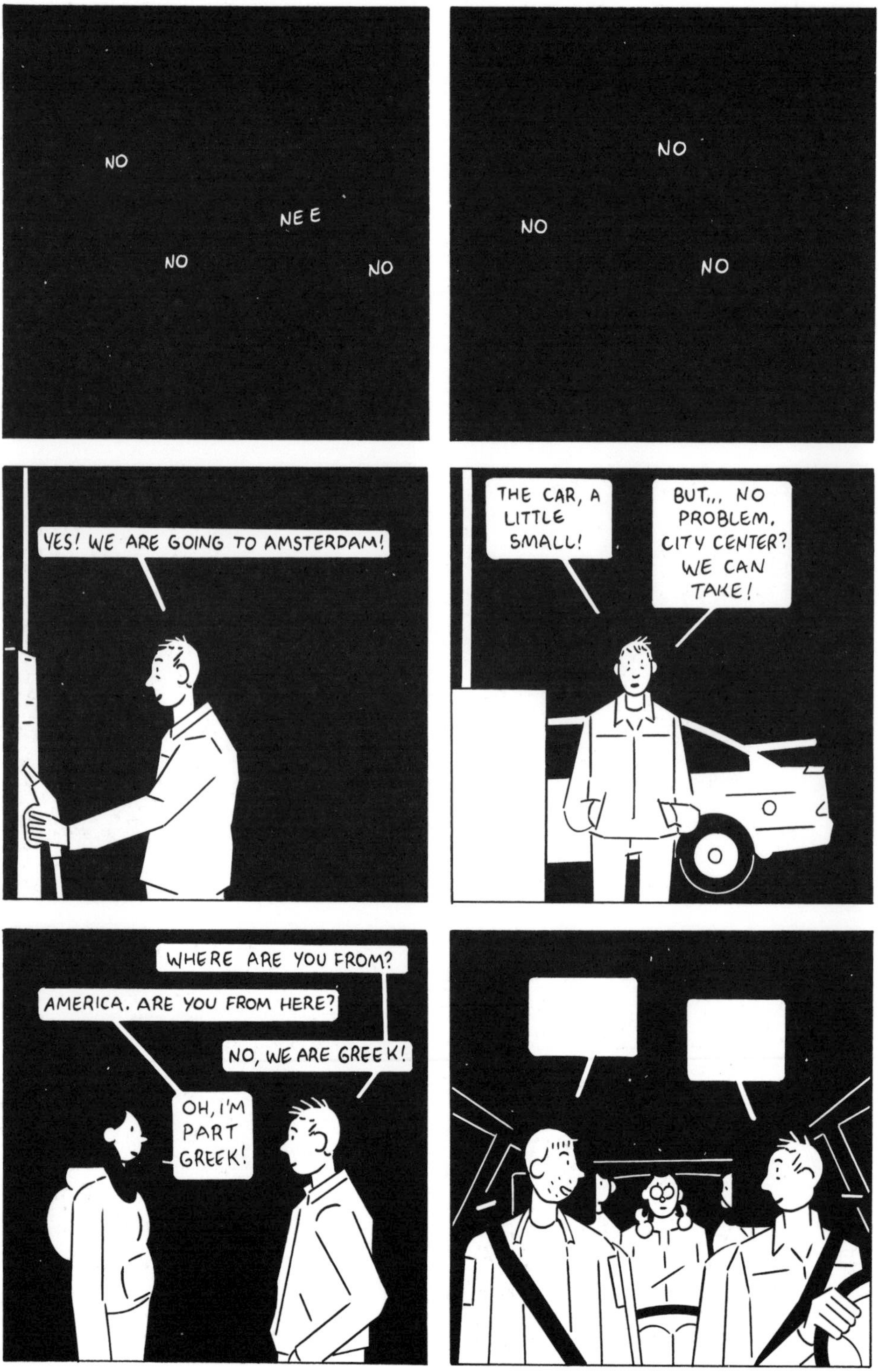
NO
NEE
NO
NO
NO
NO
NO
YES! WE ARE GOING TO AMSTERDAM!
THE CAR, A LITTLE SMALL!
BUT,,, NO PROBLEM. CITY CENTER? WE CAN TAKE!
WHERE ARE YOU FROM?
AMERICA. ARE YOU FROM HERE?
NO, WE ARE GREEK!
OH, I'M PART GREEK!

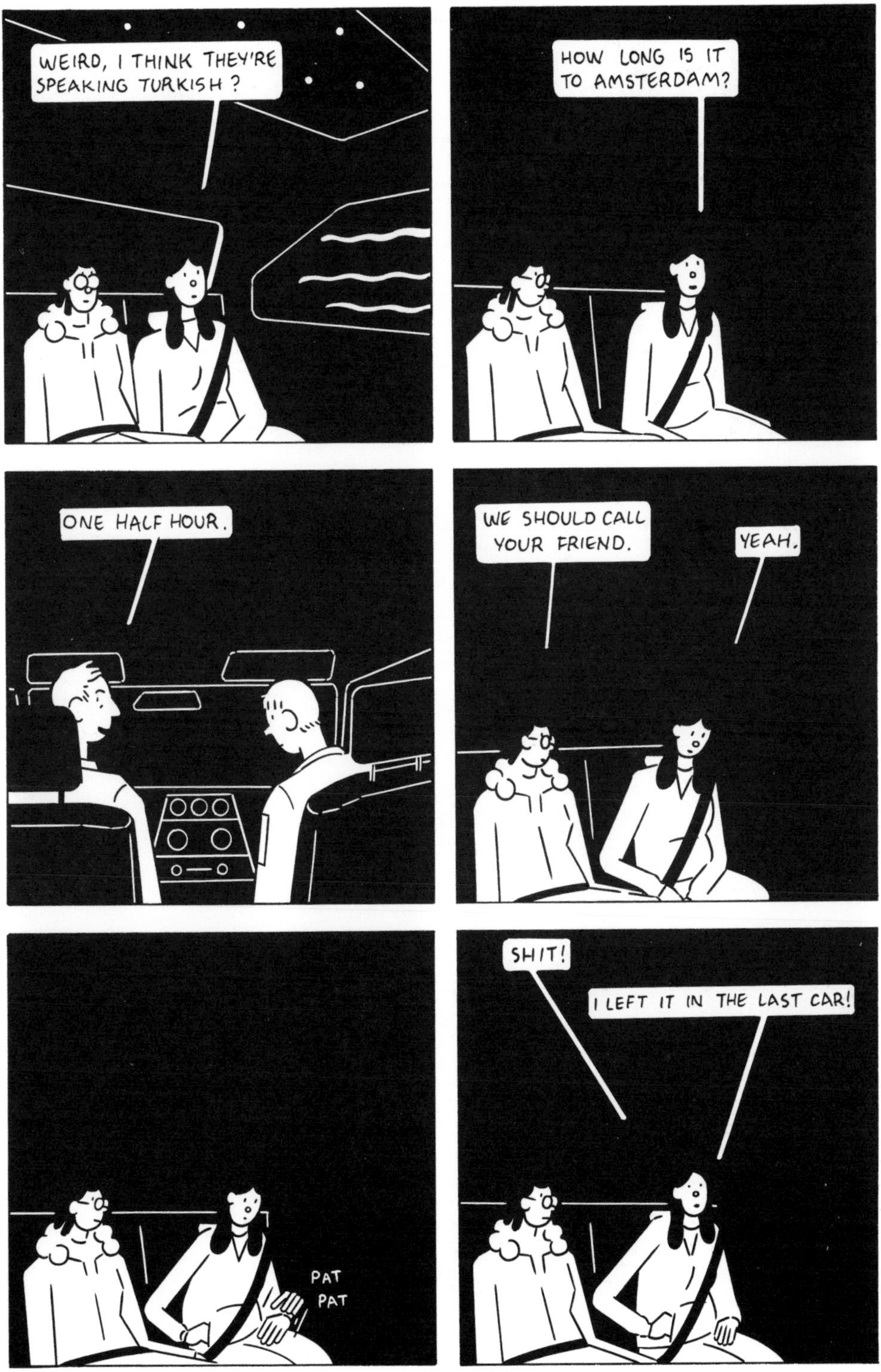
WEIRD, I THINK THEY'RE SPEAKING TURKISH ?
HOW LONG IS IT TO AMSTERDAM?
ONE HALF HOUR.
WE SHOULD CALL YOUR FRIEND.
YEAH.
PAT PAT
SHIT!
I LEFT IT IN THE LAST CAR!

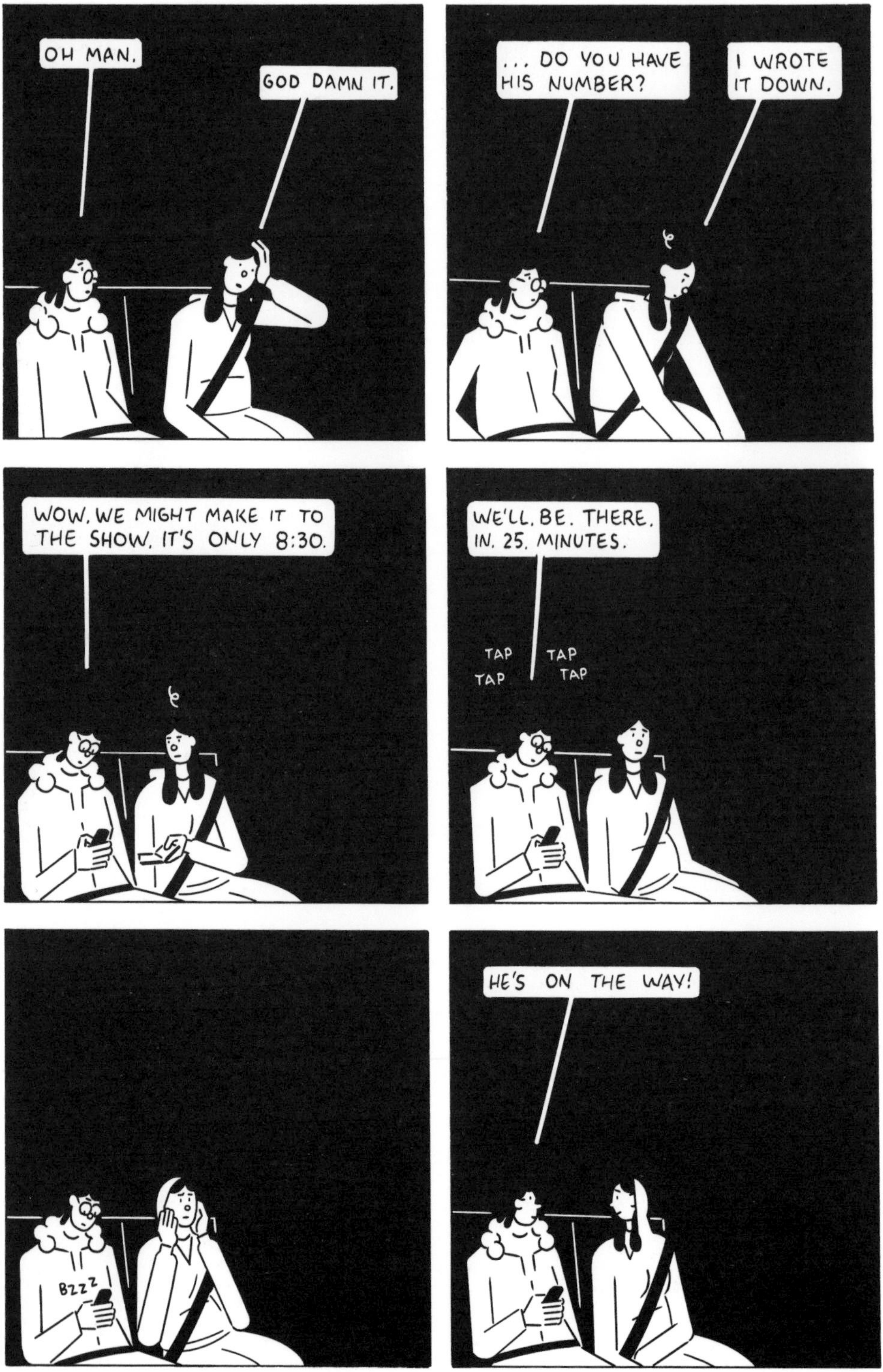
OH MAN.
GOD DAMN IT.
... DO YOU HAVE HIS NUMBER?
I WROTE IT DOWN.
WOW. WE MIGHT MAKE IT TO THE SHOW. IT'S ONLY 8:30.
WE'LL. BE. THERE. IN. 25. MINUTES.
TAP TAP
TAP TAP
BZZZ
HE'S ON THE WAY!

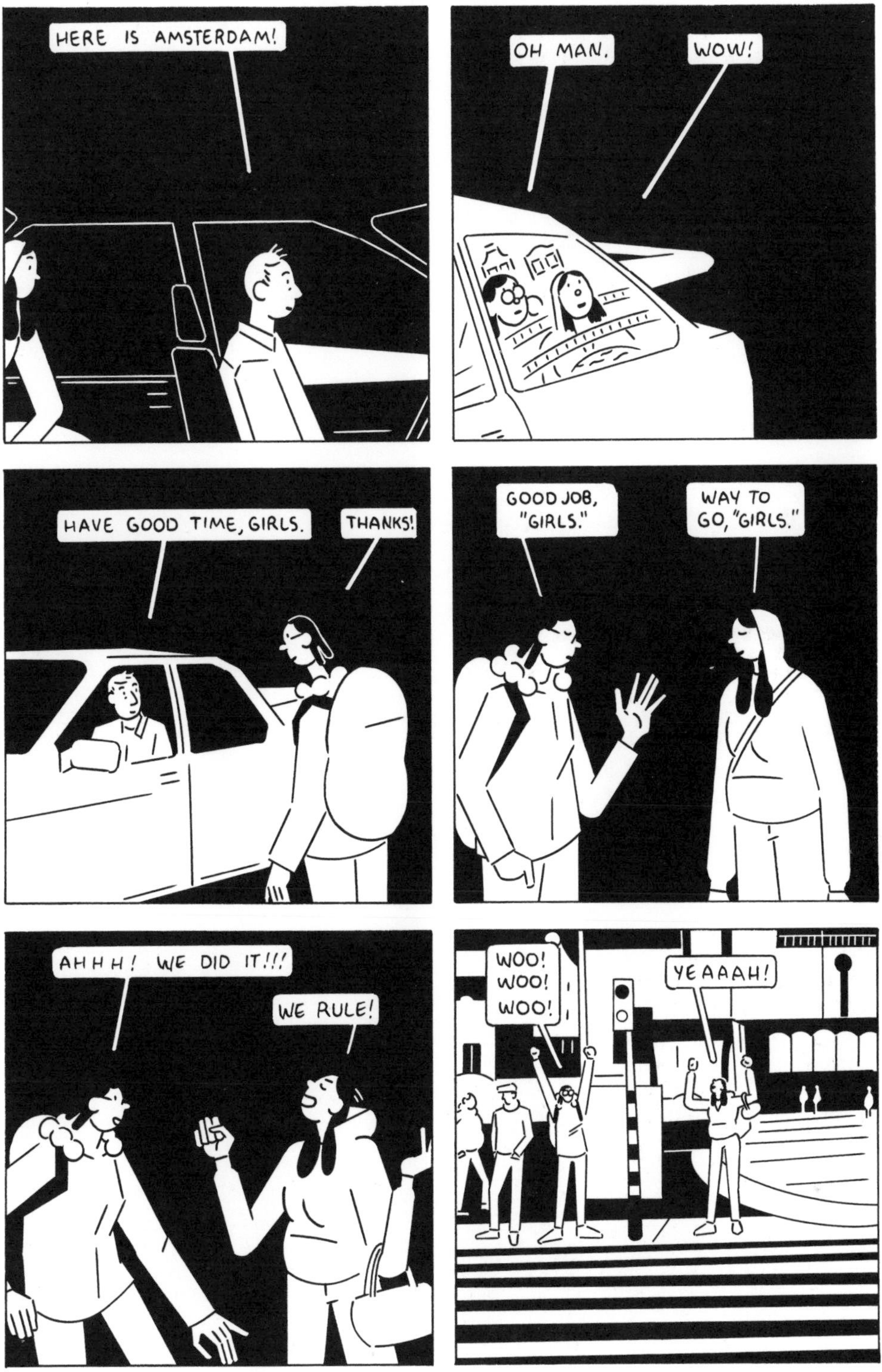
HERE IS AMSTERDAM!
OH MAN.
WOW!
HAVE GOOD TIME, GIRLS.
THANKS!
GOOD JOB, "GIRLS."
WAY TO GO, "GIRLS."
AHHH! WE DID IT!!!
WE RULE!
WOO! WOO! WOO!
YEAAAH!

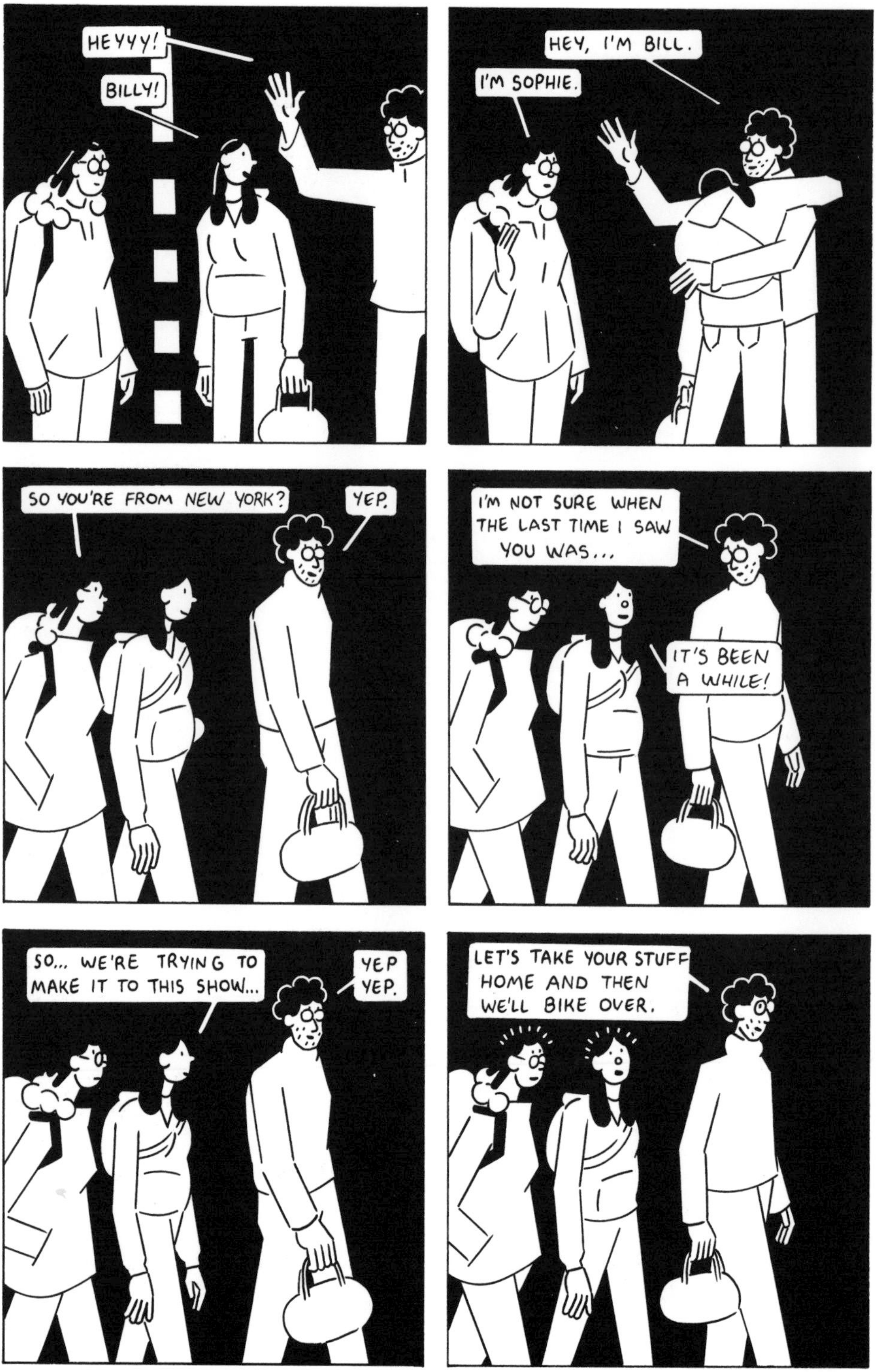
HEYYY!
BILLY!
HEY, I'M BILL.
I'M SOPHIE.
SO YOU'RE FROM NEW YORK?
YEP.
I'M NOT SURE WHEN THE LAST TIME I SAW YOU WAS...
IT'S BEEN A WHILE!
SO... WE'RE TRYING TO MAKE IT TO THIS SHOW...
YEP YEP.
LET'S TAKE YOUR STUFF HOME AND THEN WE'LL BIKE OVER.

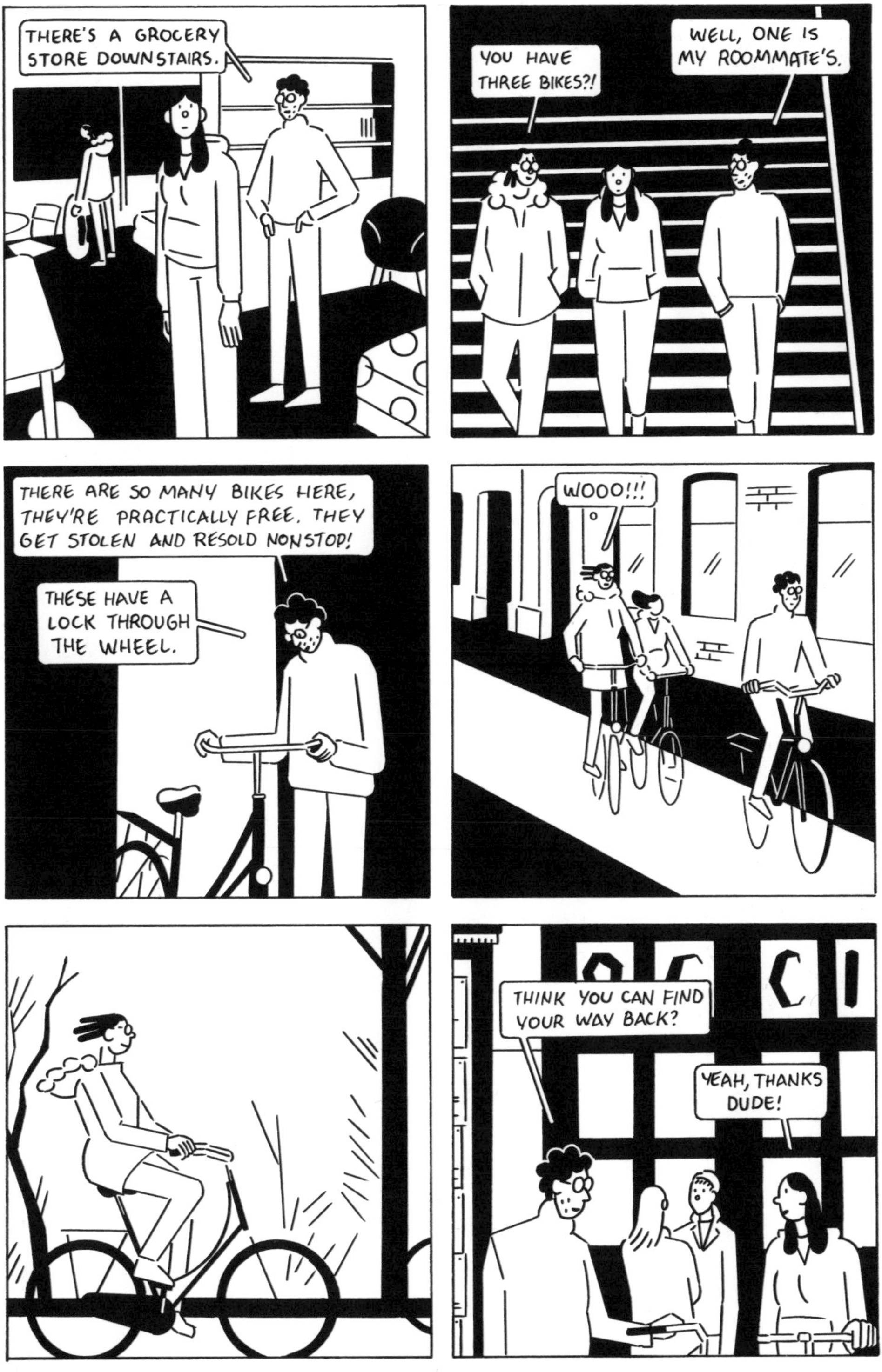
THERE'S A GROCERY STORE DOWNSTAIRS.
YOU HAVE THREE BIKES?!
WELL, ONE IS MY ROOMMATE'S.
THERE ARE SO MANY BIKES HERE, THEY'RE PRACTICALLY FREE. THEY GET STOLEN AND RESOLD NONSTOP!
THESE HAVE A LOCK THROUGH THE WHEEL.
WOOO!!!
THINK YOU CAN FIND YOUR WAY BACK?
YEAH, THANKS DUDE!

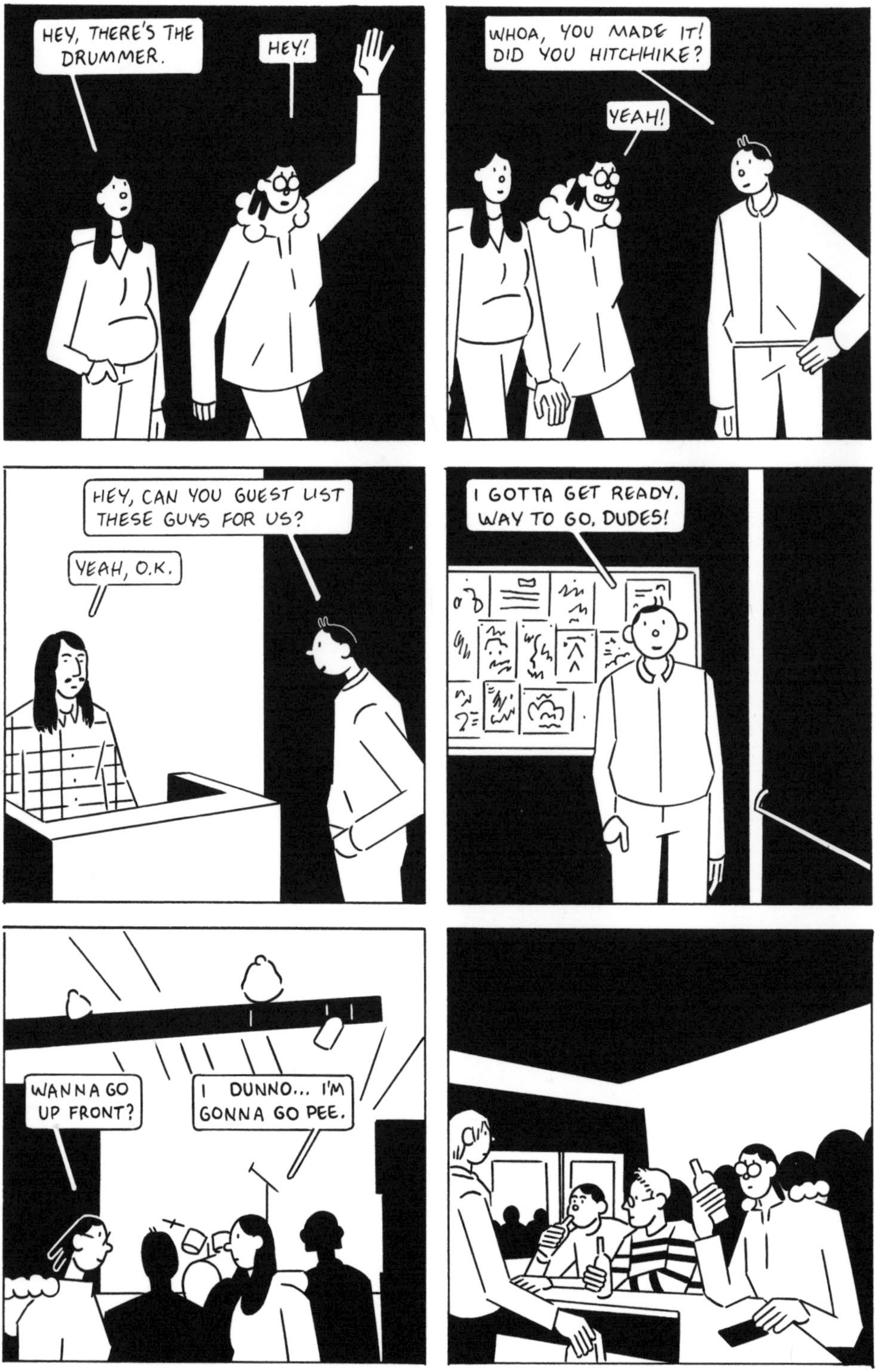
HEY, THERE'S THE DRUMMER.
HEY!
WHOA, YOU MADE IT! DID YOU HITCHHIKE?
YEAH!
HEY, CAN YOU GUEST LIST THESE GUYS FOR US?
YEAH, O.K.
I GOTTA GET READY. WAY TO GO, DUDES!
WANNA GO UP FRONT?
I DUNNO... I'M GONNA GO PEE.

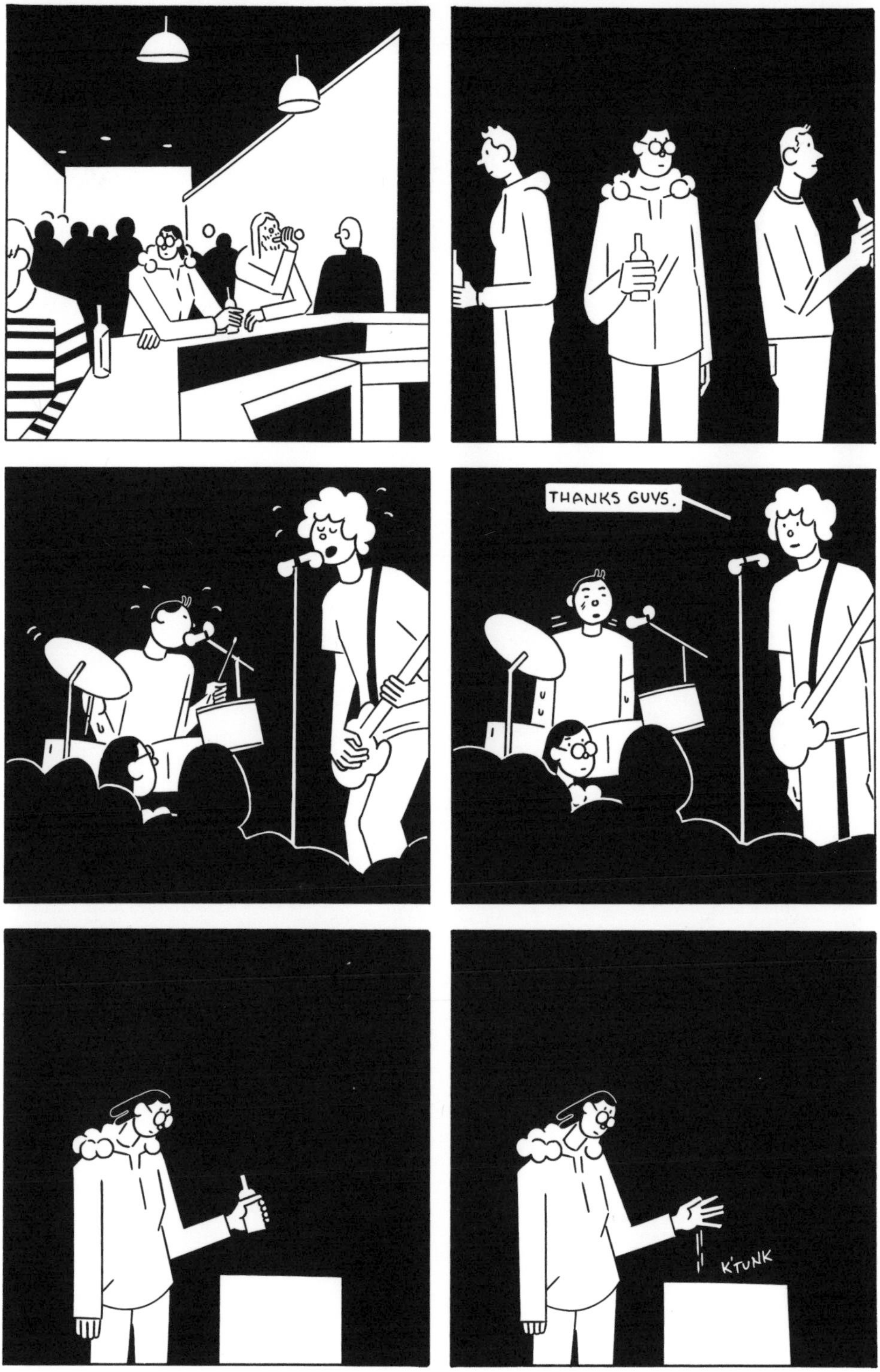
THANKS GUYS.
K'TUNK

111

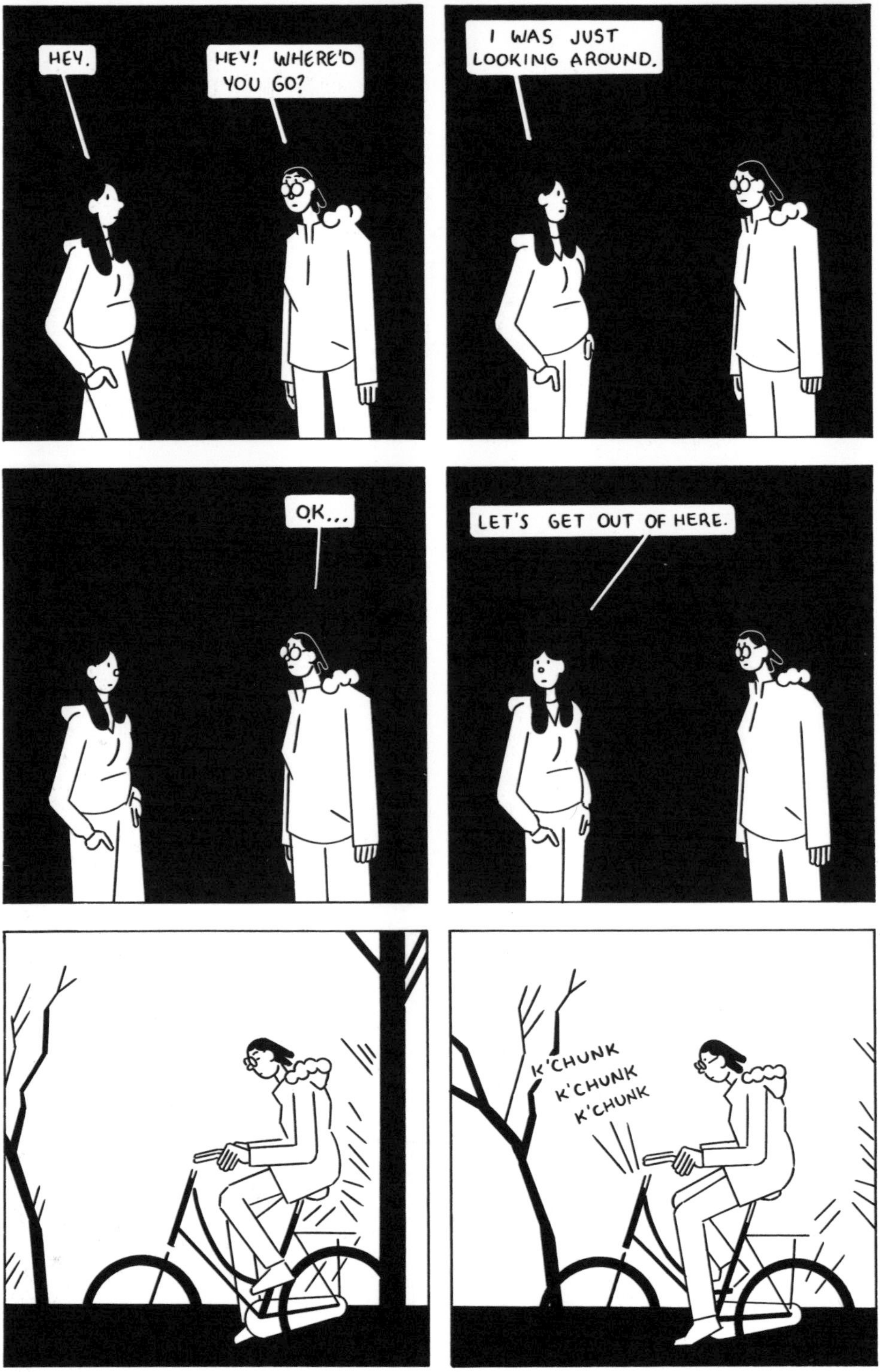
HEY.
HEY! WHERE'D YOU GO?
I WAS JUST LOOKING AROUND.
OK...
LET'S GET OUT OF HERE.
K'CHUNK
K'CHUNK
K'CHUNK

112

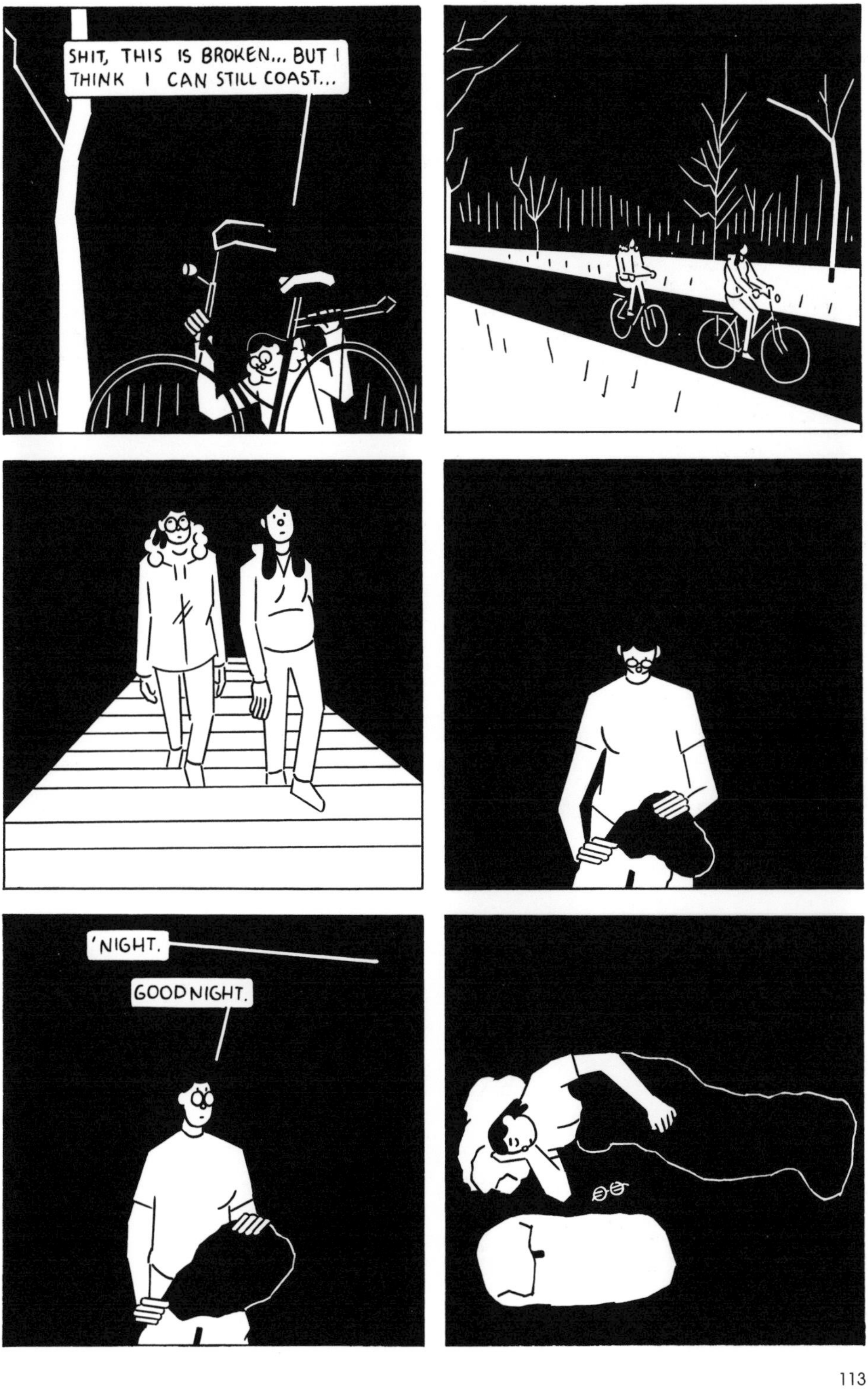
SHIT, THIS IS BROKEN... BUT I THINK I CAN STILL COAST...
'NIGHT.
GOODNIGHT.

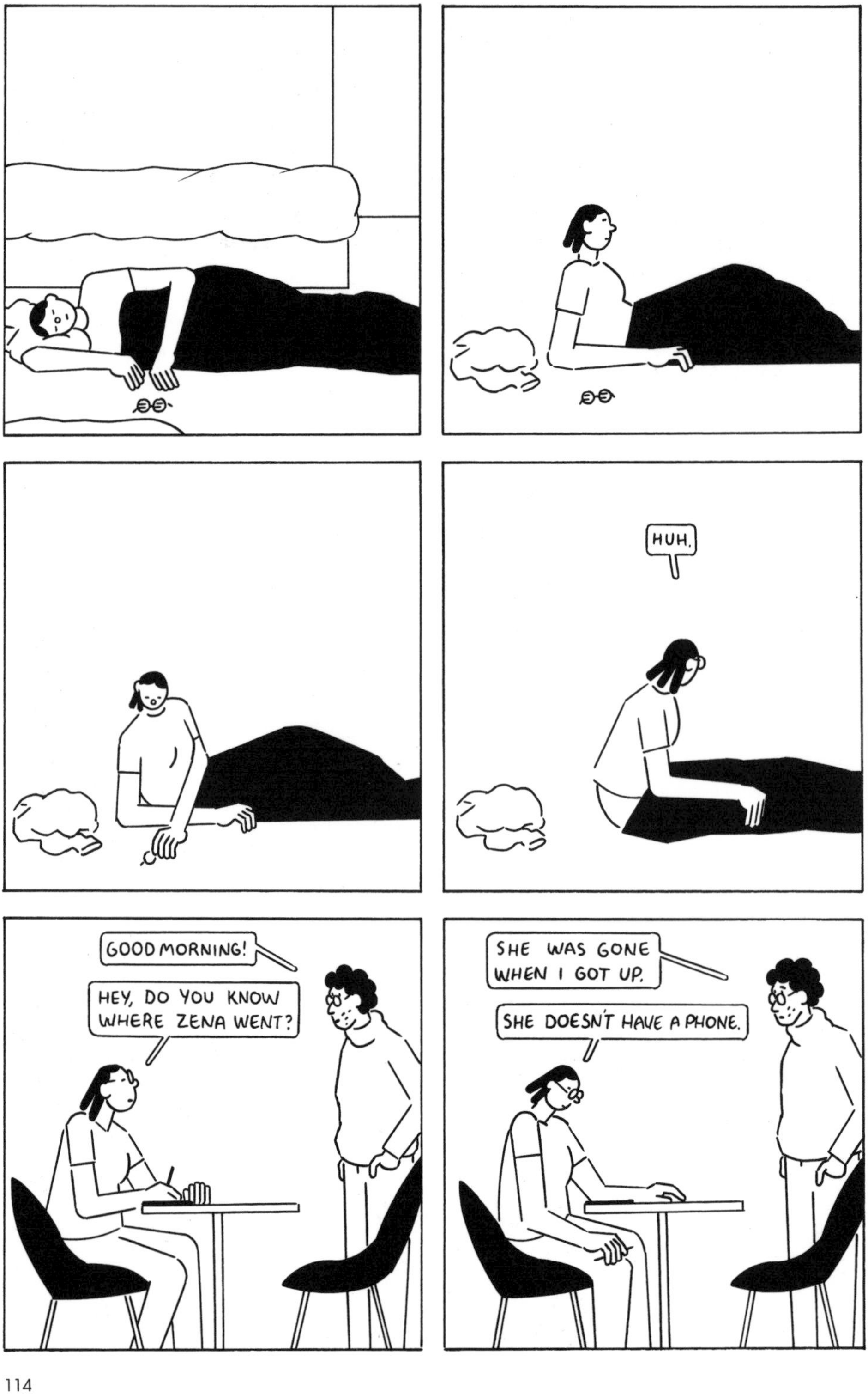
HUH.
GOOD MORNING!
HEY, DO YOU KNOW WHERE ZENA WENT?
SHE WAS GONE WHEN I GOT UP.
SHE DOESN'T HAVE A PHONE.

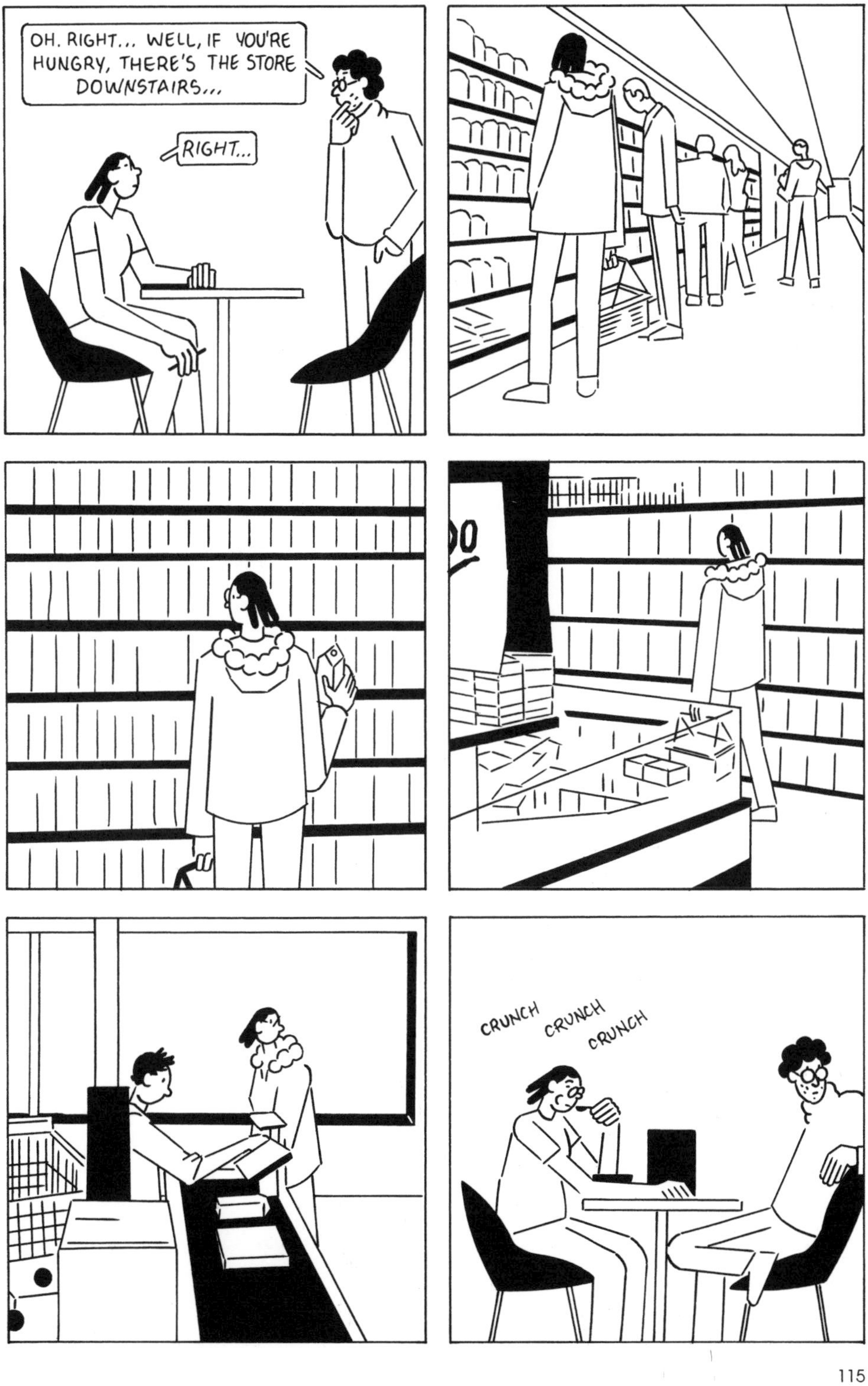
OH. RIGHT... WELL, IF YOU'RE HUNGRY, THERE'S THE STORE DOWNSTAIRS...
RIGHT...
CRUNCH
CRUNCH
CRUNCH

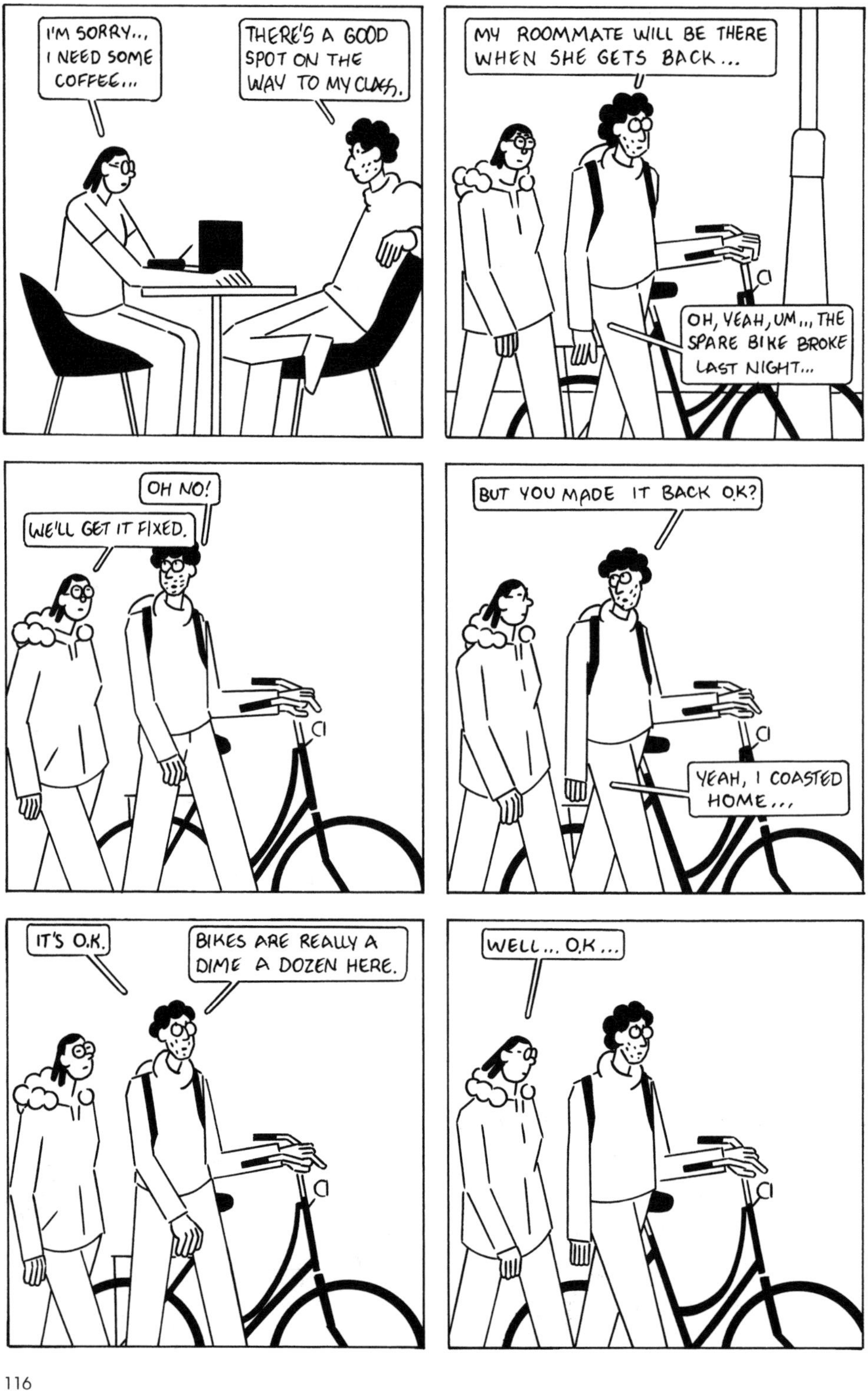
I'M SORRY... I NEED SOME COFFEE...
THERE'S A GOOD SPOT ON THE WAY TO MY CLASS.
MY ROOMMATE WILL BE THERE WHEN SHE GETS BACK...
OH, YEAH, UM... THE SPARE BIKE BROKE LAST NIGHT...
WE'LL GET IT FIXED.
OH NO!
BUT YOU MADE IT BACK O.K?
YEAH, I COASTED HOME...
IT'S O.K.
BIKES ARE REALLY A DIME A DOZEN HERE.
WELL... O.K...

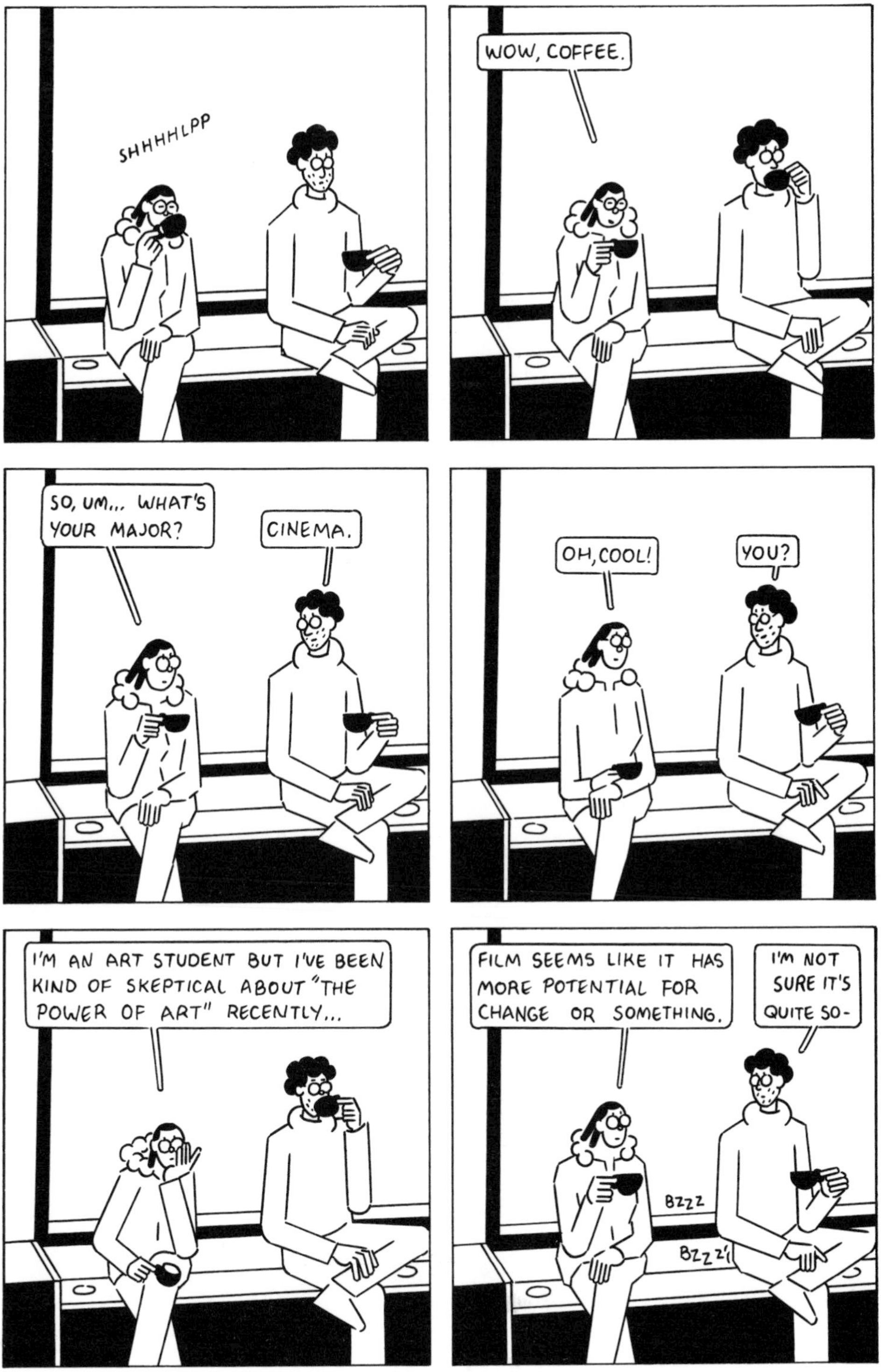
SHHHHLPP
WOW, COFFEE.
SO, UM... WHAT'S YOUR MAJOR?
CINEMA.
OH, COOL!
YOU?
I'M AN ART STUDENT BUT I'VE BEEN KIND OF SKEPTICAL ABOUT "THE POWER OF ART" RECENTLY...
FILM SEEMS LIKE IT HAS MORE POTENTIAL FOR CHANGE OR SOMETHING.
I'M NOT SURE IT'S QUITE SO-
BZZZ
BZZZ

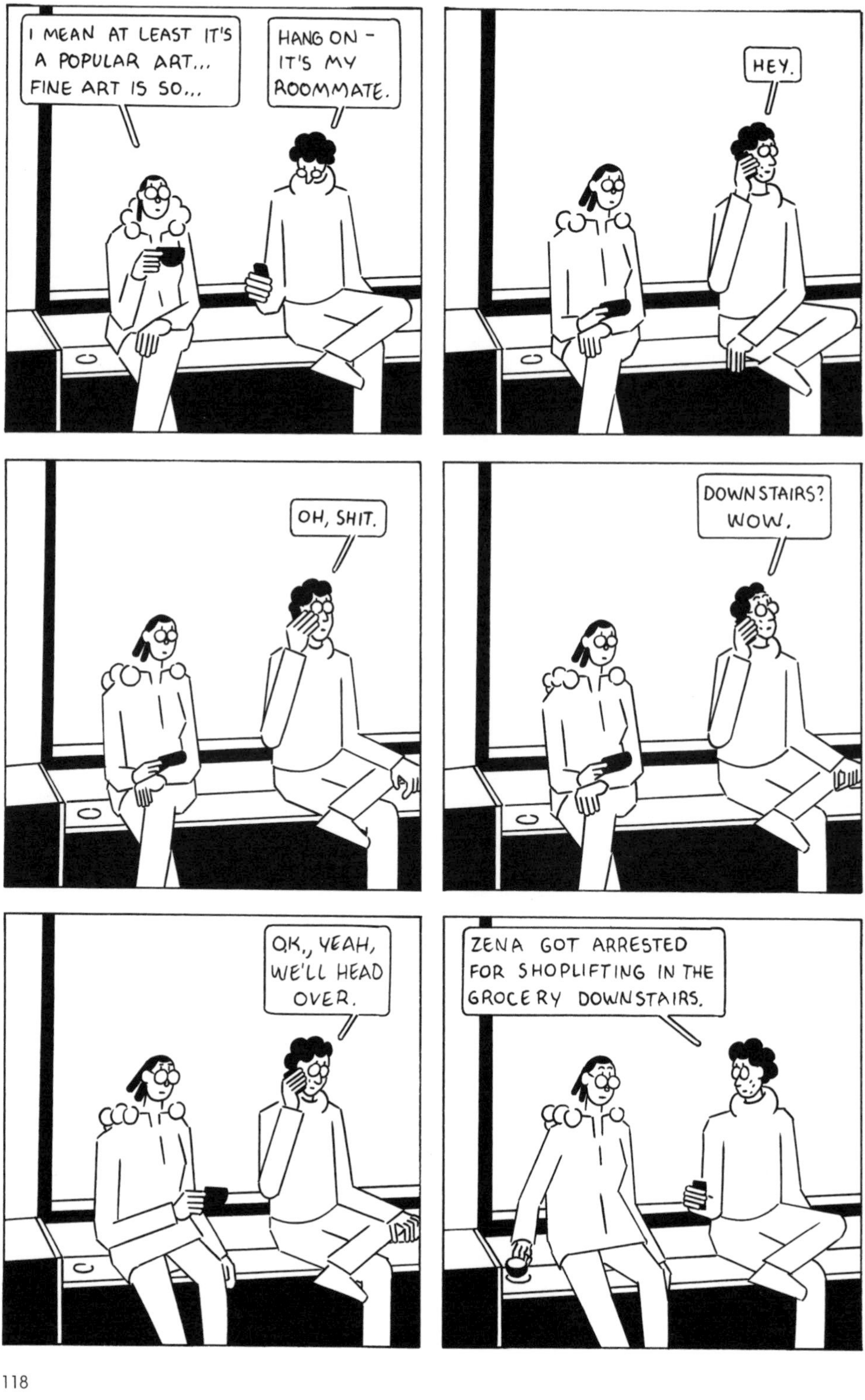
I MEAN AT LEAST IT'S A POPULAR ART... FINE ART IS SO...
HANG ON - IT'S MY ROOMMATE.
HEY.
OH, SHIT.
DOWNSTAIRS? WOW.
O.K., YEAH, WE'LL HEAD OVER.
ZENA GOT ARRESTED FOR SHOPLIFTING IN THE GROCERY DOWNSTAIRS.

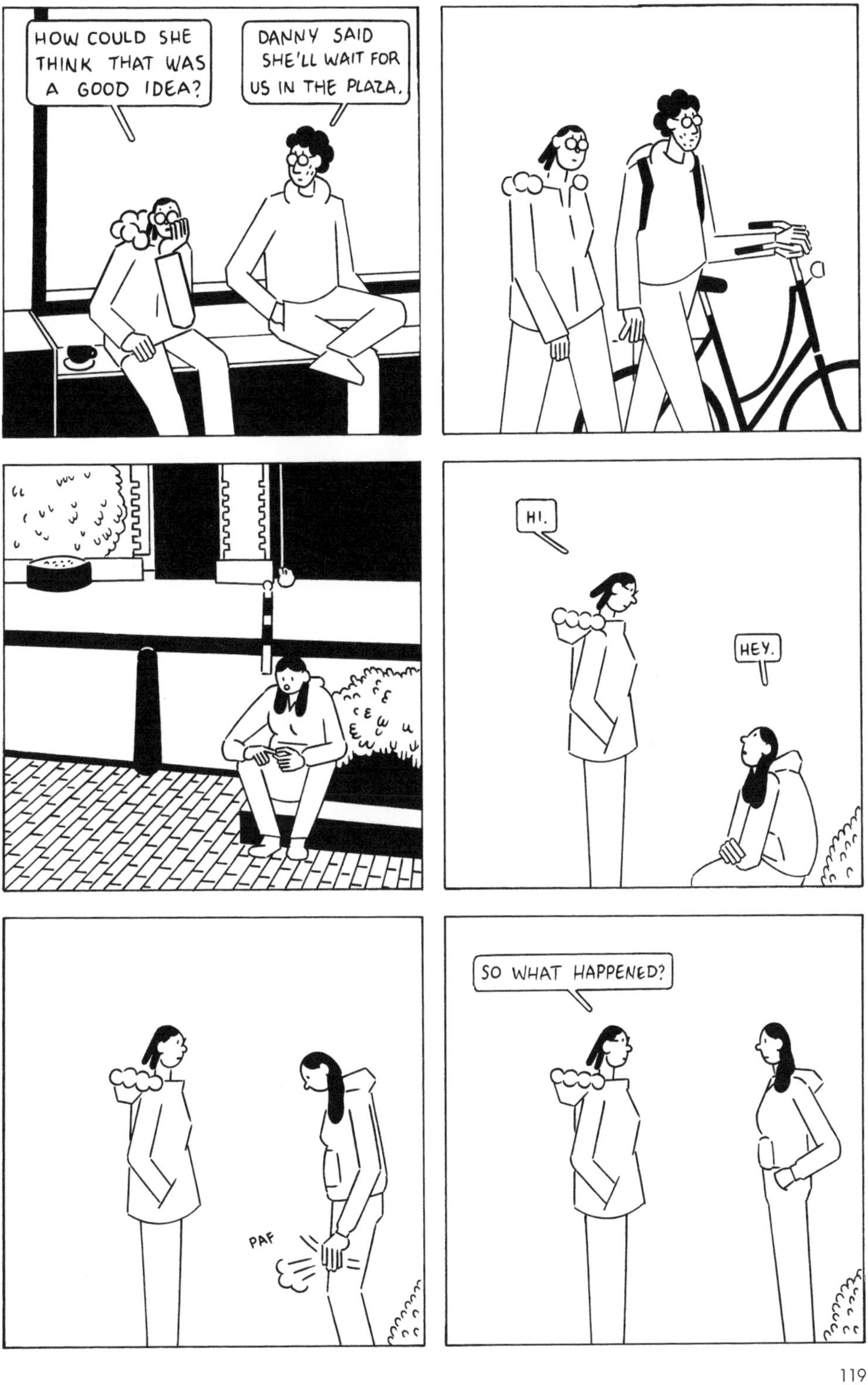
HOW COULD SHE THINK THAT WAS A GOOD IDEA?
DANNY SAID SHE'LL WAIT FOR US IN THE PLAZA.
HI.
HEY.
PAF
SO WHAT HAPPENED?

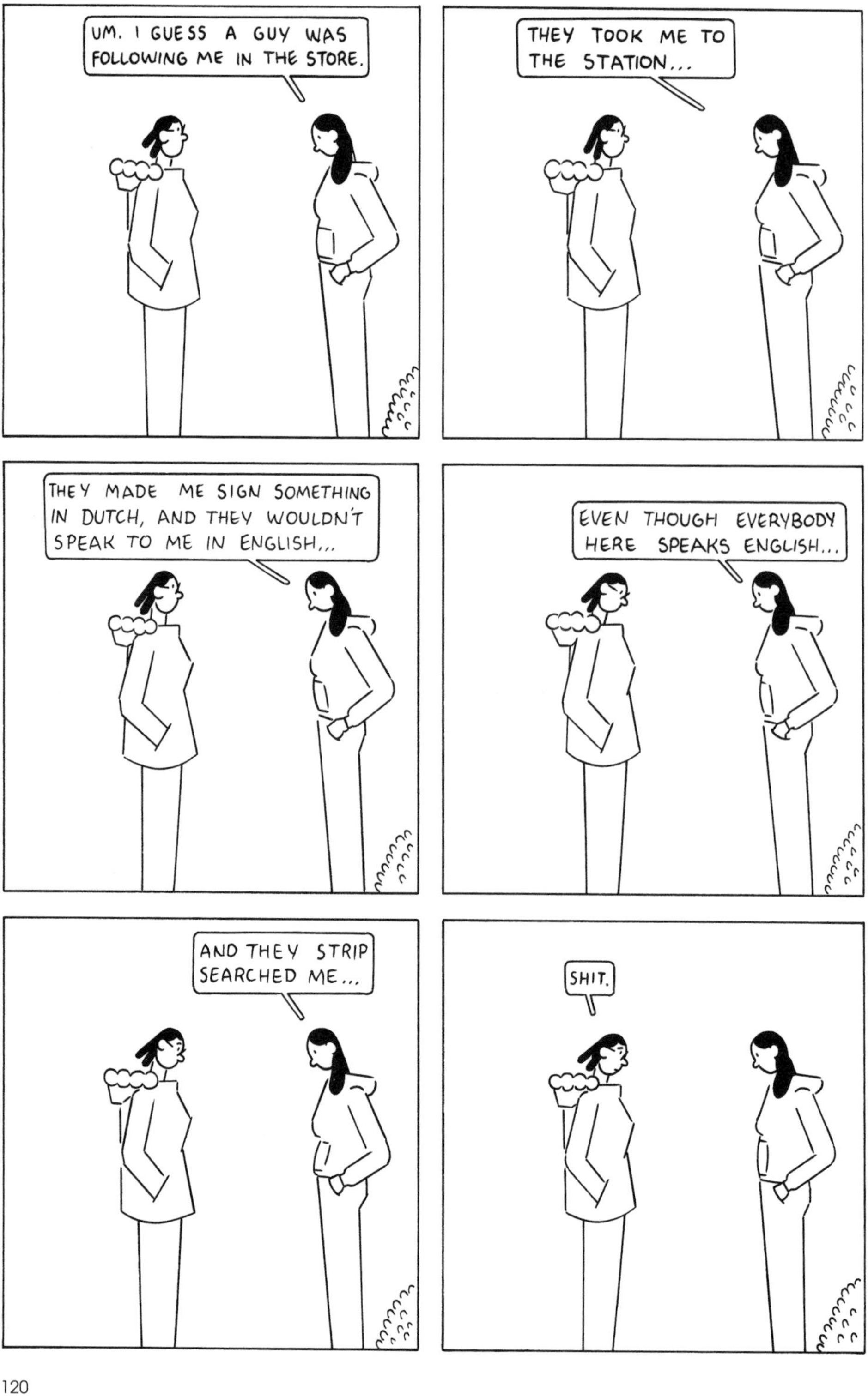
UM. I GUESS A GUY WAS FOLLOWING ME IN THE STORE.
THEY TOOK ME TO THE STATION...
THEY MADE ME SIGN SOMETHING IN DUTCH, AND THEY WOULDN'T SPEAK TO ME IN ENGLISH...
EVEN THOUGH EVERYBODY HERE SPEAKS ENGLISH...
AND THEY STRIP SEARCHED ME...
SHIT.

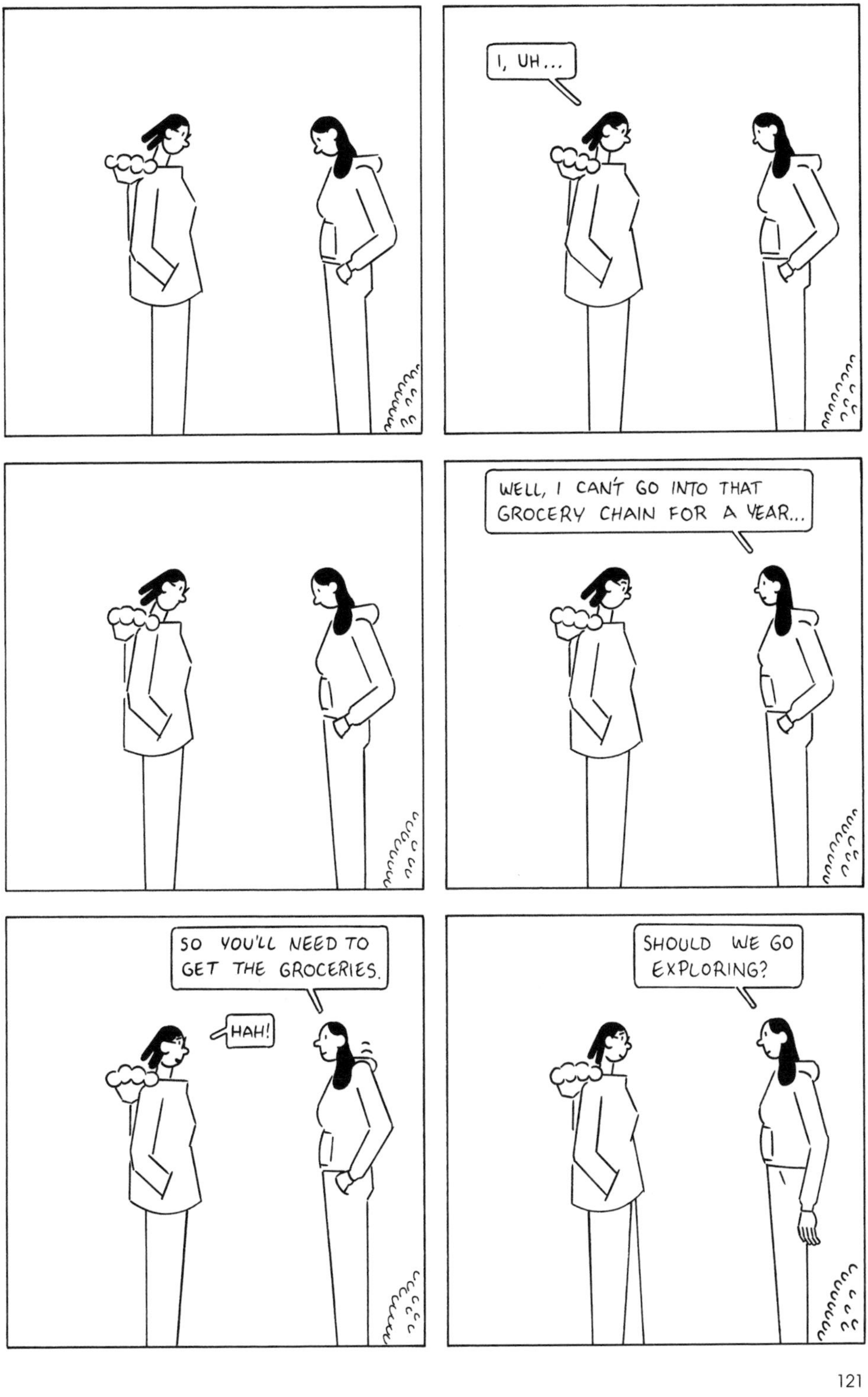
I, UH...
WELL, I CAN'T GO INTO THAT GROCERY CHAIN FOR A YEAR...
SO YOU'LL NEED TO GET THE GROCERIES.
HAH!
SHOULD WE GO EXPLORING?

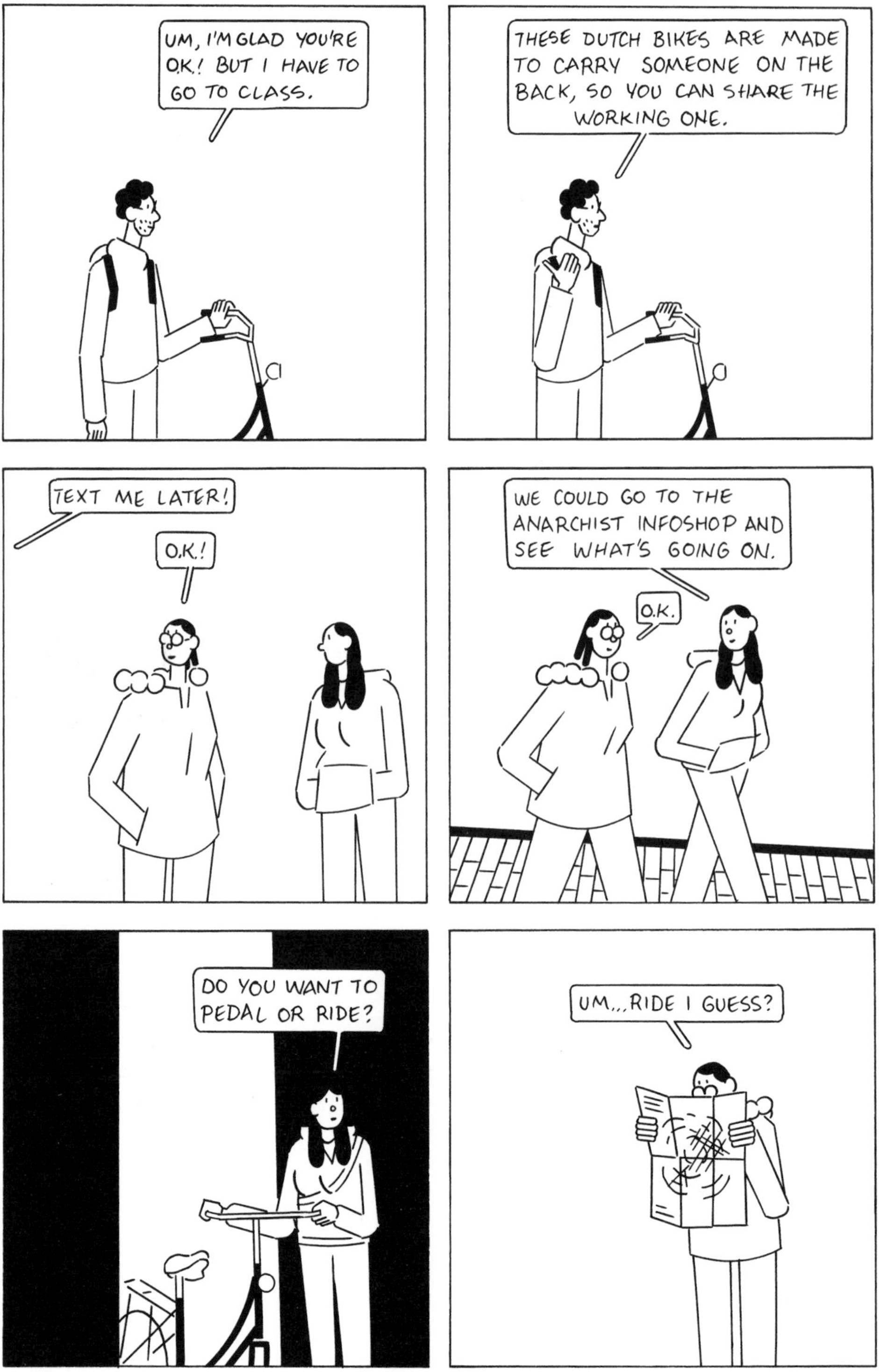
UM, I'M GLAD YOU'RE O.K.! BUT I HAVE TO GO TO CLASS.
THESE DUTCH BIKES ARE MADE TO CARRY SOMEONE ON THE BACK, SO YOU CAN SHARE THE WORKING ONE.
TEXT ME LATER!
O.K.!
WE COULD GO TO THE ANARCHIST INFOSHOP AND SEE WHAT'S GOING ON.
O.K.
DO YOU WANT TO PEDAL OR RIDE?
UM... RIDE I GUESS?

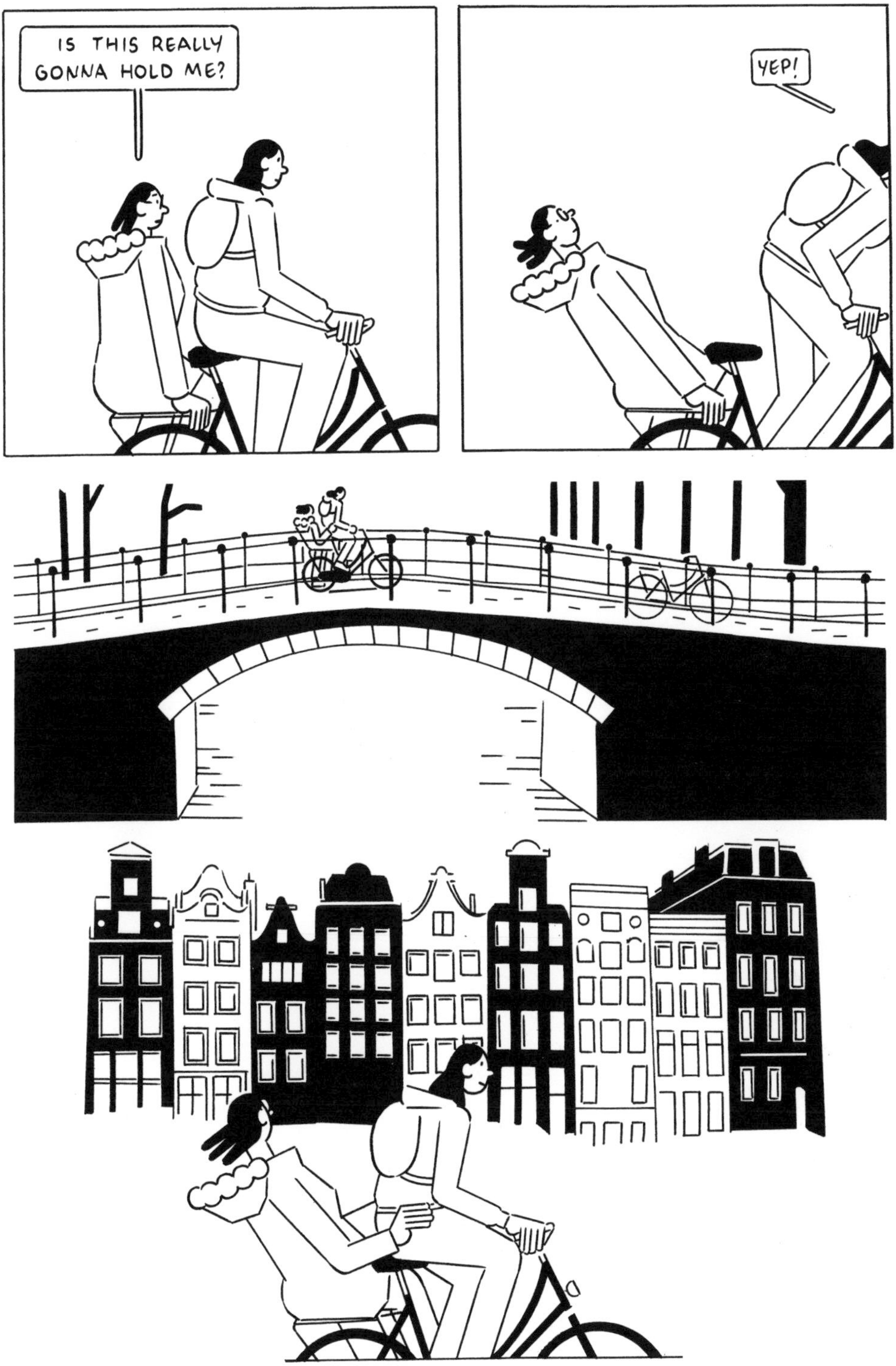
IS THIS REALLY GONNA HOLD ME?
YEP!

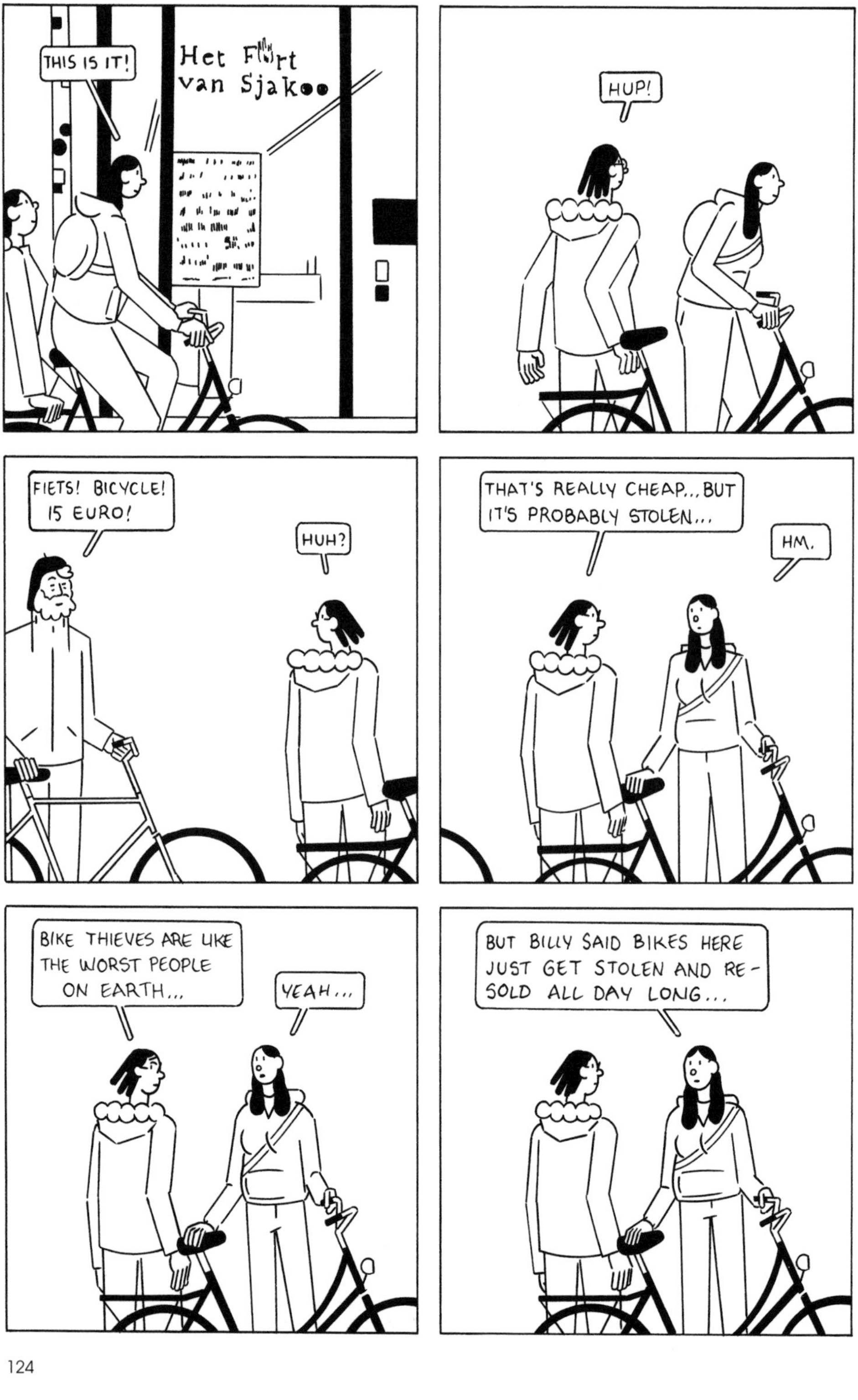
THIS IS IT!
Het Fort van Sjakoo
HUP!
FIETS! BICYCLE! 15 EURO!
HUH?
THAT'S REALLY CHEAP... BUT IT'S PROBABLY STOLEN...
HM.
BIKE THIEVES ARE LIKE THE WORST PEOPLE ON EARTH...
YEAH...
BUT BILLY SAID BIKES HERE JUST GET STOLEN AND RE-SOLD ALL DAY LONG...

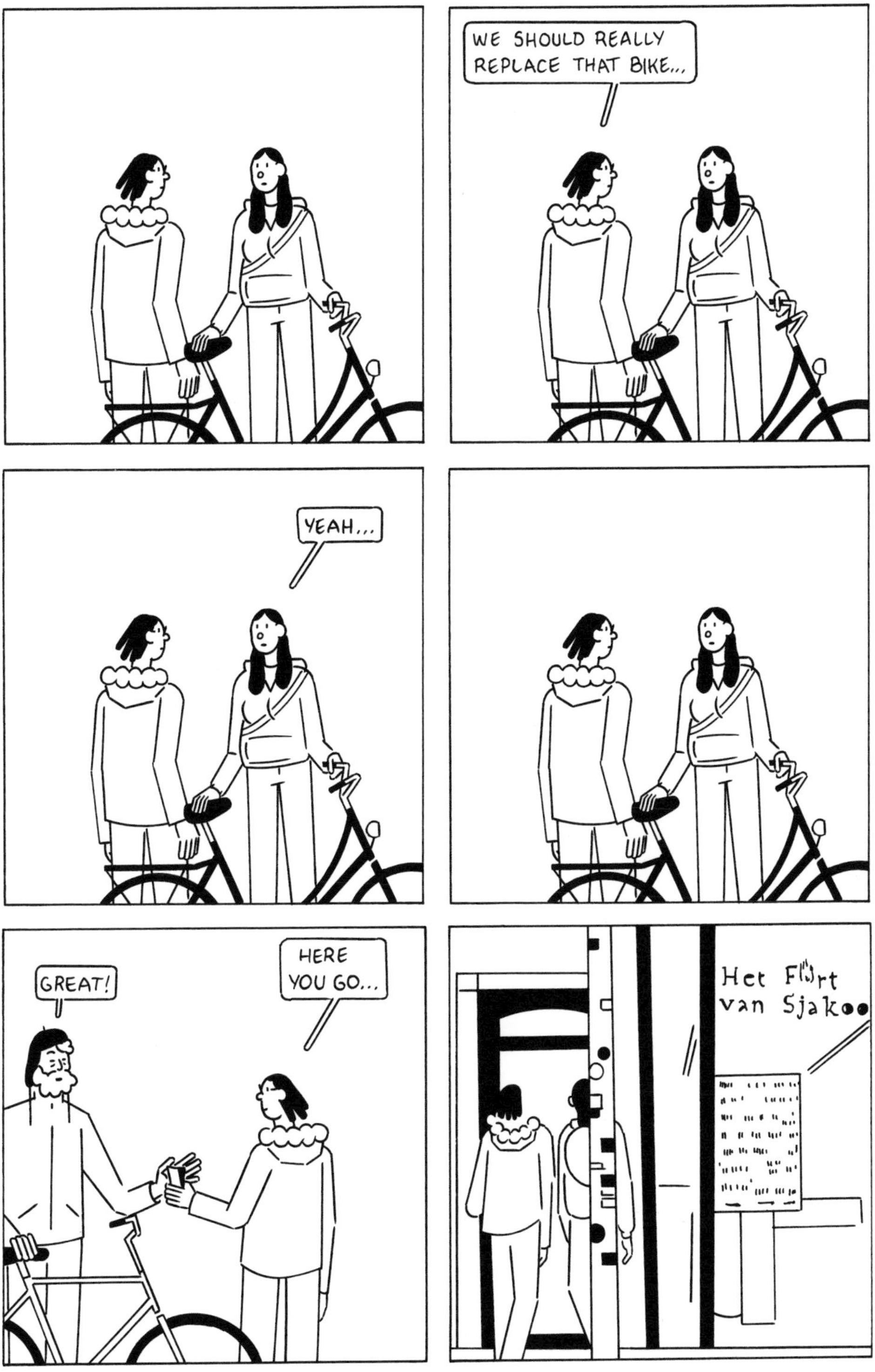
WE SHOULD REALLY REPLACE THAT BIKE...
YEAH...
GREAT!
HERE YOU GO...
Het Fort
van Sjakoo

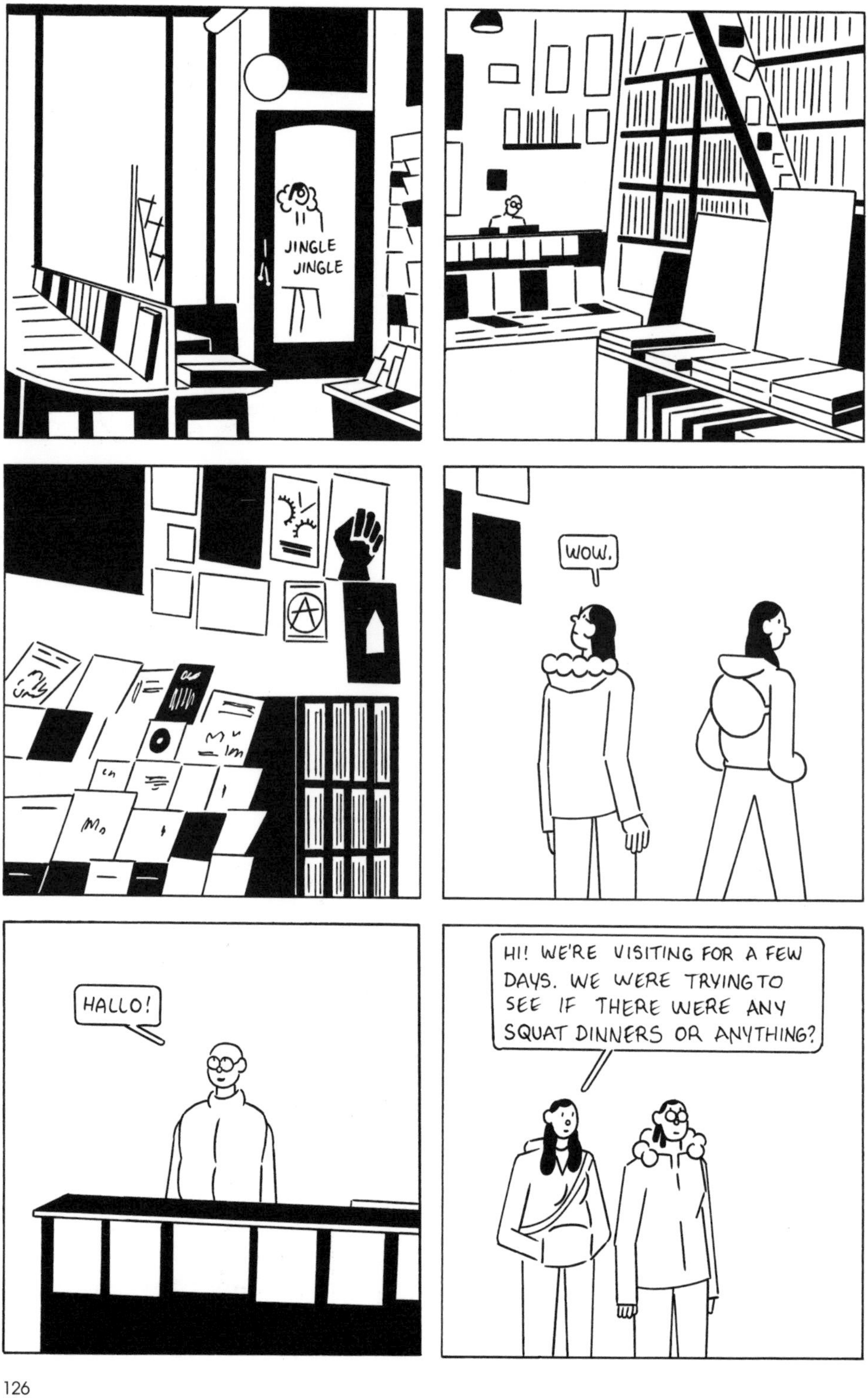
JINGLE
JINGLE
WOW.
HALLO!
HI! WE'RE VISITING FOR A FEW DAYS. WE WERE TRYING TO SEE IF THERE WERE ANY SQUAT DINNERS OR ANYTHING?

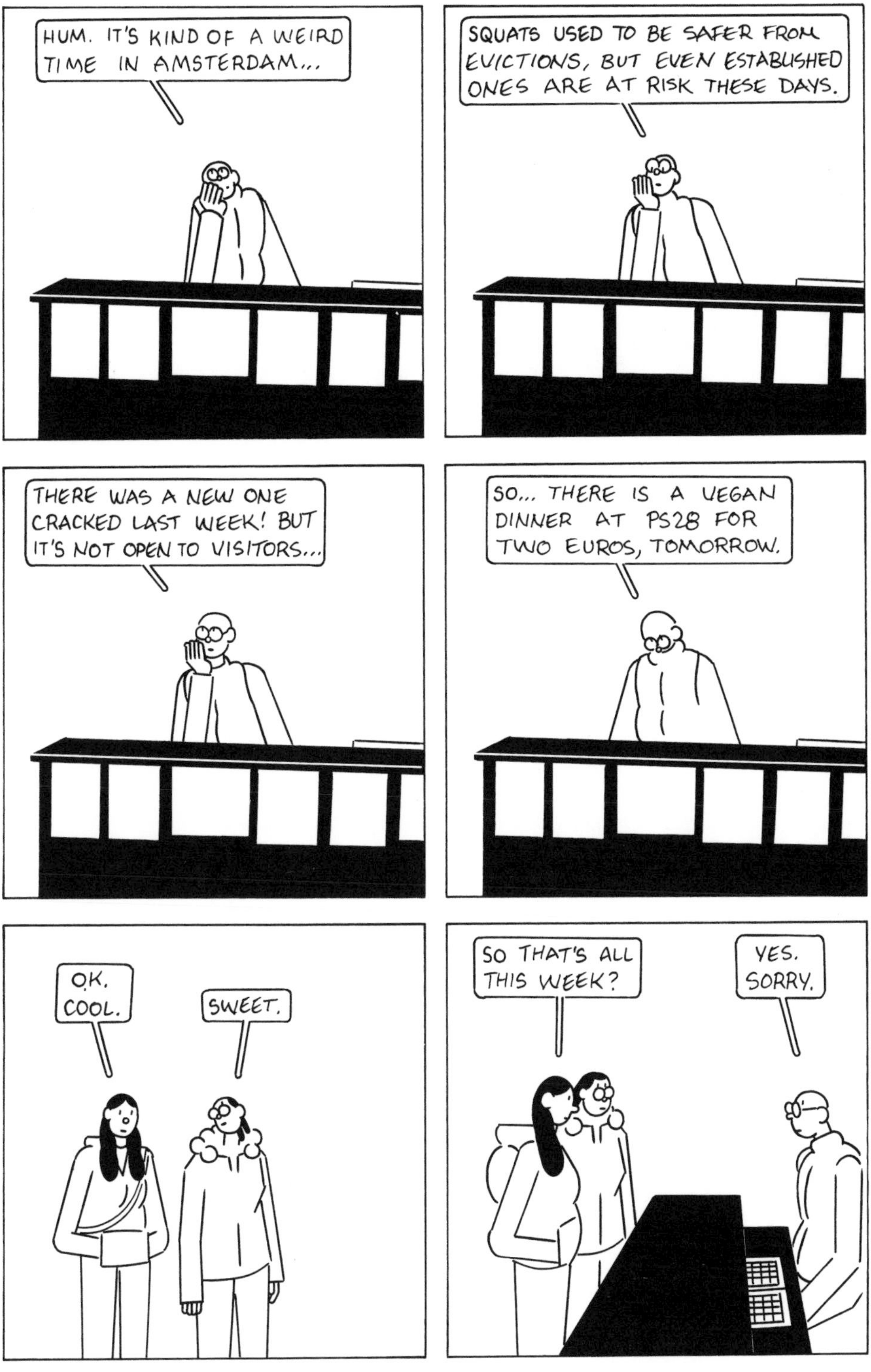

HUM. IT'S KIND OF A WEIRD TIME IN AMSTERDAM...
SQUATS USED TO BE SAFER FROM EVICTIONS, BUT EVEN ESTABLISHED ONES ARE AT RISK THESE DAYS.
THERE WAS A NEW ONE CRACKED LAST WEEK! BUT IT'S NOT OPEN TO VISITORS...
SO... THERE IS A VEGAN DINNER AT PS28 FOR TWO EUROS, TOMORROW.
O.K. COOL.
SWEET.
SO THAT'S ALL THIS WEEK?
YES. SORRY.

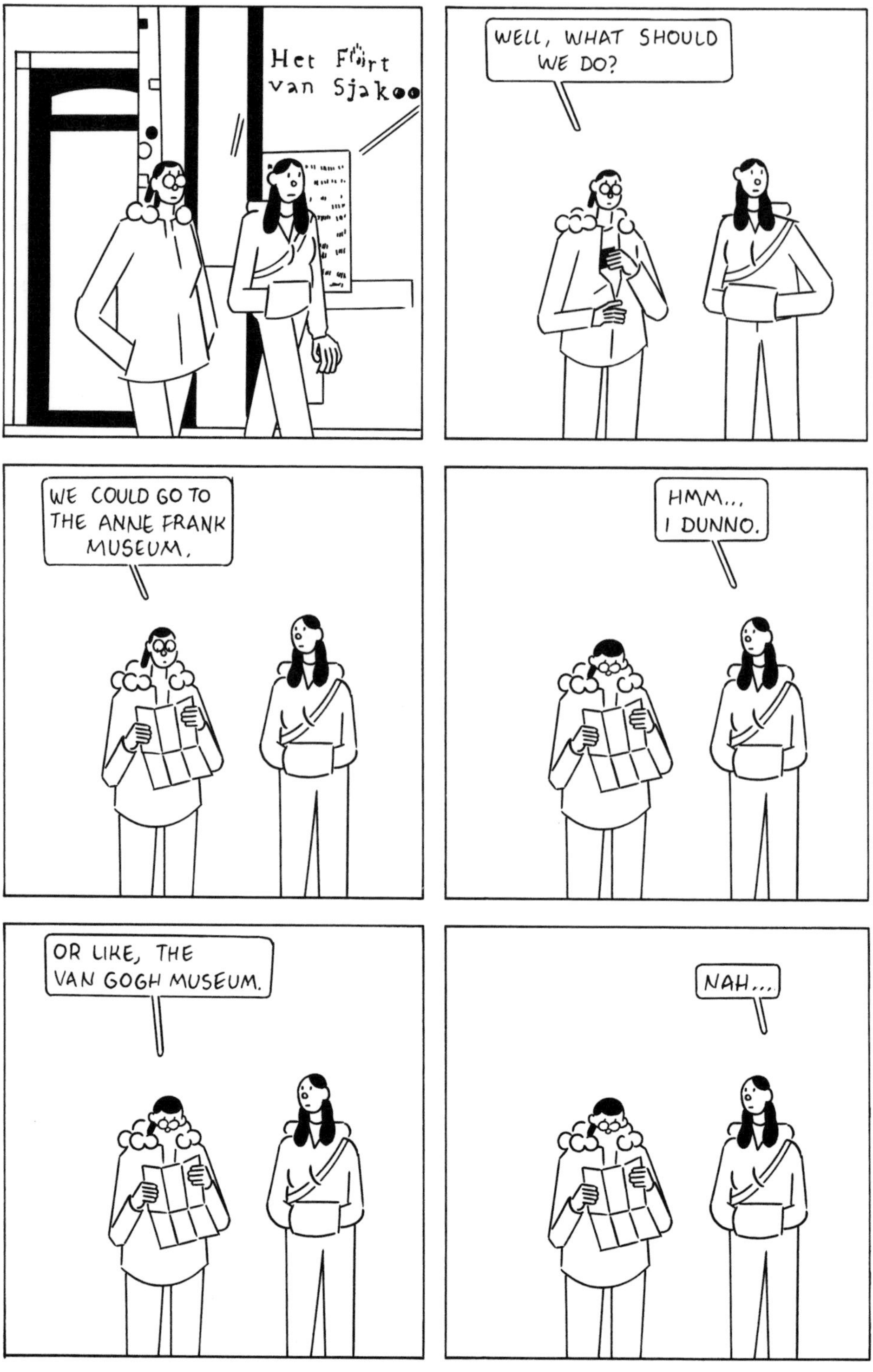
Het Fl?rt van Sjakoo
WELL, WHAT SHOULD WE DO?
WE COULD GO TO THE ANNE FRANK MUSEUM.
HMM... I DUNNO.
OR LIKE, THE VAN GOGH MUSEUM.
NAH...

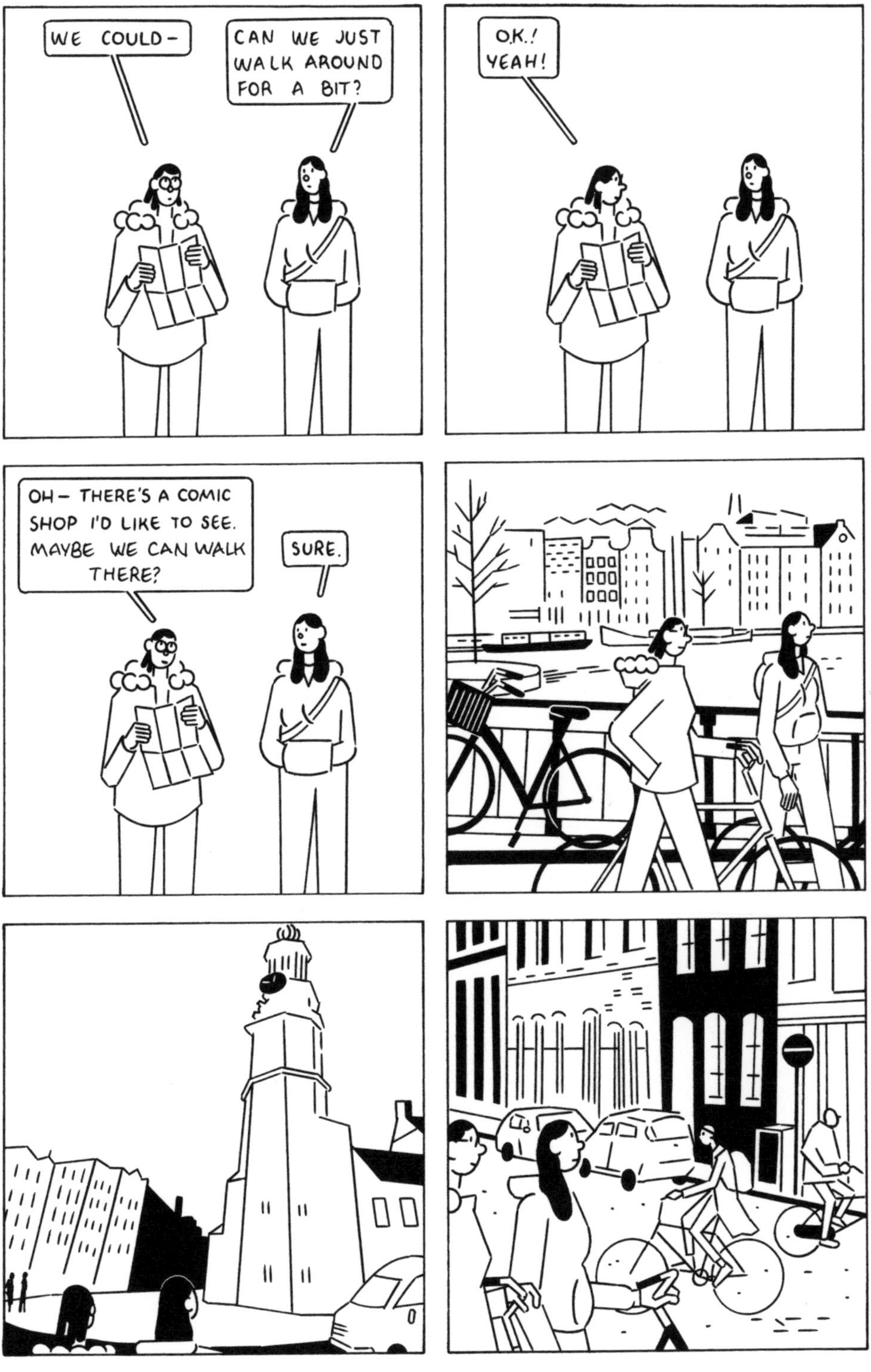
WE COULD-
CAN WE JUST WALK AROUND FOR A BIT?
O.K.! YEAH!
OH- THERE'S A COMIC SHOP I'D LIKE TO SEE. MAYBE WE CAN WALK THERE?
SURE.

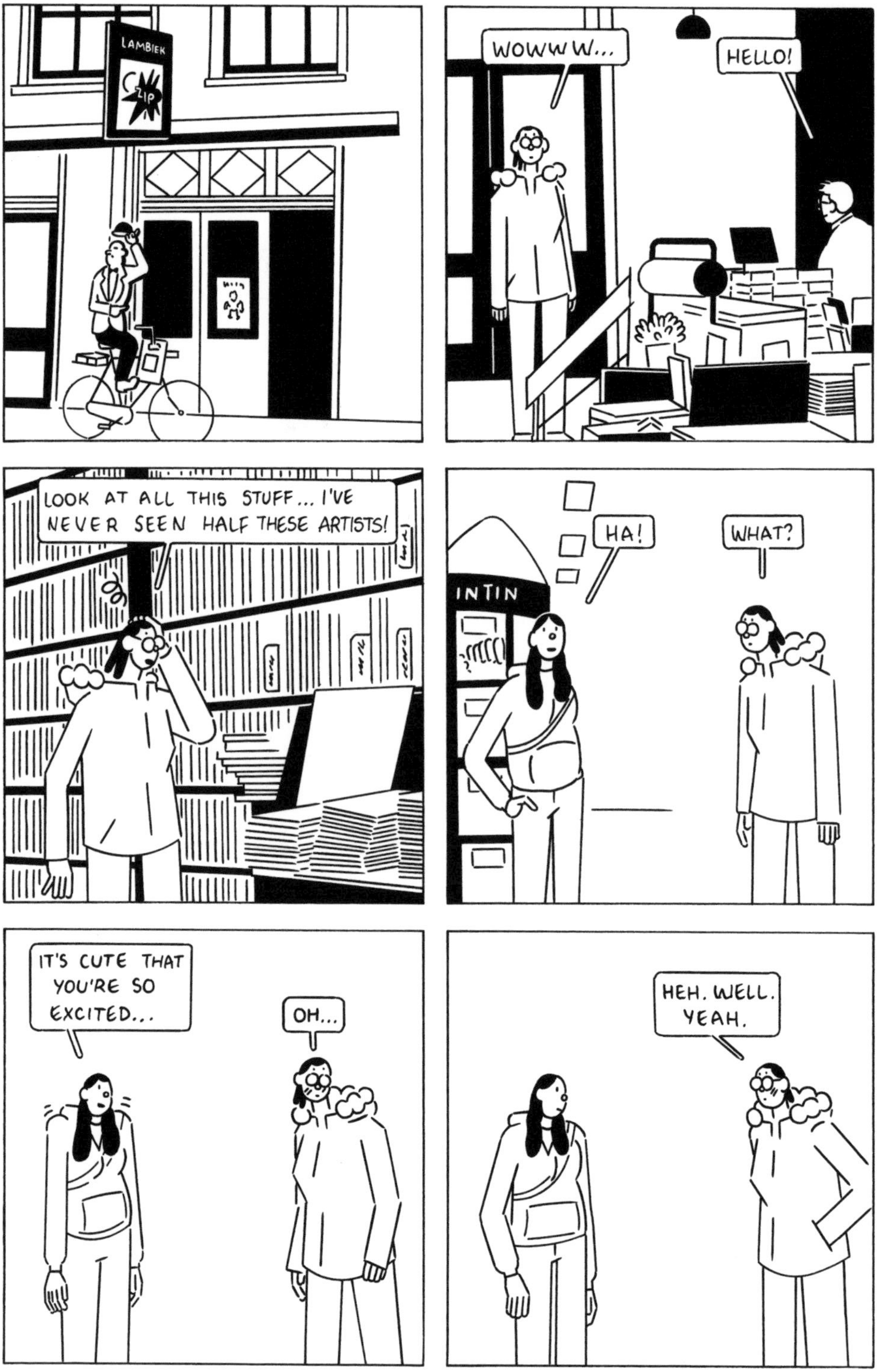
LAMBIEK
ZIP
WOWWW...
HELLO!
LOOK AT ALL THIS STUFF... I'VE NEVER SEEN HALF THESE ARTISTS!
INTIN
HA!
WHAT?
IT'S CUTE THAT YOU'RE SO EXCITED...
OH...
HEH. WELL. YEAH.

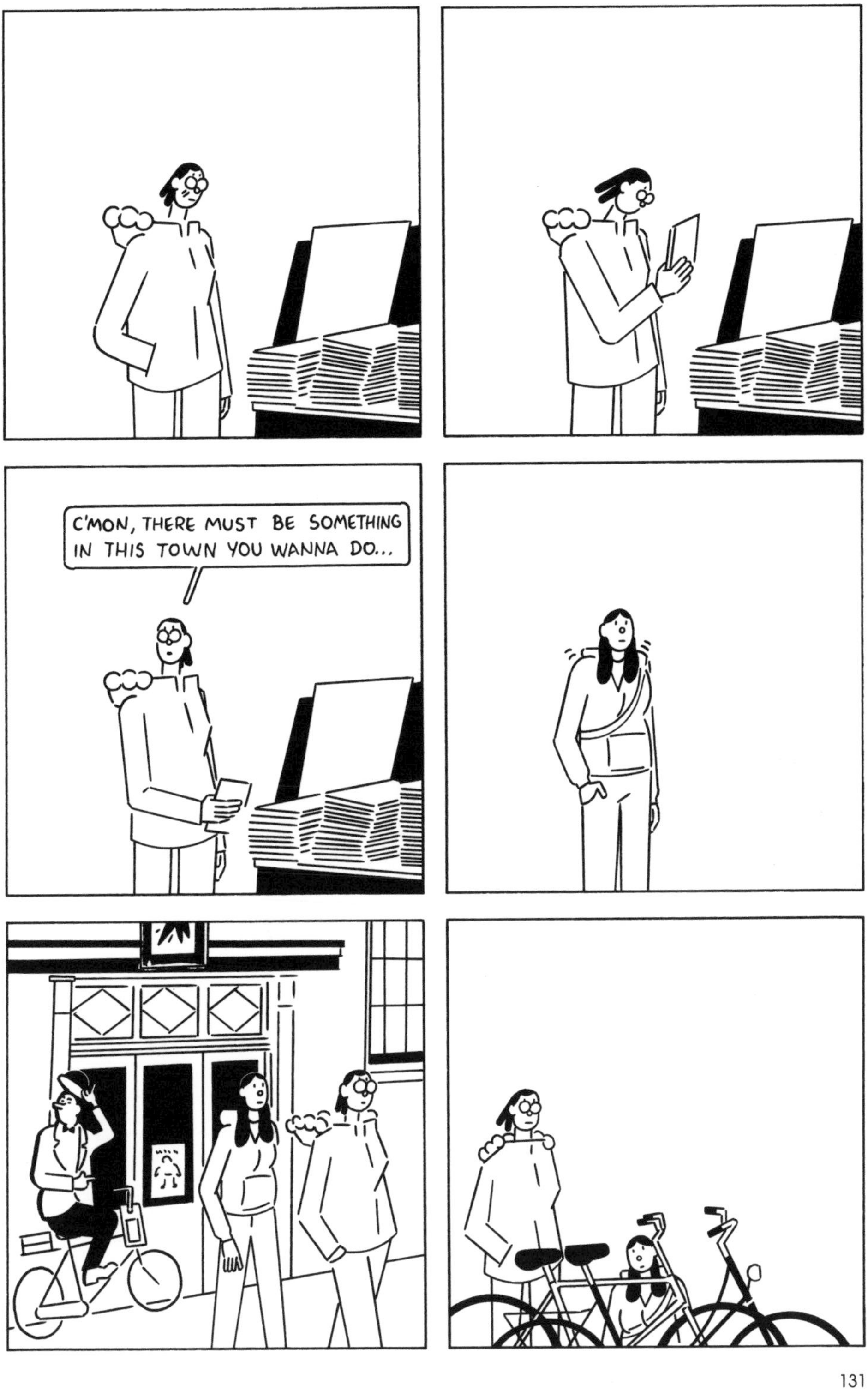
C'MON, THERE MUST BE SOMETHING IN THIS TOWN YOU WANNA DO...

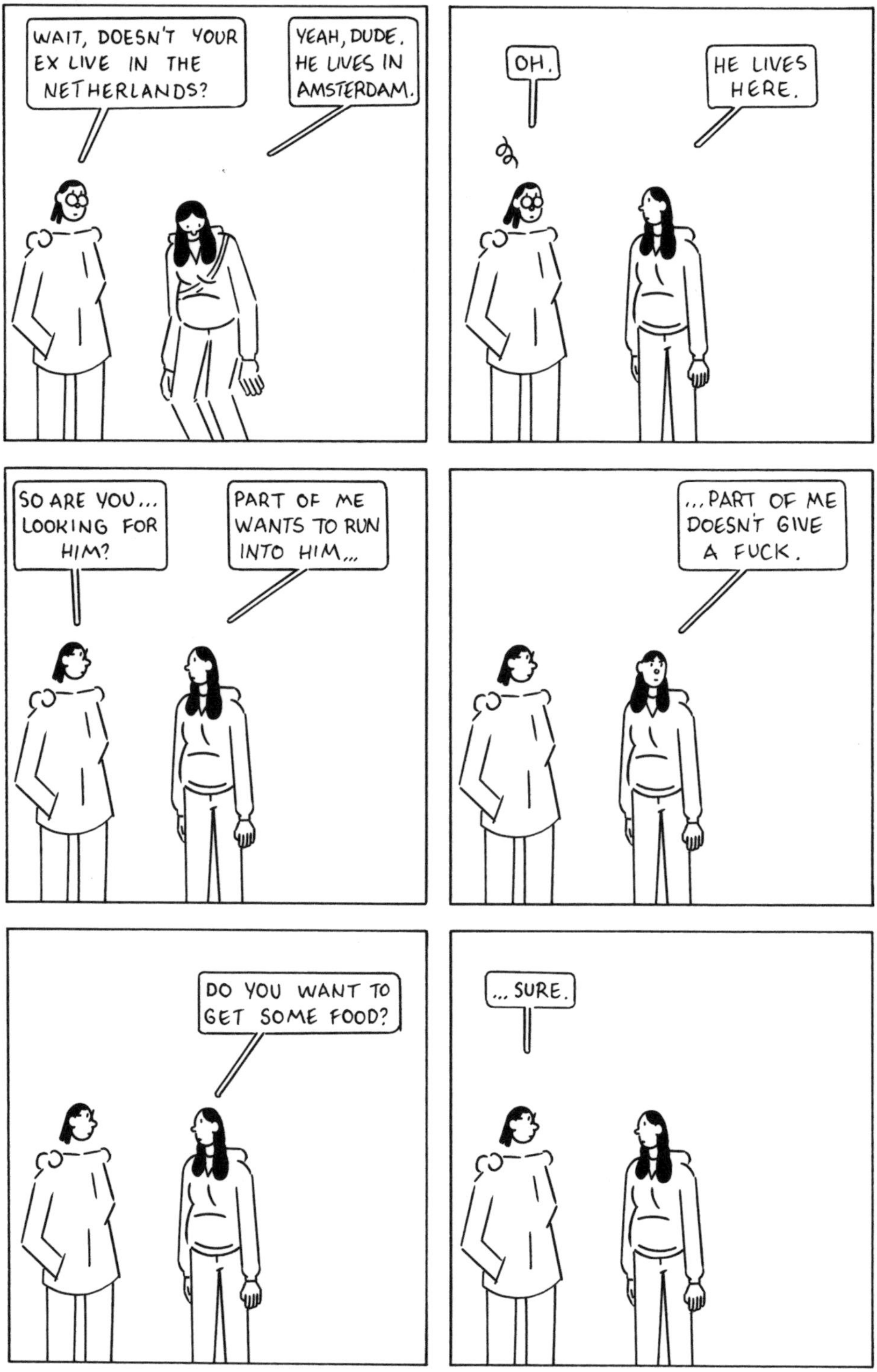
WAIT, DOESN'T YOUR EX LIVE IN THE NETHERLANDS?
YEAH, DUDE. HE LIVES IN AMSTERDAM.
OH.
HE LIVES HERE.
SO ARE YOU... LOOKING FOR HIM?
PART OF ME WANTS TO RUN INTO HIM...
...PART OF ME DOESN'T GIVE A FUCK.
DO YOU WANT TO GET SOME FOOD?
...SURE.

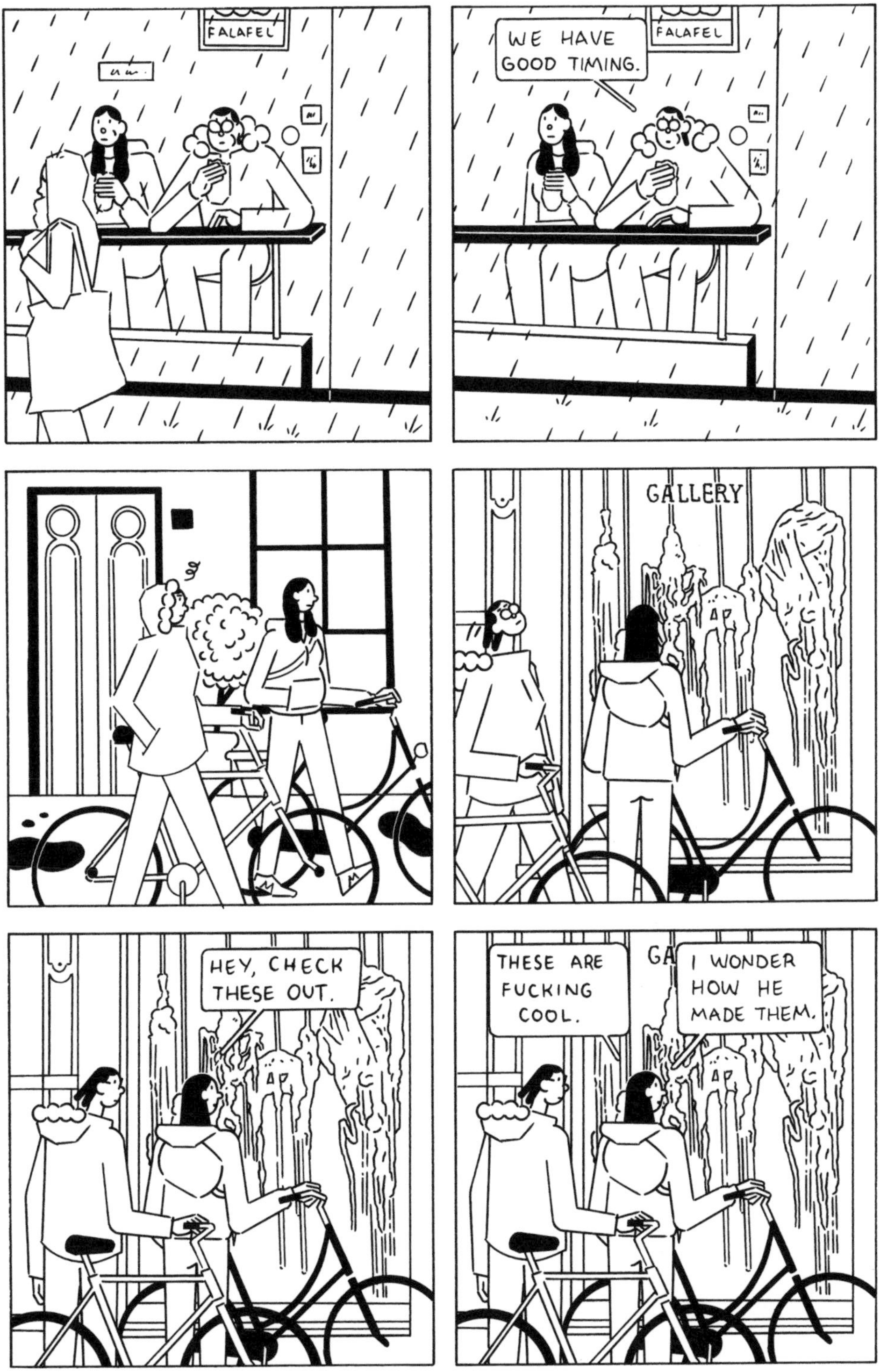
FALAFEL
FALAFEL
WE HAVE GOOD TIMING.
GALLERY
HEY, CHECK THESE OUT.
THESE ARE FUCKING COOL.
I WONDER HOW HE MADE THEM.

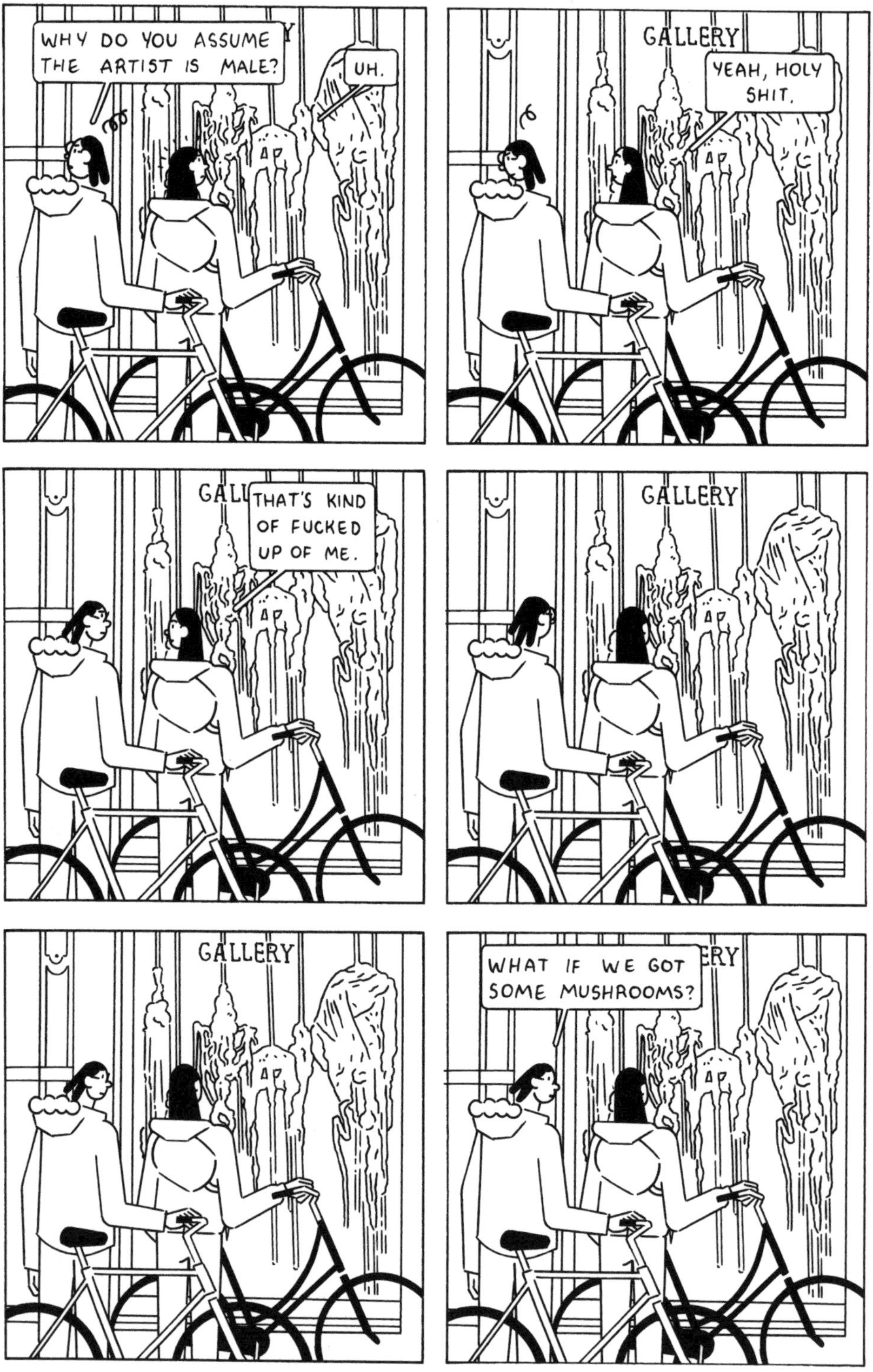
WHY DO YOU ASSUME THE ARTIST IS MALE?
UH.
GALLERY
YEAH, HOLY SHIT.
GALL
THAT'S KIND OF FUCKED UP OF ME.
GALLERY
GALLERY
WHAT IF WE GOT SOME MUSHROOMS?

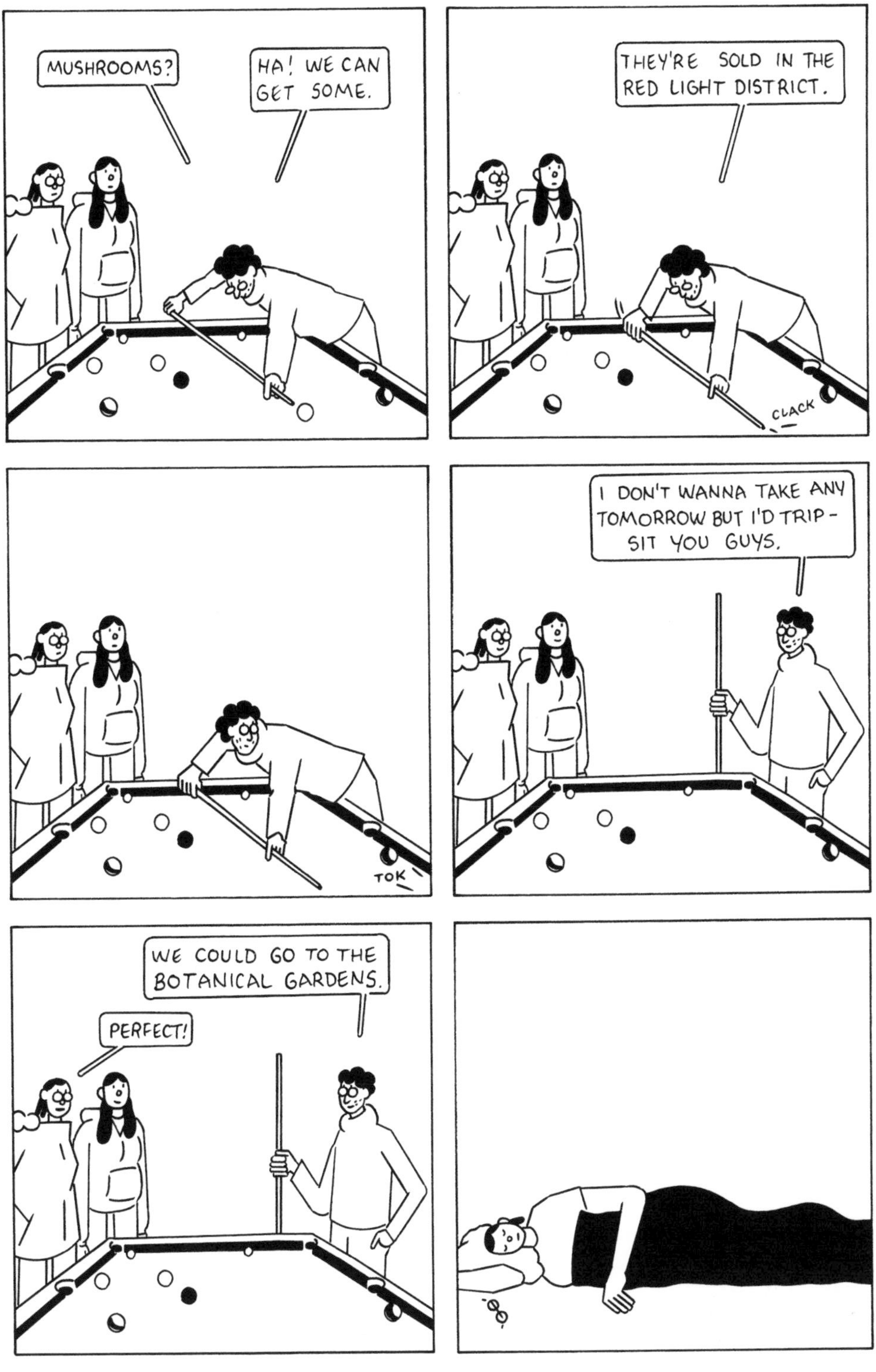
MUSHROOMS?
HA! WE CAN GET SOME.
THEY'RE SOLD IN THE RED LIGHT DISTRICT.
CLACK
TOK
I DON'T WANNA TAKE ANY TOMORROW BUT I'D TRIP-SIT YOU GUYS.
WE COULD GO TO THE BOTANICAL GARDENS.
PERFECT!

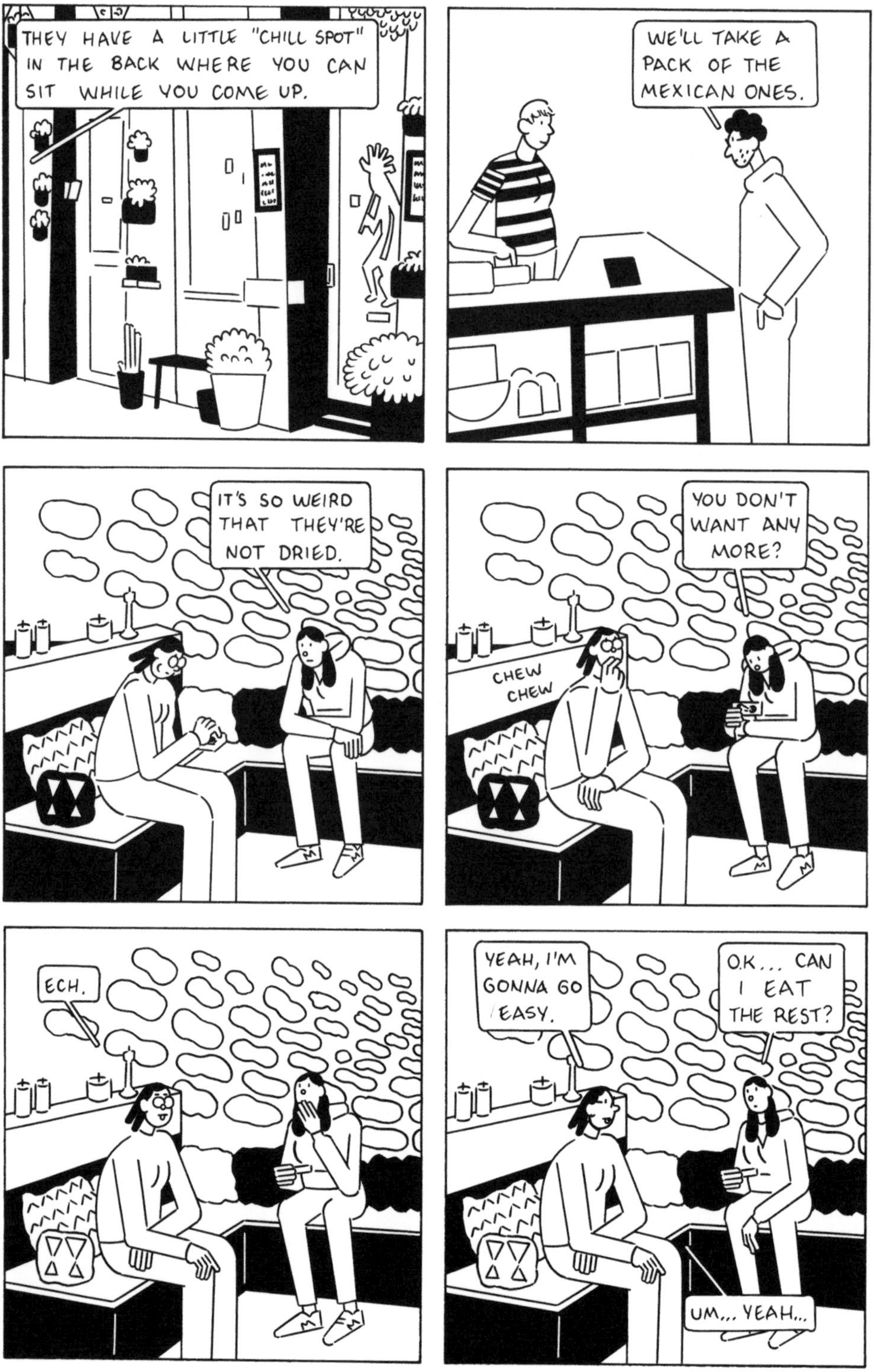
THEY HAVE A LITTLE "CHILL SPOT" IN THE BACK WHERE YOU CAN SIT WHILE YOU COME UP.
WE'LL TAKE A PACK OF THE MEXICAN ONES.
IT'S SO WEIRD THAT THEY'RE NOT DRIED.
CHEW CHEW
YOU DON'T WANT ANY MORE?
ECH.
YEAH, I'M GONNA GO EASY.
O.K... CAN I EAT THE REST?
UM... YEAH...

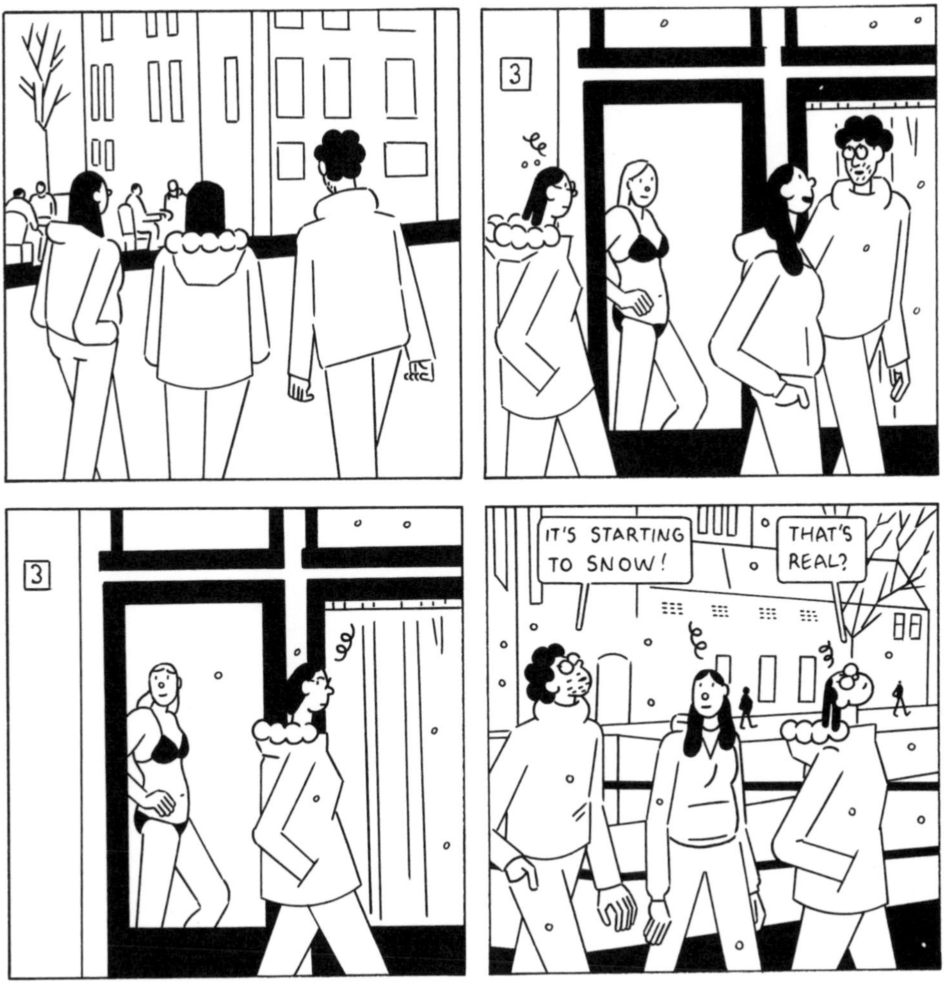
3
3
IT'S STARTING TO SNOW!
THAT'S REAL?

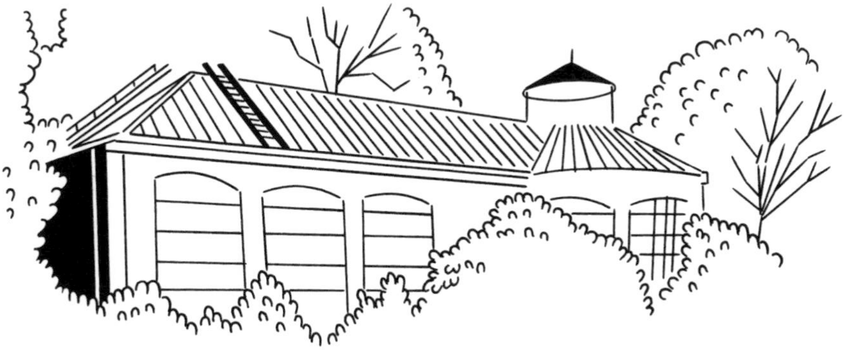

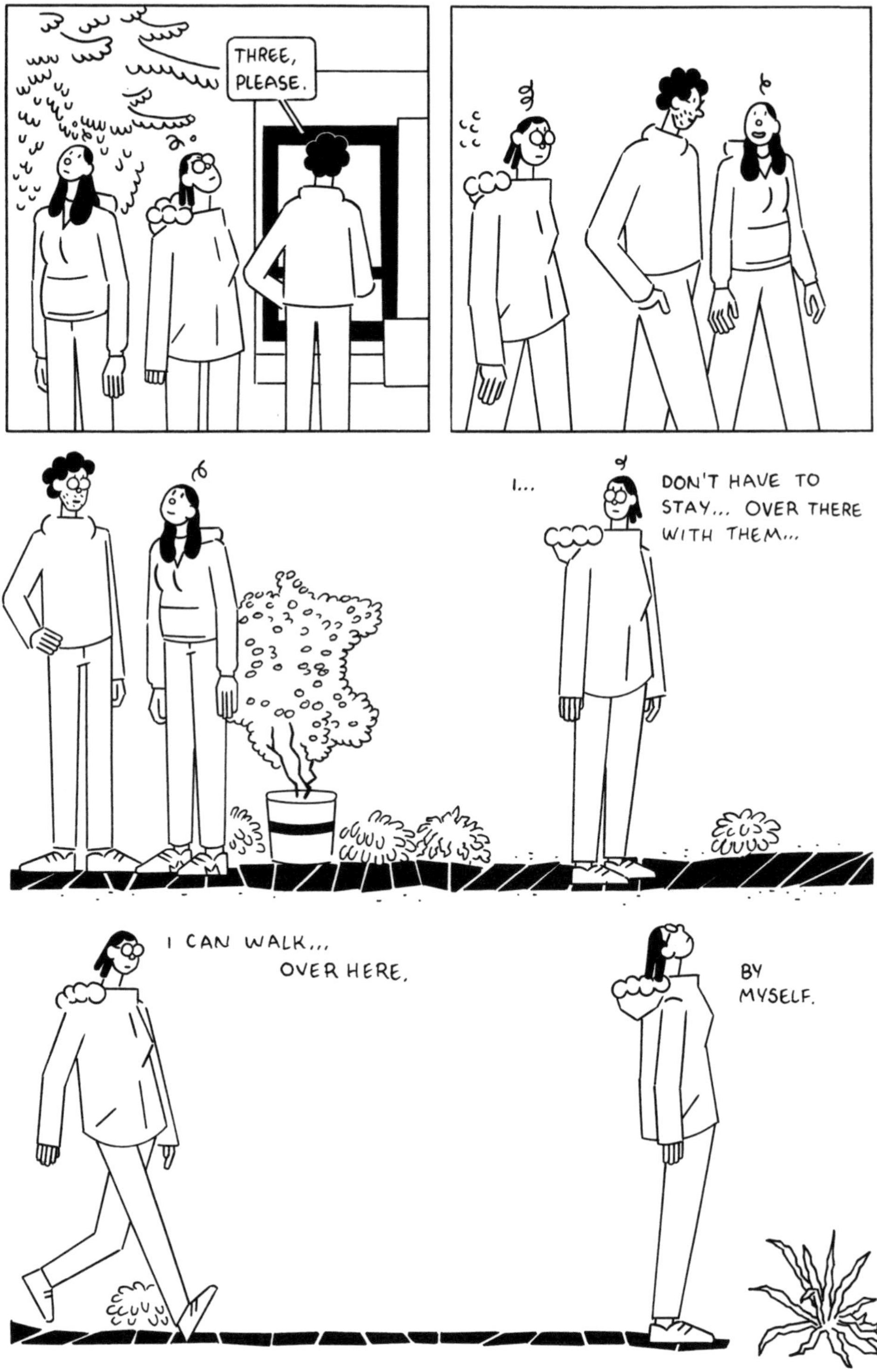

THREE, PLEASE.
I...
DON'T HAVE TO STAY... OVER THERE WITH THEM...
I CAN WALK...
OVER HERE.
BY MYSELF.

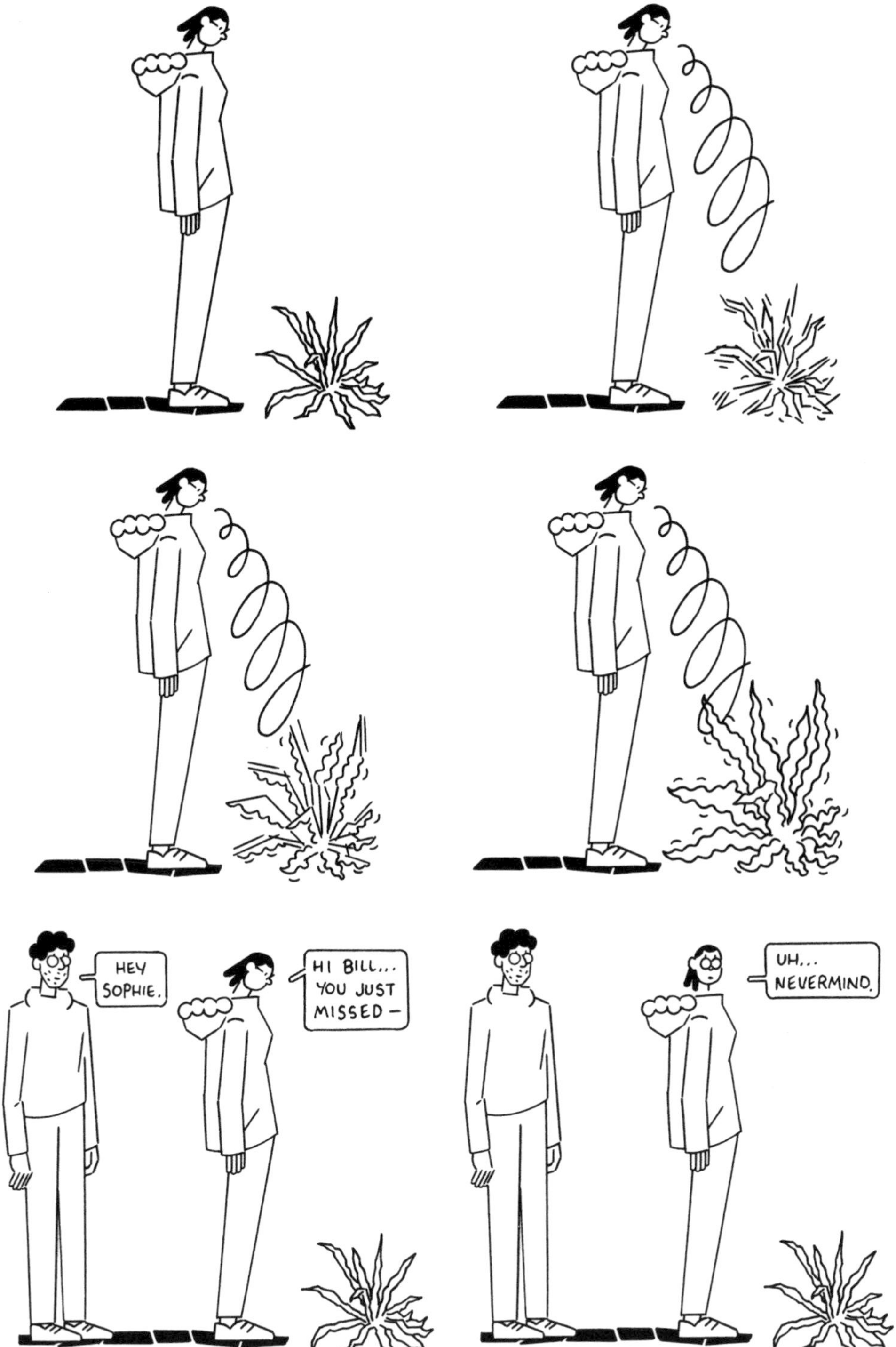
HEY SOPHIE.
HI BILL... YOU JUST MISSED—
UH... NEVERMIND.

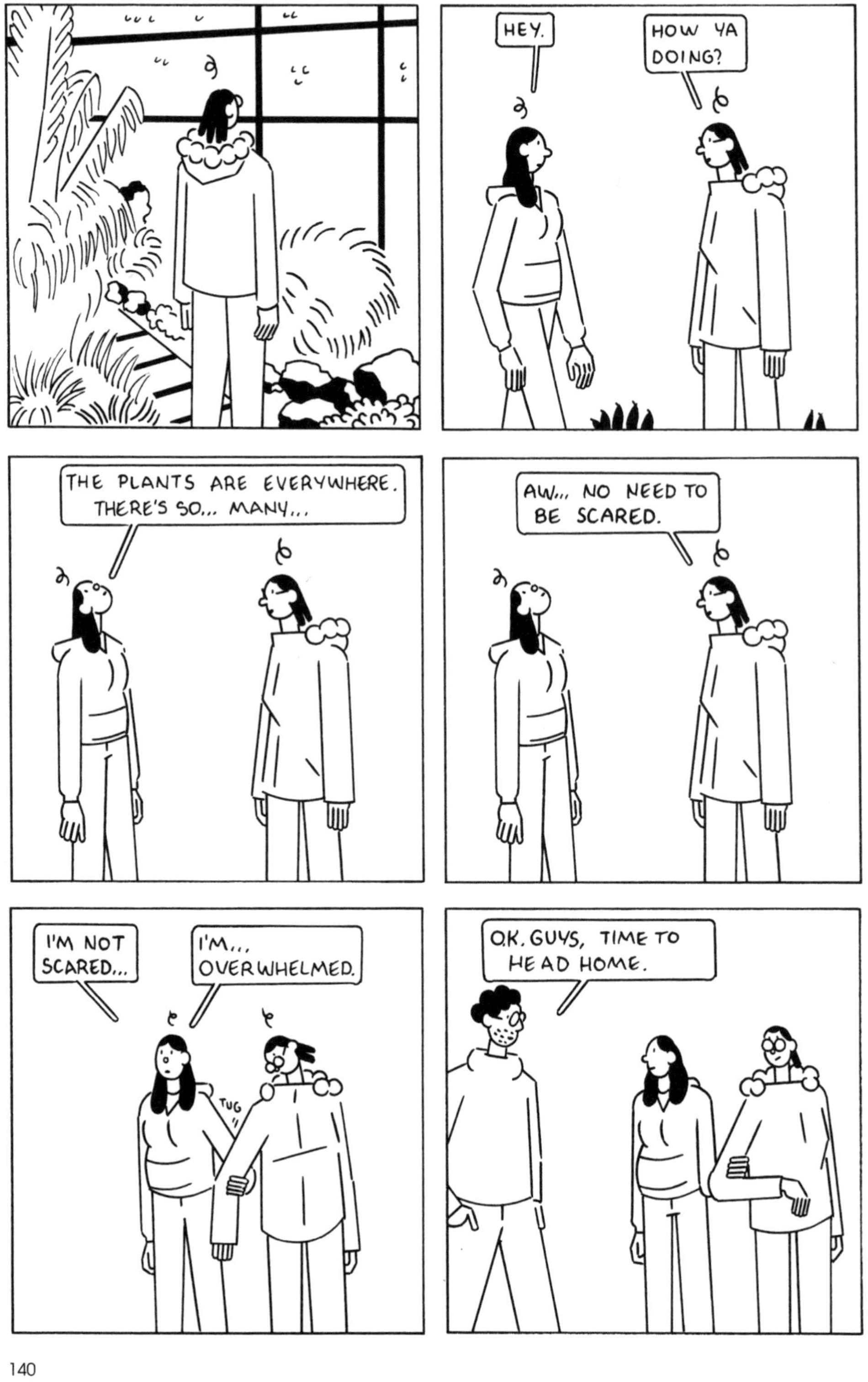
HEY.
HOW YA DOING?
THE PLANTS ARE EVERYWHERE. THERE'S SO... MANY...
AW... NO NEED TO BE SCARED.
I'M NOT SCARED...
I'M... OVERWHELMED.
TUG
O.K. GUYS, TIME TO HEAD HOME.

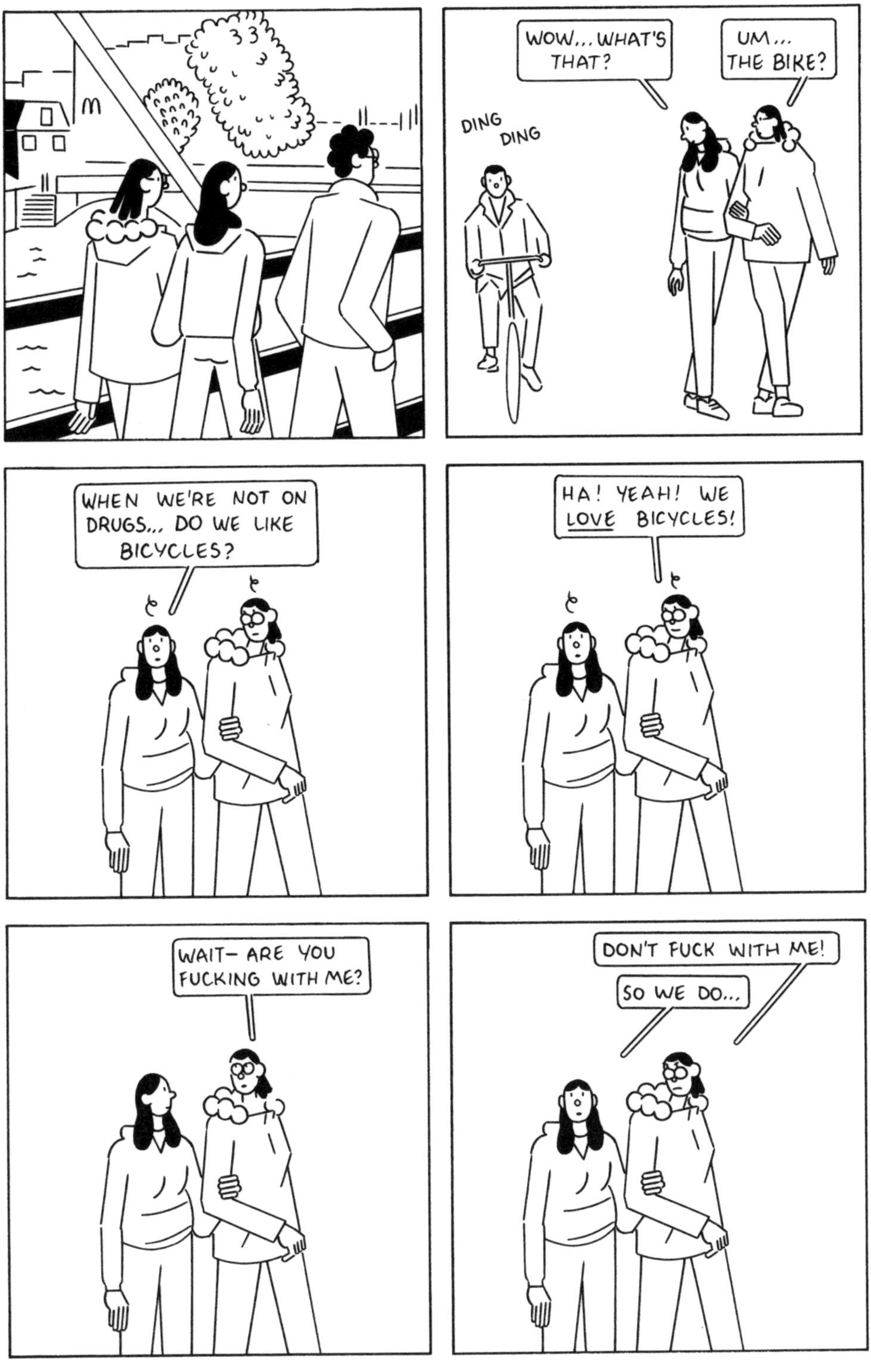
DING
DING
WOW... WHAT'S THAT?
UM... THE BIKE?
WHEN WE'RE NOT ON DRUGS... DO WE LIKE BICYCLES?
HA! YEAH! WE LOVE BICYCLES!
WAIT- ARE YOU FUCKING WITH ME?
DON'T FUCK WITH ME!
SO WE DO...

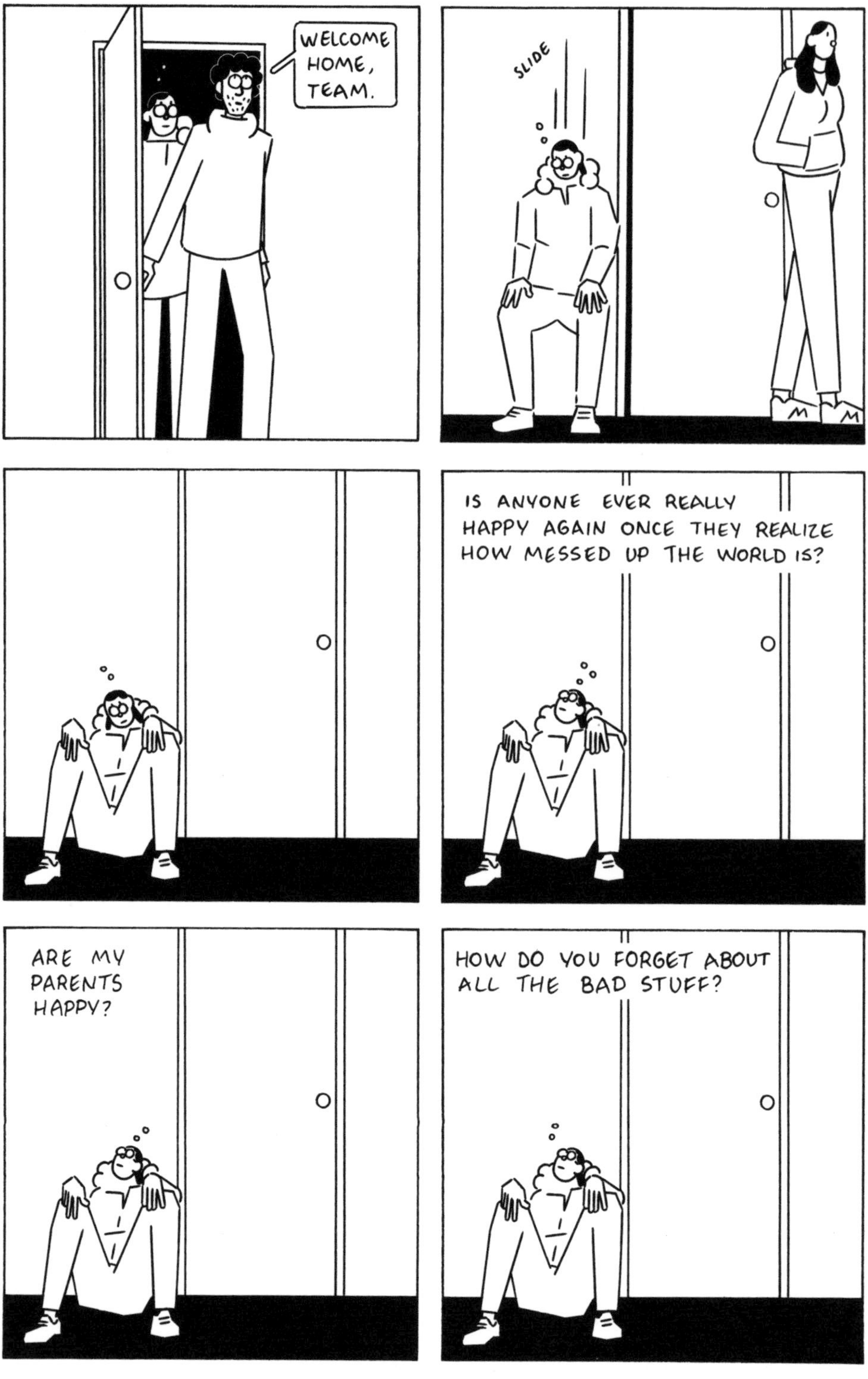
WELCOME HOME, TEAM.
SLIDE
IS ANYONE EVER REALLY HAPPY AGAIN ONCE THEY REALIZE HOW MESSED UP THE WORLD IS?
ARE MY PARENTS HAPPY?
HOW DO YOU FORGET ABOUT ALL THE BAD STUFF?

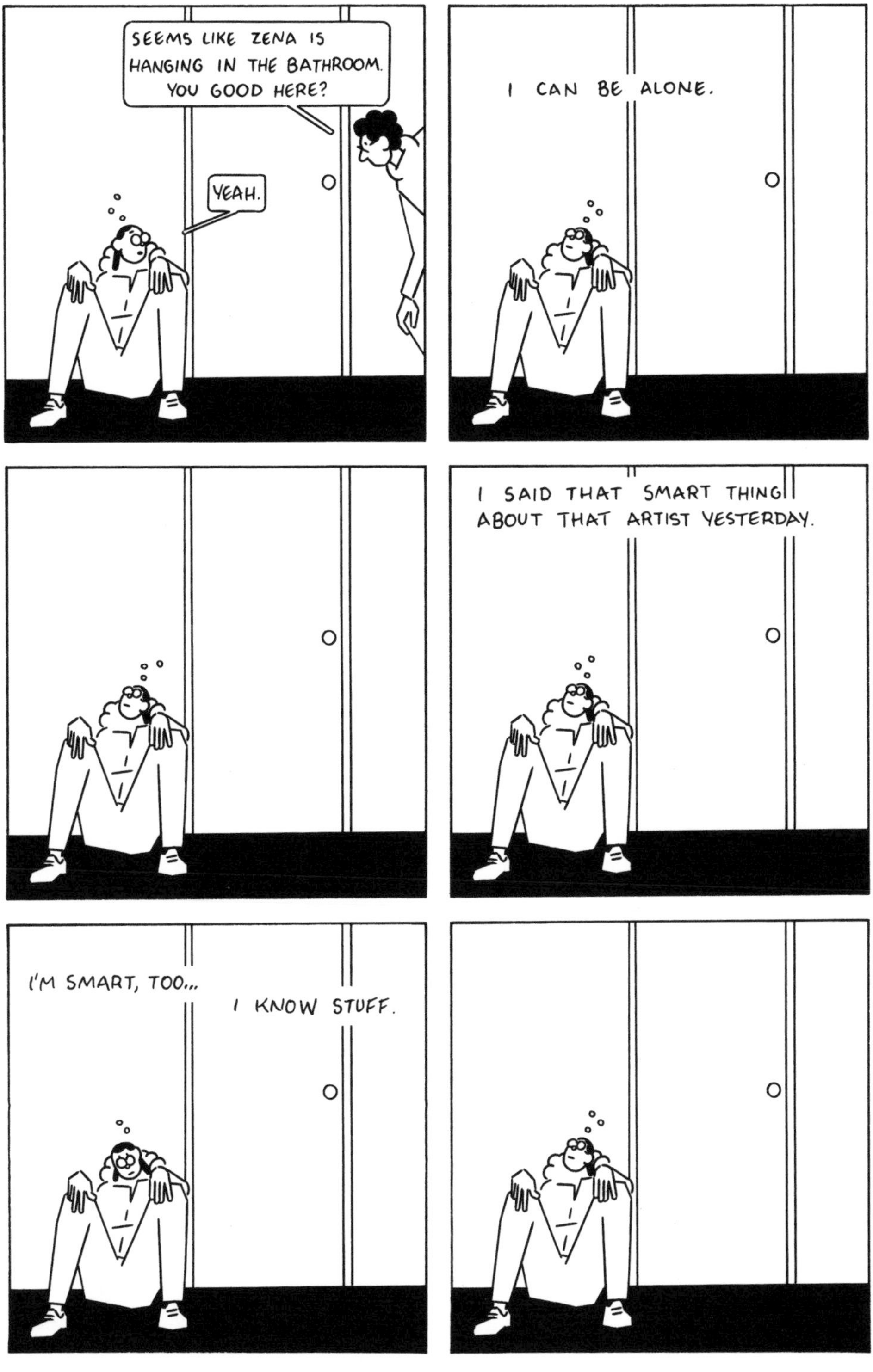
SEEMS LIKE ZENA IS HANGING IN THE BATHROOM. YOU GOOD HERE?
YEAH.
I CAN BE ALONE.
I SAID THAT SMART THING ABOUT THAT ARTIST YESTERDAY.
I'M SMART, TOO...
I KNOW STUFF.

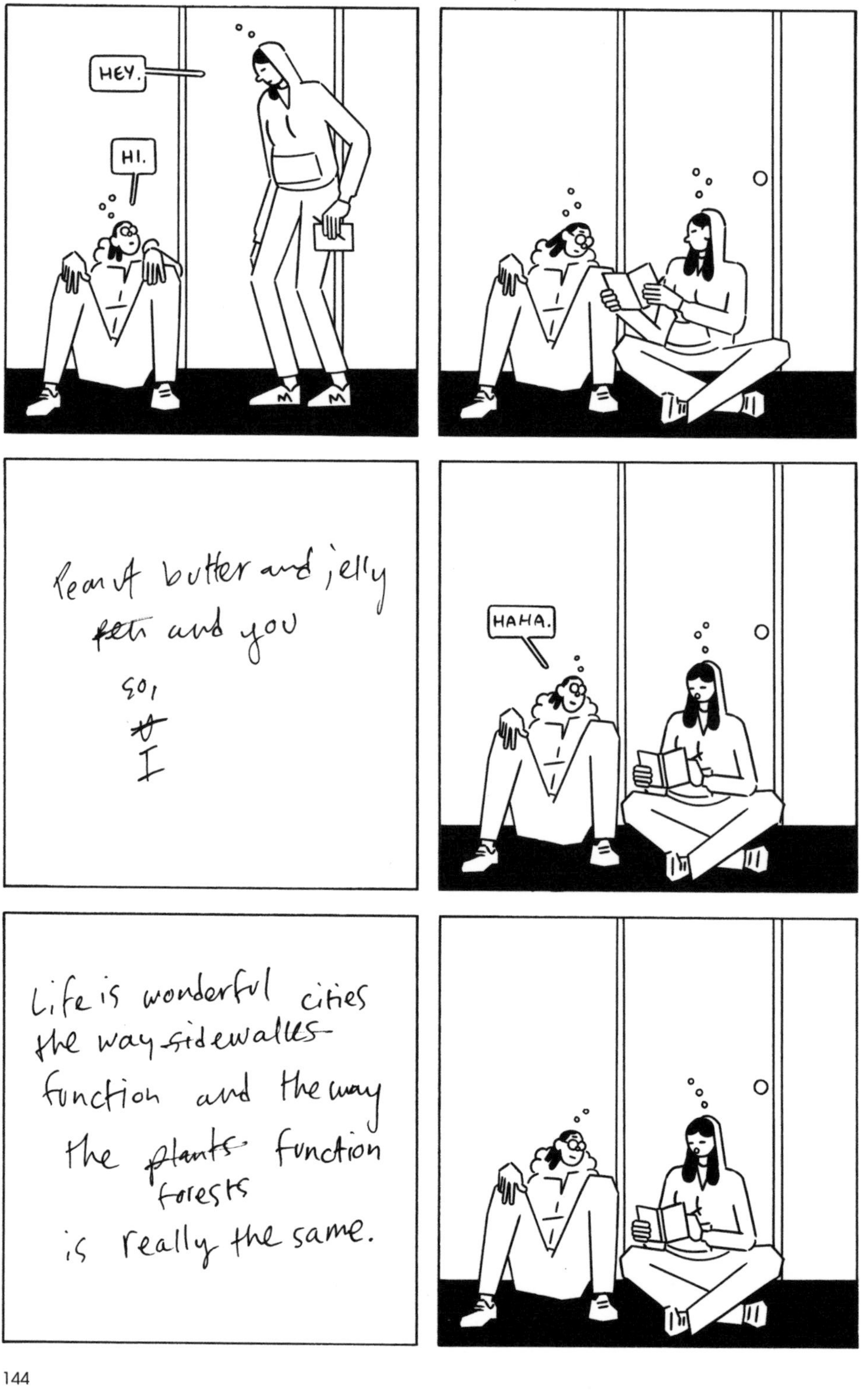
HEY.
HI.
Peanut butter and jelly
and you
I
HAHA.
Life is wonderful cities
the way ~~sidewalks~~
function and the way
the ~~plants~~ function
forests
is really the same.

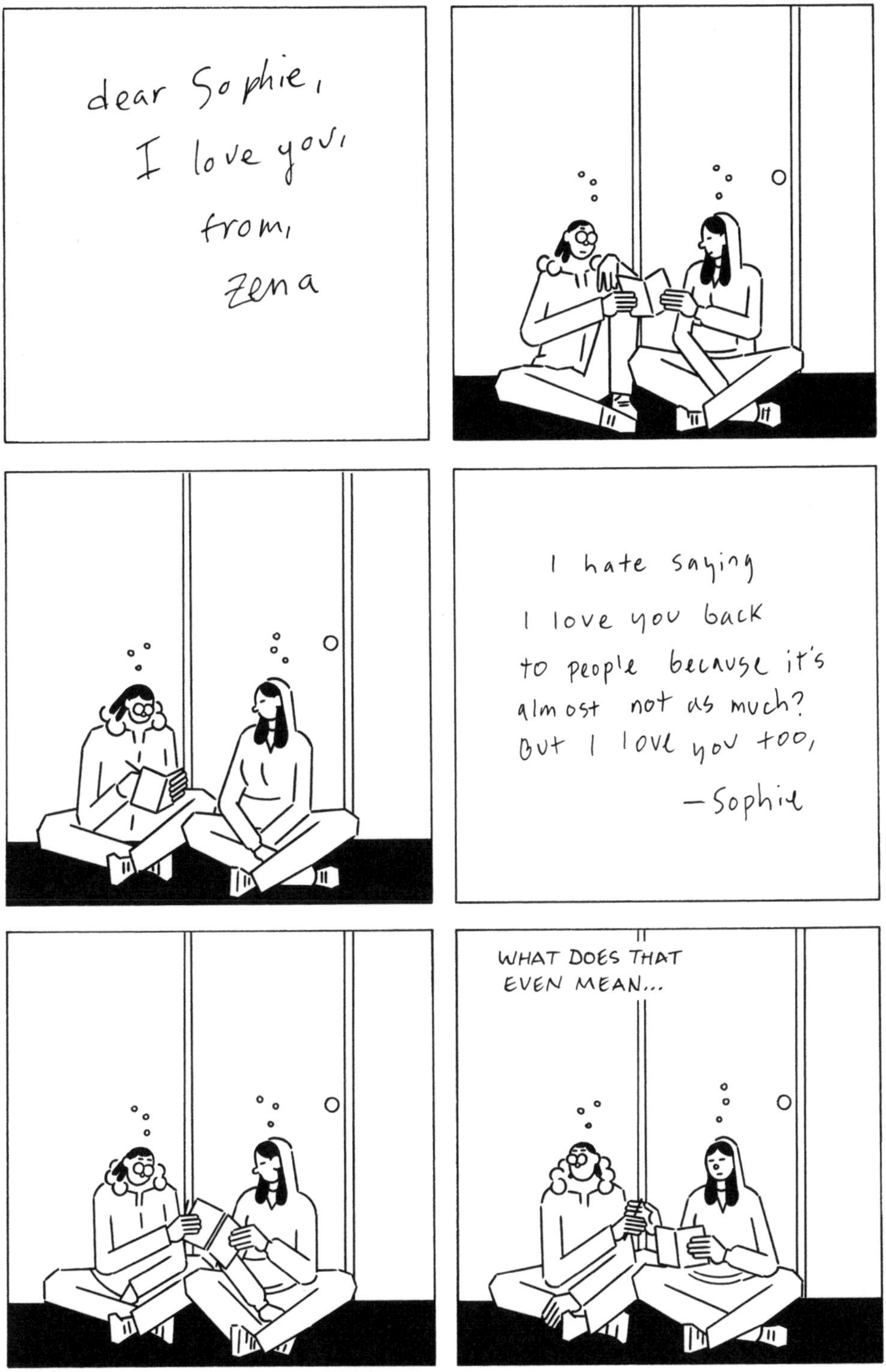
dear Sophie,
I love you,
from,
Zena
I hate saying
I love you back
to people because it's
almost not as much?
But I love you too,
—Sophie
WHAT DOES THAT
EVEN MEAN...

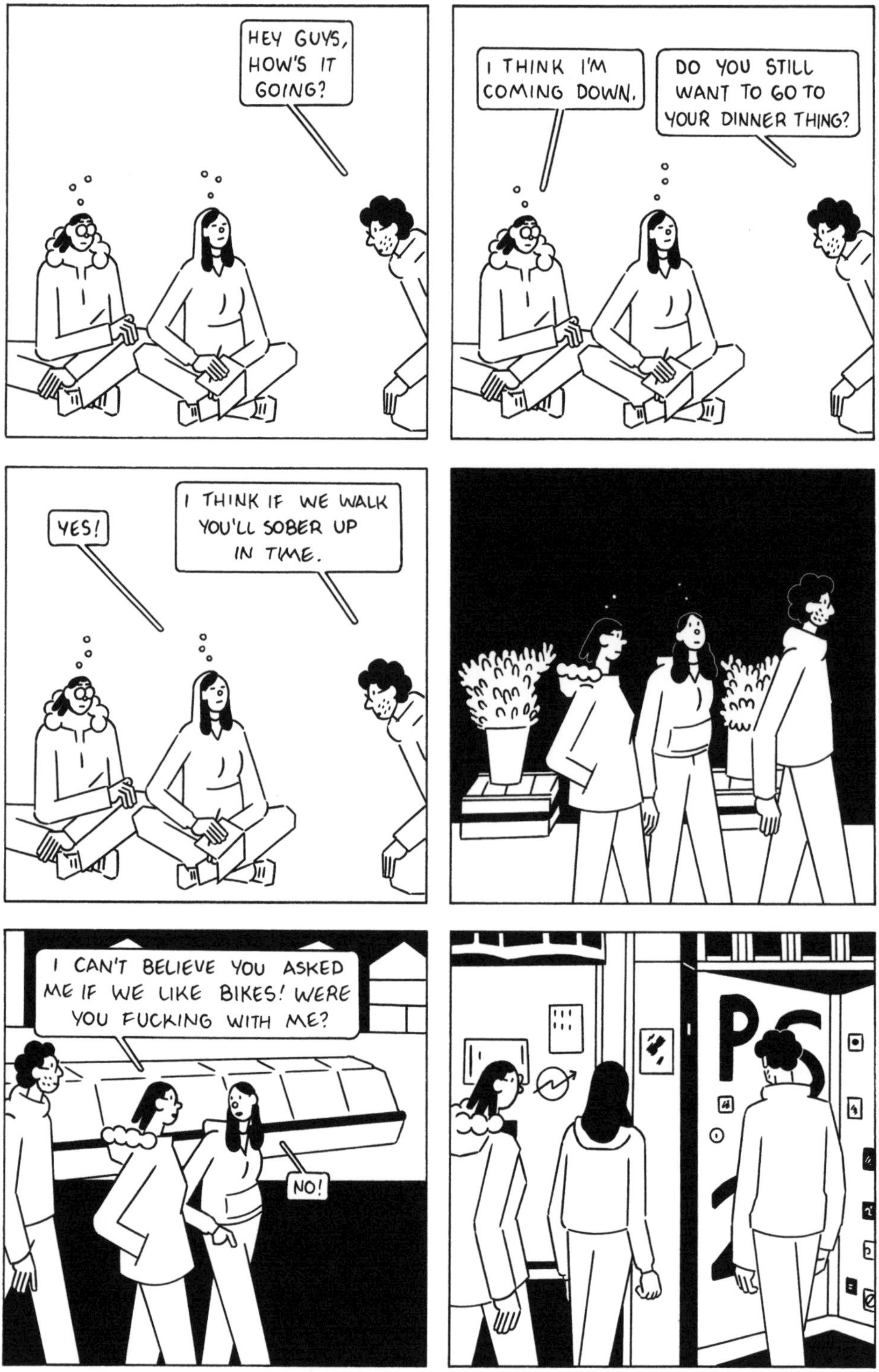
HEY GUYS, HOW'S IT GOING?
I THINK I'M COMING DOWN.
DO YOU STILL WANT TO GO TO YOUR DINNER THING?
YES!
I THINK IF WE WALK YOU'LL SOBER UP IN TIME.
I CAN'T BELIEVE YOU ASKED ME IF WE LIKE BIKES! WERE YOU FUCKING WITH ME?
NO!

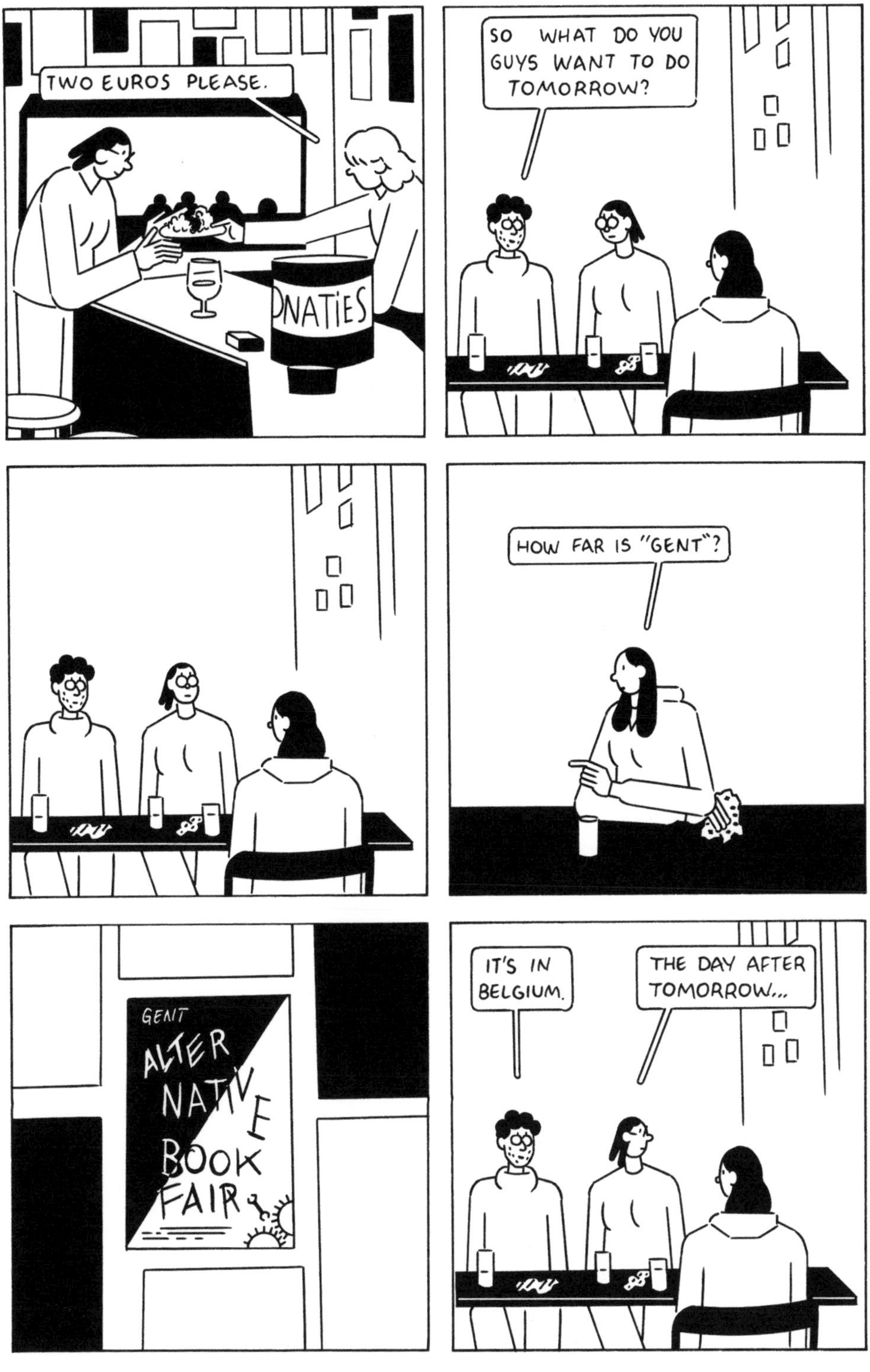
TWO EUROS PLEASE.
DONATIES
SO WHAT DO YOU GUYS WANT TO DO TOMORROW?
HOW FAR IS "GENT"?
GENT
ALTERNATIVE BOOK FAIR
IT'S IN BELGIUM.
THE DAY AFTER TOMORROW...

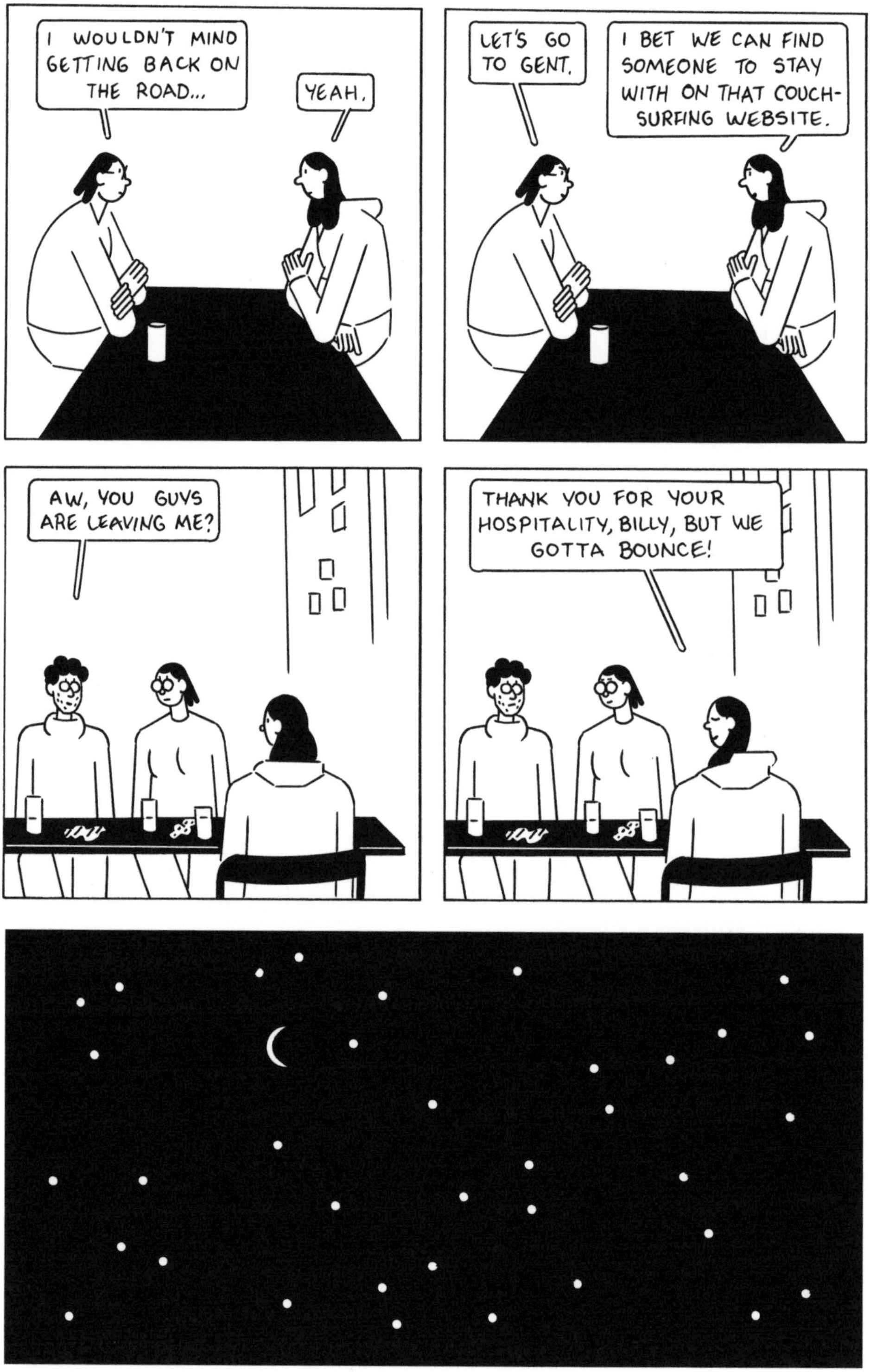
I WOULDN'T MIND GETTING BACK ON THE ROAD...
YEAH.
LET'S GO TO GENT.
I BET WE CAN FIND SOMEONE TO STAY WITH ON THAT COUCH-SURFING WEBSITE.
AW, YOU GUYS ARE LEAVING ME?
THANK YOU FOR YOUR HOSPITALITY, BILLY, BUT WE GOTTA BOUNCE!

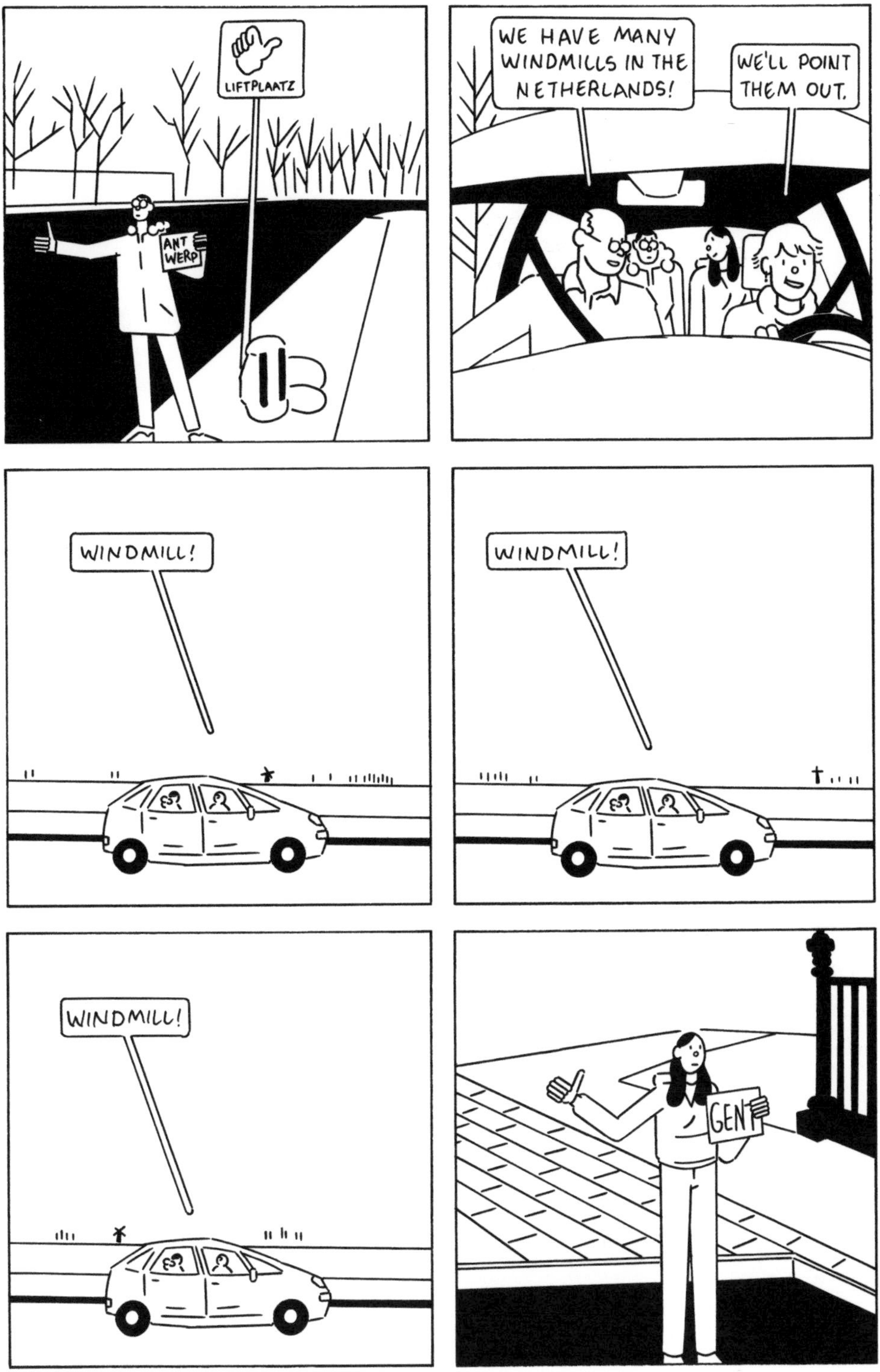
LIFTPLAATZ
ANT WERP
WE HAVE MANY WINDMILLS IN THE NETHERLANDS!
WE'LL POINT THEM OUT.
WINDMILL!
WINDMILL!
WINDMILL!
GENT

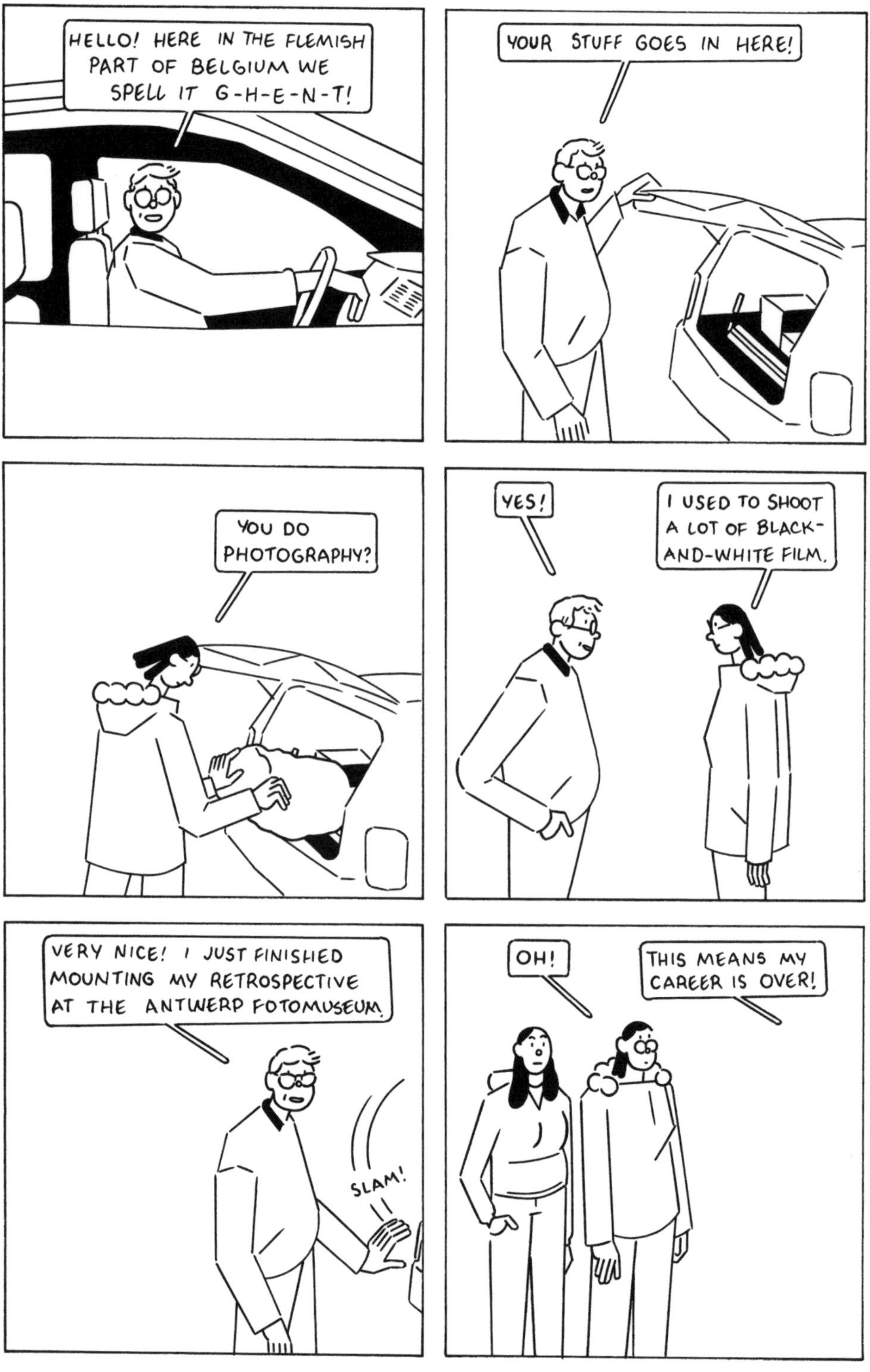
HELLO! HERE IN THE FLEMISH PART OF BELGIUM WE SPELL IT G-H-E-N-T!
YOUR STUFF GOES IN HERE!
YOU DO PHOTOGRAPHY?
YES!
I USED TO SHOOT A LOT OF BLACK-AND-WHITE FILM.
VERY NICE! I JUST FINISHED MOUNTING MY RETROSPECTIVE AT THE ANTWERP FOTOMUSEUM.
SLAM!
OH!
THIS MEANS MY CAREER IS OVER!

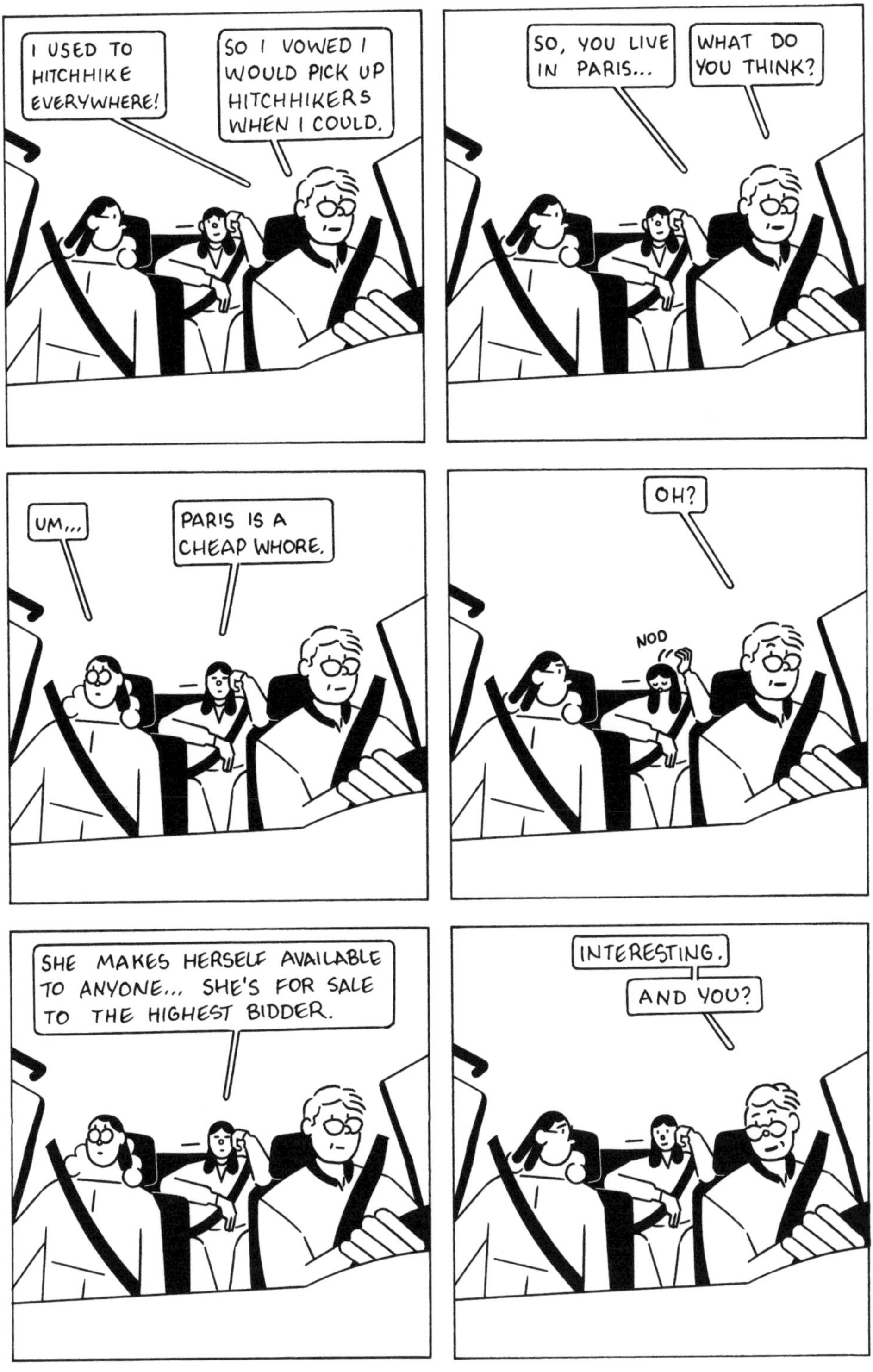
I USED TO HITCHHIKE EVERYWHERE!
SO I VOWED I WOULD PICK UP HITCHHIKERS WHEN I COULD.
SO, YOU LIVE IN PARIS...
WHAT DO YOU THINK?
UM,,,
PARIS IS A CHEAP WHORE.
OH?
NOD
SHE MAKES HERSELF AVAILABLE TO ANYONE... SHE'S FOR SALE TO THE HIGHEST BIDDER.
INTERESTING.
AND YOU?

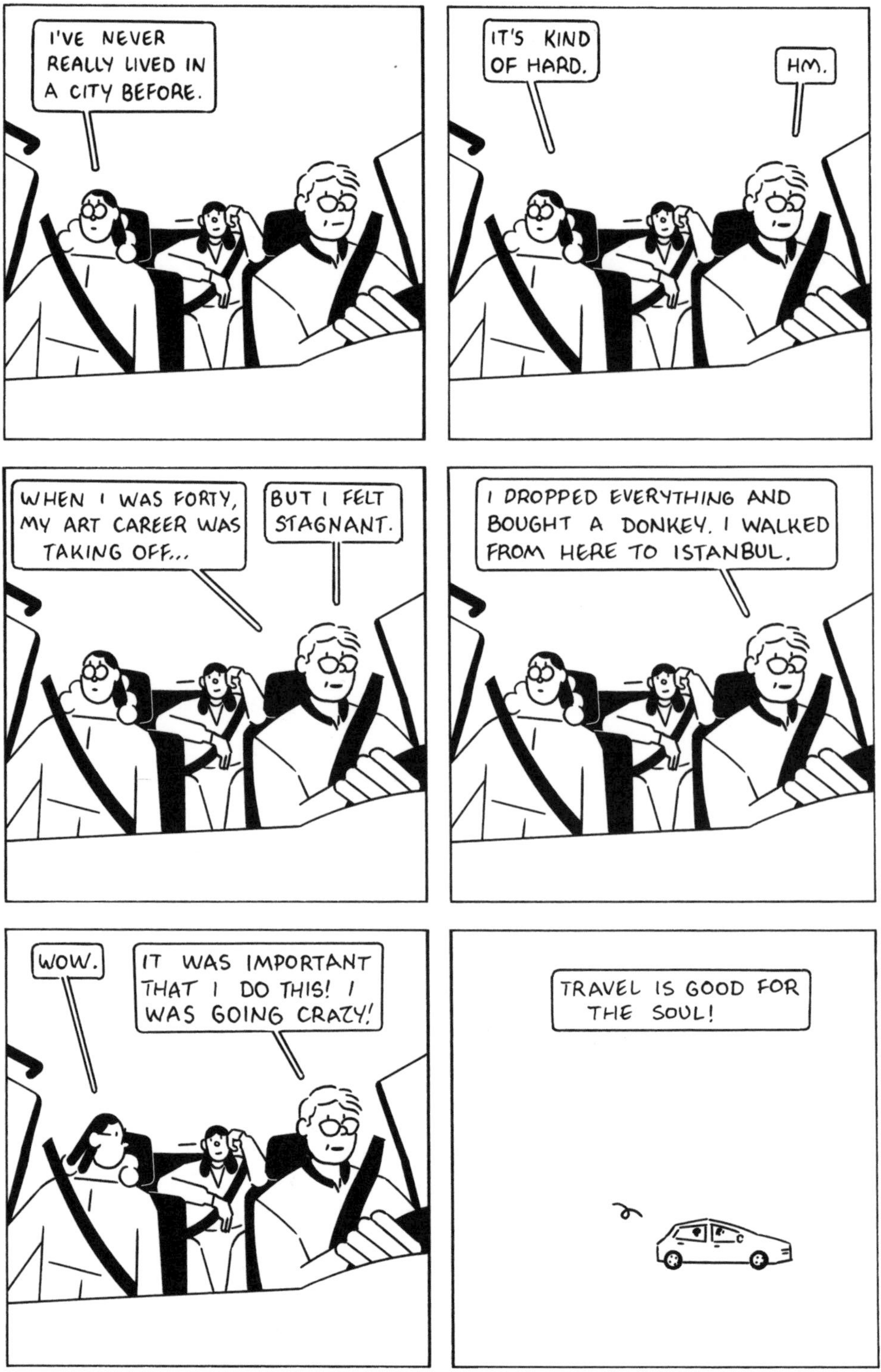
I'VE NEVER REALLY LIVED IN A CITY BEFORE.
IT'S KIND OF HARD.
HM.
WHEN I WAS FORTY, MY ART CAREER WAS TAKING OFF...
BUT I FELT STAGNANT.
I DROPPED EVERYTHING AND BOUGHT A DONKEY. I WALKED FROM HERE TO ISTANBUL.
WOW.
IT WAS IMPORTANT THAT I DO THIS! I WAS GOING CRAZY!
TRAVEL IS GOOD FOR THE SOUL!

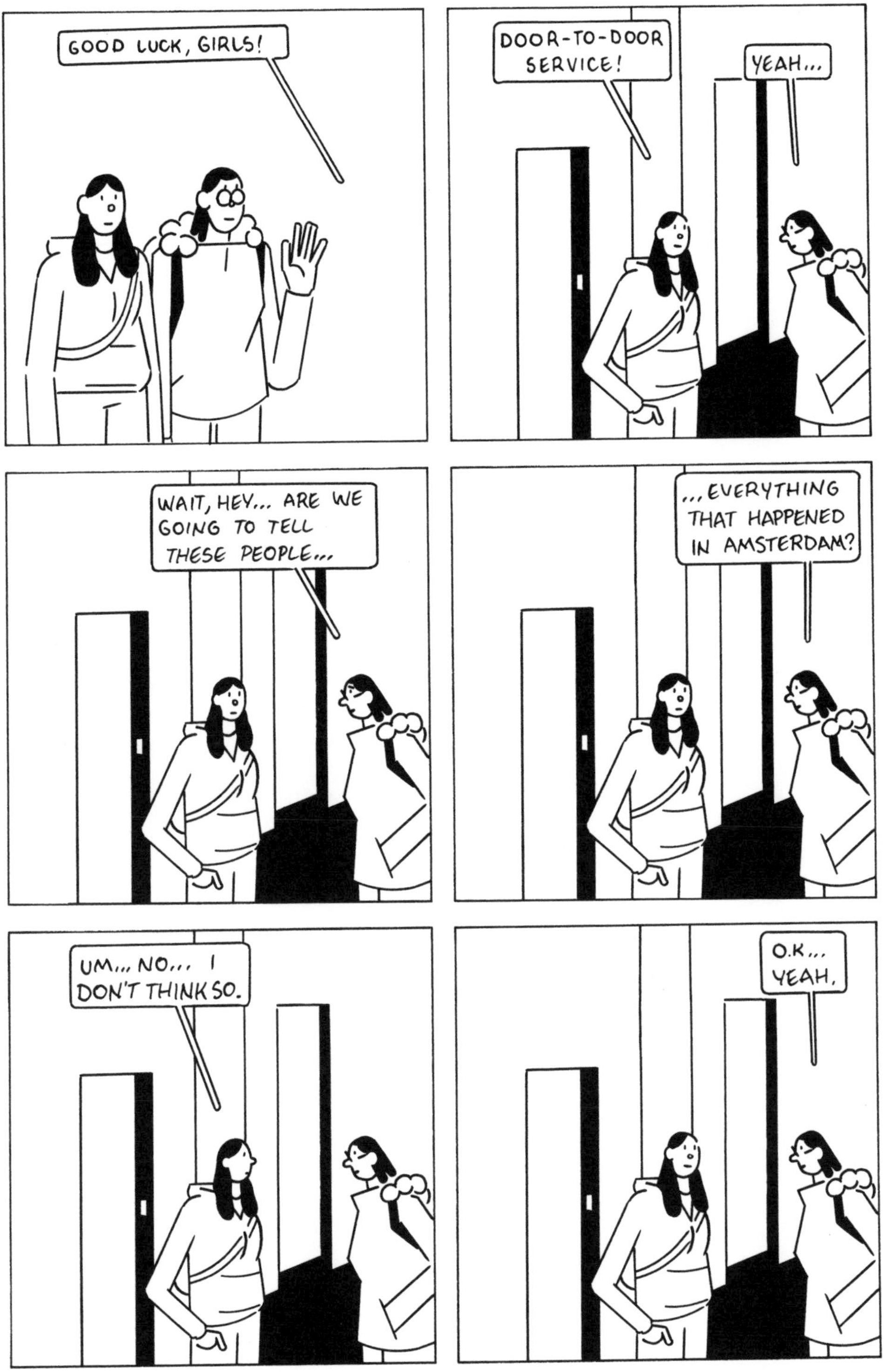
GOOD LUCK, GIRLS!
DOOR-TO-DOOR SERVICE!
YEAH...
WAIT, HEY... ARE WE GOING TO TELL THESE PEOPLE...
...EVERYTHING THAT HAPPENED IN AMSTERDAM?
UM... NO... I DON'T THINK SO.
O.K... YEAH.

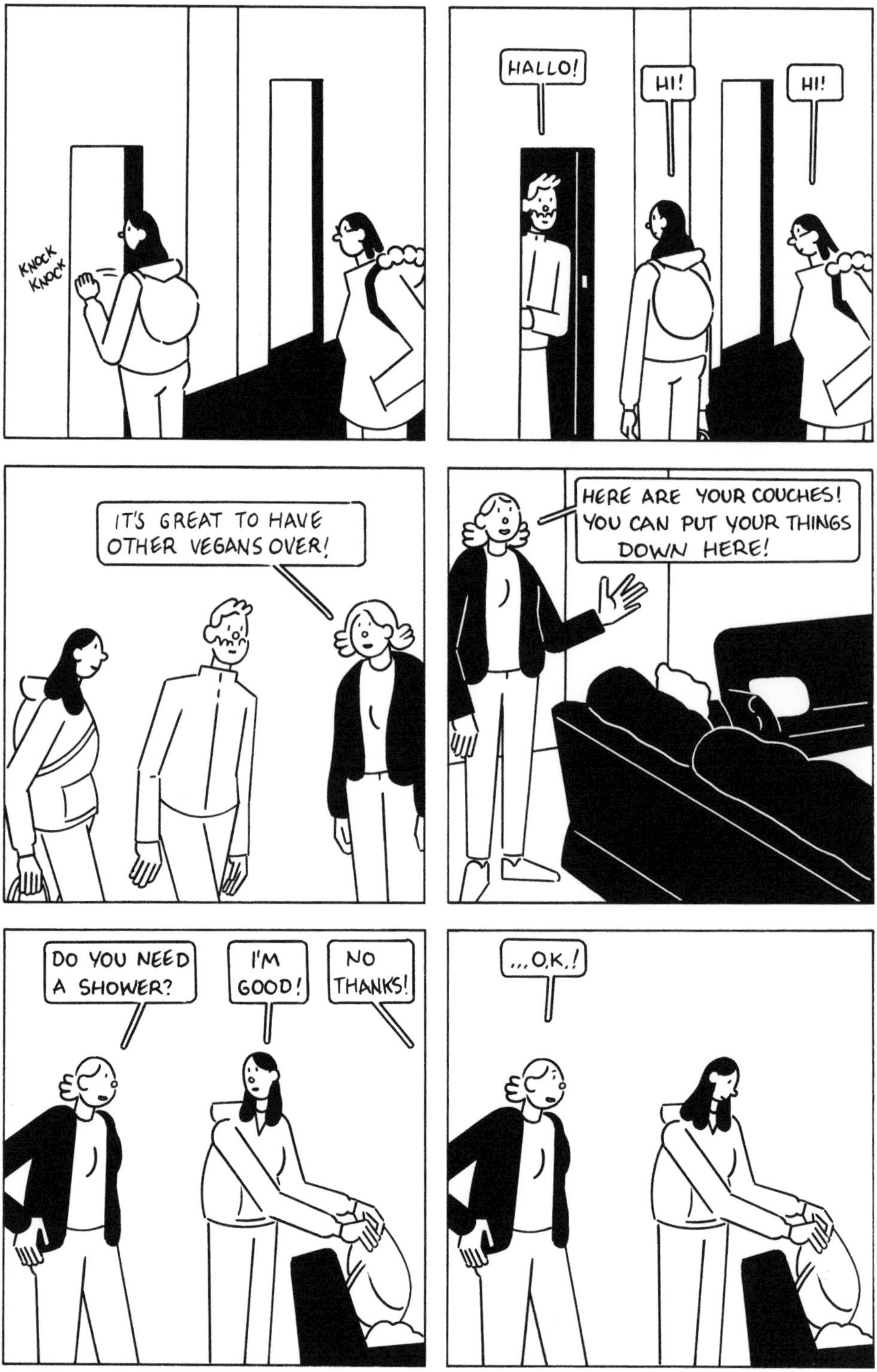
KNOCK KNOCK
HALLO!
HI!
HI!
IT'S GREAT TO HAVE OTHER VEGANS OVER!
HERE ARE YOUR COUCHES! YOU CAN PUT YOUR THINGS DOWN HERE!
DO YOU NEED A SHOWER?
I'M GOOD!
NO THANKS!
...O.K.!

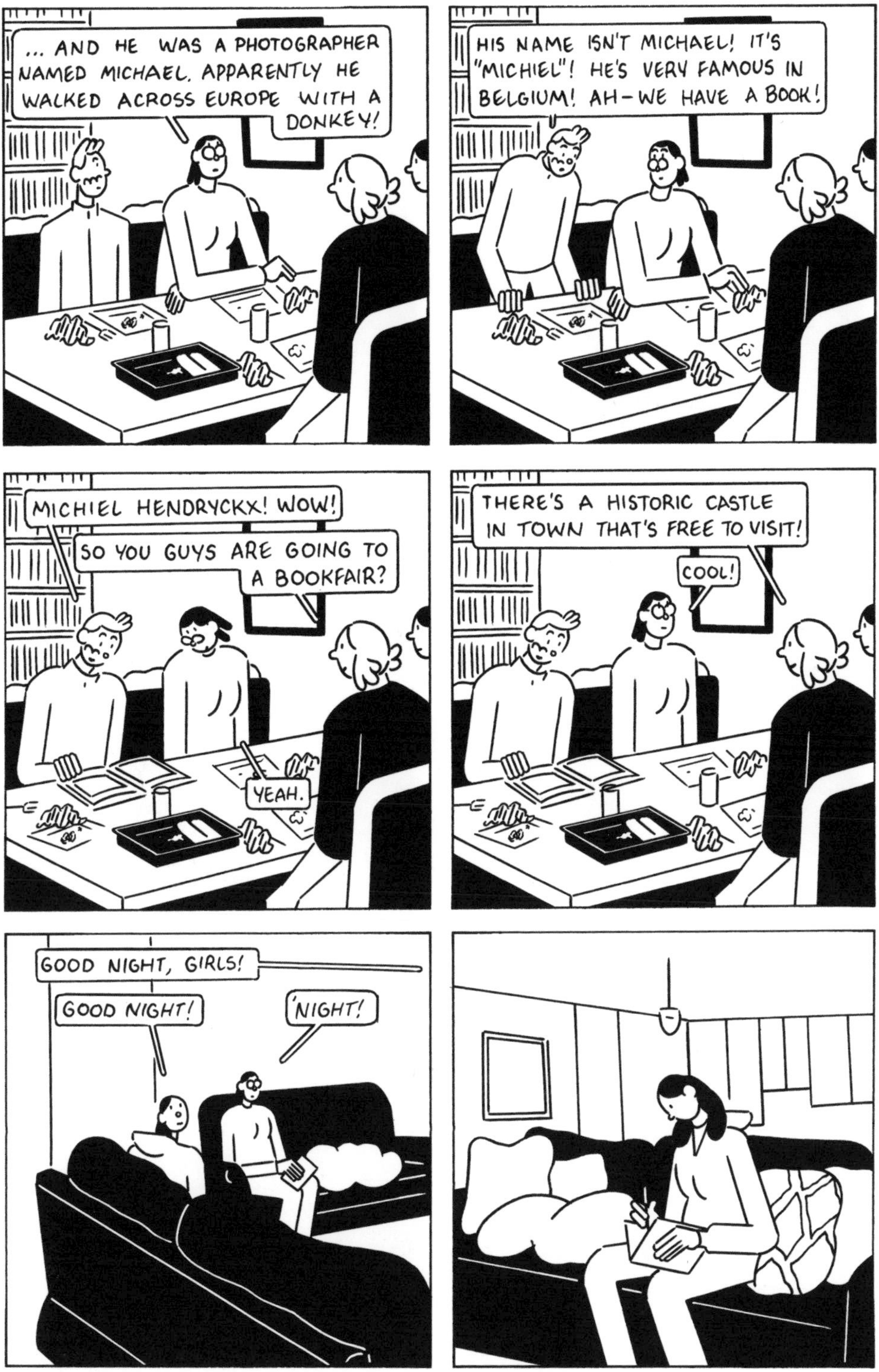
... AND HE WAS A PHOTOGRAPHER NAMED MICHAEL. APPARENTLY HE WALKED ACROSS EUROPE WITH A DONKEY!
HIS NAME ISN'T MICHAEL! IT'S "MICHIEL"! HE'S VERY FAMOUS IN BELGIUM! AH—WE HAVE A BOOK!
MICHIEL HENDRYCKX! WOW!
SO YOU GUYS ARE GOING TO A BOOKFAIR?
YEAH.
THERE'S A HISTORIC CASTLE IN TOWN THAT'S FREE TO VISIT!
COOL!
GOOD NIGHT, GIRLS!
GOOD NIGHT!
'NIGHT!

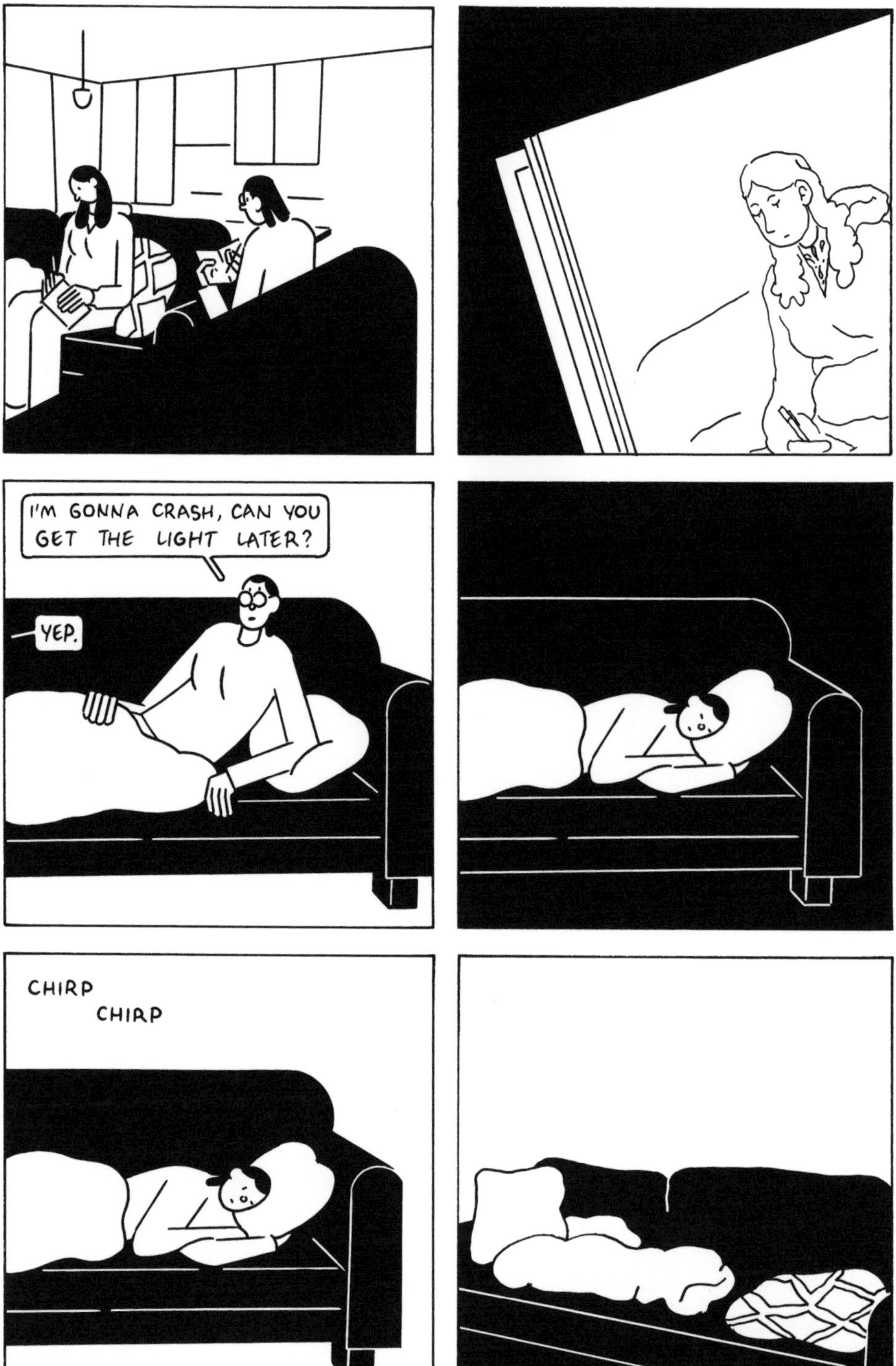
I'M GONNA CRASH, CAN YOU GET THE LIGHT LATER?
YEP.
CHIRP
CHIRP

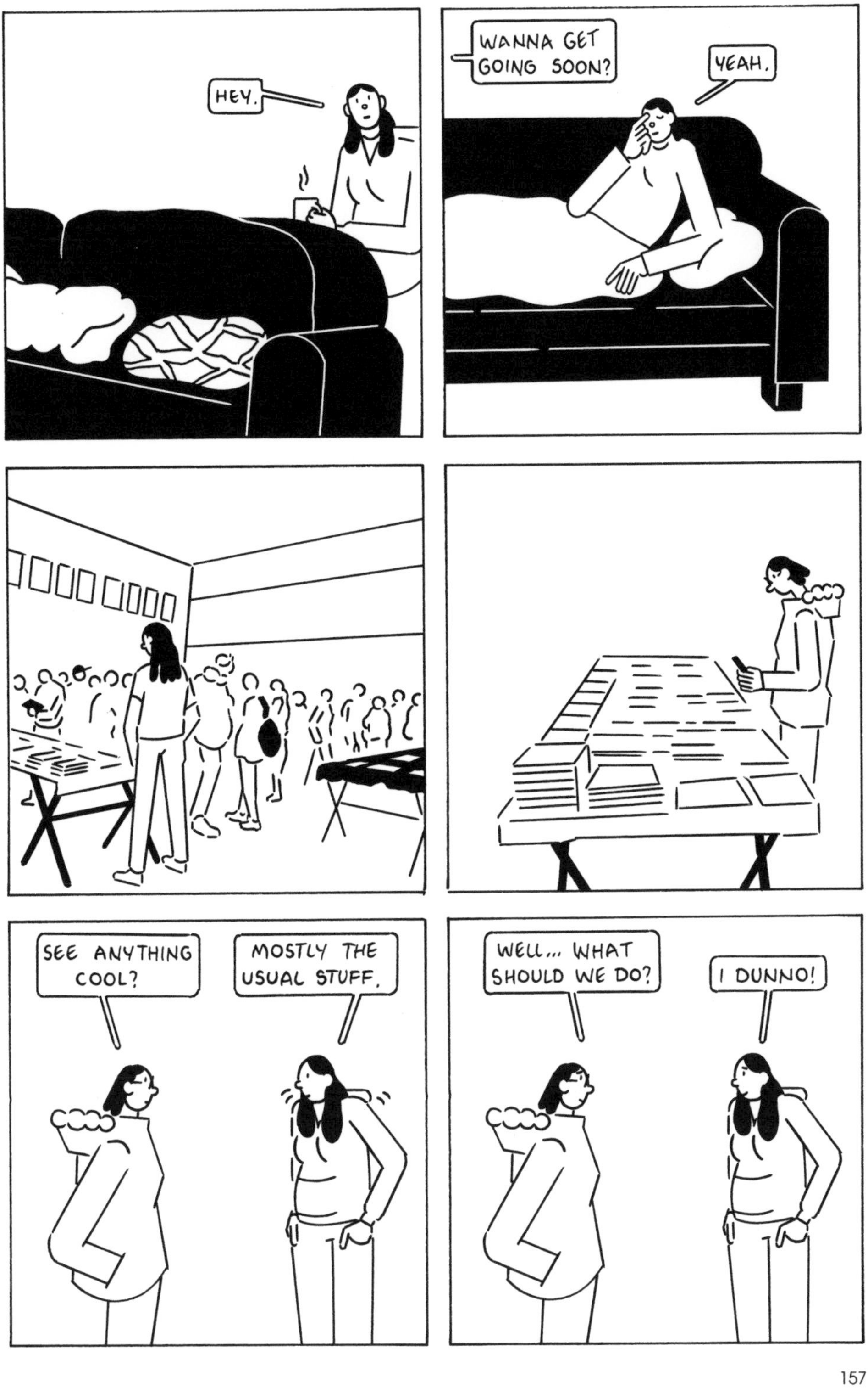
HEY.
WANNA GET GOING SOON?
YEAH.
SEE ANYTHING COOL?
MOSTLY THE USUAL STUFF.
WELL... WHAT SHOULD WE DO?
I DUNNO!

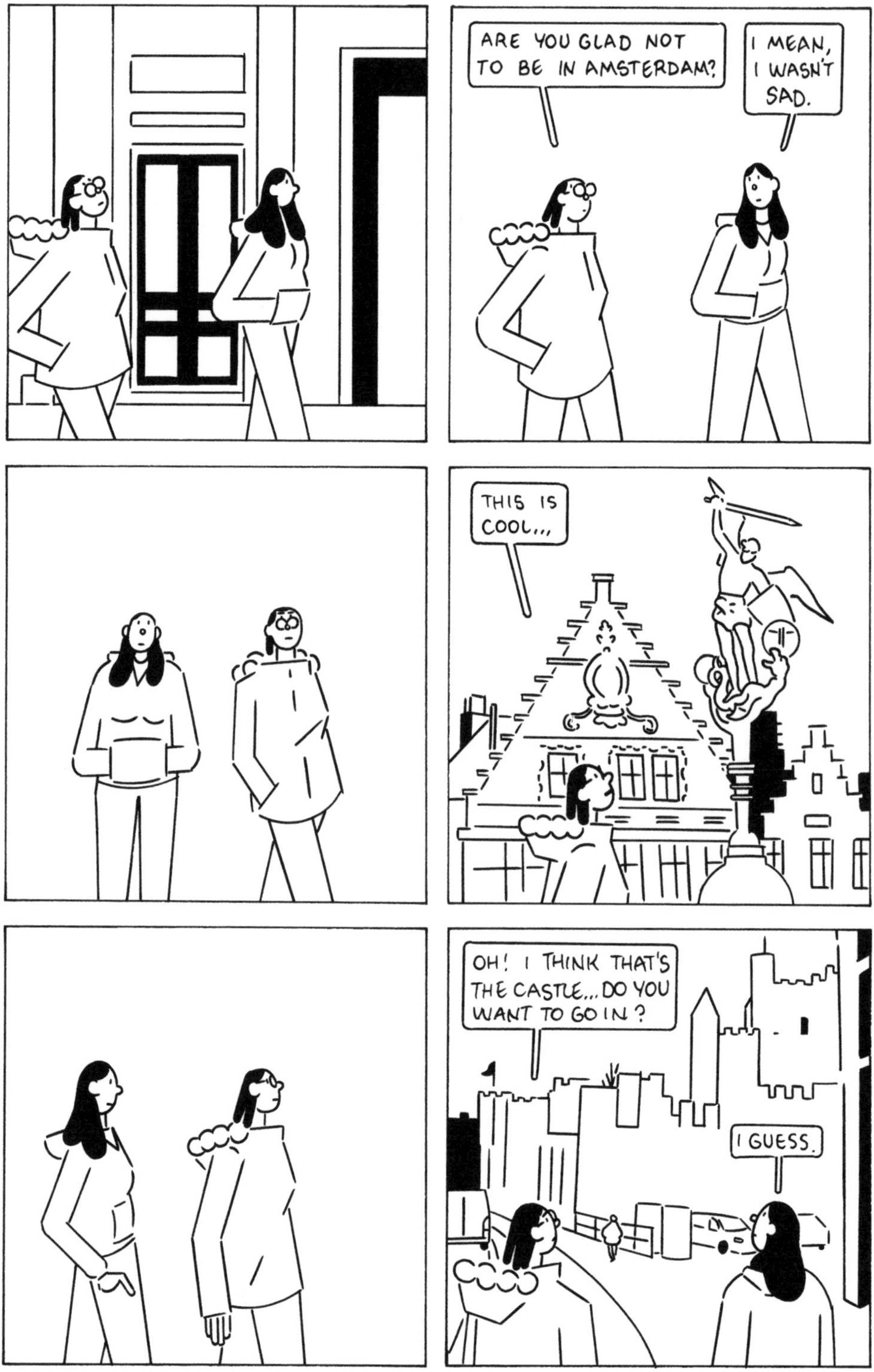
ARE YOU GLAD NOT TO BE IN AMSTERDAM?
I MEAN, I WASN'T SAD.
THIS IS COOL...
OH! I THINK THAT'S THE CASTLE... DO YOU WANT TO GO IN?
I GUESS.

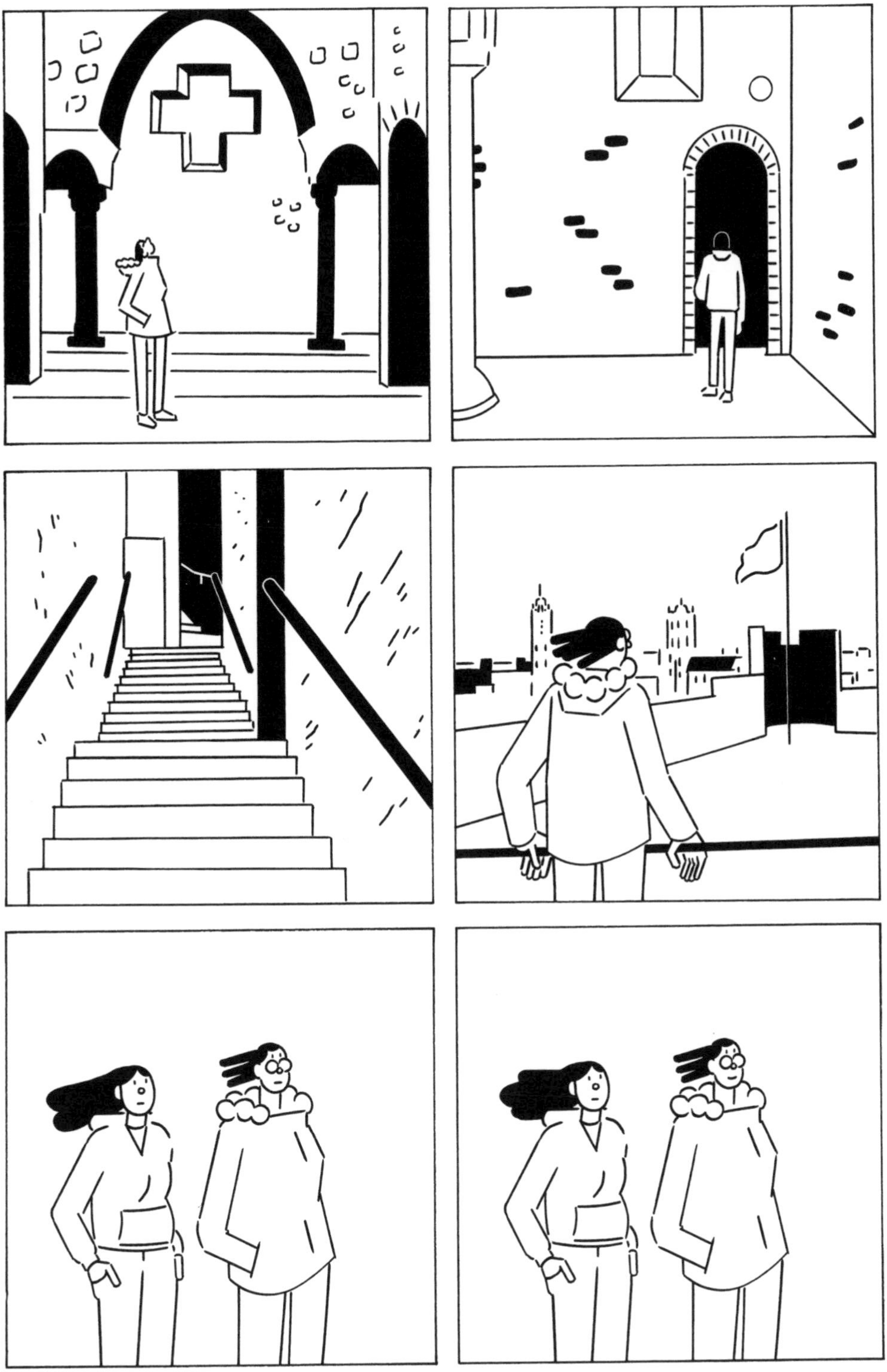

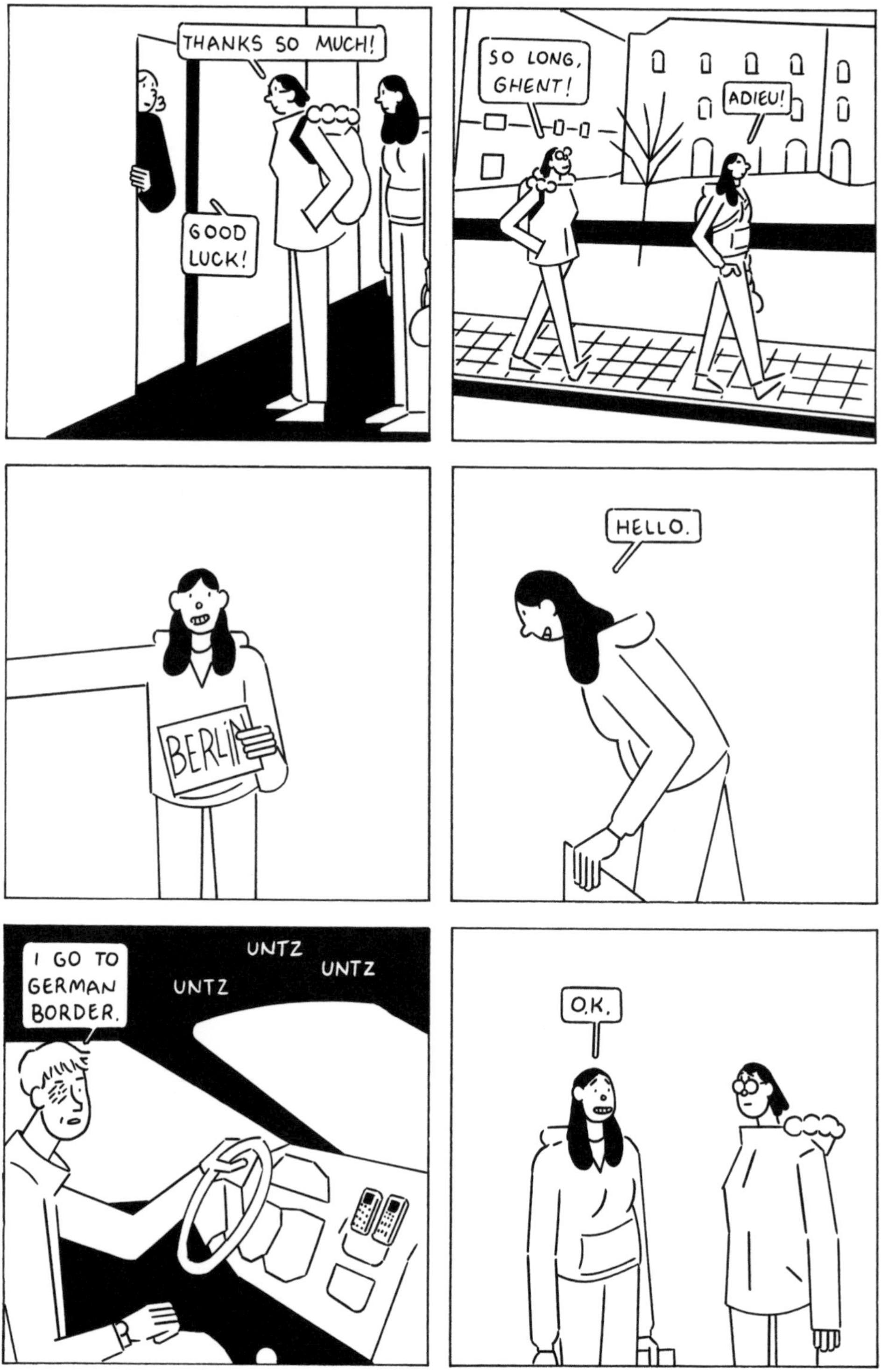
THANKS SO MUCH!
GOOD LUCK!
SO LONG, GHENT!
ADIEU!
BERLIN
HELLO.
I GO TO GERMAN BORDER.
UNTZ
UNTZ
UNTZ
O.K.

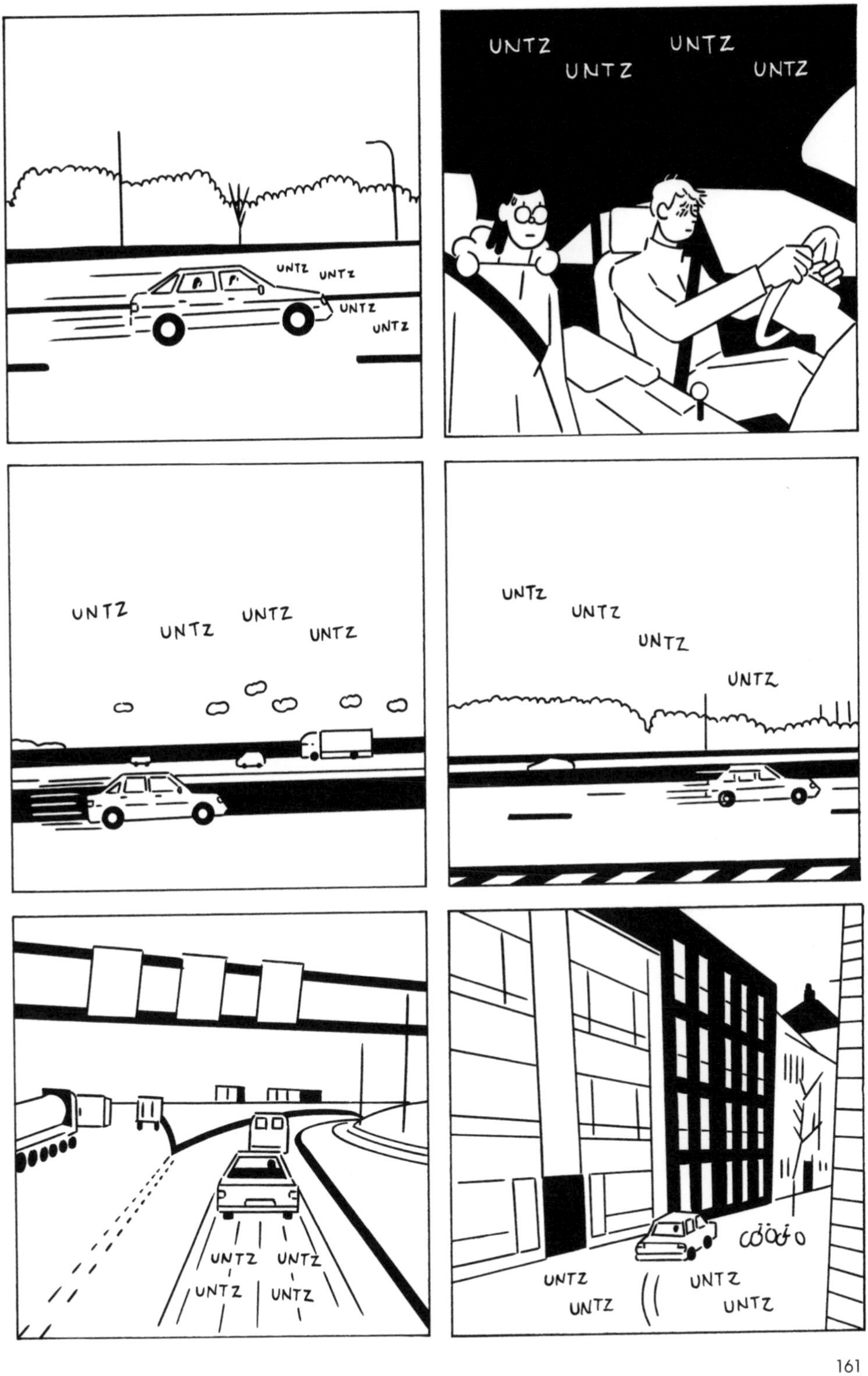
UNTZ UNTZ
UNTZ
UNTZ
UNTZ UNTZ
UNTZ UNTZ
UNTZ UNTZ
UNTZ UNTZ
UNTZ
UNTZ
UNTZ
UNTZ
UNTZ UNTZ
UNTZ UNTZ
UNTZ
UNTZ
UNTZ
UNTZ

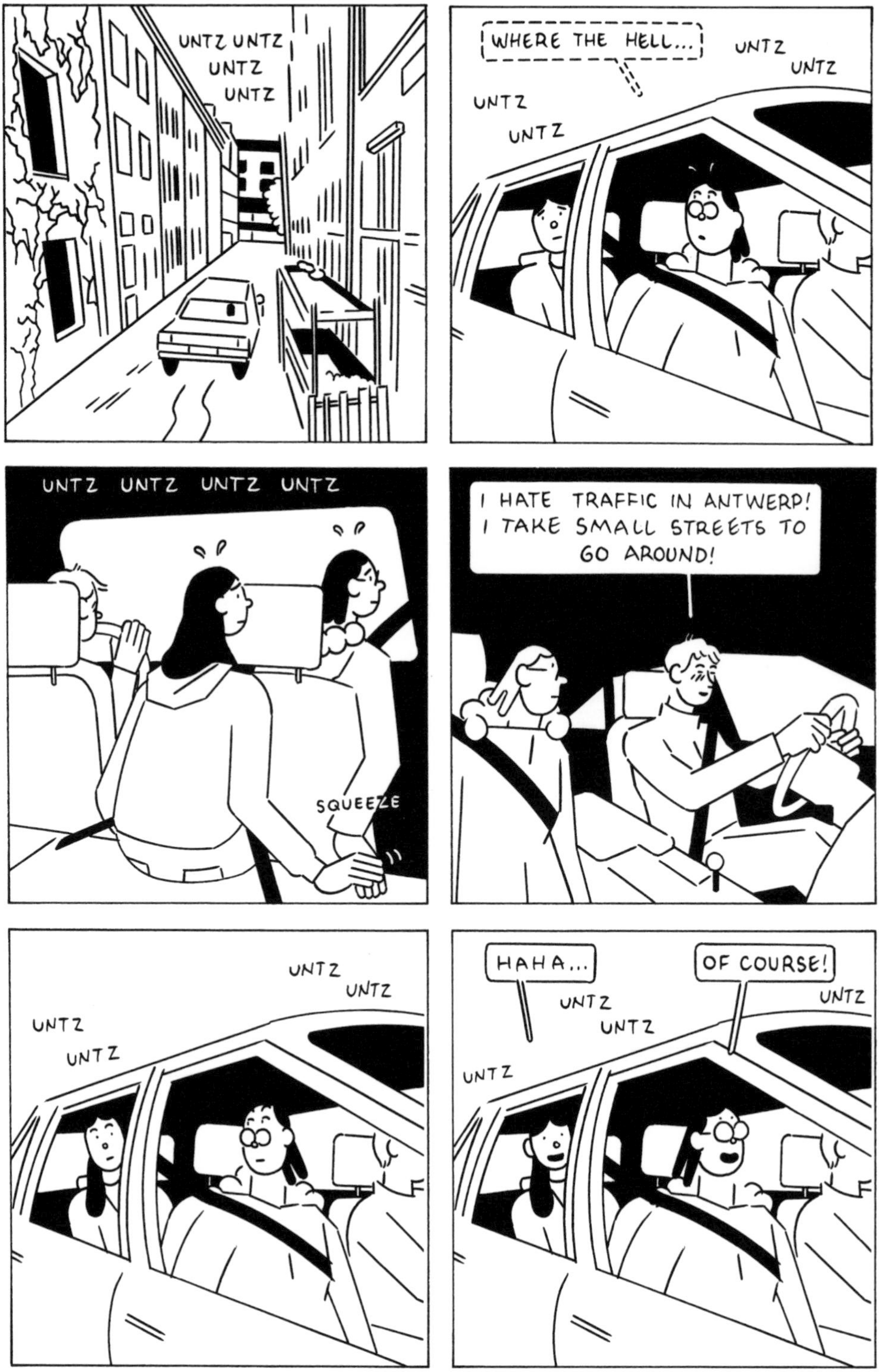
UNTZ UNTZ
UNTZ
UNTZ
WHERE THE HELL...
UNTZ
UNTZ
UNTZ
UNTZ
UNTZ UNTZ UNTZ UNTZ
SQUEEZE
I HATE TRAFFIC IN ANTWERP! I TAKE SMALL STREETS TO GO AROUND!
UNTZ
UNTZ
UNTZ
UNTZ
HAHA...
OF COURSE!
UNTZ
UNTZ
UNTZ
UNTZ

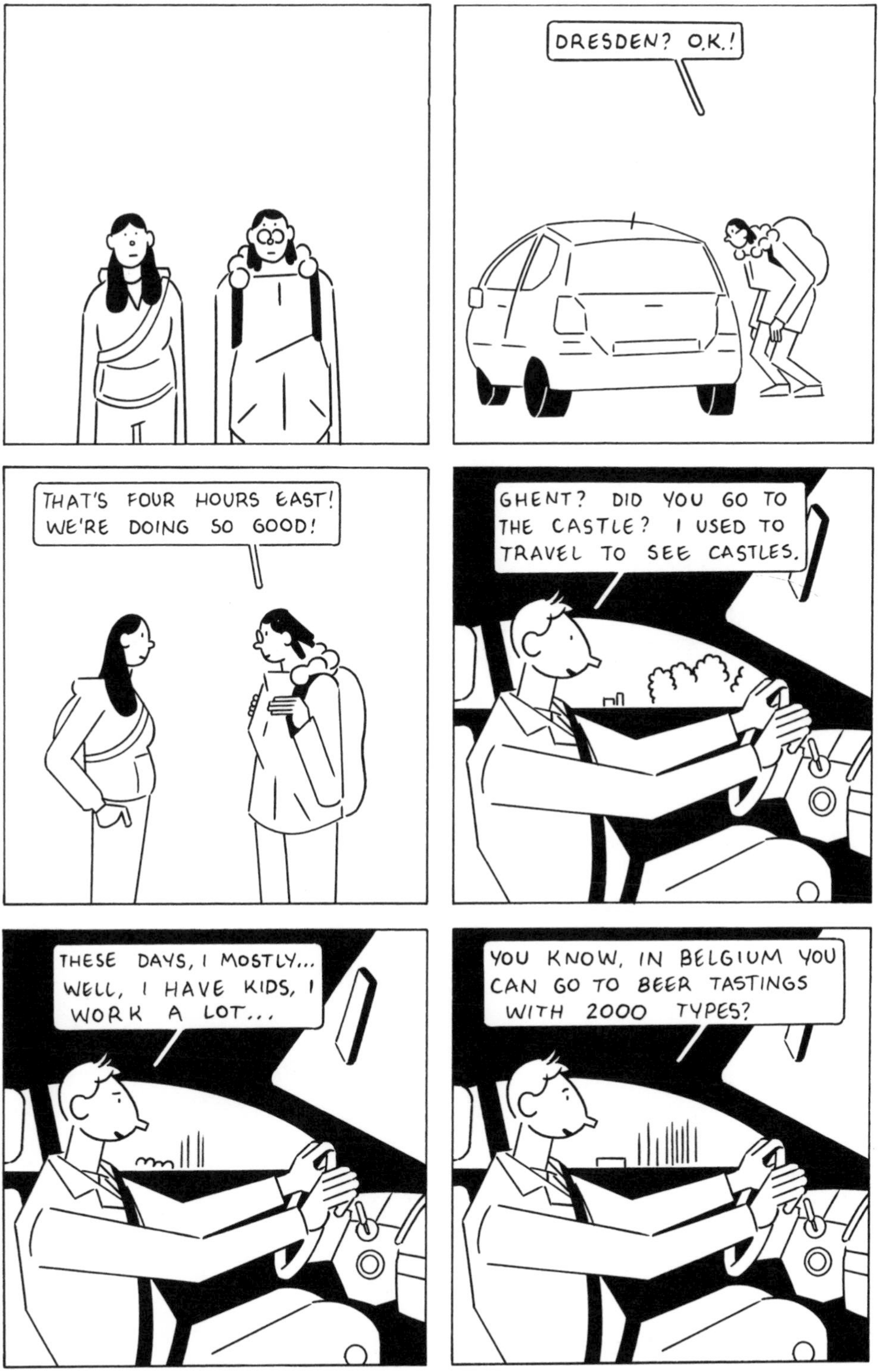

DRESDEN? O.K.!
THAT'S FOUR HOURS EAST! WE'RE DOING SO GOOD!
GHENT? DID YOU GO TO THE CASTLE? I USED TO TRAVEL TO SEE CASTLES.
THESE DAYS, I MOSTLY... WELL, I HAVE KIDS, I WORK A LOT...
YOU KNOW, IN BELGIUM YOU CAN GO TO BEER TASTINGS WITH 2000 TYPES?

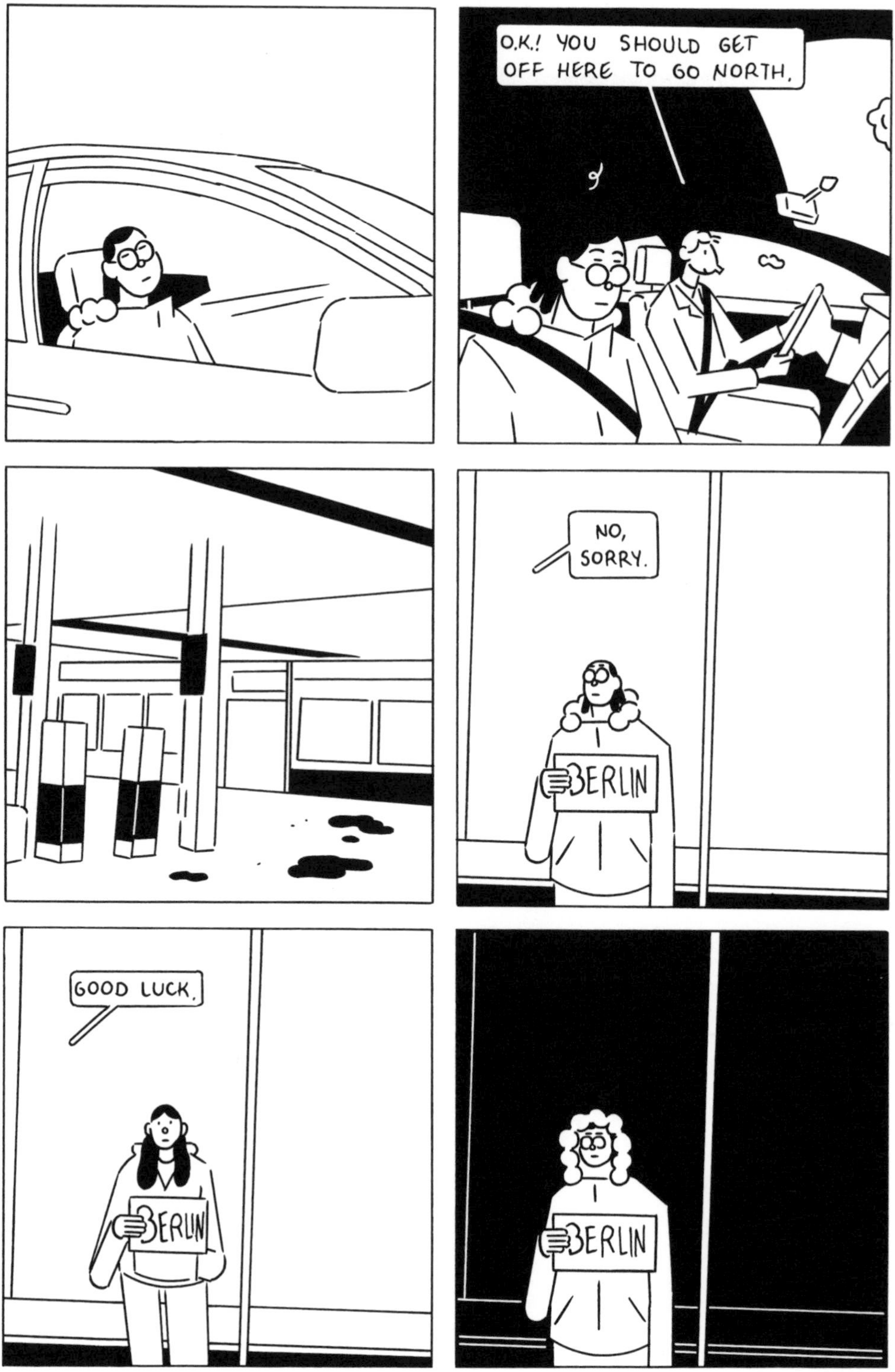
O.K.! YOU SHOULD GET OFF HERE TO GO NORTH.
NO, SORRY.
BERLIN
GOOD LUCK.
BERLIN
BERLIN

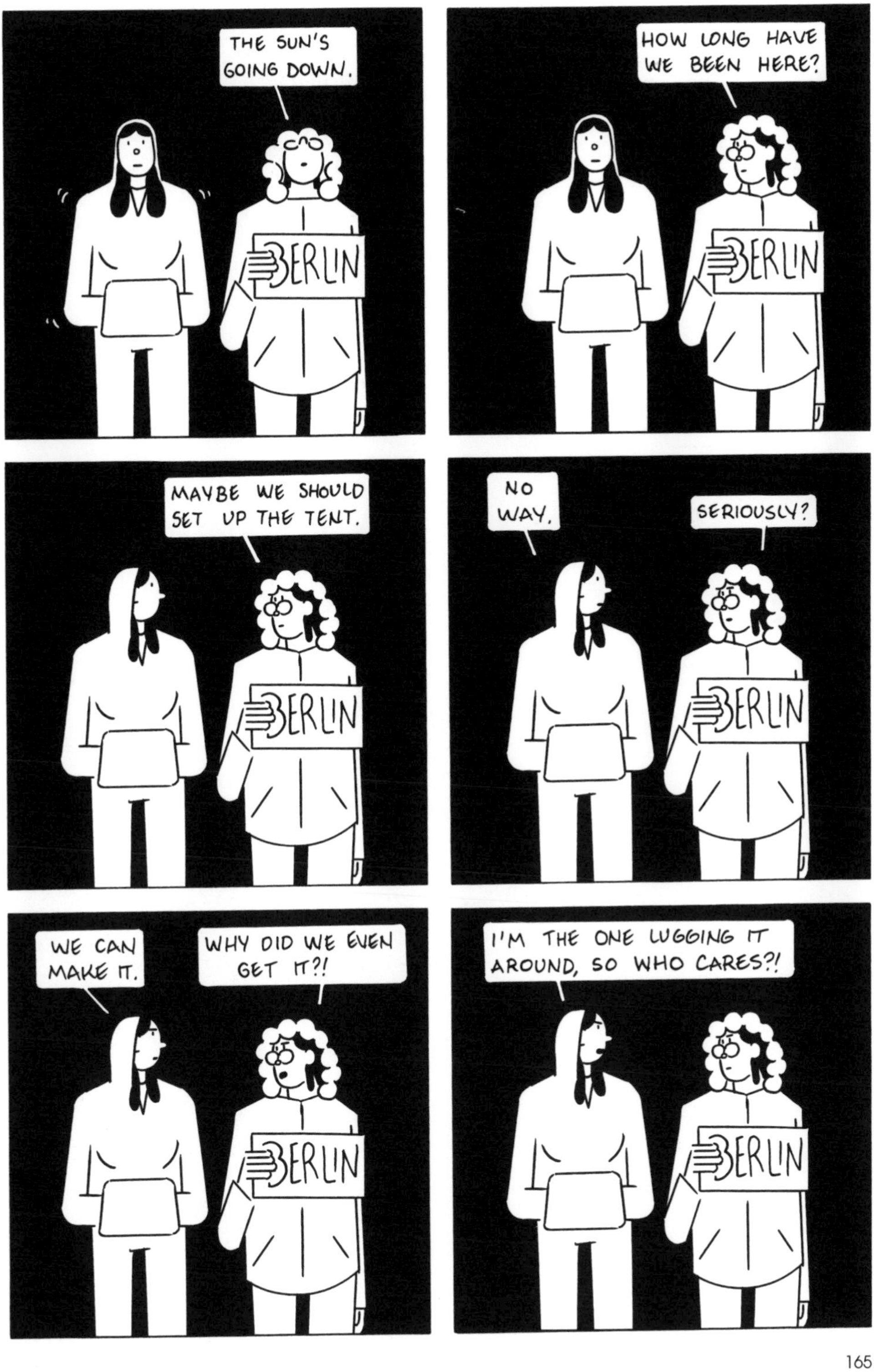
THE SUN'S GOING DOWN.
HOW LONG HAVE WE BEEN HERE?
BERLIN
MAYBE WE SHOULD SET UP THE TENT.
NO WAY.
SERIOUSLY?
WE CAN MAKE IT.
WHY DID WE EVEN GET IT?!
I'M THE ONE LUGGING IT AROUND, SO WHO CARES?!

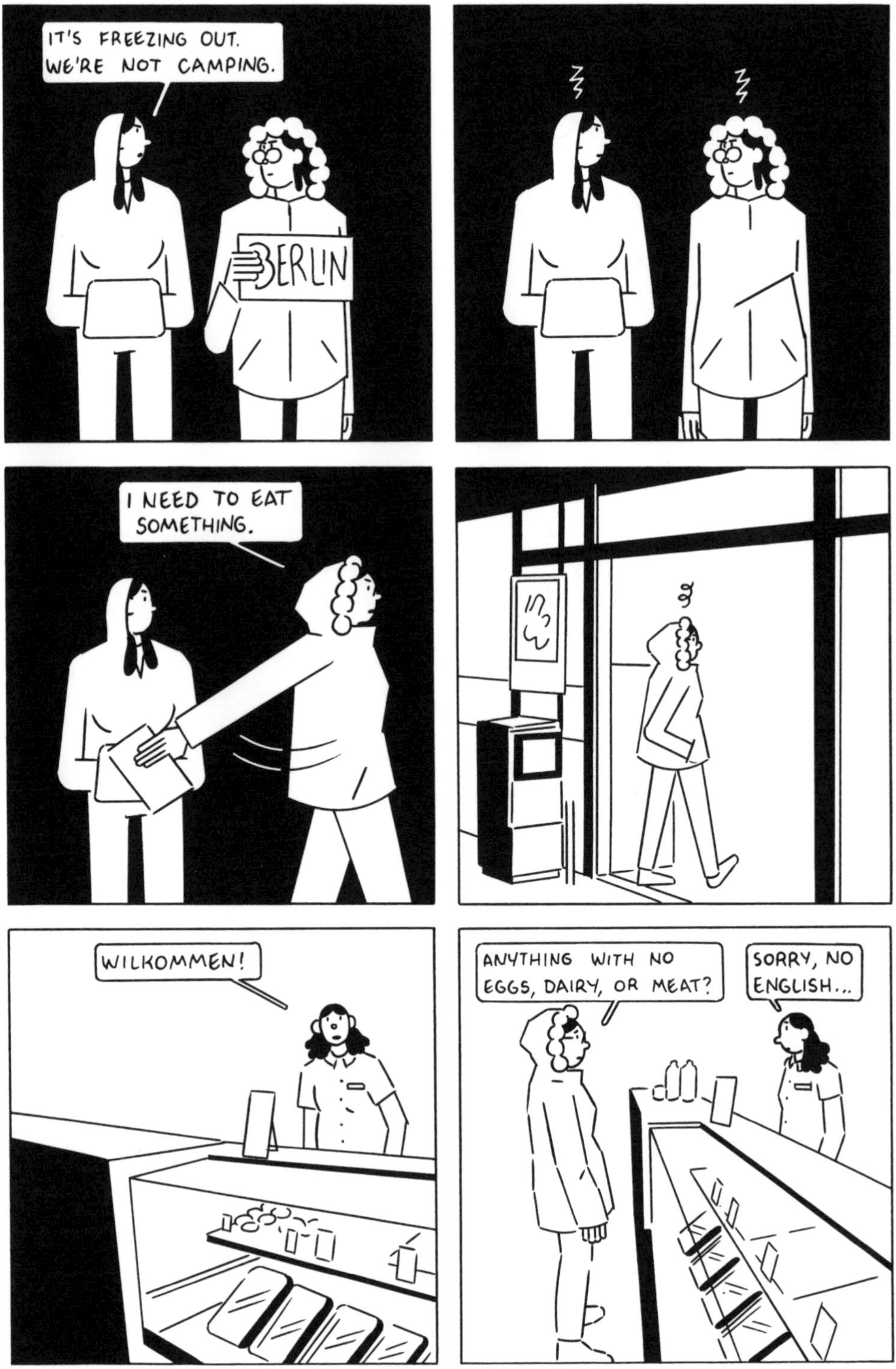
IT'S FREEZING OUT. WE'RE NOT CAMPING.
BERLIN
I NEED TO EAT SOMETHING.
WILKOMMEN!
ANYTHING WITH NO EGGS, DAIRY, OR MEAT?
SORRY, NO ENGLISH...

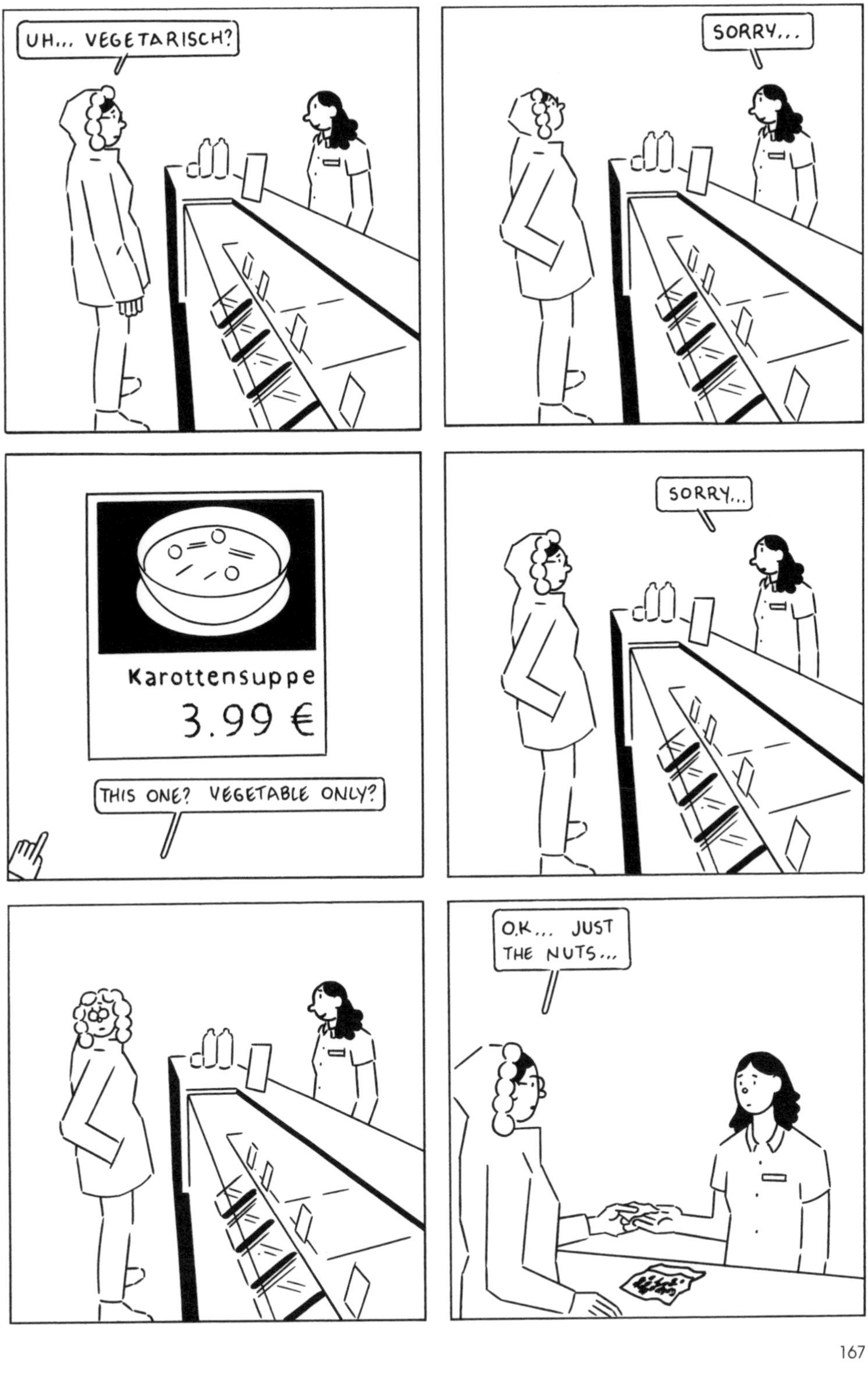
UH... VEGETARISCH?
SORRY...
Karottensuppe
3.99 €
THIS ONE? VEGETABLE ONLY?
SORRY...
O.K... JUST THE NUTS...

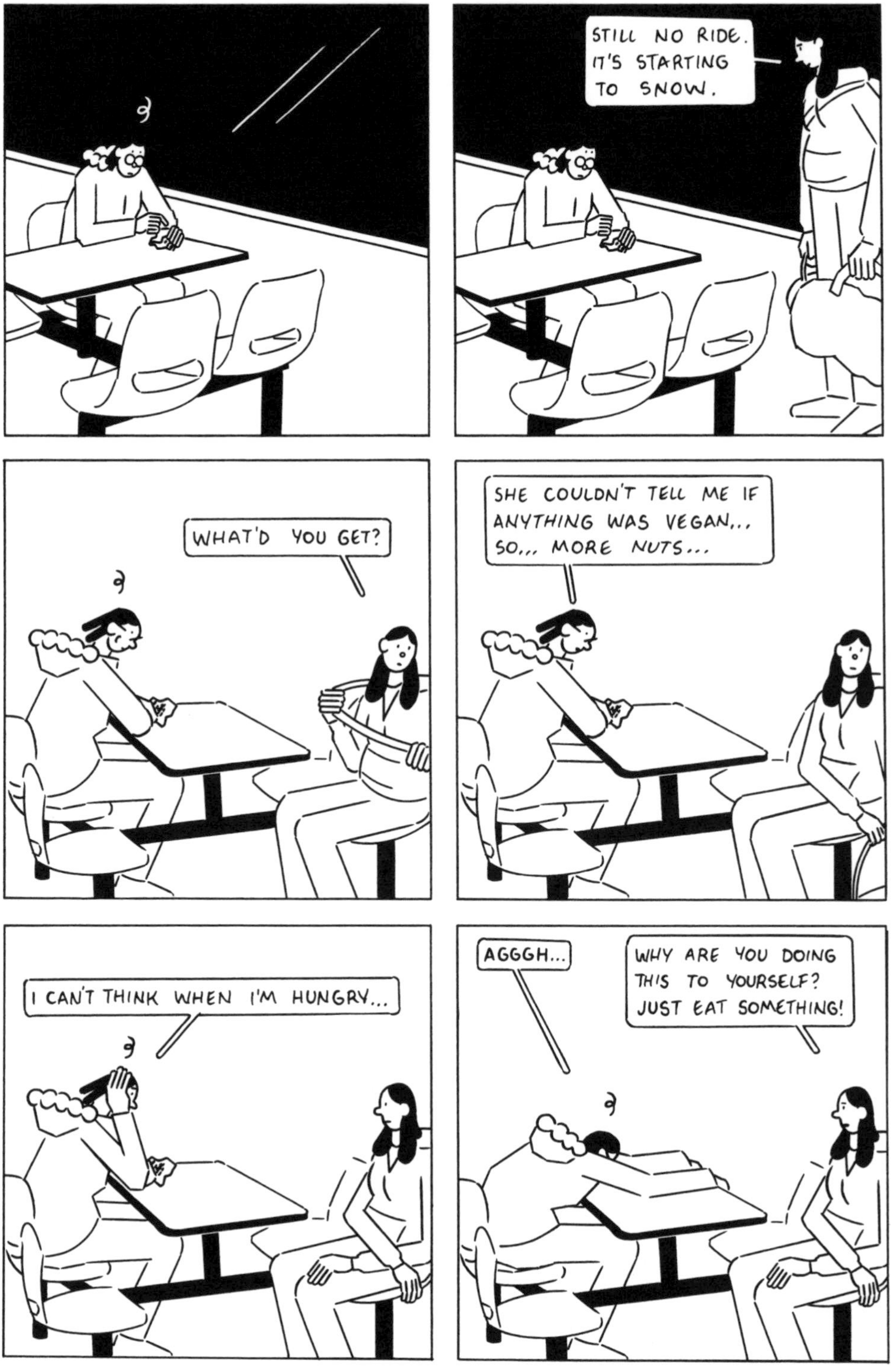
STILL NO RIDE. IT'S STARTING TO SNOW.
WHAT'D YOU GET?
SHE COULDN'T TELL ME IF ANYTHING WAS VEGAN... SO... MORE NUTS...
I CAN'T THINK WHEN I'M HUNGRY...
AGGGH...
WHY ARE YOU DOING THIS TO YOURSELF? JUST EAT SOMETHING!

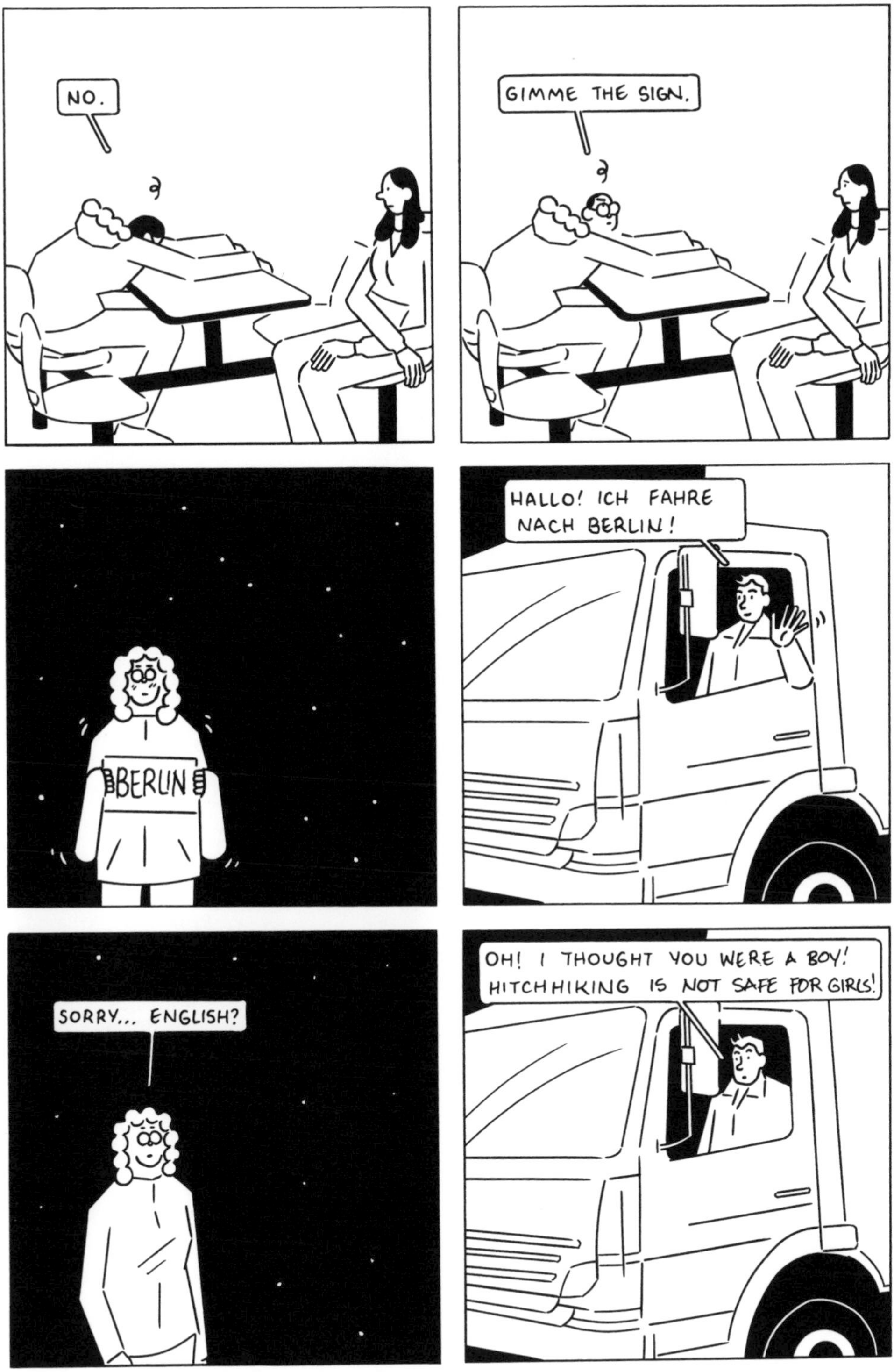
NO.
GIMME THE SIGN.
BERLIN
HALLO! ICH FAHRE NACH BERLIN!
SORRY... ENGLISH?
OH! I THOUGHT YOU WERE A BOY! HITCHHIKING IS NOT SAFE FOR GIRLS!

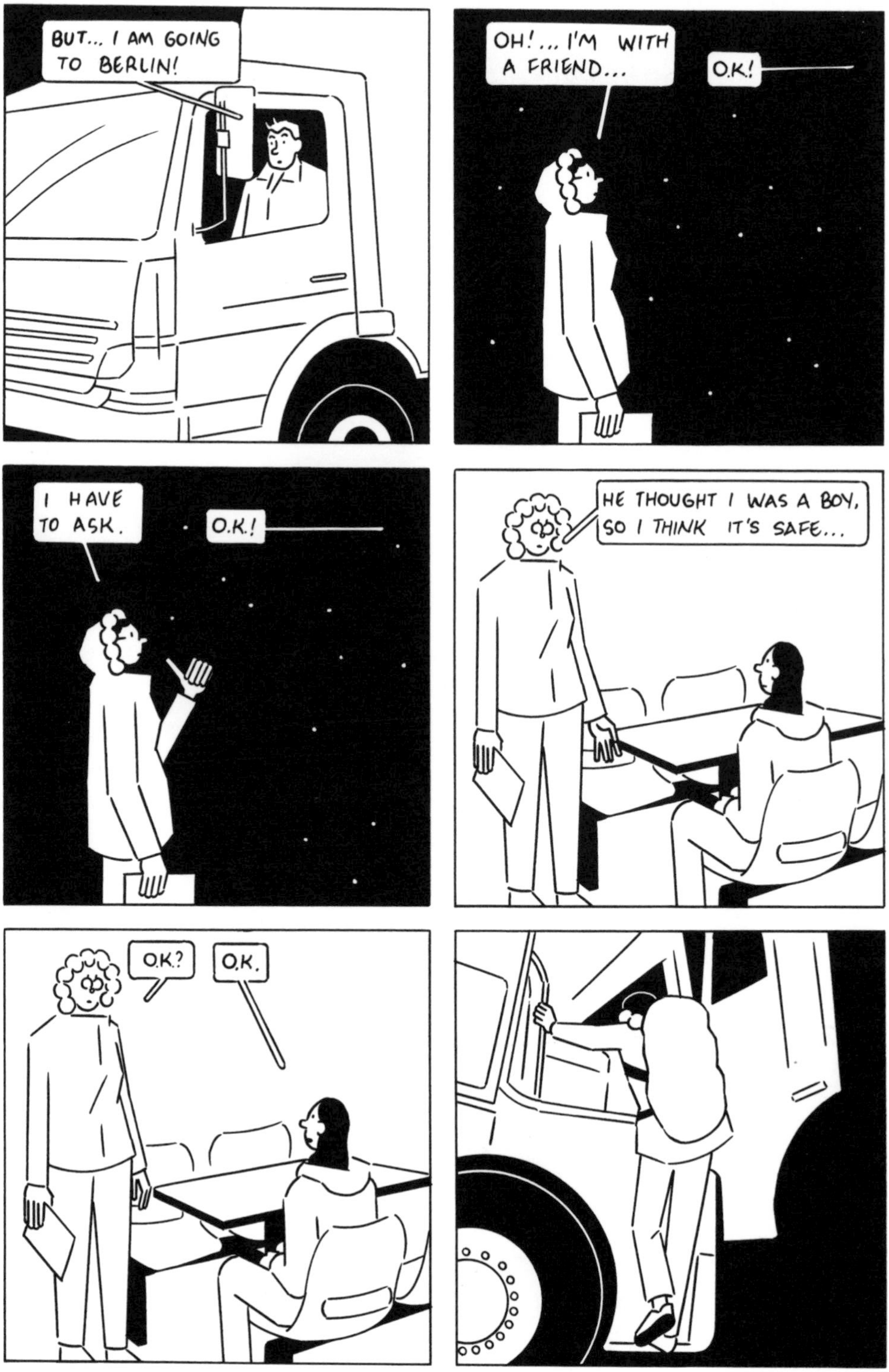
BUT... I AM GOING TO BERLIN!
OH!... I'M WITH A FRIEND...
O.K!
I HAVE TO ASK.
O.K.!
HE THOUGHT I WAS A BOY, SO I THINK IT'S SAFE...
O.K.?
O.K.

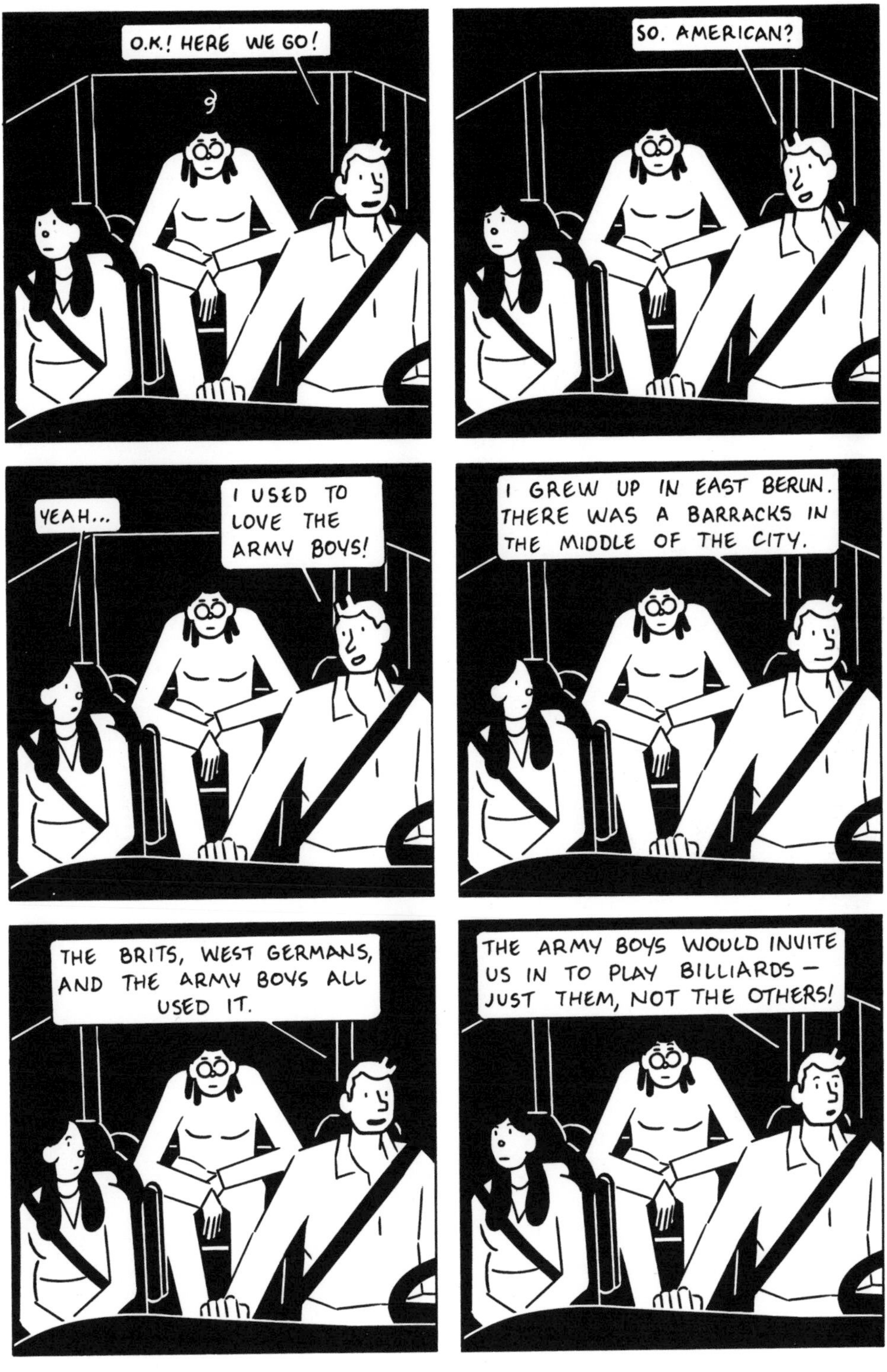
O.K.! HERE WE GO!
SO. AMERICAN?
YEAH...
I USED TO LOVE THE ARMY BOYS!
I GREW UP IN EAST BERLIN. THERE WAS A BARRACKS IN THE MIDDLE OF THE CITY.
THE BRITS, WEST GERMANS, AND THE ARMY BOYS ALL USED IT.
THE ARMY BOYS WOULD INVITE US IN TO PLAY BILLIARDS — JUST THEM, NOT THE OTHERS!

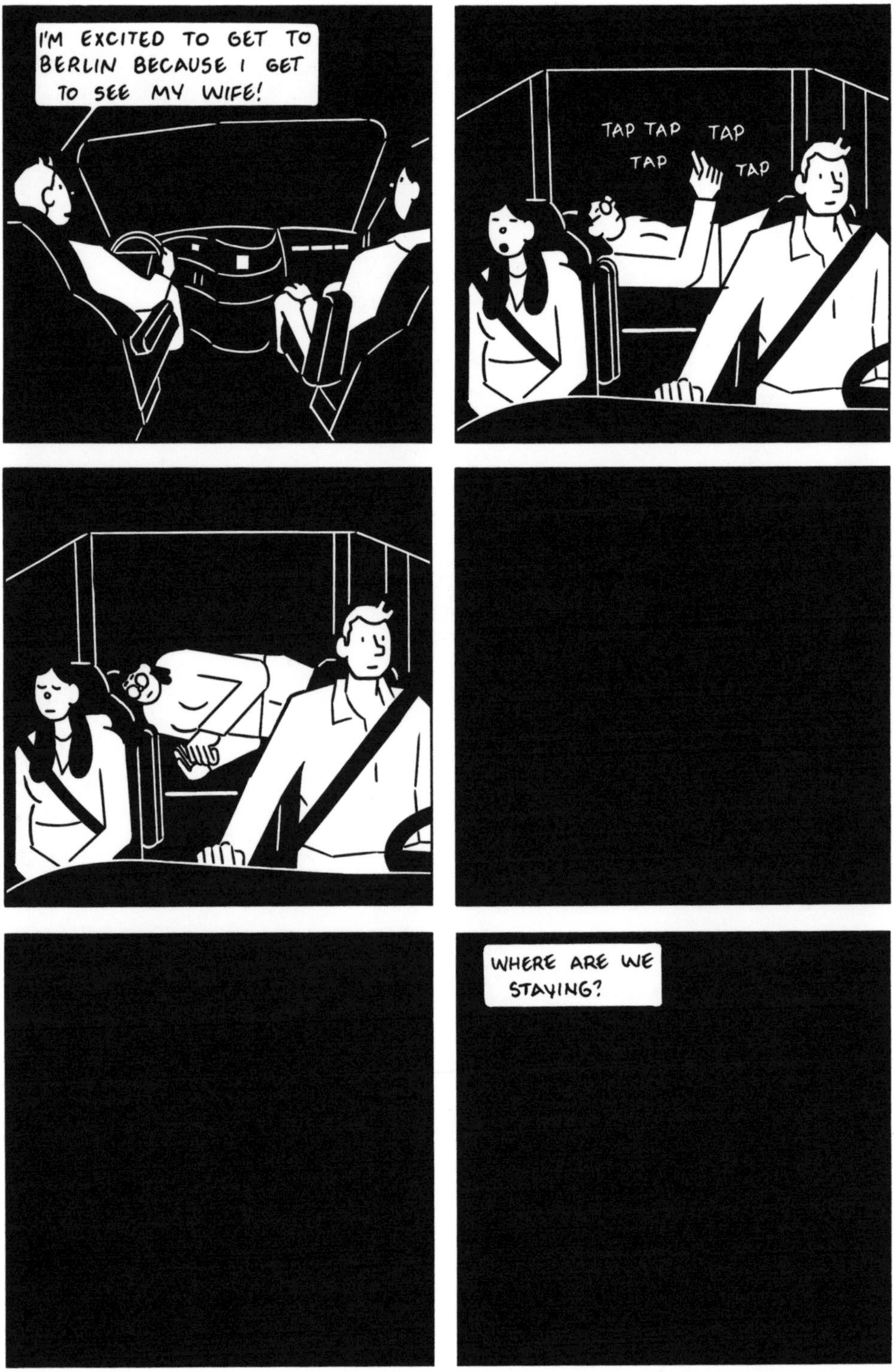
I'M EXCITED TO GET TO BERLIN BECAUSE I GET TO SEE MY WIFE!
TAP TAP TAP
TAP
TAP
WHERE ARE WE STAYING?

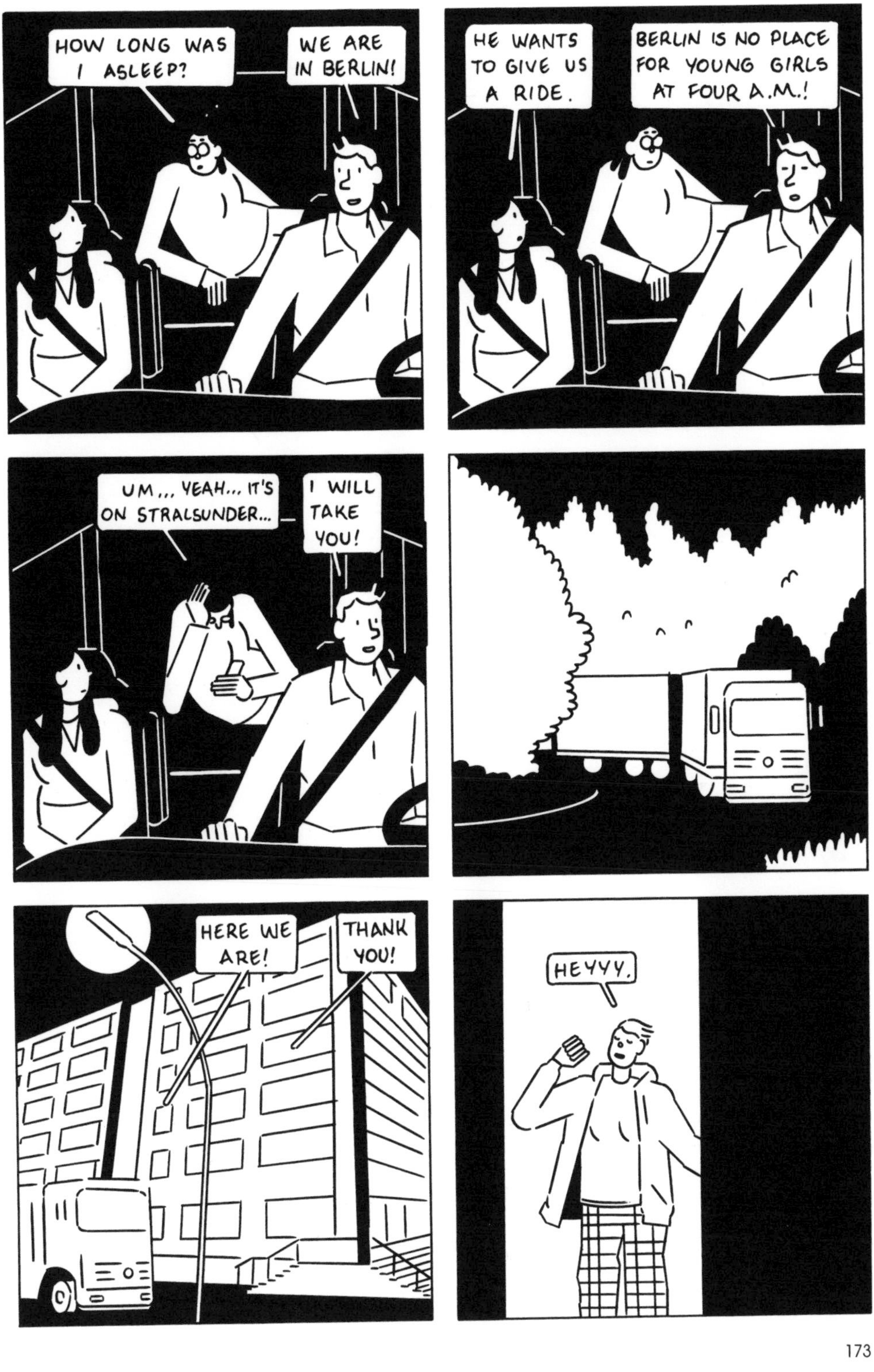
HOW LONG WAS I ASLEEP?
WE ARE IN BERLIN!
HE WANTS TO GIVE US A RIDE.
BERLIN IS NO PLACE FOR YOUNG GIRLS AT FOUR A.M.!
UM,,, YEAH... IT'S ON STRALSUNDER...
I WILL TAKE YOU!
HERE WE ARE!
THANK YOU!
HEYYY.

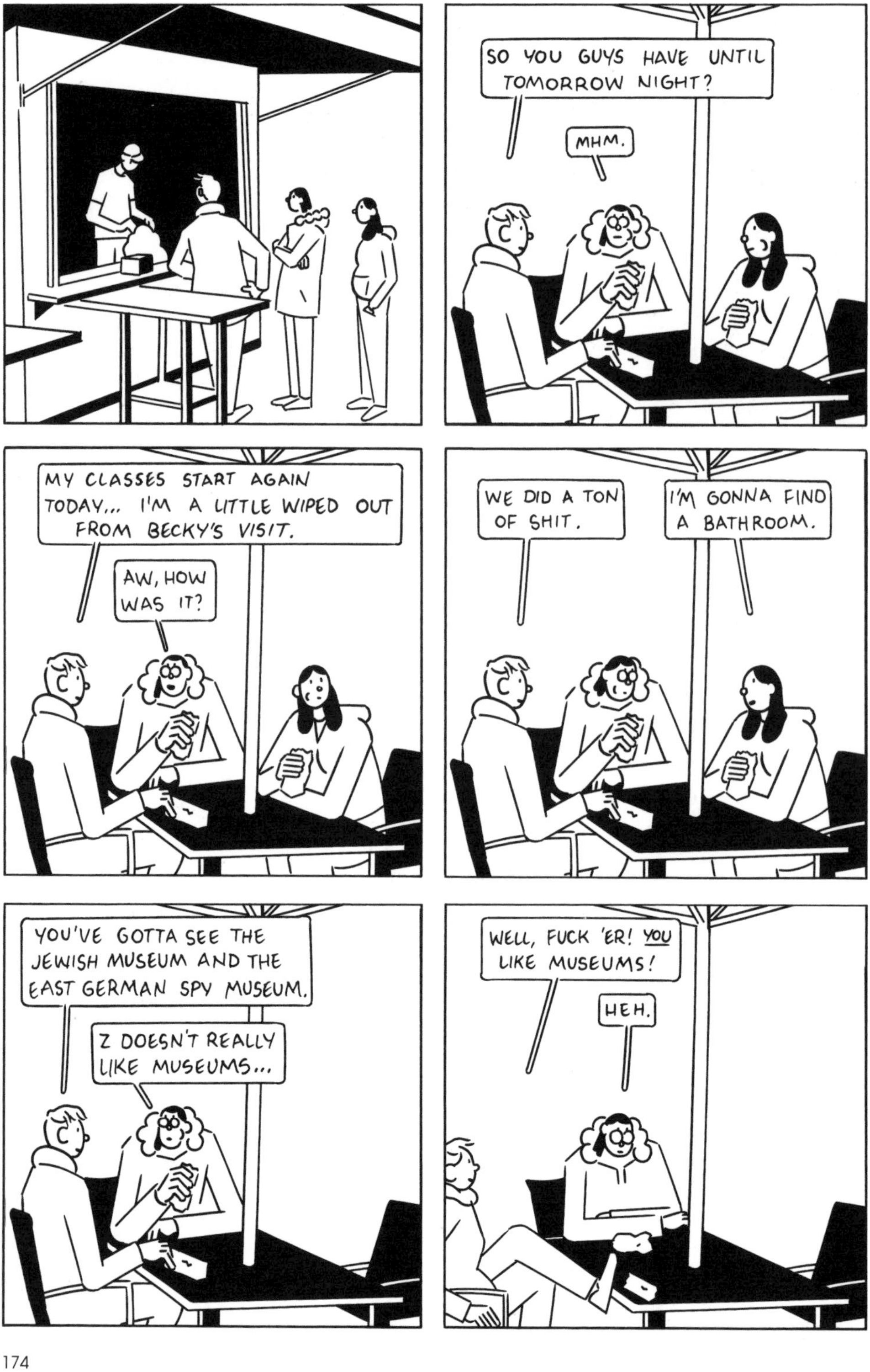

SO YOU GUYS HAVE UNTIL TOMORROW NIGHT?
MHM.
MY CLASSES START AGAIN TODAY... I'M A LITTLE WIPED OUT FROM BECKY'S VISIT.
AW, HOW WAS IT?
WE DID A TON OF SHIT.
I'M GONNA FIND A BATHROOM.
YOU'VE GOTTA SEE THE JEWISH MUSEUM AND THE EAST GERMAN SPY MUSEUM.
Z DOESN'T REALLY LIKE MUSEUMS...
WELL, FUCK 'ER! YOU LIKE MUSEUMS!
HEH.

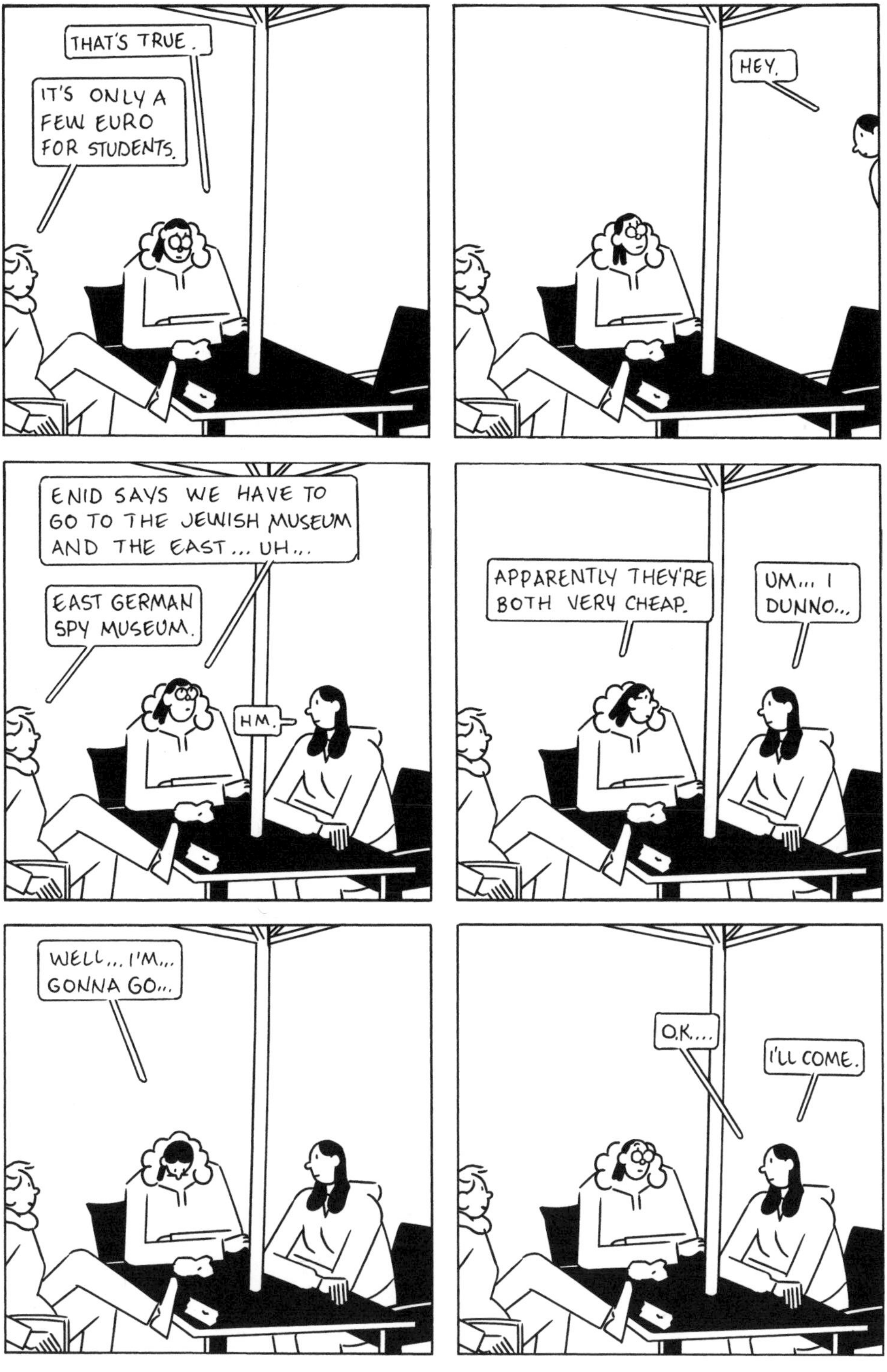
THAT'S TRUE.
IT'S ONLY A FEW EURO FOR STUDENTS.
HEY.
ENID SAYS WE HAVE TO GO TO THE JEWISH MUSEUM AND THE EAST... UH...
EAST GERMAN SPY MUSEUM.
HM.
APPARENTLY THEY'RE BOTH VERY CHEAP.
UM... I DUNNO...
WELL... I'M... GONNA GO...
O.K....
I'LL COME.

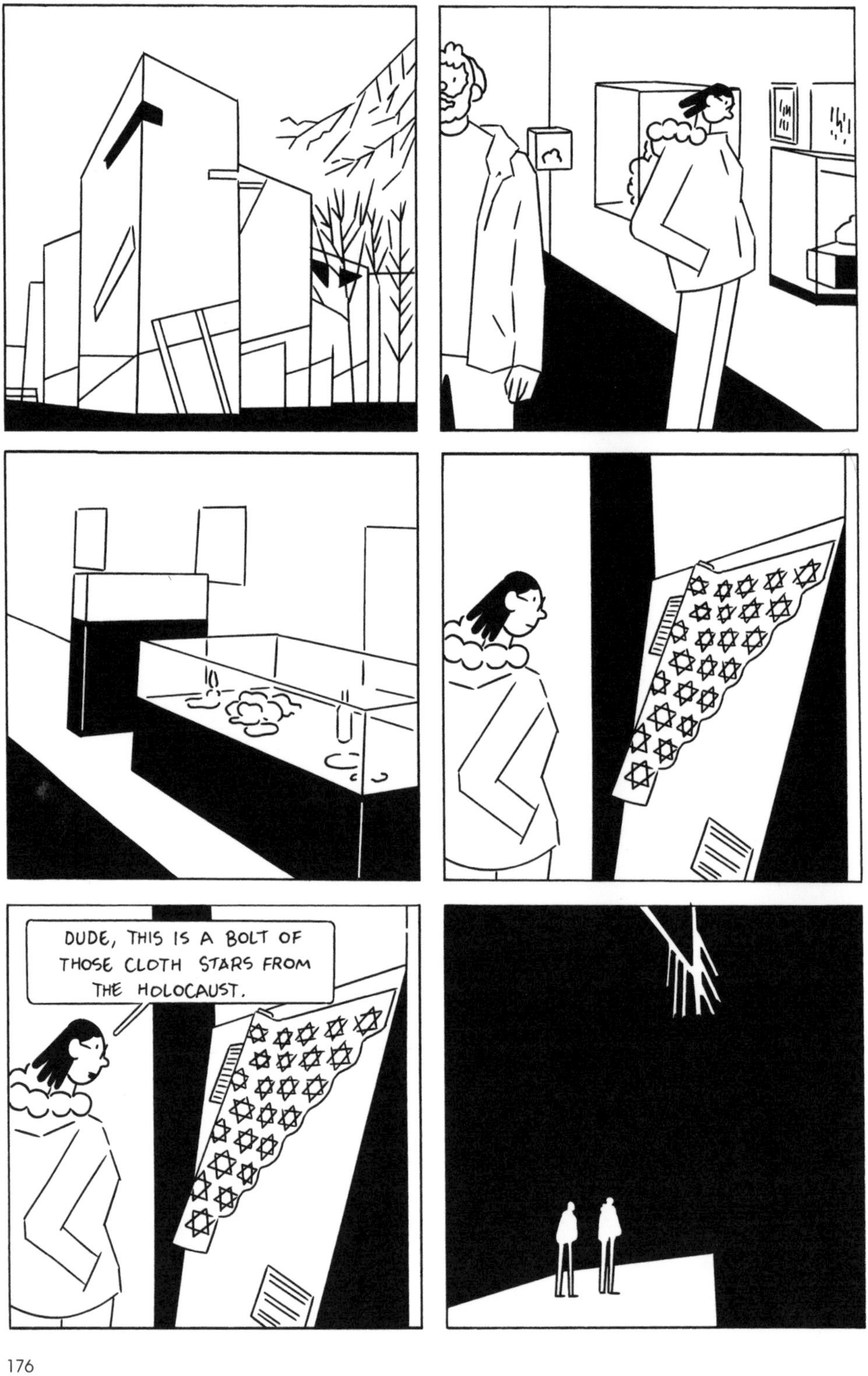
DUDE, THIS IS A BOLT OF THOSE CLOTH STARS FROM THE HOLOCAUST.

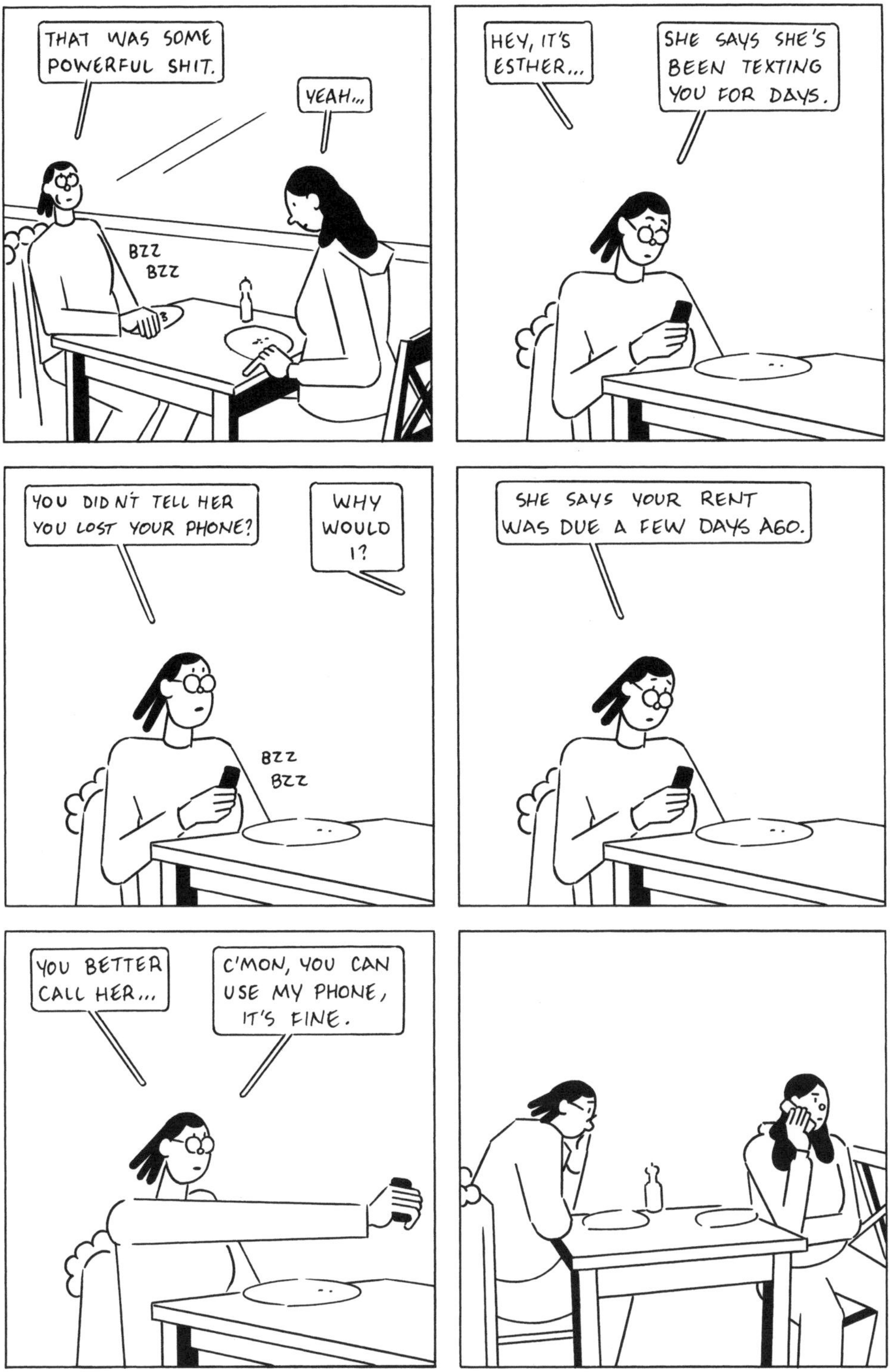
THAT WAS SOME POWERFUL SHIT.
YEAH...
BZZ BZZ
HEY, IT'S ESTHER...
SHE SAYS SHE'S BEEN TEXTING YOU FOR DAYS.
YOU DIDN'T TELL HER YOU LOST YOUR PHONE?
WHY WOULD I?
BZZ BZZ
SHE SAYS YOUR RENT WAS DUE A FEW DAYS AGO.
YOU BETTER CALL HER...
C'MON, YOU CAN USE MY PHONE, IT'S FINE.

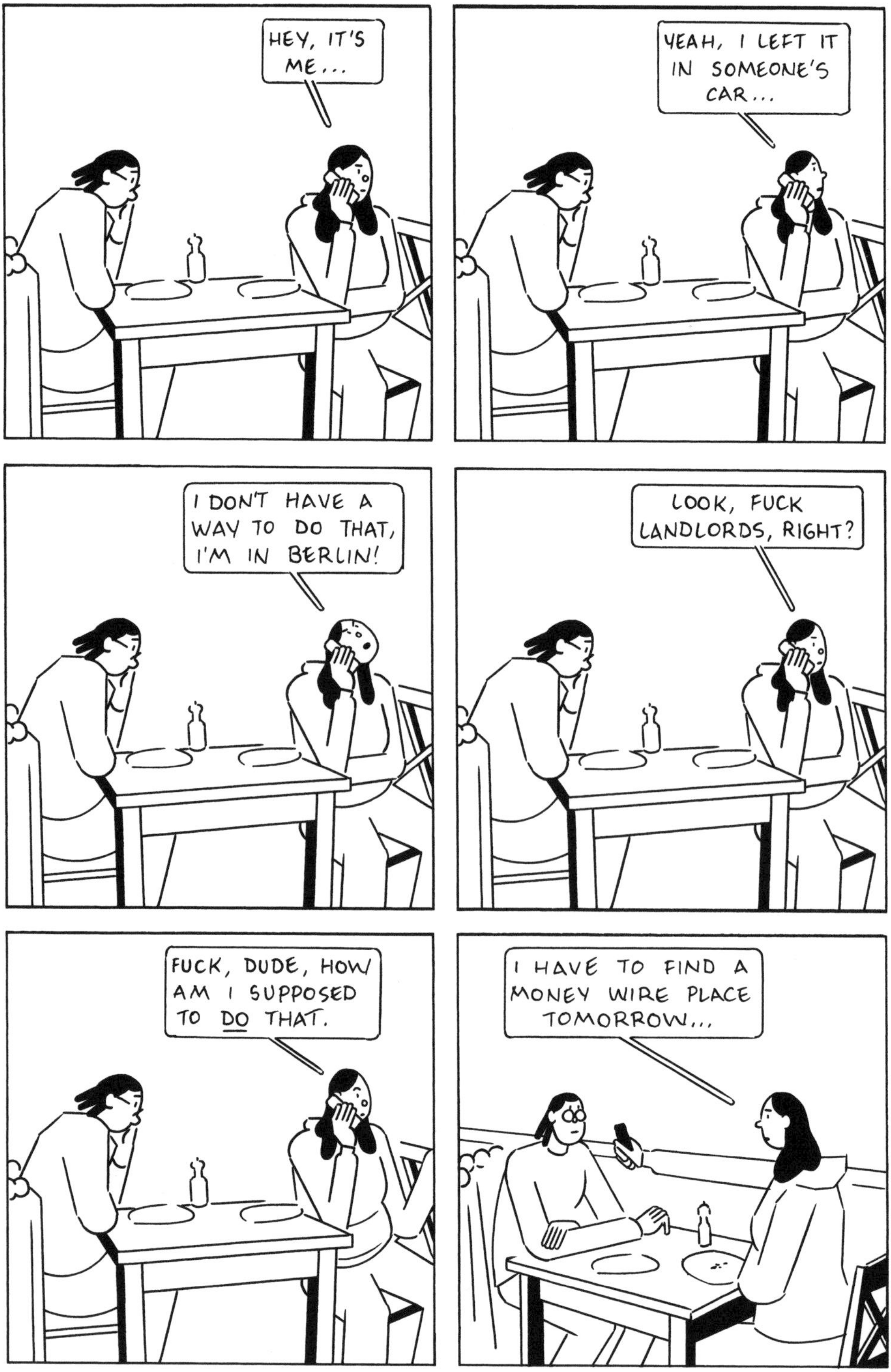
HEY, IT'S ME...
YEAH, I LEFT IT IN SOMEONE'S CAR...
I DON'T HAVE A WAY TO DO THAT, I'M IN BERLIN!
LOOK, FUCK LANDLORDS, RIGHT?
FUCK, DUDE, HOW AM I SUPPOSED TO DO THAT.
I HAVE TO FIND A MONEY WIRE PLACE TOMORROW...

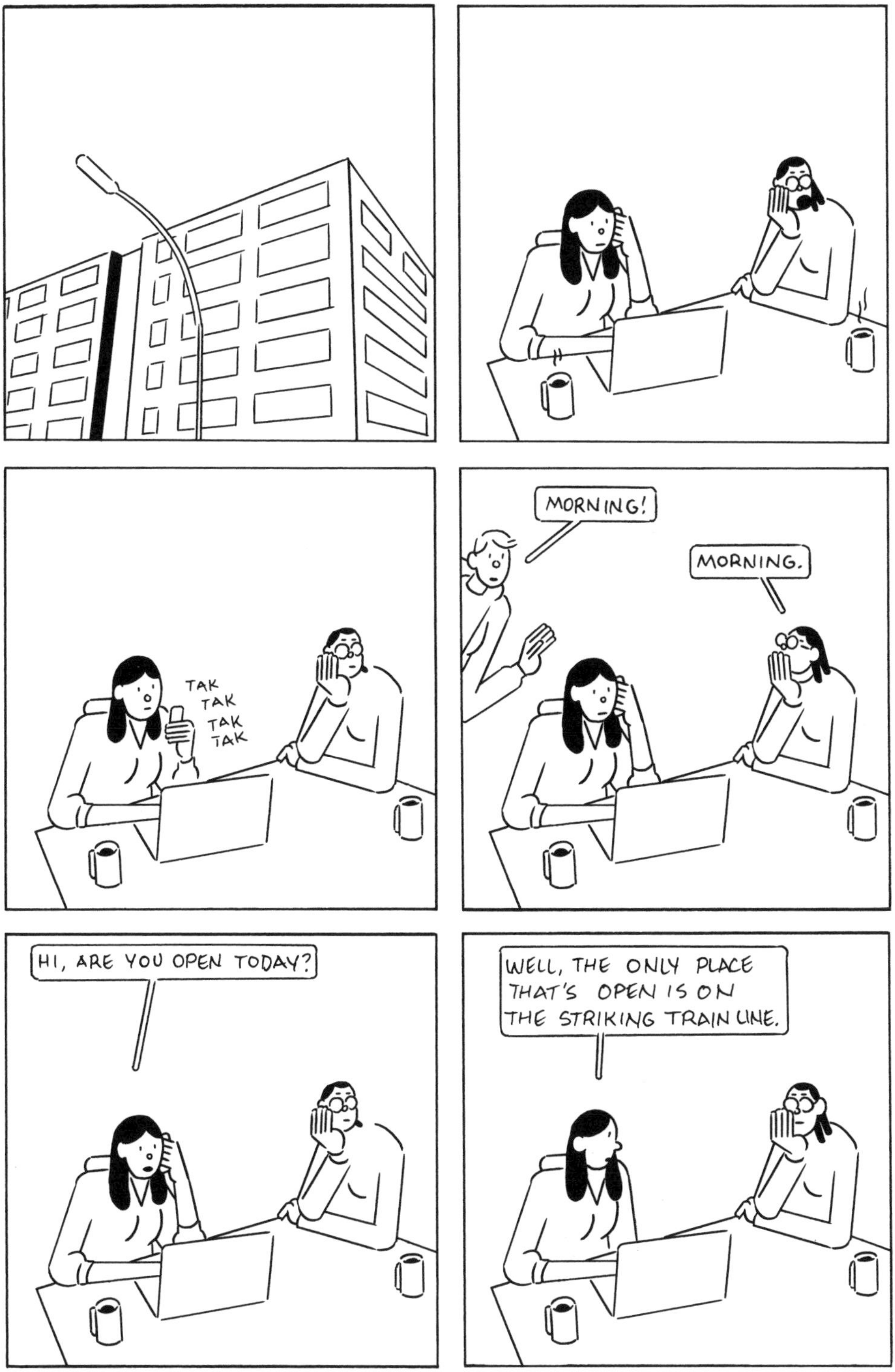
TAK
TAK
TAK
TAK
MORNING!
MORNING.
HI, ARE YOU OPEN TODAY?
WELL, THE ONLY PLACE THAT'S OPEN IS ON THE STRIKING TRAIN LINE.

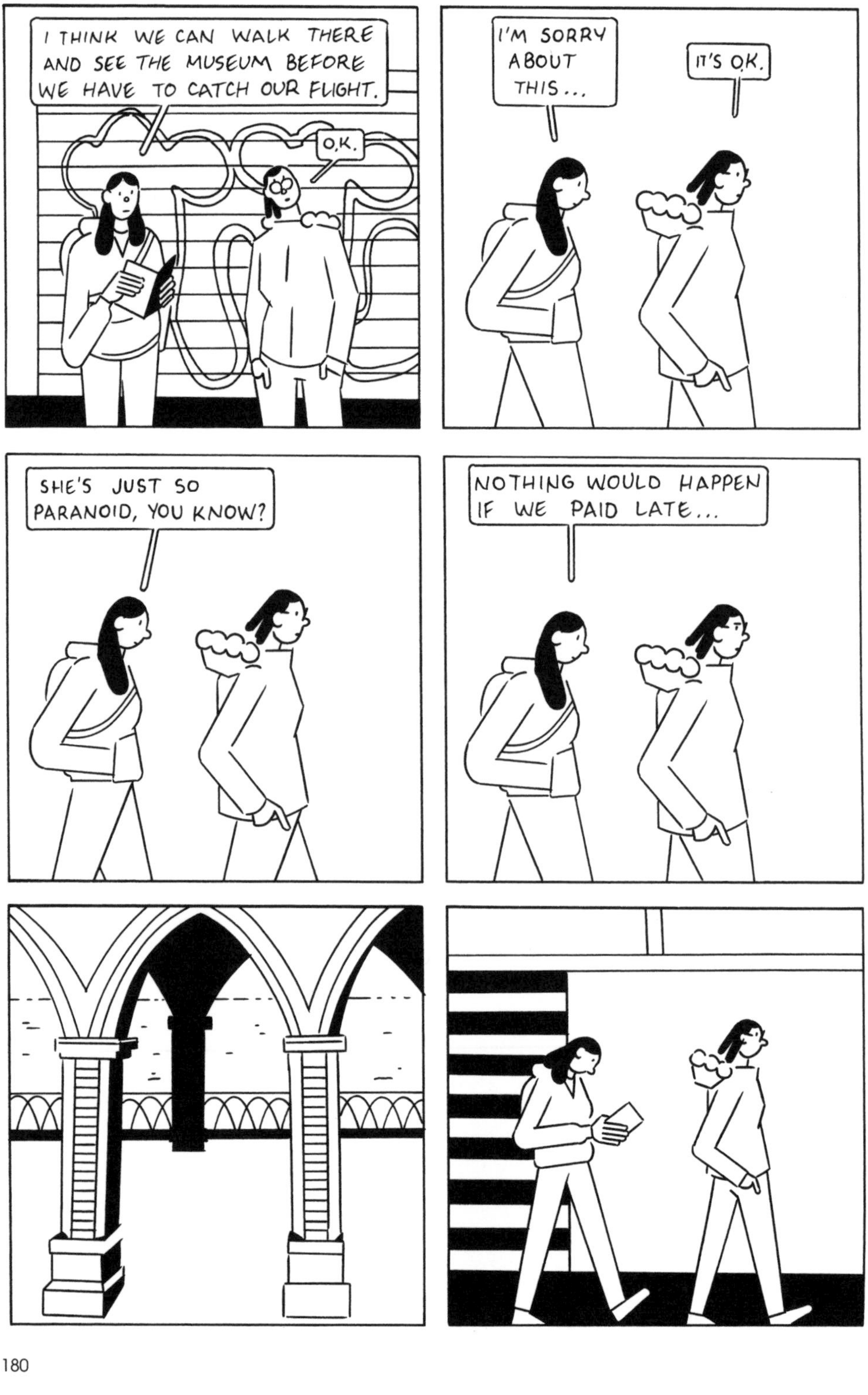
I THINK WE CAN WALK THERE AND SEE THE MUSEUM BEFORE WE HAVE TO CATCH OUR FLIGHT.
O.K.
I'M SORRY ABOUT THIS...
IT'S O.K.
SHE'S JUST SO PARANOID, YOU KNOW?
NOTHING WOULD HAPPEN IF WE PAID LATE...

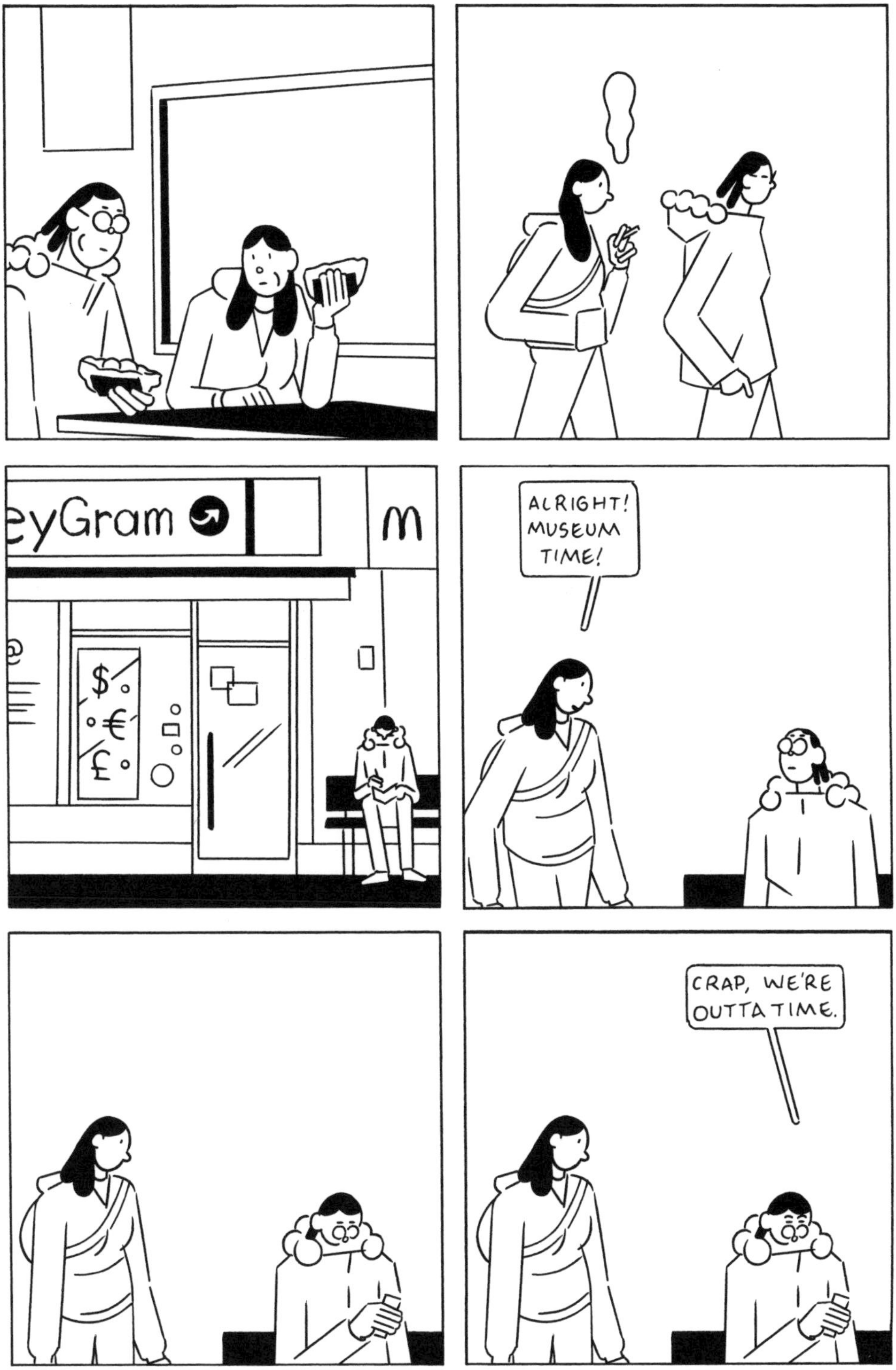
eyGram
m
$
€
£
@
ALRIGHT! MUSEUM TIME!
CRAP, WE'RE OUTTA TIME.

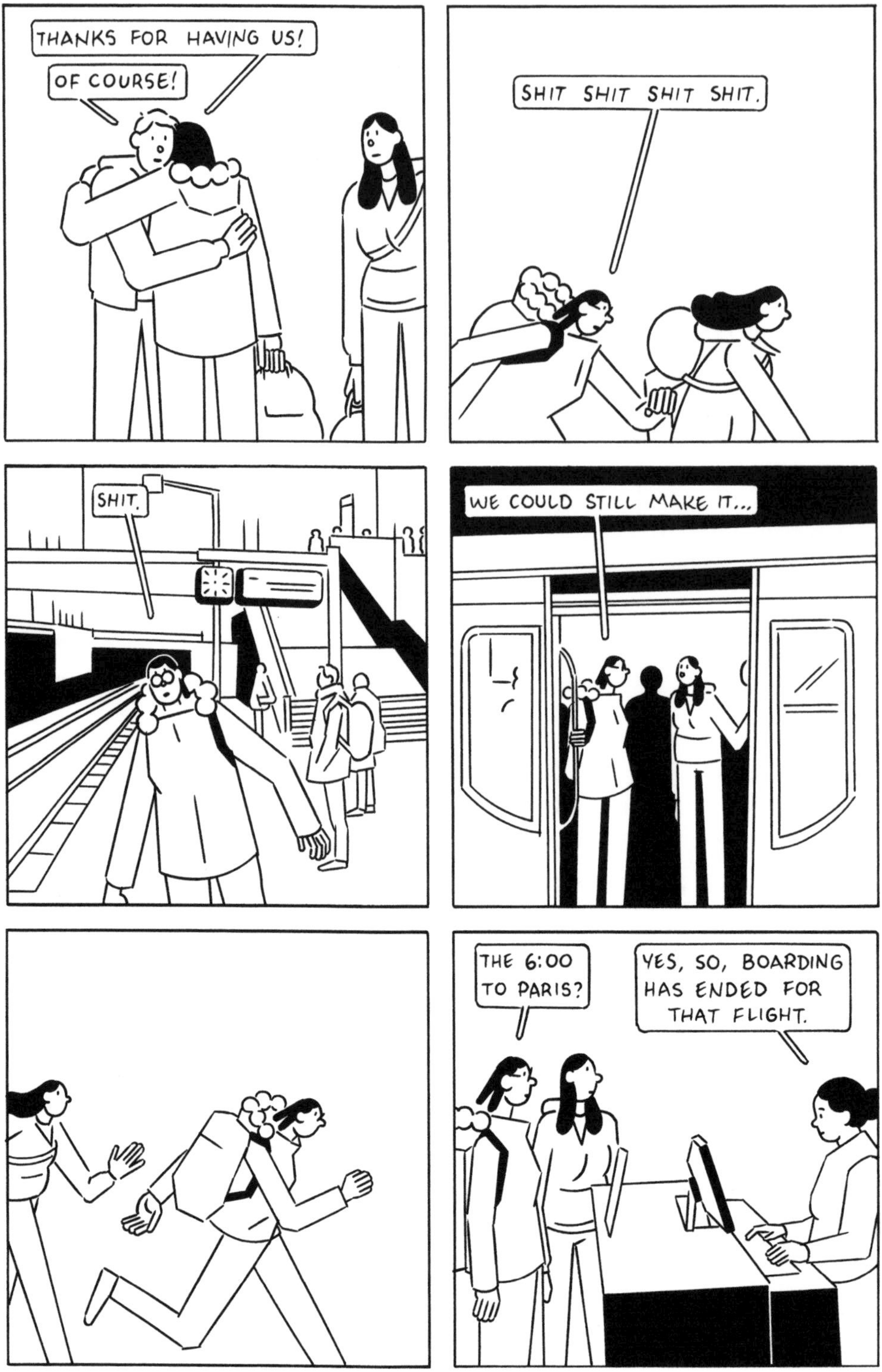
THANKS FOR HAVING US!
OF COURSE!
SHIT SHIT SHIT SHIT.
SHIT.
WE COULD STILL MAKE IT...
THE 6:00 TO PARIS?
YES, SO, BOARDING HAS ENDED FOR THAT FLIGHT.

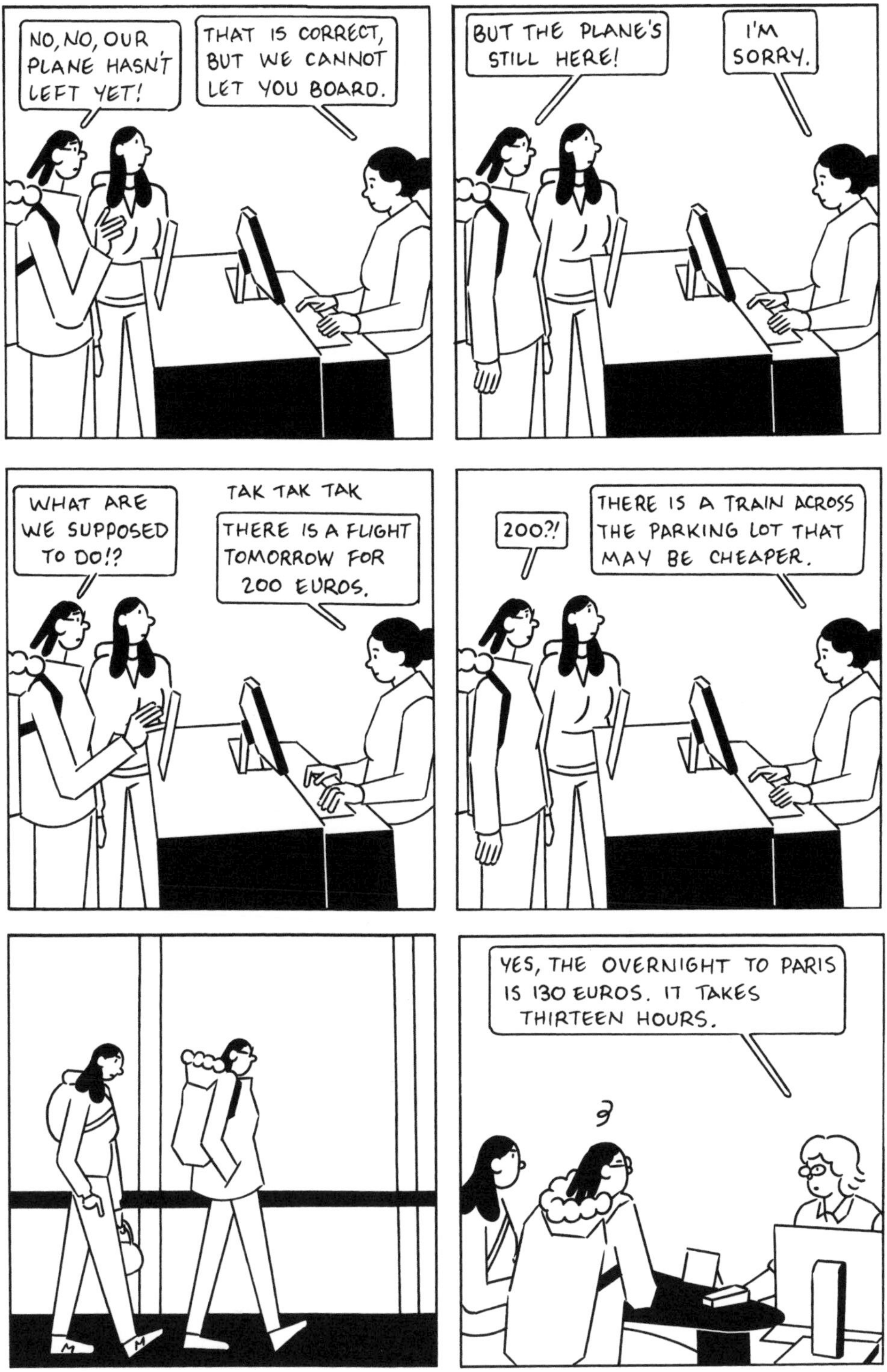
NO, NO, OUR PLANE HASN'T LEFT YET!
THAT IS CORRECT, BUT WE CANNOT LET YOU BOARD.
BUT THE PLANE'S STILL HERE!
I'M SORRY.
WHAT ARE WE SUPPOSED TO DO!?
TAK TAK TAK
THERE IS A FLIGHT TOMORROW FOR 200 EUROS.
200?!
THERE IS A TRAIN ACROSS THE PARKING LOT THAT MAY BE CHEAPER.
YES, THE OVERNIGHT TO PARIS IS 130 EUROS. IT TAKES THIRTEEN HOURS.

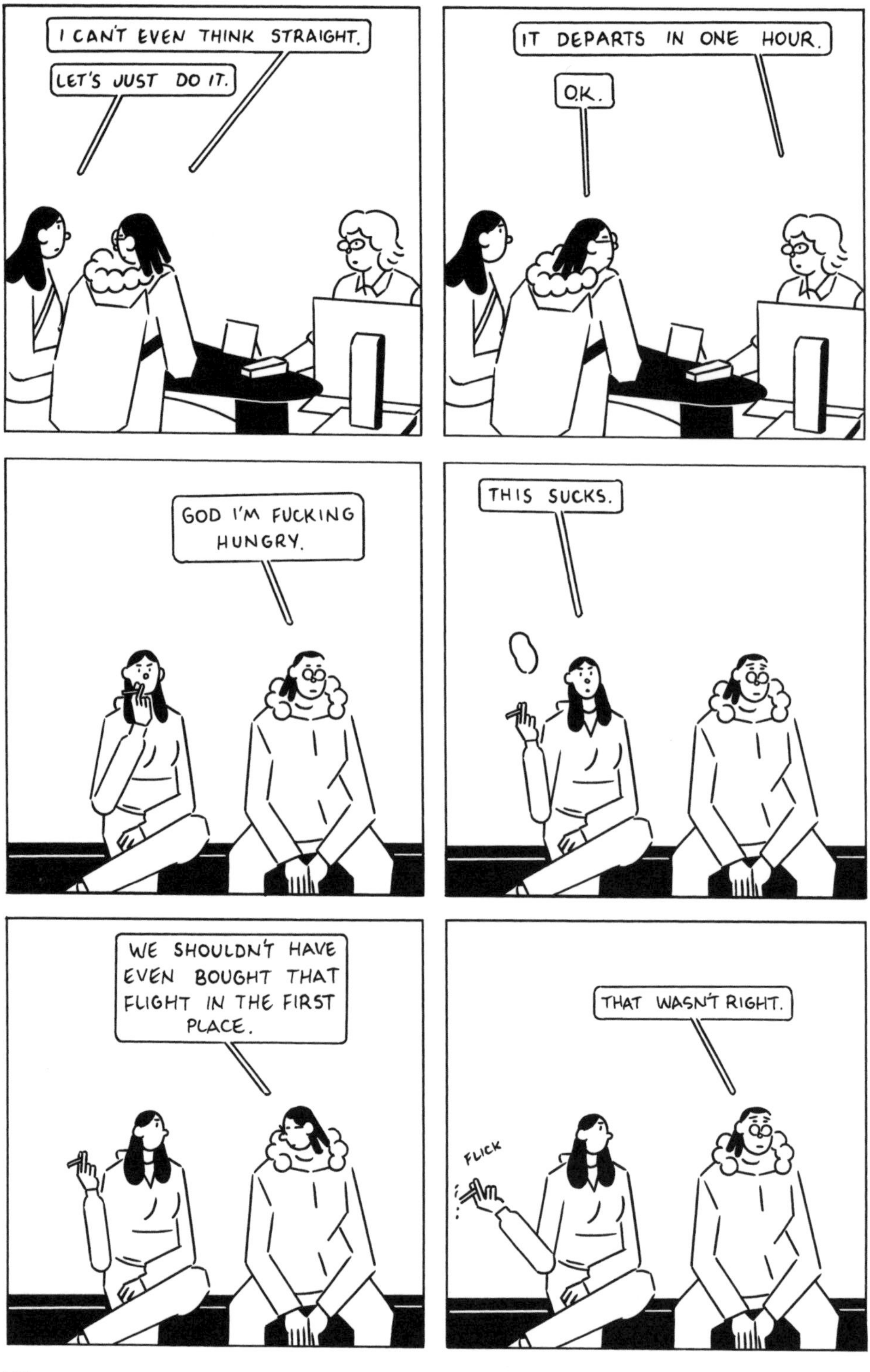
I CAN'T EVEN THINK STRAIGHT.
LET'S JUST DO IT.
IT DEPARTS IN ONE HOUR.
O.K.
GOD I'M FUCKING HUNGRY.
THIS SUCKS.
WE SHOULDN'T HAVE EVEN BOUGHT THAT FLIGHT IN THE FIRST PLACE.
FLICK
THAT WASN'T RIGHT.

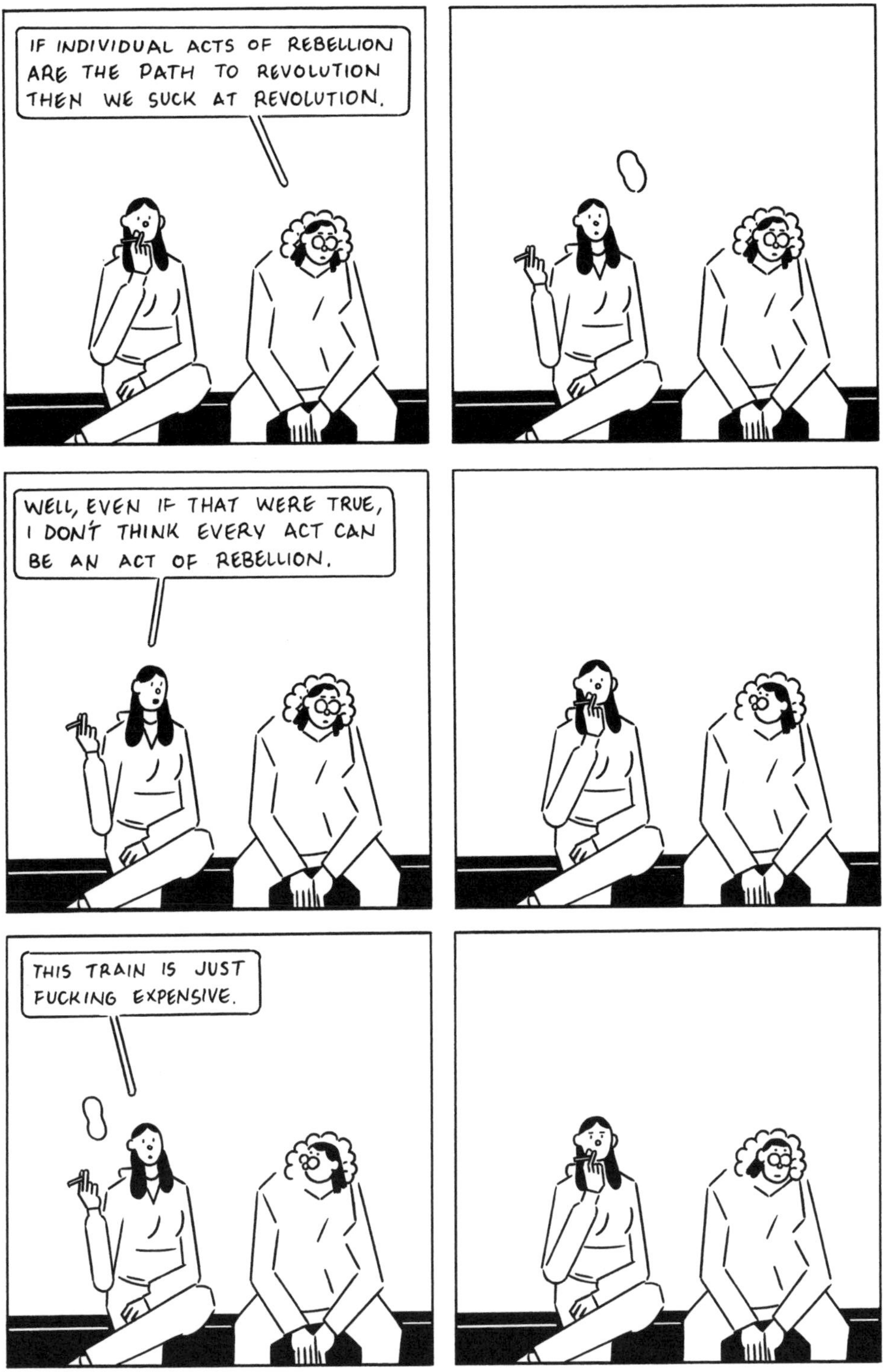
IF INDIVIDUAL ACTS OF REBELLION ARE THE PATH TO REVOLUTION THEN WE SUCK AT REVOLUTION.
WELL, EVEN IF THAT WERE TRUE, I DON'T THINK EVERY ACT CAN BE AN ACT OF REBELLION.
THIS TRAIN IS JUST FUCKING EXPENSIVE.

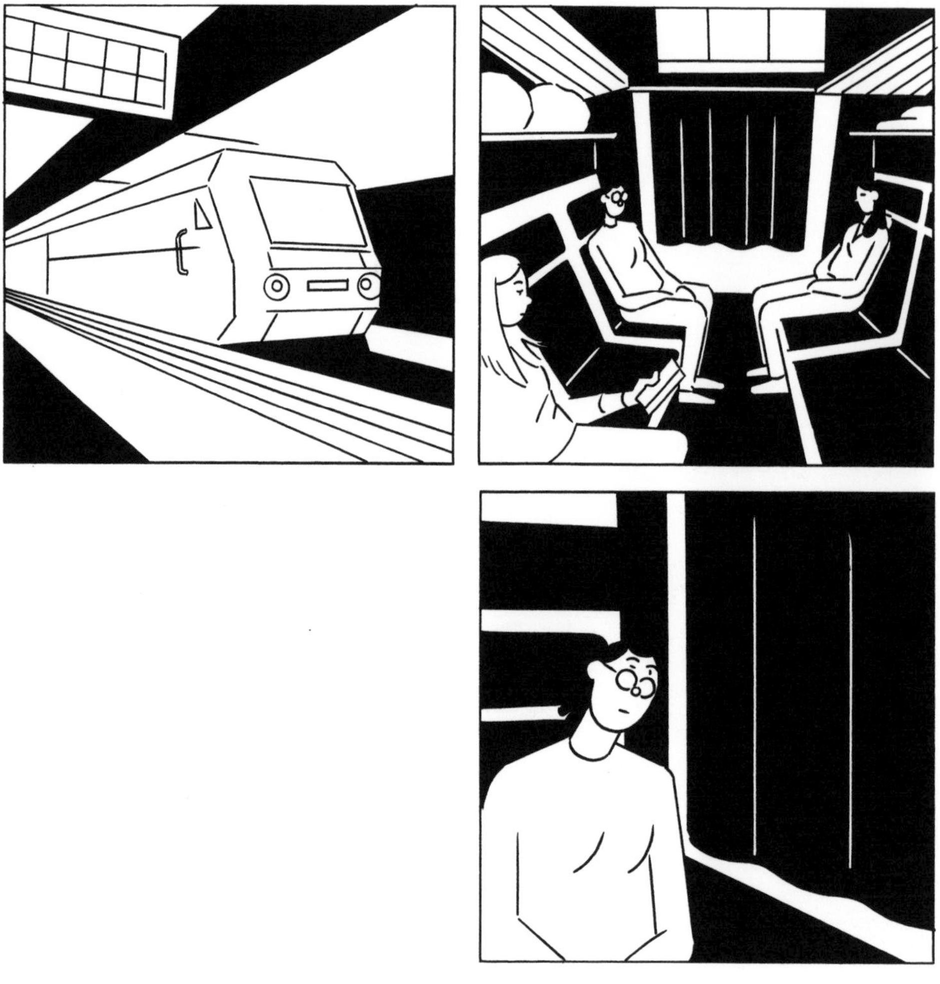

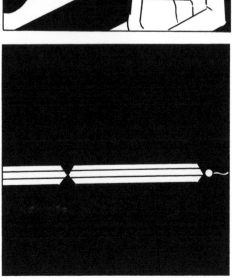

カリス

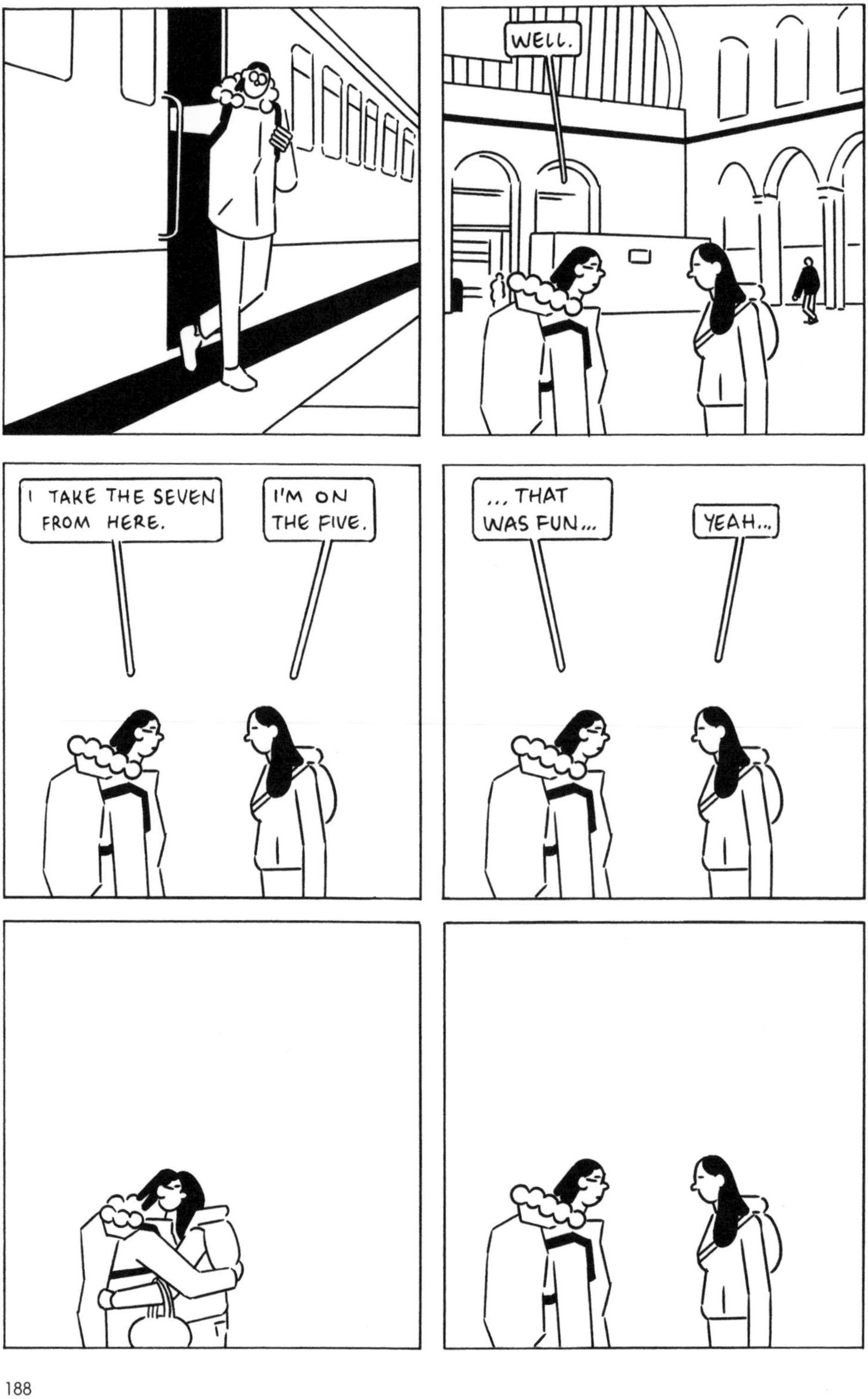
WELL.
I TAKE THE SEVEN FROM HERE.
I'M ON THE FIVE.
... THAT WAS FUN...
YEAH...

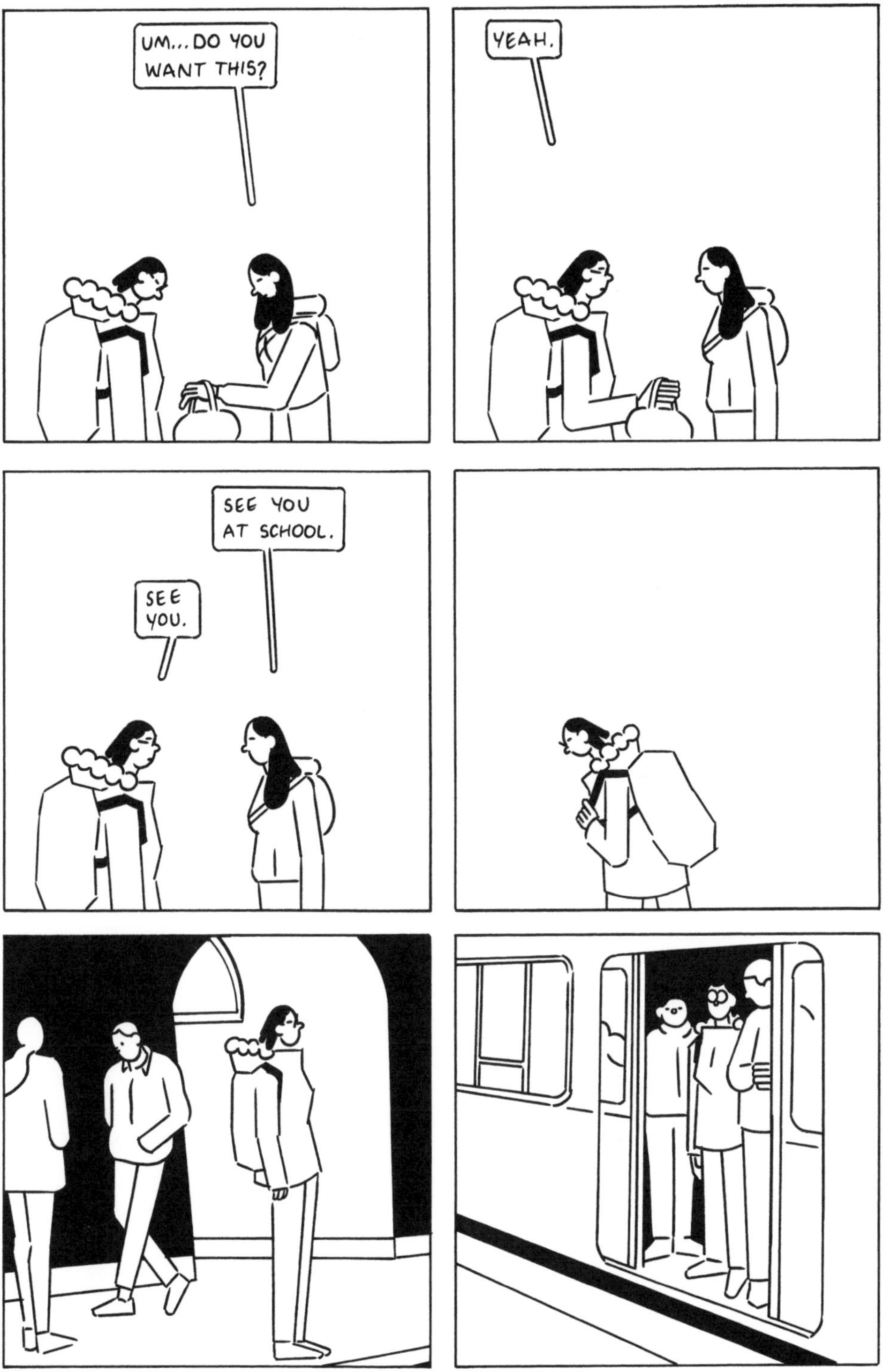
UM... DO YOU WANT THIS?
YEAH.
SEE YOU AT SCHOOL.
SEE YOU.

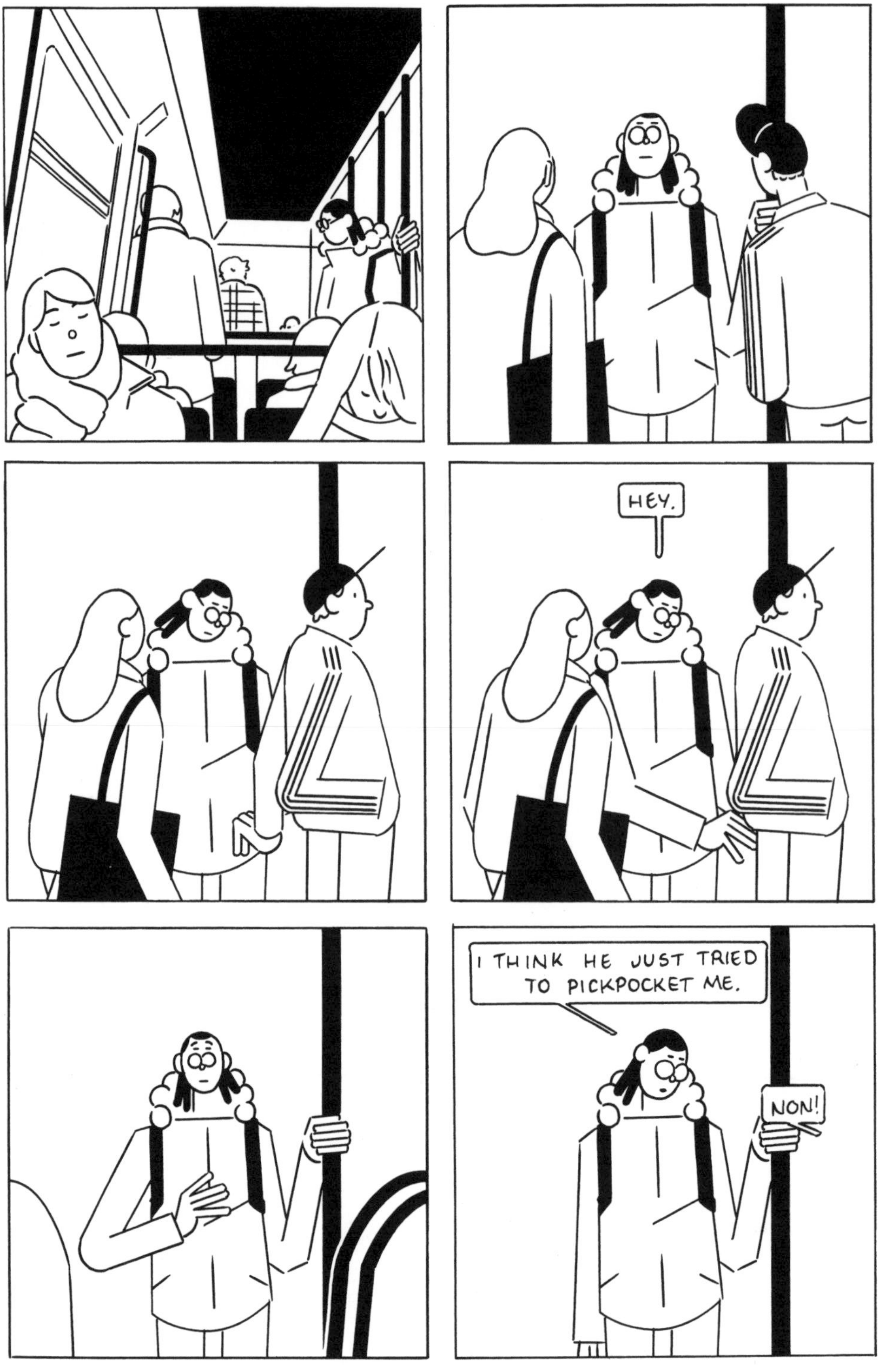
HEY.
I THINK HE JUST TRIED TO PICKPOCKET ME.
NON!

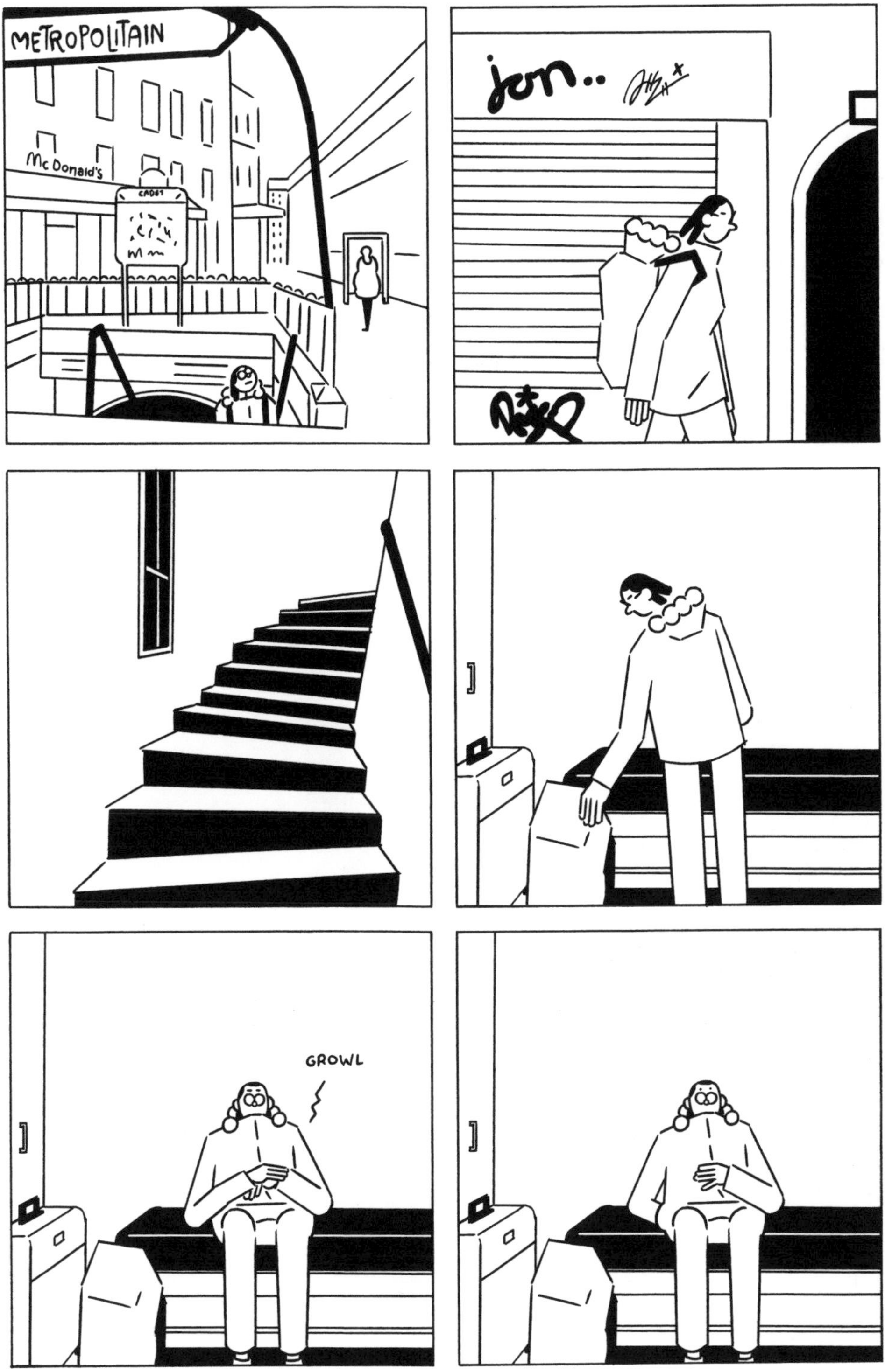
METROPOLITAIN
McDonald's
jon..
GROWL

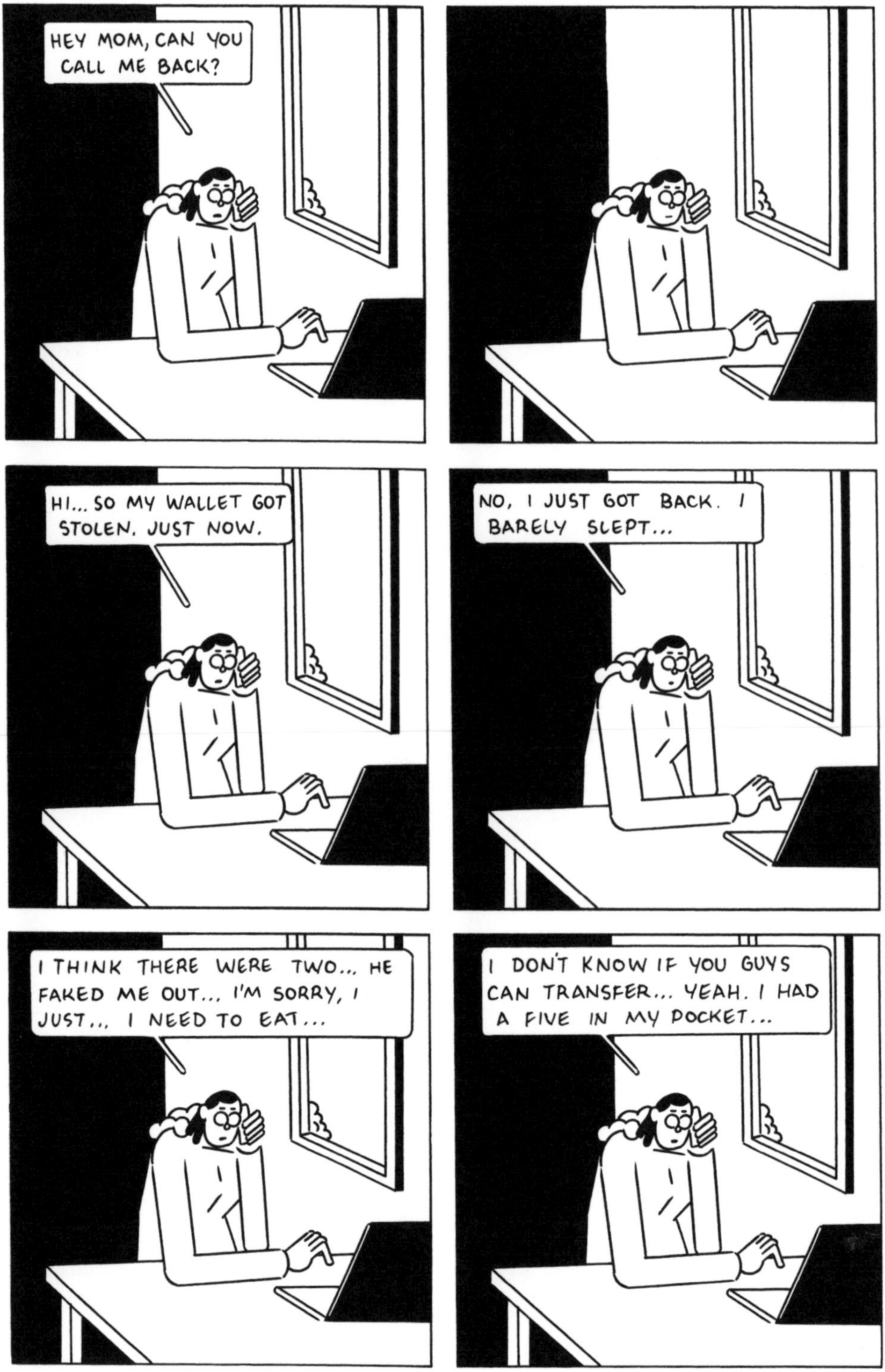
HEY MOM, CAN YOU CALL ME BACK?
HI... SO MY WALLET GOT STOLEN. JUST NOW.
NO, I JUST GOT BACK. I BARELY SLEPT...
I THINK THERE WERE TWO... HE FAKED ME OUT... I'M SORRY, I JUST... I NEED TO EAT...
I DON'T KNOW IF YOU GUYS CAN TRANSFER... YEAH. I HAD A FIVE IN MY POCKET...

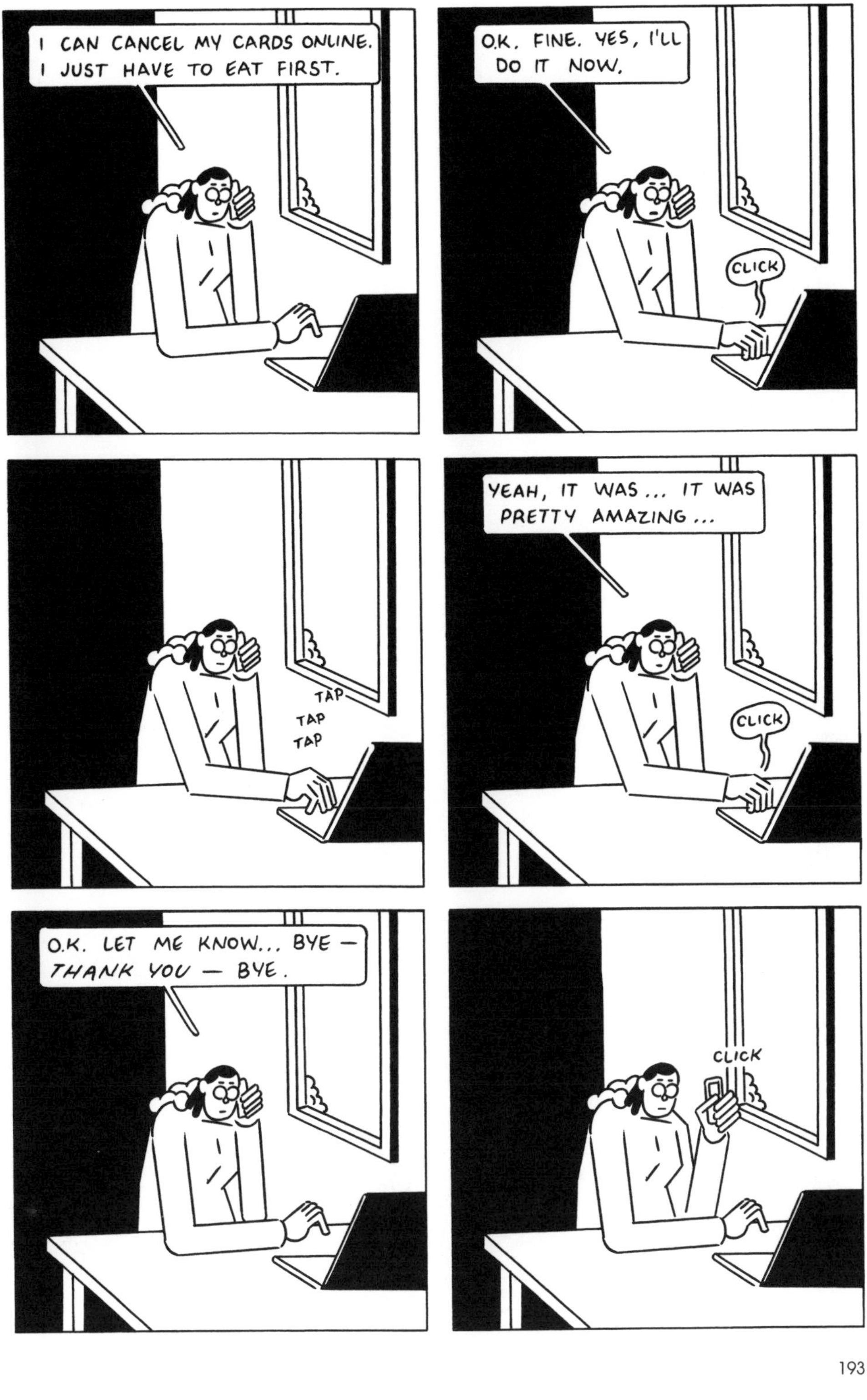

I CAN CANCEL MY CARDS ONLINE. I JUST HAVE TO EAT FIRST.
O.K. FINE. YES, I'LL DO IT NOW.
CLICK
TAP
TAP
TAP
YEAH, IT WAS... IT WAS PRETTY AMAZING...
CLICK
O.K. LET ME KNOW... BYE — *THANK YOU* — BYE.
CLICK

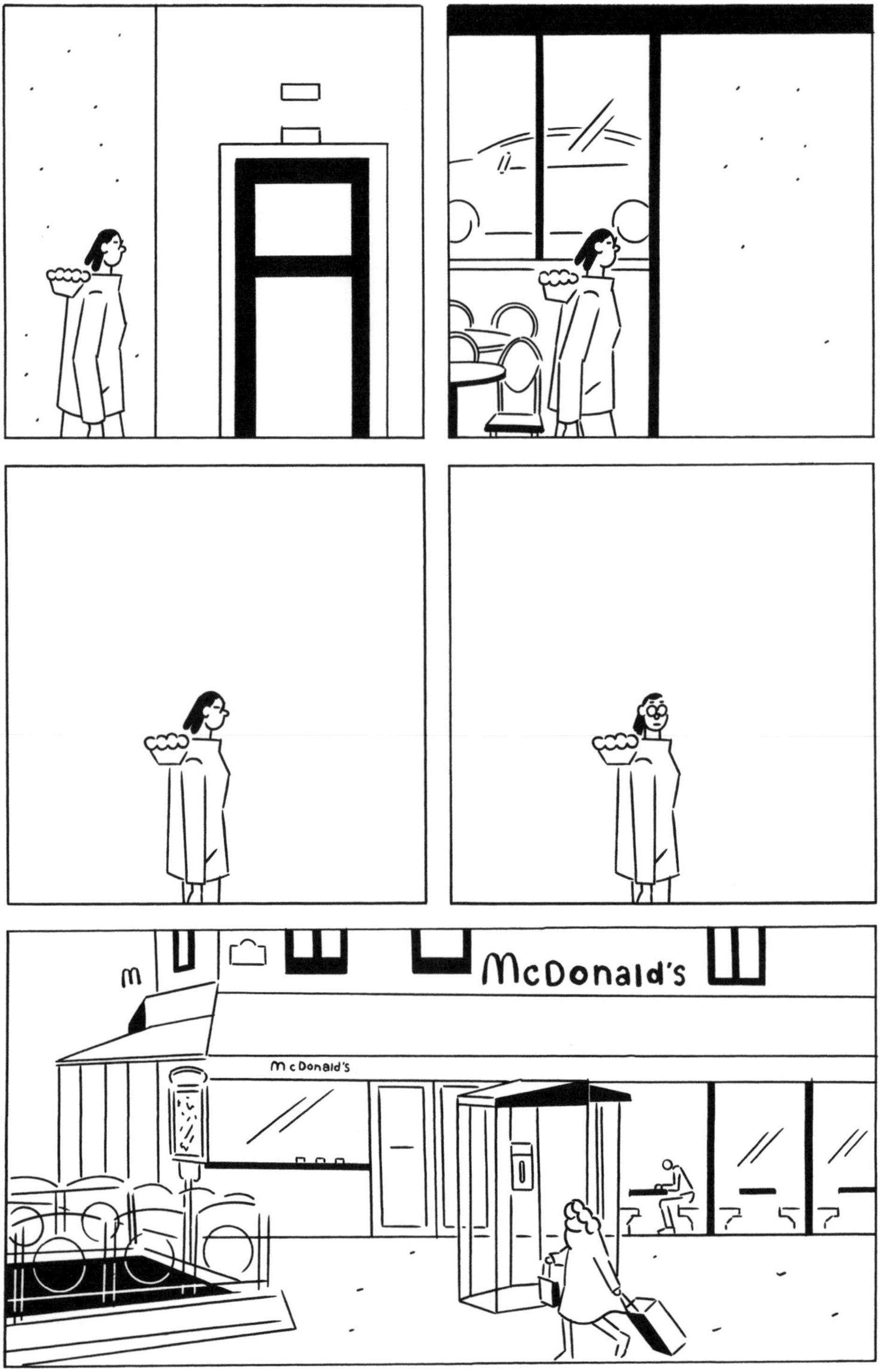
m
McDonald's
McDonald's

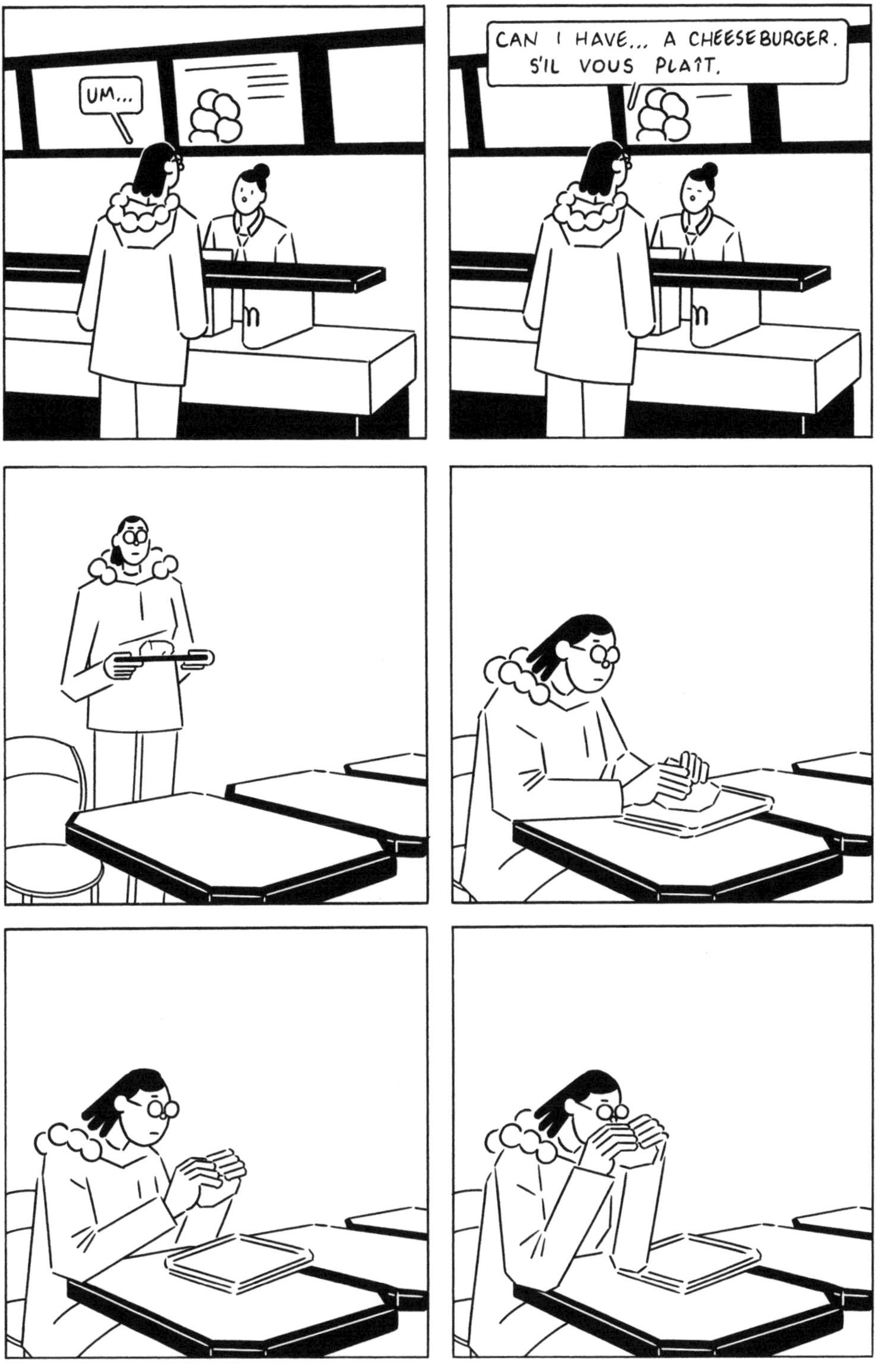
UM...
CAN I HAVE... A CHEESEBURGER. S'IL VOUS PLAIT.

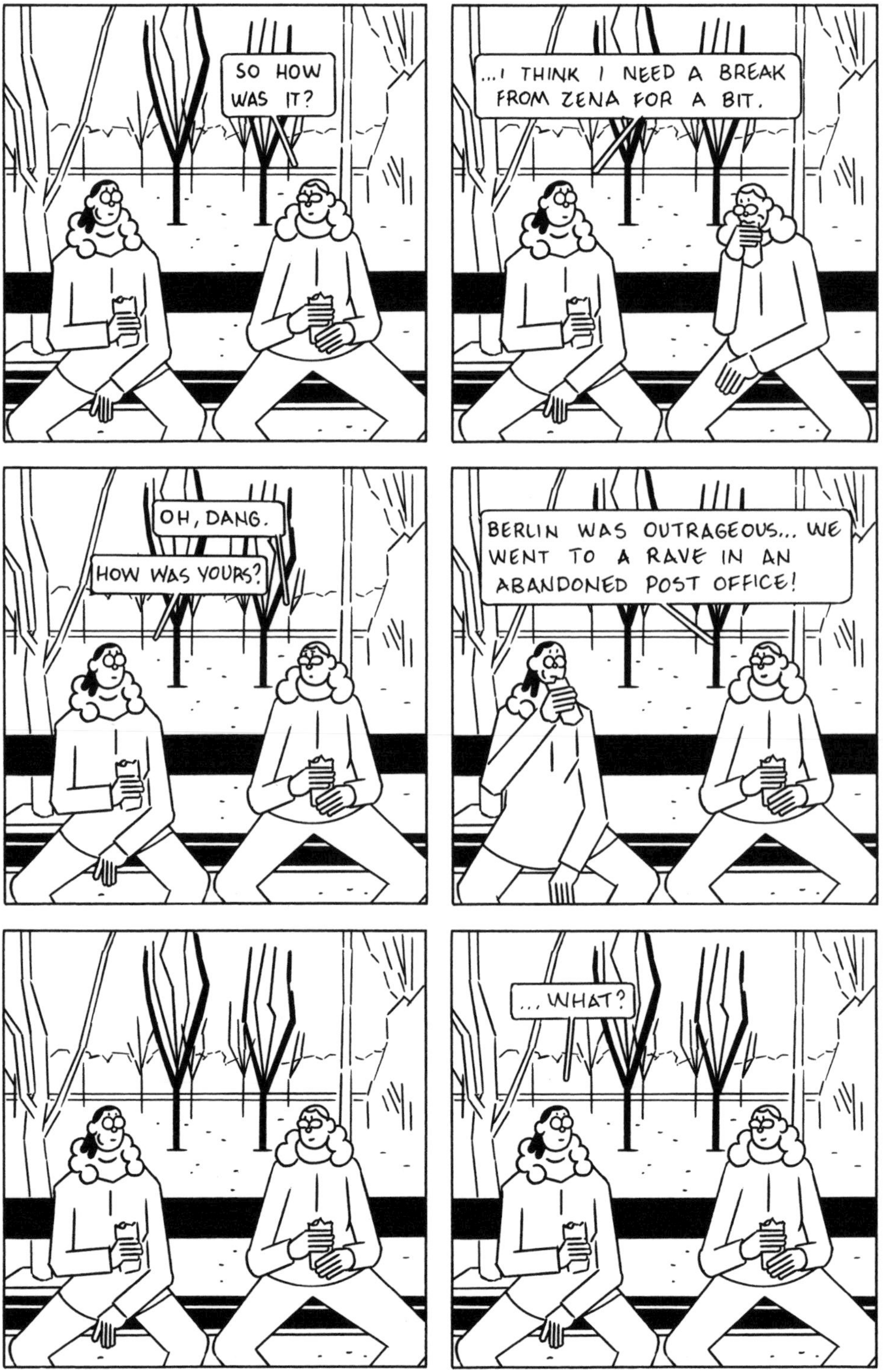
SO HOW WAS IT?
...I THINK I NEED A BREAK FROM ZENA FOR A BIT.
OH, DANG.
HOW WAS YOURS?
BERLIN WAS OUTRAGEOUS... WE WENT TO A RAVE IN AN ABANDONED POST OFFICE!
...WHAT?

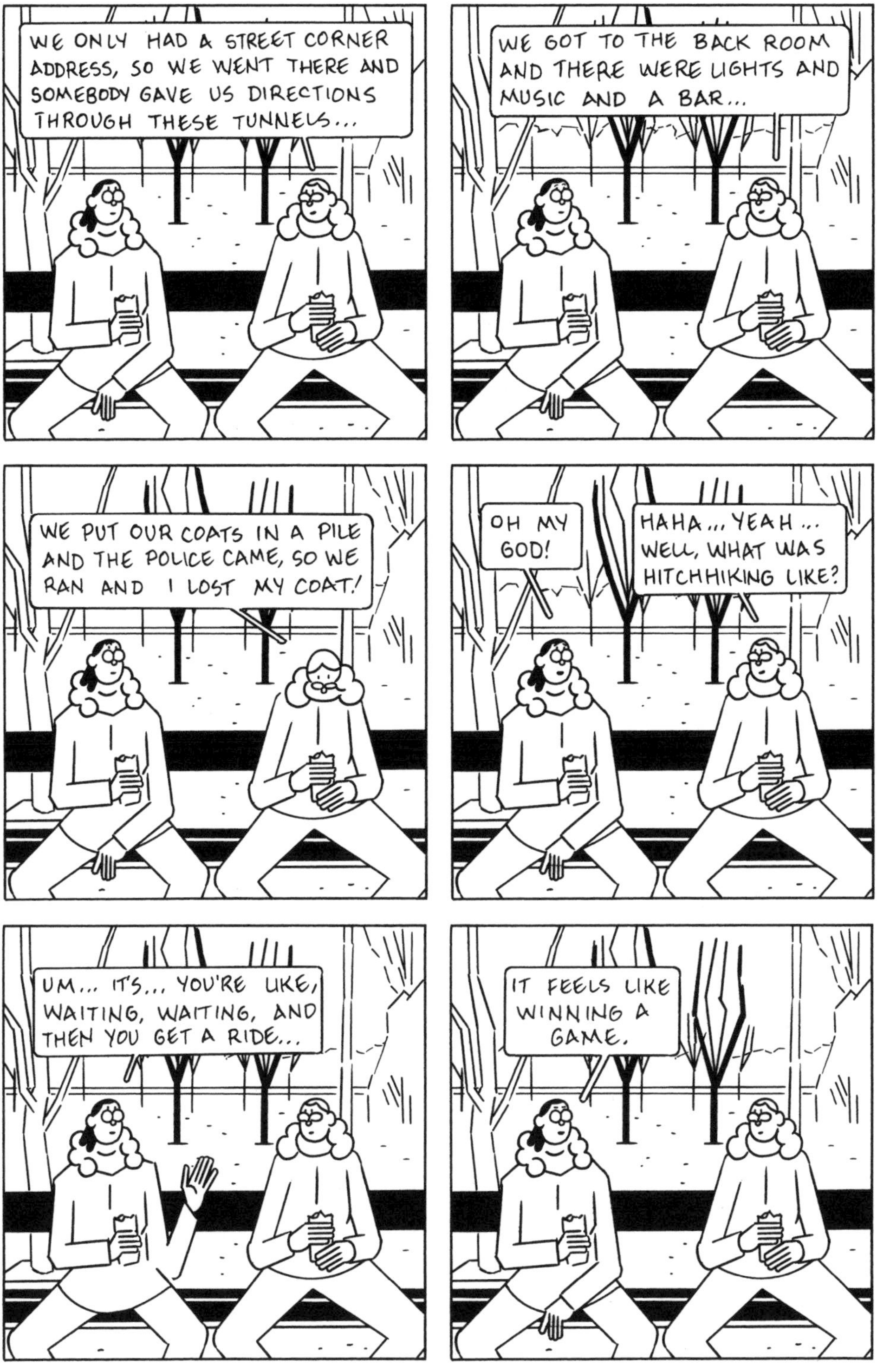
WE ONLY HAD A STREET CORNER ADDRESS, SO WE WENT THERE AND SOMEBODY GAVE US DIRECTIONS THROUGH THESE TUNNELS...
WE GOT TO THE BACK ROOM AND THERE WERE LIGHTS AND MUSIC AND A BAR...
WE PUT OUR COATS IN A PILE AND THE POLICE CAME, SO WE RAN AND I LOST MY COAT!
OH MY GOD!
HAHA... YEAH... WELL, WHAT WAS HITCHHIKING LIKE?
UM... IT'S... YOU'RE LIKE, WAITING, WAITING, AND THEN YOU GET A RIDE...
IT FEELS LIKE WINNING A GAME.

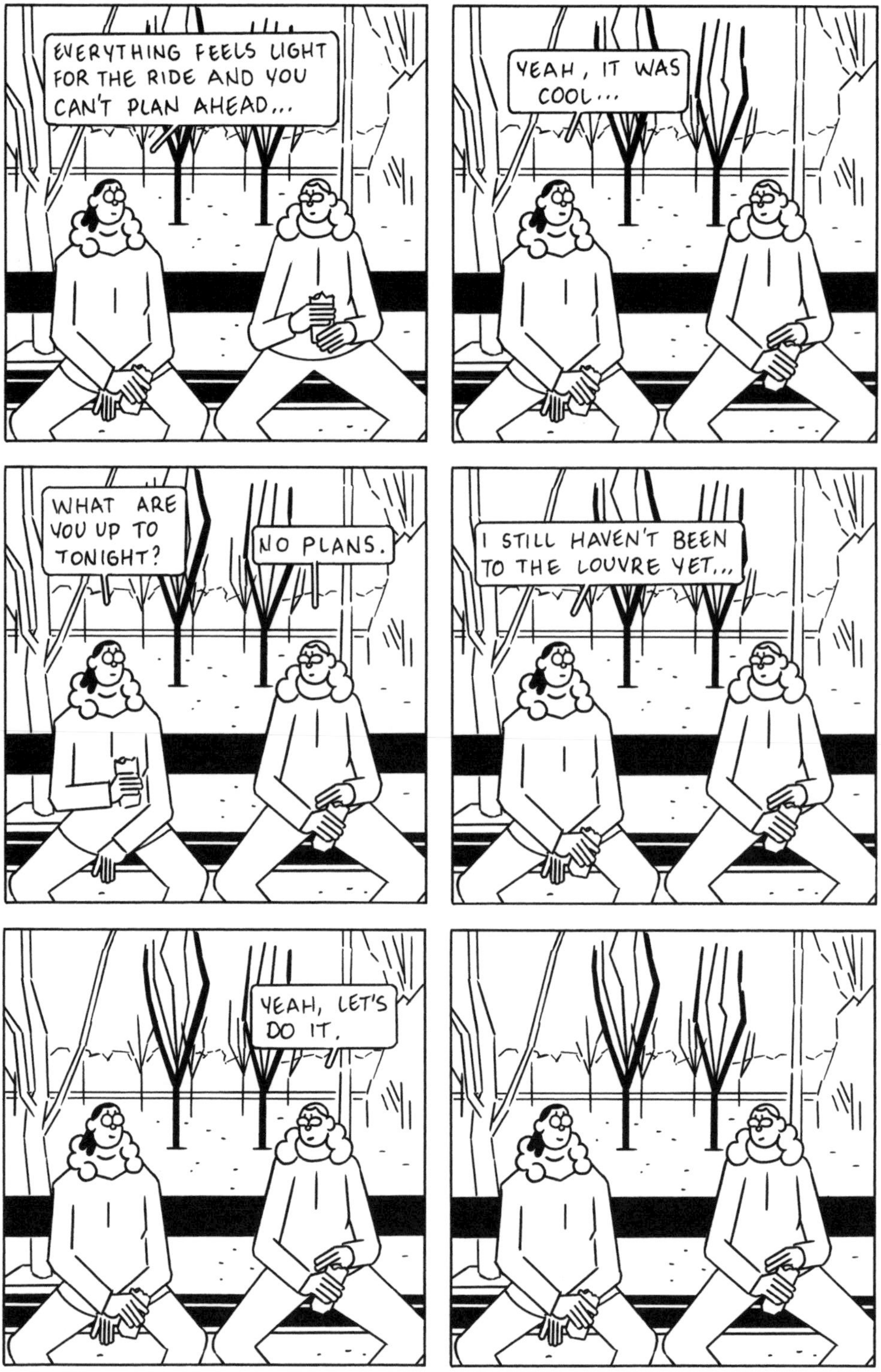
EVERYTHING FEELS LIGHT FOR THE RIDE AND YOU CAN'T PLAN AHEAD...
YEAH, IT WAS COOL...
WHAT ARE YOU UP TO TONIGHT?
NO PLANS.
I STILL HAVEN'T BEEN TO THE LOUVRE YET...
YEAH, LET'S DO IT.

THANKS TO my parents, who told me all their stories and only got mildly upset when I tried to follow in their footsteps.

Thanks to the old friends who helped me to figure out who I am.

I am grateful to the Center for Cartoon Studies, who gave me the Fellowship where I began working seriously on this story, and to my friends and eventual teachers and classmates there, whose critiques were invaluable.

Thanks to Jason Lutes, whose feedback and encouragement allowed me to finally stop rewriting and go for it.

Thanks to the MacDowell Colony, who gave me time and space to begin the project's final phase.

Thanks to Drawn & Quarterly for helping bring this into the world.

Thanks to Dan Nott, Jon Chadurjian, Marta Chudolinska, and Chris Green for being my weekly virtual work buddies and helping me make it to the end. Thanks to ST.

Thanks again to Chris Green for stepping in as my assistant during the final months, reassembling my scattered drawings and finishing the spot blacks with clear-eyed enthusiasm.

And to Hannah Cummins: your support has been unfailing during a process that took a lot longer than you may have anticipated. I hope I can offer the same to you.

SOPHIE YANOW is an artist and writer based in the San Francisco Bay Area. *The Contradictions* is her first book with Drawn & Quarterly, the webcomic of which won an Eisner Award and was nominated for the Ringo and Harvey awards. Yanow is also the author of *What is a Glacier?* and *War of Streets and Houses*. Her comics have appeared in *The New Yorker*, *The Guardian*, *Los Angeles Review of Books*, and *The Nib*. She has been a MacDowell Colony Fellow, and her translation of Dominique Goblet's *Pretending is Lying* received the Scott Moncrieff prize for translation from French. Yanow has taught at the Center for Cartoon Studies, the New Hampshire Institute of Art, and The Animation Workshop in Denmark.